SHIʿI COSMOPOLITANISMS IN AFRICA

PUBLIC CULTURES OF THE MIDDLE EAST AND NORTH AFRICA

Paul A. Silverstein, Susan Slyomovics, and Ted Swedenburg, *editors*

SHI^cI COSMOPOLITANISMS IN AFRICA

Lebanese Migration and Religious Conversion in Senegal

Mara A. Leichtman

Indiana University Press

Bloomington and Indianapolis

This book is a publication of

Indiana University Press
Office of Scholarly Publishing
Herman B Wells Library 350
1320 East 10th Street
Bloomington, Indiana 47405 USA

iupress.indiana.edu

⊖ The paper used in this publication meets the minimum requirements of the American National Standard for Information Sciences—Permanence of Paper for Printed Library Materials, ANSI Z39.48–1992.

Manufactured in the United States of America

Library of Congress Cataloging-in-Publication Data

Leichtman, Mara, author.
  Shiʿi cosmopolitanisms in Africa : Lebanese migration and religious conversion in Senegal / Mara A. Leichtman.
    pages cm. — (Public cultures of the Middle East and North Africa)
    Includes bibliographical references and index.
  ISBN 978-0-253-01599-0 (cl : alk. paper) — ISBN 978-0-253-01601-0 (pb : alk. paper) — ISBN 978-0-253-01605-8 (eb) 1. Shiʿah—Senegal. 2. Shiites—Senegal. 3. Lebanese—Senegal—Religion. 4. Lebanon—Emigration and immigration. 5. Conversion—Shiʿah. 6. Shiʿah—Relations—Sunnites. 7. Sunnites—Relations—Shiʿah. I. Title. II. Series: Public cultures of the Middle East and North Africa.
  BP192.7.S38L45 2015
  297.8209663—dc23

2014048975

1 2 3 4 5 20 19 18 17 16 15

For Samir, whose love for Senegal has touched me deeply. In memory of my Uncle Zell, with whom I enjoyed many Lebanese meals.

Contents

Preface
Islam and Politics

Africa is increasingly playing a role in U.S. foreign policy and the Western fight against terrorism. The 1998 bombings of U.S. embassies in Kenya and Tanzania, 2008 coup in Mauritania (where attacks against European tourists led to the canceling of the Paris-to-Dakar rally), 2012 coups in Mali and Guinea Bissau, piracy off the coast of Somalia, Invisible Children's viral Kony 2012 video campaign, and growing visibility of Nigeria's Boko Haram movement brought Africa into America's immediate agenda. Journalists and diplomats focus on al-Qaʾida's role in Africa, seeing "extremists" or "terrorists" everywhere, yet sometimes lacking concrete proof of their activities.

Douglas Farah, a former Washington Post correspondent who described himself as "covering largely poor and obscure West African countries" (2004:9), published a book entitled *Blood from Stones: The Secret Financial Network of Terror.* The back cover reads, in an exaggerated manner: "After 9/11, at a great risk to his own life, Farah hung out with drugged out killers and arms traffickers in West Africa to trace the links between the underground diamond trade and international terrorism." What surprised me was not his accusation that Lebanese Shiʿa were using Liberian blood diamonds to finance Hizbullah, but his use, interchangeably, of Hizbullah and al-Qaʾida, linking these two organizations in the same sentences as if they were one and the same. In 2011, the *New York Times* ran a series of articles vaguely outlining similarly unproven "accusations."[1] Does this connection really exist?

Knowledge is often produced through less-than-objective media coverage, and for many in the West, Africa is a land of poverty, starvation, war, and "fundamentalism." French celebrity journalist Pierre Péan wrote his own sensationalist account entitled *Manipulations Africaines* (2001), linking the 1989 Libyan bombing of UTA flight 772 to Hizbullah's 1987 taking of French hostages (freed by Senegal's Shaykh al-Zayn). Both Péan and Farah claim to uncover networks of Arab "terrorists" on the African continent, blaming Africa's chaos for allowing such men to run loose and conduct illicit, unmonitored activities. Farah's reporting in particular was widely quoted and formed the basis for U.S. military and policy reports on Lebanese involvement in conflict diamonds, concluding with the need for "those prosecuting the Global War on Terrorism" to carefully monitor West Africa (Laremont and Gregorian 2006:34; see also Gberie 2002; Levitt 2004; Middle East Intelligence Bulletin 2004). Laremont and Gregorian go so far as to state (citing Farah) that "emerging research suggests that Al-Qaeda, Hizbullah, and AMAL have occasionally merged their terrorist-financing initiatives" (2006:30), although they admit difficulty in determining whether al-Qaʾida continues to engage in illicit diamond trading in West Africa. Gberie leaps to conclusions with the following statement: "Lebanese involvement with the RUF [Sierra Leone's guerilla movement Revolutionary United Front] is also largely anecdotal, but in both cases the stories are supported by generations of shady business practice, and by the strong interest of some Lebanese in the virulent politics of the Middle East" (2002:16). Nevertheless, the Middle East Intelligence Bulletin (2004) acknowledges that "although al-Qaeda and Hezbollah are usually mentioned in the same breath when terrorist links to the diamond trade are discussed, the two organizations have been involved in very different capacities." Whereas Senegal is not cited in the reports about diamonds, Levitt (2004) does suggest, citing Israeli intelligence reports, that Senegal is the "secondary centre for Hizbullah's fundraising activity in Africa" after Ivory Coast. On June 11, 2013, the U.S. Treasury blacklisted four Lebanese Shiʿa in West Africa, including a restaurant owner in Dakar, for allegedly fundraising for Hizbullah.[2]

Despite the focus of these journalists and policy analysts on Hizbullah's influence in Africa, many scholars of Islam in Senegal and Senegalese religious leaders had little, if any, knowledge of the existence of Shiʿi Islam in Dakar. When I described my project to them, responses ranged from denial, to disbelief, to confusing a reformist Sunni movement with Shiʿi Islam. A Senegalese graduate student, upon hearing me present my research on Senegalese converts to Shiʿi Islam, questioned why I would research a community that was obviously so insignificant he had never heard of them. How could Western journalists and government officials be so sure these "terrorists" existed when Senegalese scholars were equally certain they did not?

This study documents the beginnings of a Shiʿi movement in Senegal. It does not uncover additional terrorist networks in Africa, reveal the money trail from Senegal to Lebanon, or disclose Hizbullah's West African headquarters, real or imaginary. My focus is not on Shiʿi Islam as a "fundamentalist" Islam, but on Shiʿi Islam as a religious identity and way of being. Religion is part of Lebanese and Senegalese lives, and is crucial in the formation of subjects within the national Senegalese state and transnational Muslim community, yet it is not a static force. Both local and global influences help shape religious identities: French colonialism, Senegalese politics of Africanization, the Lebanese Civil War, the Iranian Revolution, and the 2006 Lebanon War, to name only a few historical events. Lebanese and Senegalese are torn between North and South and "between Islam and the West" (Gellar 1982), all the while struggling to create their own Arab and/or African identity. Is Islam religious or political? Can Islam be Westernized, Arab-ized, or Africanized? Must one choose among these influences, or can one live a cosmopolitan life betwixt and between these different worlds? Are these worlds, indeed, so very different? This book provides an account of the everyday lives of the predominantly Shiʿi Lebanese community in Senegal, focusing on their changing religious, ethnic, and national identities. These subjectivities are placed in the context of the politics of globalization and cosmopolitanism, postcolonialism in Africa, and conflict in the Middle East.

Senegal's Lebanese community is only one part of the story of Shiʿi cosmopolitanism in West Africa. Levitt (2004) writes (citing Israeli intelligence reports) that "'in recent years, many foreign students, including from Uganda and other African countries, are sent to study theology in Iranian universities' as a means of recruiting and training them as Hizbullah operatives or Iranian intelligence agents." Over the past few decades, Senegalese have begun to "convert" from Sunni to Shiʿi Islam, but this book demonstrates that their Shiʿi identity is linked to an intellectual and textual tradition of an "authentic" Islam, not to nationalist politics in the Middle East, although they respect Ayatollah Khomeini's ideologies. Shiʿi Islam for Senegalese converts is therefore adaptable to a distinctly Senegalese understanding and is a means to bypass the authority and power of Sufi leaders and create their own agency and following. Becoming Shiʿa is also one way certain Senegalese, especially those who are highly educated and relatively affluent, attempt to escape the colonial legacy, the failure of the Senegalese state, and growing structural inequalities in their country through adopting while adapting a religious model that for them has been successful elsewhere in combating the West. The book thus explores the process of becoming Shiʿa in Senegal in the context of tensions between local and global Islamic forces. It is an investigation of two very different communities who share a common minority religious interpretation of Islam in a predominantly Sunni Muslim country: Lebanese migrants and Senegalese converts.

Acknowledgments

I WOULD LIKE TO begin with a special note of appreciation for Shaykh ʿAbdul Munʿam al-Zayn, who allowed me full access at Dakar's Lebanese Islamic Institute and engaged me in numerous discussions about religion in both Senegal and Lebanon. Coming to a determination to work with an American Jewish anthropologist after 9/11 and during the buildup to the 2003 U.S.-led invasion of Iraq is not a decision every shaykh would make. I struggled greatly with how to treat the inevitable religion question. During my initial stay in Senegal during the summer of 2000, I would respond when asked my religion that I was not religious. This was interpreted to mean that I was atheist and therefore did not believe in *anything*, an unacceptable phenomenon in Senegal (as well as in Lebanon). After a number of shocked and outwardly disapproving reactions from pious Lebanese, who informed me that no good Muslim or Christian would ever welcome an atheist into their homes, I decided that it was better to openly address my Jewish heritage.

Therefore during Ramadan 2002, when a woman approached me in Shaykh al-Zayn's mosque during the Friday afternoon prayer, I informed her that I was American and Jewish in response to her prodding. This displeased the shaykh, who remarked that it only takes the talk of one woman for the entire community to know. Word quickly spread around Shaykh al-Zayn's congregation that an American Jewish "spy" was in his audience. Although he responded to dozens of phone calls by explaining that he was aware of my presence and that I was (then) a student, the community informed him that he could not be sure that I was not a spy. He advised me to stop going to mosque for my safety. Reluctantly I obeyed.

One week later I had another meeting with the shaykh. He now told me that he was receiving phone calls asking where the American had gone and whether he forbade her from attending his lectures. He recounted a parable of Juha, the Arab fool. Juha and his father were riding a donkey, but Juha begins to feel sorry for the donkey for having too heavy a load, so he tells his father to step down. People watched Juha riding while his elderly father walked and criticized him, so he, too, gets off the donkey and walks next to his father, leaving the fortunate ass with no load at all. The moral of the story is no matter what you do, ride or walk, be present at lectures or absent, people will talk. I self-consciously resumed my attendance of the Islamic Institute lectures for the remainder of Ramadan.

My own liminal position and the multiple registers of language, religion, and culture through which I conducted participant observation enabled the uniqueness of my reflections on this transcultural project. My identity as an American,

Jew, and woman was always in the back of Lebanese and Senegalese minds, and while some never ceased to be suspicious, especially in light of world events, with time and persistence I won enough trust to carry out my research. Occasionally, interest in learning more about my religion led to a detailed comparison of Judaism and Islam, which I found to be beneficial. I was always an anomaly in the community, but I eventually became an accepted anomaly.

This project spanned thirteen years and four continents. Research was made possible by awards from the Andrew Mellon Foundation (2000 and 2001, administered by Brown University), Fulbright Program, Population Council, and National Science Foundation (2002–2003). Additional research in Senegal (2006, 2007, 2008, 2009, 2013) and leave from teaching at Michigan State University were facilitated by MSU's Intramural Research Grants Program, Muslim Studies Program, Center for Advanced Study of International Development, African Studies Center, and Department of Anthropology. A National Institute of Child Health and Human Development fellowship through Brown's Population Studies and Training Center funded my graduate training. The University of Michigan and the Center for Middle East and North African Studies served as an excellent base from which to write (2004–2005). I was a visiting fellow at Zentrum Moderner Orient, Berlin (2007), and the (former) International Institute for the Study of Islam in the Modern World, Leiden (2008).

I am greatly indebted to the many people who assisted and supported me along the way, including my teachers David Kertzer, Bill Beeman, Phil Leis, Calvin Goldscheider, and Mamadou Diouf. Calvin and Mamadou read more drafts than anybody else and were instrumental in helping me shape ideas. At Brown I was grateful for the support of Jan Brunson, Pilapa Esara, Lacey Gale, Susi Keefe, Audrey Mouser, Simone Poliandri, Isabel Rodrigues, Dan Smith, and Bruce Whitehouse. Colleagues at MSU advised me on the writing process. In particular I wish to thank Beth Drexler, Kiki Edozie, Emine Evered, Anne Ferguson, Steve Gold, Walter Hawthorne, Leslie Moch, James Pritchett, and Karin Zitzewitz. Andrea Louie and Jyotsna Singh critiqued drafts of my introduction.

Feedback from countless presentations pushed my analysis to new levels. Portions of revised written work were commented on by Irfan Ahmad, Joost Beuving, Muçahit Bilici, Sean Brotherton, Lara Deeb, Mamadou Diouf, Frances Hasso, Marloes Janson, Kai Kresse, Peter Mandaville, Sabrina Mervin, Augustus Richard Norton, Zakia Salime, Jim Searing (a spirited discussant at ASA days before his untimely death), Roschanack Shaery-Eisenlohr, Paul Silverstein, Benjamin Soares, Ted Swedenburg, and anonymous journal reviewers. My understanding of cosmopolitanism was enhanced by conversations with Robert Hefner, Bruce Lawrence, and Dorothea Schulz. The long and grueling work of research, writing, and revising would not have been possible without the moral support of friends and colleagues, in particular Zain Abdullah, Erin Augis, Sandi Bellinger, Ruah Bhay,

Aly Drame, Maribeth Gainard, Rola Husseini, Kate McClellan, Babak Raḥimi, Zakia Salime, Lucia Volk, and Nikolai Wenzel. My mother has always supported my education and nontraditional career.

Research in Senegal depended on the assistance, friendship, and hospitality of too many to thank by name; I also wish to respect their privacy and anonymity. The Lebanese community welcomed me at events, invited me for meals, and partook in many conversations. Samir's dedication to my research was essential. The Attye and Sarraf families opened their homes to me. Father Tony Fakhry often received me at Dakar's Maronite Mission. Senegalese Shiʿa invited me into their community and enthusiastically shared their religious experiences. At Université Cheikh Anta Diop, Ibrahima Thioub shared his own research on the Lebanese of Senegal and lent me Boumedouha's dissertation, which I had been chasing for years. Babacar Samb spent hours with me contemplating Islam. I am indebted to Diegane Sene, then of CESTI, for aiding me in my newspaper search and allowing me to photocopy the many French colonial archival documents he collected on Lebanese in Senegal. Sidy Lamine Niass of *Wal Fadjri* and Babacar Niang, now of *Al-Madina*, led me to Senegalese Shiʿa and dubbed cassettes of Islamic radio programs. Cheikh Diop of IFAN searched for articles in Senegalese newspapers on Shiʿi Islam and the Lebanese community. Charles Becker shared demographic sources from his impressive personal library. The American Cultural Center assisted with contacts and bureaucracy.

The German Orient Institute was an ideal base in Beirut the summer of 2000. Anja Peleikis connected me with many acquaintances in Lebanon. Abir Bassam and Ali Badawi occasionally served as guides and translators. Souha Tarraf-Najib shared her research on the history of Senegal's Lebanese community. Many other scholars, journalists, government officials, religious leaders, and NGO workers helped formulate my impressions of Lebanon's relationship with its emigrant communities in Africa.

In Paris, Sabrina Mervin meticulously sharpened my knowledge about Lebanese Shiʿa. Jean Schmitz included me in his scholarly community of Africanists and eased my access to Paris's libraries. Fabienne Samson-Ndaw invited me to join a research group at the Centre d'Etudes Africaines at EHESS. Abu Sahra generously hosted me and engaged in dialogue about Islam on many occasions. At Oxford, Nadim Shehadi allowed me access to the unpublished dissertations housed at the Centre for Lebanese Studies. I compared Lebanese communities in Anglophone and Francophone Africa with Xerxes Malki. I am grateful to the Imam al-Khuʾi Foundation in London and Paris for furthering my understanding of Shiʿi Islam.

Birama Diagne, Mohamad Cama, and Patricia Pereiro transcribed French-language cassettes. Noémi Tousignant and Meadow Dibble-Dieng translated quotations from French into English. Doaa Darwish and Ebraima K. M. Saidy transcribed and translated Arabic cassettes. Assan Sarr translated Wolof recordings. Cengiz Salman conducted a literature review. Adrianne Daggett created the maps used in this book. I am grateful to Paul Silverstein for soliciting my work for the Public Cultures of the Middle East and North Africa series. The careful read and critique of my manuscript by Robert Launay and one anonymous reviewer helped me improve this book. Rebecca Tolen and her staff at Indiana University Press guided the manuscript through the review and editing process. All remaining errors are my own. All photographs were taken by the author unless otherwise noted in the captions.

Portions of this book are revisions of and elaborations on previously published work. An earlier version of chapter 3 appeared in Frances Trix, John Walbridge, and Linda Walbridge's edited volume *Muslim Voices and Lives in the Contemporary World* (Palgrave Macmillan, 2008). An earlier version of chapter 4 was published in *International Journal of Middle East Studies* 42 (2): 269–290, 2010. A portion of chapter 6 appeared in *Journal of Religion in Africa* 39 (3): 319–351, 2009. Some of the material in chapter 7 appeared in Mamadou Diouf and Mara A. Leichtman, editors, *New Perspectives on Islam in Senegal: Conversion, Migration, Wealth, Power, and Femininity* (Palgrave Macmillan, 2009).

Note on Transliteration

Throughout the book I use a simplified version of the *International Journal of Middle East Studies* guidelines for the transliteration of Arabic words. All diacritical marks have been omitted, except the ayn (ʿ) and glottal stop hamza (ʾ). At times I use the broken Arabic plural (e.g., *marajiʿ*); however, for additional simplicity, I add the English "s" to indicate plurals of more familiar Arabic words (e.g., *fatwas*). When using direct quotes, I preserve the transliteration used in the original text; as a result certain words appear in multiple spellings. Names and places are transcribed according to their most common English or French spelling (e.g., Beirut not Bayrut; Diourbel not Jurbel).

SHI'I COSMOPOLITANISMS IN AFRICA

Introduction

Locating Cosmopolitan Shi'i Islamic Movements in Senegal

DAKAR IS LOCATED on the Atlantic coast at the westernmost edge of the African mainland, a strategic position and major port for transatlantic and European trade, including the export of slaves from the sixteenth to nineteenth centuries. Recognized as a French *commune* in 1872, and replacing Saint-Louis as the capital of French West Africa in 1902, Dakar was accessible by both sea and land, linked to Bamako by a major railroad. Racial and social segregation marked the process of urbanization during the colonial period. Today the cosmopolitan city retains its position as a West African financial center and migrant destination— as well as a port of (increasingly clandestine) departure in this neoliberal age of economic crisis.

Travelers to Dakar, and to other West African cities, encounter a very visible and established minority trading community. Lebanese migrants were ghettoized by French colonial officers in a particular central section of Dakar Plateau. This combined business and residential quarter is covered in dust, blown south from the Sahara desert, mixed with trash, empty boxes, discarded containers, and swarming with flies. Streets are a buzz of activity, crowded with cars and trucks, motorcycles, merchandise carts, people shopping, selling items, yelling, spitting, coughing, greeting. In the shops one often encounters a Lebanese proprietor, with a few Lebanese employees or coworkers, often family members, while the majority of the employees are Senegalese (sometimes Guineans or *métis*). A cacophony of languages can be heard: Wolof, Pular, French, Arabic.

The Lebanese businessmen are savvy, and shop names are intentionally evocative to attract customers, such as Bed Bath and Beyond (of no affiliation with the trademarked American chain) and Al Pacino's Dream Shop (which sells African cloth). One man gave me a midnight tour of the plastics factory he managed, one of five in Dakar, all Lebanese-owned and engaged in fierce competition for the West African market. Senegalese workers operating expensive machinery from Europe manned the twenty-four-hour factory. Our tour began with barrels of colored plastic beads, melted and pressed into molds. Most important, however, was the labeling process at the end of the production cycle, which marked products as "Made in the USA" and even "Made in Harlem"! (The neighborhood known as "Little Senegal" in Harlem is home to the largest Senegalese population in the United States [Abdullah 2010; Kane 2011; Stoller 2002].) Finished products ranged from chairs and tables, to buckets, basins, and bowls, to smaller cosmetics cases. The plastics factory worked together with the Lebanese-run cosmetics factory to package their products. The manager told me that his wife once bought an inexpensive face powder and marveled at the low price she paid for an American product. When he verified that her purchase was produced in his factory, his wife was furious that even she had been deceived by such marketing ploys.

Once populated almost exclusively by Lebanese, this business district is becoming more mixed with Senegalese merchants, who are edging out Lebanese competition in an increasingly brutal economic climate. Some Lebanese were forced to shift to other business sectors; others even relocated to more affordable and remote areas of Dakar. Known as *baol-baol,* many Murid Sufis are rural-to-urban migrants, coming from the Baol region in Senegal, and dominating Dakar's informal economy. Setting up shop on the street in front of their Lebanese competitors enables them to undercut Lebanese business by selling the same product at a fraction of the price without overhead costs. I was once walking through the bustling Sandaga market and was accosted by one of these hawkers who begged me to buy from him and not from the Lebanese.

On Friday afternoons the marketplace is transformed by the call to prayer broadcasting from the loudspeakers of nearby minarets. Lebanese shops are either closed or staffed temporarily by female relatives as male shopkeepers head to the Lebanese Shiʿi mosque for the communal prayer. Some Senegalese Muslims join the Lebanese in prayer, as crowds of Senegalese Sufi merchants convert city streets into sanctified spaces, prostrating publicly on squares of cardboard or burlap sacks. The soothing sounds of Islam mysteriously replace the honking horns from frequently congested traffic, streets empty of cars; even the usually aggressive taxi drivers, desperate for passengers they can overcharge, are nowhere to be found. The intense economic rivalry in Dakar dissipates into religious coexistence and at times even collaboration as Muslims. Just as cosmopolitanism is the key to economic success in Senegal, it is also an important factor in religious transitions over time, for Lebanese as well as indigenous Senegalese Muslims. It is this sacred space, very much in constant interaction with the profane—the economic as well as the political—that this book explores.

What is at stake for religion in an increasingly globalized world unchained yet bounded by processes of migration, cosmopolitanism, and governmentality? To answer this question, I focus on religious ties between Senegalese, Lebanese in Senegal, and Lebanon, within a larger context of French colonialism and "global" Shiʿi Islam, referring to the religio-political fervor originating in Iran that spread to Shiʿi Muslims around the world. I am less interested in the cosmopolitanism of the individual migrant/traveler and more in religion as a global movement. Research using the now dominant frameworks of globalization, transnationalism, multiculturalism, and cosmopolitanism has often neglected to incorporate religion, or religion has been sidestepped, reduced to either totalitarian orthodoxies or false consciousness (although fine exceptions do exist). The following chapters illustrate diverse forms of cosmopolitanism as envisaged and practiced by two Shiʿi Muslim minorities—one diasporic, the other indigenous—in a Sunni Muslim-majority country. My discussion explores the interrelationship among theories of cosmopolitanism, migration, and religious transformation, while paying attention to intricacies of these theories in colonial, as well as postcolonial and neoliberal, Africa.

I begin with an examination of how Lebanese identity adapted over time from religious sectarianism to "secular" ethnicity, when religion ceased to divide Muslim and Christian migrants and instead became a shared element of Lebanese diasporic culture. Situating this predominantly Muslim population in its Senegalese context led me in two different directions. First, I examine Lebanese Shiʿa as part of the Lebanese community as a whole, including its Christian minority. Following Simpson and Kresse, who posit that "any conception of 'cosmopolitan society' . . . ought to reflect the historical struggles on which it builds" (2008:2), the first part of this book provides a history of Lebanese settlement in Senegal. Lebanese first adapted to being a minority by emphasizing Lebanese ethnicity over religious denomination. Uniting as an ethnic group helped counter discrimination first under French colonialism and later from the independent Senegalese state. More recently, external constraints have begun to threaten Lebanese coexistence in Senegal as the 2006 Lebanon War revived sectarian divisions. Responses to the war from Dakar were particularly significant because a majority of Lebanese in Senegal had never visited Lebanon. Shiʿi Islam began to stand for Lebanese nationalism, and the shaykh had more success in strengthening the community's identification as Lebanese than in turning them into pious Shiʿa. This identity change is one variation of Shiʿi cosmopolitanism, as Shiʿi Islam for Lebanese in Senegal links religious observance to ethno-national belonging.

Second, I explore Lebanese interactions with Senegalese Muslims, specifically Senegalese who "converted" to Shiʿi Islam over the past few decades, who are cosmopolitan in different ways than the Lebanese. In contrast to many Lebanese, who are multilingual in French, Wolof, and Lebanese Arabic, yet mostly illiterate in classical Arabic, Senegalese Shiʿi leaders are fluent in Arabic, and many have university degrees from the Middle East. Senegal's Shiʿa choose their persuasion due to social connections with other *Arabisants* and cite intellectual reasons, finding that Shiʿi religious literature convincingly answers their questions about Islam. Arabic enables them to access Shiʿi religious texts, interact with other Shiʿa, and be part of a global Islamic movement. Shiʿi Islam makes it possible for converts to escape the local power of Senegal's Sufi leaders by creating an alternative Islamic network. They spread knowledge about Shiʿi Islam in Wolof or other local languages, first to friends and family, and ultimately to a larger population through teaching, conferences, holiday celebrations, and media publicity.

Whereas Lebanese of different denominations came together in Senegal as one ethnic group, religion trumped African ethnicity for Senegalese converts. Members of Senegal's myriad ethnic groups and (initially) various Sufi orders collaborated in the common goal of propagating their new faith. While inscribing their intervention in the local religious imaginary through reworking history and tradition, Senegalese Shiʿa are able to go beyond established ties of Senegal's Sunni reformist movements with Saudi Arabia and of local Sufi orders with the Senegalese state and (re)negotiate new international linkages with Iran and Lebanon. The result is what I call "conversion" to push theories of religious change to a new level as Senegalese simultaneously search for their place both outside and inside their traditions.

Even though Senegalese converts share Shiʿi Islam with Lebanese coreligionists, the two populations remain almost entirely apart. They do not regularly socialize, and Senegalese converts envision themselves as more intellectually Shiʿa than Lebanese businessmen. Lebanese Shaykh al-Zayn, who established Dakar's Islamic Social Institute in 1978, is a central figure in both communities. He is not the only Shiʿi influence; the spread of the 1979 Iranian Revolution to West Africa also led to heightened religio-political identity. Some Senegalese converts were brought to Shiʿi Islam through their relationships with Lebanese, and some pray regularly at the Lebanese Islamic Institute and are employed by Shaykh al-Zayn to manage daily affairs, lead religious services, and teach Arabic. Certain Lebanese are also present at Senegalese Shiʿi events. Examining these groups together enables an evaluation of the development of a global Shiʿi Islam that affects local communities in diverse ways.

Becoming a "citizen of the world" through travel, migration, business contacts, homeland politics, religious networks, conversion, and education impacts national culture and nationalism. Whereas Lebanon remains the ideological homeland of Lebanese Shiʿa, Senegalese converts create a distinctly Senegalese Shiʿism. For them, as Shiʿi Islam travels to Africa it loses the (often political) spirit that exemplifies religion in countries of origin: Iran's revolutionary undertones or Lebanon's resistance forces. These processes provide new evidence for reformulating theories of cosmopolitanism to correspond with the complex relationship between religion, migration, conversion, and ethnicity/nationalism. Thus Shiʿi rituals— and the global and local allegiances inherent in their performances—have distinct meanings for Lebanese migrants and Senegalese converts.

In bringing together these two case studies through an analysis of the intersection of multiple sites of local and global Islam (French colonialism, Lebanese migration, Iranian revolution, Senegalese conversion) this book challenges the notion that Islam is "counter-cosmopolitan." First developed by Appiah (2006), this argument has been taken up by other scholars—particularly political scientists such as Held (2010) in the post-9/11 context—and critiqued by anthropologists and Islamic studies scholars. Lebanese migrants and Senegalese converts strategically mold cosmopolitan ethics in ways that enable each minority community to assert political autochthony. Religion, for Lebanese, becomes secularized in an inclusive ethno-national identity that, despite increasing sectarian tensions, unites Muslims and Christians as "Afro-Lebanese." In contrast, Shiʿi Islam brings members of Senegalese ethnic groups together in an alternative network that preaches religious reform with an aim of overcoming the state's economic failures. Religion thus provides a universalizing and differentiating identity that supersedes previous colonial categories of "race" and "ethnicity." Lebanese migrants and Senegalese converts transform the conceptual framework of Shiʿi Islam into a humanitarian and thus (locally) universal one from which everyone can benefit. Through education, health care, economic development, working for peace in rebel separatist territories, and assisting during national tragedies, Shiʿi Islam is deradicalized and familiarized as it caters to the African (and sometimes Lebanese) public good. This humanism is also reinforced by the universalist language of Shaykh al-Zayn and Senegalese Shiʿi leaders knowing when to emphasize Shiʿi Islam as an all-inclusive (not foreign minority branch of) Islam.

In highlighting the dynamic and heterogeneous nature of contemporary identifications, I examine Muslim cosmopolitanism as articulated through engagement with history, colonialism, the state, political-economy, global Islamic movements, and the imagination of nations. I understand cosmopolitanism to be a heuristic concept and contested category of practice, a disposition or form of experience that refers to a variety of imagination, a specific cultural and social condition that allows Muslims to inhabit the contemporary world, and a future possibility grounded in present-day realities (Leichtman and Schulz 2012). I argue for the centrality of religious traditions and networks to projects of cosmopolitanism, and probe the secular post-Enlightenment and elitist bias inherent in much of the cosmopolitan literature. I envision Muslim cosmopolitanism to be at once universalist in identifying (to some extent) with the global Islamic *umma* (Muslim community-at-large) and rooted in particular local histories. Although this book focuses primarily on Shiʿi Muslim cosmopolitanism, I also examine other models of cosmopolitanism: French colonial cosmopolitanism and the cosmopolitan political ideologies of Lebanese Michel Chiha, Senegalese Leopold Sedar Senghor, and Iranian Ayatollah Ruhollah Khomeini—all of whom in different ways reconfigured a universalism that was a function of European/Christian, Arab, African, or Islamic particularities.

On Transnationalism and Cosmopolitanism

My previous scholarship examined Lebanese migrants (Leichtman 2005; Leichtman 2010; Leichtman 2013) and Senegalese converts (Leichtman 2009) in a transnational framework. But as I previously argued, the transnationalism approach has its limitations (Leichtman 2005). Many studies have a geographical bias, examining immigrants in North America and Europe without comparison to other world regions, and ignore the impact of colonialism. I argued that transnationalism could not be limited only to sending and receiving countries. Relationships between migrant, home country, host country, and tertiary countries are key factors in the creation of transnational community and are especially important in examining transnational ties among South–South migrants. I also suggested that definitions of transnationalism for second and later generations must be modified. Movement between home and host country and economic and political embeddedness are no longer central criteria. Instead, ethnic groups maintain transnational characteristics through self-identification and definition by others, imagining the motherland, and upholding political and religious ideologies. In order to more effectively bring together case studies of Lebanese migrants and Senegalese converts as examples of vernacularization of global Shiʿi Islamic movements in Dakar, I ground my analysis instead in the literature on cosmopolitanism.

While also a problematic concept, cosmopolitanism, as I envision it, makes possible a move beyond political boundaries of geographic borders inherent in notions of transnationalism. I draw from the literature I find most relevant to the African context.[1] Vertovec and Cohen define cosmopolitanism as "something that simultaneously: (a) transcends the seemingly exhausted nation-state model; (b) is able to mediate actions and ideals oriented both to the universal and the particular, the global and the local; (c) is culturally anti-essentialist; and (d) is capable of representing variously complex repertoires of allegiance, identity and interest" (2003:4). Cosmopolitanism—as anthropologists have emphasized and on which I draw—remains grounded in the local. Beck argues that "what is distinctive about cosmopolitanization is that it is *internal* and it is internalized *from within* national societies or local cultures" (2006:72–73). Similarly Werbner insists that "for anthropologists, cosmopolitanism is as much a local engagement *within* postcolonial states—with cultural pluralism, global rights movements, ideas about democracy and the right to dissent—as beyond their borders" (2008:4–5). In these notions of cosmopolitanism the global remains important, but the focus shifts to local contexts that are concurrently shaped by while also influencing the global.

The struggle for survival in postcolonial and neoliberal Senegal during economic and political crises puts pressure on local communities to expand their networks in creative ways. This book outlines the varied approaches of Lebanese and Senegalese Shiʿa, two distinct communities as envisioned by the Senegalese state. The moral and ethical foundations of the cosmopolitan outlook provide a framework for understanding both Shiʿi minority communities, whereas transnationalism is best applied to studies of migrant communities and not to indigenous populations who do not necessarily move across borders. Cosmopolitanism simultaneously transcends as it is defined by the political. This book will illustrate the relationship between cosmopolitanism, Islam, and politics, stressing the agency between, and the political structure of, state and society in Senegal. Faisal Devji's *The Terrorist in Search of Humanity*, however polemic, provides an intriguing model for establishing the ethics of Muslim cosmopolitanism.

Devji examines Osama bin Laden and al-Qaʾida as an example of militancy's endeavor to found a global politics outside of inherited forms and institutions. As al-Qaʾida outgrew (or could not be confined by) established traditional politics, global media "did not simply represent or even influence politics but actually took its place" (2008:3). Devji provocatively suggests that al-Qaʾida "has abandoned the nation state and with it Islamic law as a model, claiming territory only in the abstract terms of a global caliphate" (4). In this way he maintains that local forms of Islamic militancy are increasingly mediated by global conditions—not the other way around. Politics governing citizens of nation-states are replaced with an ethical form of Muslims as human beings and "contemporary representatives of human suffering" (7)—no different, Devji declares, from other NGOs dedicated to humanitarian work. Human rights and humanitarianism provide militants with terms by which to imagine global Muslim politics of the future.

My goal is to historicize the conflict between ethics and politics in the context of Shiʿi Islamic movements. Following Devji's analysis, the earlier 1979 Iranian Revolution and 2006 Lebanon War can be compared to al-Qaʾida, not in terms of particular Islamist agendas, but in attempts at universalism and global dissemination to other Muslim contexts. As Khomeini's ideologies traveled, the revolution's violence and distinctly Iranian political message likewise transformed into Muslim pride and Islamic humanitarianism. Lebanese Shaykh ʿAbdul Munʿam al-Zayn founded West Africa's first Lebanese and Shiʿi Islamic institute precisely at the time of Iran's revolution (chapter 3). The revolution's legacy continued to live on as Senegalese converts in the 1980s and 1990s sought knowledge about Shiʿi jurisprudence and translated religious proselytizing into Shiʿi Islamic NGOs working toward economic development. Likewise in 2006 Hizbullah won the public opinion war against Israel through gaining international support (including Senegal), resulting in mass protests against the war's human rights violations and humanitarian assistance to victims. Thus unlike transnationalism, an inefficient concept constrained as a political category by nation-state boundaries, cosmopolitanism allows deeper engagement with processes of globalization and localization. In this book I describe cosmopolitanism in a variety of ways: historical moments (Lebanese migration, French colonialism, the Iranian Revolution, the

2006 Lebanon War), identity shifts ("secular" Lebanese ethnicity, Senegalese religious conversion), and constant tensions between the moral and the political (Lebanese affective ties to Lebanon, Senegalese proclamations that Shiʻi Islam is distinctly *African*).

It is, in fact, the ethical dimension of cosmopolitanism that enables analysis of the political. Politics can be understood as claims on and of the state, as duties, rights, and obligations of (foreign-born or native) citizens. There is also a politics of cosmopolitanism—to say cosmopolitanism is political makes it meaningful and gives it consequences, such as foreign and domestic policies in response to 9/11. I am making a distinction between the two. It is not my goal to address the politics of 9/11, even though much of the literature on Muslim cosmopolitanism derives from that historical moment in examining Muslim "terrorism" or in responding to such scholarship. I do not agree with the position that considers Muslims to be "counter-cosmopolitans." Cosmopolitanism is, however, a fundamental ethical conflict for Islam. If cosmopolitanism, according to Appiah (2006), is "universality plus difference," can religious minorities such as Shiʻa in Senegal promote a cosmopolitanism highlighting difference before universality, or promote a universality that will apply to a particular delineated group? This book will outline such strategies.

Considering Cosmopolitanism in Anthropology

Cosmopolitanism has become the new buzzword of the past two decades. Some of its meanings can be traced to Cynics or Stoics in Greek antiquity, others to Immanuel Kant's eighteenth-century elaborations. Some authors even posit a *new* cosmopolitanism linked to contemporary processes of globalization, deregulation of markets, postnationalism, migration, and feminism.[2] Derived from the Greek conjunction of "world" (*cosmos*) and "city" (*polis*), cosmopolitanism describes a "citizen of the world," one who is not rootless but embedded in concentric circles of identity (Nussbaum 1994).

Given the considerable conceptual indeterminacy of the term (for Pollock et al. 2000:577–578, "specifying cosmopolitanism positively and definitely is an uncosmopolitan thing to do"), there is ample room for scholars to attribute to it various advantages. Hannerz (2004) highlights the concept's use for anthropologists as they move back and forth between "the local" and "the global," blurring the initial, problematic contrast between the two. Ho (2002; 2006) goes beyond this binary in demonstrating how debates about cosmopolitan forms of self-understanding are neither local, national, nor global, but recognize how forms of identity arise from wider linkages. Werbner (2008) envisions a new anthropology of cosmopolitanism, grounded ethically in ideas of tolerance, inclusiveness, hospitality, personal autonomy, and emancipation. This challenges the concept's articulations in other disciplines: rejecting the view that cosmopolitanism is only and singularly elitist; suggesting that cosmopolitanism's fundamental values are not necessarily "Western"; insisting that not all postcolonial cosmopolitans are travelers or need to reside or move permanently beyond their nations and cultures; and stressing that cosmopolitanism reflects striving for universal ideals and local multiculturalisms within a particular field of power. For anthropologists, *vernacular cosmopolitanism,* an "oxymoron that joins contradictory notions of local specificity and universal enlightenment" (Werbner 2006:496), has been particularly popular, highlighting the plurality of practices that constitute and result from regionally diverse historicities and worldviews.

The understanding of cosmopolitanism that I am most interested in here—applicable to both Lebanese migrants and Senegalese converts—"presents diasporas, the interplay of oral and literate traditions, the relations among village, nation, and transnational society as matters of multiple memberships and mixture" (Calhoun 2003:540). This cosmopolitanism of participation actively incorporates, rather than merely tolerates, ethnicity and recognizes that cosmopolitanism cannot be detached from local culture. Culture, never static and always highly fluid, is autochthonous and remains grounded in its roots. For Lebanese migrants in Senegal this cosmopolitanism brings together Lebanese Muslims and Christians in a celebration of Lebanese national culture. For Senegalese converts, Shiʿi Islam transcends ethnic groups, draws from Shiʿi resources in Iran and Lebanon, yet remains true to Senegalese culture. However, I disagree with Calhoun's assertion that this notion of cosmopolitanism is disconnected from politics. As this book will demonstrate, Shiʿi Muslim cosmopolitanism—at least in the Senegalese context—is inescapably political.

The cosmopolitanism framework can be used to analyze the politics of communities envisaged in *marginality* (Bhabha 1996). The Shiʿi concept of *taqiyya* (dissimulation), practiced when necessary by Shiʿa in Senegal (chapter 7), can be evaluated according to Brink-Danan's model of minority cosmopolitanism. Brink-Danan (2011) debates the aspect of "choice" inherent in cosmopolitanism, understood as actively and publicly pursuing difference, and questions how this changes for individuals and communities already marked as "different." She writes: "Being a Jewish cosmopolitan [in Turkey] means not only knowing about different ways of being, but knowing in which contexts one should (and should not) perform difference" (448). Similarities between Jews and Shiʿa as persecuted religious minorities have long been drawn. Lebanese Shiʿa in Dakar privately commemorate ʿAshura, avoiding the public processions popular in some Muslim countries and even the West, and their only public demonstration (in support of Lebanon during the 2006 war with Israel) incorporated symbols of simultaneous patriotism as Senegalese (chapter 4). Diasporans, such as Lebanese, have long insisted on their right to combine transnational loyalty and local citizenship. Lebanese also draw on their past: the Phoenician diaspora of the Old World, Beirut's cos mopolitanism, their history as protected traders and sojourners, which enabled them to become "postnational" citizens (Soysal 1994). On the other hand, unlike Jews in Turkey and Lebanese in Senegal, Senegal's Shiʿa have recently begun to publicly perform their difference, hoping to spread their cosmopolitan religious vision of choice to Sufi compatriots (chapter 7). The label of "cosmopolitan," despite fervent claims of patriotism and efforts to demonstrate assimilation, is not universally and positively accepted.

Muslim Cosmopolitanism

I have thus far outlined an ethical model of cosmopolitanism capable of theorizing a global religious movement while remaining rooted in local culture and history. This flexible cosmopolitanism can be creatively molded, celebrated, or hidden in response to minority identity politics and the reality that difference, especially ethnic and religious difference, is not universally applauded. Religion is an essential cultural component, and cosmopolitanism is a relevant framework not only for anthropology, but also for Islamic studies. In the afterword to *Rethinking Islamic Studies—From Orientalism to Cosmopolitanism,* Lawrence asks: "*What are the distinctions between orthodox, normative, and "folk" Islam? . . .* Ironically, those who ask these questions today are no longer best identified as either Muslim or non-Muslim, but rather as citizens of the world. . . . Religion qua cosmopolitanism confers a special benefit for the study of Islam. . . . Instead of privileging or deriding one religious tradition vis-à-vis others, it shows the boundedness of religious communities within a larger complex of commercial exchange and social comity best etched by the term *oikoumene*" (2010:303–304).

This application of cosmopolitanism, as a moving beyond boundaries and categorization of various strands of Islam, can thus provide a solution to the long-debated question in anthropology of how to study Islam. Anthropologists began in the 1960s to focus on Muslim societies in newly independent Asian and North African states. Geertz (1968) and Gellner (1981) borrowed from Orientalism (and colonialism) in employing the distinction between orthodox and unorthodox or heterodox Islam. El-Zein (1977) proposed the existence of multiple *islams,* and many anthropologists began to treat Islam as a plural phenomenon, divided among "modernists" and "traditionalists" (Bowen 1993) or "high" and "low" Islam (inspired by Redfield 1956). Scholars attached ethnic and geographic qualifiers to the religion, describing various islams around the world.

Africa was no exception. Senegal had been an important focus of academic scholarship, with Islam an especially dominant theme since the colonial period. Policymakers and scholars simplified Islam in Senegal by dividing it into two variants: "African Islam," or what some have referred to as "traditional Islam," associated with Sufi orders, and Islamic reformist movements, perceived to have originated outside of Africa (Westerlund and Rosander 1997; Villalón 2004). French officers first made this distinction with colonial policies envisioning *Islam noir* as distinct from "orthodoxy," which mainly referred to Muslim practices in North Africa and the Middle East. The term *Islam noir* captured the colonial perception of Islam south of the Sahara defined as the product of spiritual and ritualistic transactions between Islam and "African traditional religions." African Islam was seen as less "pure," less literate, and more magical than Arab Islam, and flexible enough to be incorporated into French so-called Muslim policy (chapter 1).

Asad (1986) countered this tendency in making the influential case for treating Islam as a discursive tradition and considering Islam in relation to those discourses that sought to instruct practitioners regarding the correct form and purpose of a given practice. He thus emphasized the importance of orthodoxy, but in a different way from Orientalists and anthropologists such as Gellner. Simpson and Kresse (2008:26) envision these competing interpretations of Islamic orthodoxy and legitimacy as rival forms of cosmopolitanism, which share the goal of uniting Muslims by focusing on universal standards and practices, yet propagate a sectarian agenda that gave rise to disunity and factionalism. I prefer instead to visualize Muslim cosmopolitanism as a way to bridge various "local" and "global" Islamic traditions by escaping the problematic dichotomy that has haunted the field for too long.

Asad's work, according to Lawrence, was the precursor to a Muslim cosmopolitanism that redefines "Islam apart from both fundamentalists/Islamists and their statist/nationalist opponents" (2010:306). At once local and ideological, Muslim cosmopolitanism can be contrasted to Arabocentrism, where the *sunna*, the Prophet's example, is privileged over Arabic language and (especially Saudi) norms. This is important for African Muslims who are not native Arabic speakers and have a contentious historical relationship with the Arab world. Incorporating an anthropological understanding of cosmopolitanism enables a moving beyond the humanities-based definition Lawrence applies to Muslim cosmopolitanism, favoring Islamic texts and traditions.

We must also move beyond contemporary Western-centric political understandings of cosmopolitanism. Lincoln (2003) examines how 9/11—and other major political moments—transformed the way we think about religion; Calhoun (2003:531) likewise credits these tragic events for giving "renewed emphasis to the image of Islam as the bad other to liberalism and progress." An exploration of Muslim cosmopolitan practices and competences must unfortunately take account of the discursive parameters that, since at least September 11, have inflected scholarly debate on whether "Muslims" or "Islam" should be conceived as part or as the Other of a new cosmopolitan order of things.

9/11 is a central example in Held's new book on cosmopolitanism, which counsels the wider Islamic community "to reaffirm the compatibility of Islam with the universal, cosmopolitan principles that put life, and the free development of all human beings, at their centre" (2010:138). Held presents cosmopolitanism and (a certain strand of) Islam as mutually exclusive, which assumes that Muslims today are at odds with cosmopolitanism, or at best have not embraced such—*universal*—Enlightenment ideals. Similarly, Appiah (2006) labels all "global Muslim fundamentalists" as *counter-cosmopolitans*. Drawing exclusively from Roy (2004) and using his term *neofundamentalists,* Appiah suggests that their unitary normative vision for how all human beings should live goes against the *pluralism* and *fallibilism* inherent in the notion of cosmopolitanism. Lawrence (n.d.) argues, contra Appiah, that Muslim cosmopolitanism must displace terrorism as the referent of assumed "difference" between Muslim and non-Muslim moderns. Yet in so arguing, Lawrence also falls into the same trap of a "contaminated cosmopolitanism" (Appiah 2006) by continuing to oppose cosmopolitanism to terrorism as its binary *-ism*. Kahn (2008) reminds us that Kant's vision was grounded in a particular set of "cultural" presuppositions that were masculinist, white, and middle class, and there is no reason why global cosmopolitan Islam cannot also generate its own exclusions like classical Western so-called normative cosmopolitanism.

Establishing the historical existence of cosmopolitanism in the Muslim world demonstrates that Islam has always been cosmopolitan and that the concept is not limited to Western Enlightenment ideals. Scholars have illustrated how Muslims link cosmopolitanism to the Prophet Muhammad (Hoesterey 2012; Mandaville 2007); describe "premodern Islamic cosmopolitanism" (Zaman 2005); and locate the golden age of Middle Eastern cosmopolitanism in Istanbul (Lawrence 2012), Cairo, and Alexandria (Zubaida 2002) during European imperial dominance. History has created societies in which differences are recognized and individuals are, however unevenly, equipped with skills to navigate through such differences, what Simpson and Kresse call "struggling with history" (2008:15). This book similarly takes a historical—as well as contemporary—approach.

I raise these debates to highlight the problematic nature of cosmopolitanism as a concept for the study of both Muslim (see also MacLean 2012) *and* non-Muslim societies. The judgmental conclusions of Held and Appiah, among others, suggest another recent debate among social theorists provoked by a question posed on the Social Science Research Council's blog, *The Imminent Frame,* asking "Is Critique Secular?" In response, a conference held at University of California—Berkeley focused this discussion around inflammatory discourses arising from the 2005 Danish cartoon affair, when a right-wing newspaper published a series of cartoons unflatteringly satirizing the Prophet Muhammad. Prominent scholars raised questions regarding the nature of critical theory, which, like cosmopolitanism, is presumed to be grounded in Western-centric Kantian visions of Enlightenment.

Asad (2009) and Mahmood (2009) emphasized in different ways how the secular and the religious are not opposed but are intertwined historically and con-

ceptually, making it impossible to inquire into one without engaging the other.
Like the notion of critique, cosmopolitanism also introduces dangers of liberal
bias, and behind it, the same old dominant power relations. There are religious,
progressive, and secular varieties of cosmopolitanism. Mahmood and Lawrence,
among others, have pointed out that pluralism leads to the problem of relativism,
a concept long debated in anthropology. These issues raise a number of questions:
Can we avoid the ever-slippery slope of relativism? Does one have to be secular
to be cosmopolitan? Can one be secular, when dominant notions of secularism
are rooted in Christianity? Can there be religious tolerance without universalism? Must cosmopolitanism have an opposite (which Lawrence [n.d.] claims is
terrorism but for Geertz [1973] is a more accepted *parochialism*)? Like Mahmood
and her colleagues I do not seek a "yes" or "no" answer to the question "is critique
secular?"; my goal is merely to raise, not to answer, and not even to fully engage
with, all these questions.

Ahmad (2011) contends that there are non-Enlightenment modes of critique
and makes a case for Islamic critique as a competing non-Western modality. Similar arguments have been made for Muslim cosmopolitanism. Therefore the questions I entertain result from how many of the debates outlined above still center
around Euro-American topics: how secular liberalism applies to how Muslims
are perceived *in the West*. Are these same debates regarding freedom and blasphemy, secular criticism and religious reason, relevant in a Muslim context? How
are minorities, who follow a different branch of the same religion, perceived in
Africa? Are Lebanese Arabs who are racially distinct (as are Muslims in Europe)
treated differently than African religious minorities (who can more easily claim
autochthony)? Like all trendy terms, *Muslim cosmopolitanism* can be envisioned
as a provisional category until we come up with a better concept. This, however,
does not take away from the value of debating its application in various contexts.

Citizenship, Autochthony, and African Cosmopolitanism

I leave behind academic debates regarding Muslim cosmopolitanism in returning
to the Senegalese context. Although cosmopolites may strive to be "citizens of the
world," they are, more importantly, citizens of the country in which they reside. Yet
not all citizens are governed equally. The following chapters examine how Lebanese migrants and Senegalese converts creatively maneuver in different ways the
ethics of cosmopolitanism and Shiʿi Islam to lay claim to autochthony in order to
advance politically as a minority community in Senegal.

Mamdani (1996) argues that we cannot separate the political institutions of
contemporary Africa from their colonial legacy, particularly in regard to "race"
and "ethnicity." Providing primary examples from countries that experienced
British indirect rule, Mamdani demonstrates how natives were said to belong to
ethnic groups but nonnatives were identified racially. Whereas civil law was em-

bedded in a discourse of rights, customary law was embedded in tradition and authenticity. The hierarchy of race included master races and subject races, where Lebanese nonnatives were subject to French colonizers and later the Senegalese state (led by indigenous subject ethnicities). Subject races usually performed a middleman function, their position marked by economic privilege and preferential legal treatment. Nationalism became a native struggle to gain recognition as a transethnic identity—as an "African" race—in order to tap into the rights of civil society. Racially marked nonnative Lebanese thereby strove to be accepted as an indigenous ethnicity so as to claim Africanness. In contrast, Senegalese converts united as a panethnic religious group with the intention of overcoming state failures. To assert basic citizen rights—or compensate for the dearth of citizen services in a resource-weak state—each group had to establish autochthony.

New—or not so new—religious movements can be examined as contestations of sovereignty and competition to the state. They can also be understood as a function of, but certainly not reduced to, globalized neoliberal conditions. Debates about cosmopolitanism tie into recent discussions in African studies of autochthony (Comaroffs 2000 and 2001; Geschiere 2009; Geschiere and Nyamnjoh 2000; McGovern 2011 and 2013), cultural politics of indigeneity and commodification of ethnicity (Comaroffs 2009; Hodgson 2011), and sovereignty (Hansen and Stepputat 2005; Piot 2010), which have been dominating questions of citizenship and belonging. Geschiere and Nyamnjoh argue that "cosmopolitanism and autochthony are like conjoined twins: a fascination with globalization's open horizons is accompanied by determined efforts towards boundary-making and closure, expressed in terms of belonging and exclusion" (2000:425). For Geschiere (2009), *autochthony* means "to be born from the soil," the most authentic and primordial form of belonging. Similarly the Comaroffs define autochthony as "elevating to a first-principle the ineffable interests and connections, at once material and moral, that flow from 'native' rootedness, and special rights, in *a place of birth* . . . it resonates with deeply felt populist fears—and with the proclivity of citizens of all stripes to deflect shared anxieties onto outsiders" (2001:635). So, too, in Senegal does ethnic citizenship become invariably defined against "strangers" and those who do not "belong."

Yet Senegal is also the land of *teranga*, Wolof for hospitality—an embodiment of cosmopolitanism, where it is considered rude not to shake a stranger's hand. Senegalese take pride in their languages and customs and welcome (certain) visitors into their homes. The perfunctory American greeting "hi, how are you?" requiring only a "fine, and you?" in lieu of a literal response, is transformed into a series of detailed questions in Senegal, inquiring about one's day, health, and family. Senegalese are willing to talk all afternoon to a foreigner about their country, ethnic group, and religion. Many Senegalese are also Indophiles who appreciate Bollywood films and Indian dance (Steene 2008; see also Larkin 1997).

Ironically, Senegal—with its teranga—is also characterized by Geschiere as one of several African countries fearful and excluding of "strangers." Although he does not develop the Senegalese case, Geschiere suggests that because of the strong connection between Senegal's ruling party and Sufi orders, autochthony movements remained limited to the country's periphery. Such movements were particularly salient in the southern Casamance region, where rebels formed a secessionist faction against the state, and where Islamization was historically less successful than elsewhere in the country (2009:261–262n5). Autochthony, however, is also at play in Dakar, most obviously displayed through Senegalese interactions with Lebanese, but also behind efforts of Senegalese Shiʿa to demonstrate how Shiʿi Islam is not a foreign religion at odds with Sufi Islam.

Ideas of autochthony are linked to processes of globalization. Mbembe (2002) polarizes Africa between localism and cosmopolitanism. He describes an African mentality that negates the existence of the individual in favor of the group and defines the nation as the sum total of its differences and the particularities of each of its cultures. This divisively puts strangers—*allogènes*—at odds with nationals—*autochthones,* who have access to public space and nationality. Mbembe outlines two types of cosmopolitanism. Migrants, responding to the marginalization of allogènes, embrace a cosmopolitanism that serves to integrate them in distinct spatial strategies of various religious, economic, and cultural networks. The Lebanese community in Senegal has long attempted to establish itself through formal and informal economic channels, behind the scenes as financial backers of Senegalese politicians who would offer them protection, and as public givers of charity to those less fortunate (chapter 2). Ideas that immigrants profited more than autochthons or stole from them coveted economic opportunities led to xenophobia, to which Lebanese responded by uniting as an ethnic group to advocate for common needs. French colonial officials hoped their anti-Lebanese campaigns in West Africa in the 1930s would spread these sentiments to the "native" Senegalese population (chapter 1). Lebanese were not the only targets for xenophobia, as evidenced by Senegalese-Mauritanian tensions in 1989. Geschiere and Nyamnjoh (2000) posit that autochthony discourses can be so supple as to even accommodate a switch from one Other to another. Ironically Senegalese—and Lebanese who were once their primary scapegoats—can be heard today discussing the recent wave of Chinese immigrants as "parasites" who do not invest in Senegal.

Mbembe describes a second type of cosmopolitanism of elites who strive to reconstruct African identity through reenchanting their customs and traditions in a local reappropriation of symbolic resources of globalization. The cosmopolitanism of literate Arabic-educated Senegalese differs from that of the political elite Mbembe refers to, whose cosmopolitanism is the product of mimicry. Yet both serve as intermediaries between localities, the state, and international networks, and can bridge their access to international resources with local sentiments of belonging. Inspired by Iranian and Lebanese influences, Senegalese converts to Shi'i Islam have vernacularized this branch of Islam to become nationally and "authentically" *Senegalese*. Senegal's openness to religious plurality enables such groups to promote a cosmopolitan religious tolerance of others.

These two groups of Shi'i cosmopolitans in Senegal—Lebanese migrants and Senegalese Arabisants—are positioned to contribute to debates about Senegalese nationalism. In contrast to Anderson's (1983) *Imagined Communities,* which reflected one articulation of nationalism in the pre-globalization era, scholars argue that today's more cosmopolitan reimagination of nationhood as embracing internal difference and "multiculturalism" still falls victim to dichotomous categorizations as autochthon or alien, indigene or other. The Comaroffs write: "While most human beings still live as citizens *in* nation-states, they tend only to be conditionally, partially, and situationally citizens *of* nation-states" (2001:634). Senegal is no exception, precisely at a time when global capitalism seems to be threatening sovereign borders and displacing traditional politics.[3]

Senegal is faced with economic crisis, which has led to increasing wealth disparities, rising rent and food prices, rapid urbanization and unemployment, a decrease in public services offered by the state (in particular regular and debilitating power outages and the pungently sporadic collection of trash), and frequent university strikes (by faculty and students). This has contributed to Senegalese distrust of foreigners and envy of their perceived wealth, a sentiment not confined only to the most prominent of "foreigners," the Lebanese, but also extended to Mauritanians, Moroccans, Cape Verdeans, French, and most recently Chinese. French colonial production of the peanut monocrop and postindependence structural adjustment policies damaged the Senegalese economy, which was further exacerbated when President Abdoulaye Wade ascended to power in 2000. Pushing foreign investment as key to his campaign of *sopi* (change), massive urban construction projects, led by his son Karim under the slogan "generation of concrete," aimed to showcase Dakar as a venue for international organizations anxious to relocate from Abidjan's crises. The project's completion was timed for the (delayed) 2008 Organization of the Islamic Conference meeting in Dakar.

Yet Dakar's renovated airport and the newest of Senegal's luxurious five-star hotels, privatizing what was once public beach along the city's scenic corniche, will not benefit Senegal's poor or those living outside the capital. Senegalese suffered tremendously from incapacitating traffic jams, increased air pollution, and business loss during the multiyear construction project (which also made my fieldwork difficult). Economic desperation has become epitomized by willingness to risk lives and borrowed capital to make the clandestine and perilous voyage by pirogues, fishing boats never meant to travel six hundred miles to Spain's Canary Islands or other international destinations. This crisis further affected life-cycle events by delaying age of marriage because unemployed young men cannot afford expensive dowries and remain at the mercy of financial expectations of both extended family and religious leaders (Buggenhagen 2012). A 1967 law prohibiting excessive spending in family ceremonies remains a hotly debated political issue today. The majority of Senegalese are faced with increasing pressures to migrate. Kane (2011) emphasizes that this cannot be analyzed as a function of Senegal's economic situation alone without also considering the moral economy for success and prestige, where migration has come to replace education as a paradigm for social mobility. Yet I do not agree with Melly (2010) that absent migrants are the only ones who can belong in Dakar. The "perils of belonging" (Geschiere 2009) is one theme of this book.

Thus Senegal falls into the postcolonial paradox described by the Comaroffs, where nations must open up their frontiers in order to partake in the global economy and facilitate the inflow of wealth, while at the same time securing and regulating their borders to attract the "right" kind of migrants and businesses. In this way cosmopolitanism occurs simultaneously with autochthony movements and challenges the sovereignty of the Senegalese state. Hansen and Stepputat (2005:10–11) stress that today "sovereignty as embodied in citizens sharing territory and culture, and sharing the right to exclude and punish 'strangers,' has become a political common sense." The production of sovereignty and the linking of people to land and ethnicity to territory as an ideology of autochthony are often exclusive projects that inadvertently produce large numbers of poor, marginalized, or ethnic others as outsiders who are excluded as citizens.

The state finds itself in constant competition with other centers of sovereignty as excluded citizens seek alternative means of empowerment. The development of religious movements is one contemporary form of social mobilization in Africa. This is also a process by which Africa integrates itself into the international system, such as via connections between Lebanese in Senegal and Lebanon or Senegalese converts and Iran. Africans join religious movements in a quest for a better world, in addition to classic methods of extraversion, which include emigration and an appeal to international aid (Bayart 2000).[4] Yet in contrast to the global proliferation of what the Comaroffs have characterized as "occult economies" (2001), the growth of Shiʿi Islam in Senegal is not grounded in the (real or imagined) need to conjure wealth through magical means that defy explanation. In fact, the Muslim half of Africa is conveniently forgotten as certain otherwise meticulous scholars generalize "the experience of Africa—where charismatic Christianity and occult imaginaries have transformed the cultural landscape in the last ten years" (Piot 2010:10).[5] Shiʿi Islam's success is due instead to its ability to link religious explanations, based on Islamic texts, with basic training grounded in practices of grassroots development. Neoliberalism has reconfigured relationships between the governing and the governed, power and knowledge, sovereignty and territoriality. NGOs as practitioners of humanity give value to marginalized populations and challenge political spaces of inclusion and exclusion demarcated by nation-states (Ong 2006; Hodgson 2011). For Shiʿa in Senegal, founding institutions in the name of religion alone no longer suffices. These must also be official state-registered NGOs, which provide legitimacy for minority communities to carry out their religious work, grounded in economic development, which attracts a growing membership whose needs are not met by the Senegalese state. Public performances of religious sovereignty thus become necessary, exhibited through conferences, media broadcasts, religious rituals, the opening of new schools, and neighborhood events that offer free health evaluations. Religious organizations— as an ethical form of the Muslim humanitarianism described by Devji—claim to be nonpolitical even though their offerings contribute to filling the gap left by state inefficiencies.

Chapter Summary

This book is based on a total of approximately two years of ethnographic research in Senegal, consisting of repeated trips to Dakar of various lengths (ranging from ten days to one and a half years) between 2000 and 2013. I began this project with a one-month stay in Beirut the summer of 2000, where I also returned briefly in 2001 and 2007. Visits to Shiʿi organizations based in London and Paris provided additional insight into Shiʿi cosmopolitanism.

This book is divided into two parts. Part 1, which comprises four chapters, focuses on the history of Lebanese migration to Senegal and the social, economic, and religious development of the community over several generations. It explains how Lebanese Muslims and Christians (almost evenly proportioned in the first generation) came together as a secular "Afro-Lebanese" ethnic group in response to empire politics and colonial rivalries, which caused continuous tensions between religion, ethnicity, race, and nationalism. Part 2 contains three chapters that explore the expansion of Shiʿi Islam among Senegalese, discussing competing Lebanese, Iranian, and indigenous African leadership and featuring conversion stories.

History and cosmopolitanism come into play in this book in various ways. Using Senegal's national archives and secondary sources, chapter 1 presents French strategies in *Afrique Occidentale Française,* in particular the colonial administration's position on Islam in West Africa and changing policies toward Lebanese migration. While portraying itself as a "Muslim power," the French civilizing mission reinforced racial notions of autochthony through prohibiting Lebanese from praying in public spaces, attending religious school, and living in popular Senegalese residential quarters. Colonialists endeavored to control the importation of publications in Arabic, especially those that had taken an anti-French position on other colonies or glorified revolt in the Middle East. This chapter details anti-

Lebanese campaigns of the 1950s and Lebanese efforts to fight back using transnational ties.

Chapter 2 examines Leopold Sedar Senghor's philosophy of Negritude and his cosmopolitan articulation of the place of Arabs within Africa. It discusses Lebanese economic, political, and cultural integration in Senegal and perceptions of race and racism. Independence in 1960 raised questions of belonging for the Lebanese community, tied to policies of Africanization and hostility by Senegalese, as well as continuing instabilities in Lebanon. Lebanese efforts to gain acceptance as a "Senegalese" ethnic group attempted to shift colonial racial discourses to a more inclusive and tolerant notion of postcolonial nationalism.

Chapter 3 introduces the life and work of Shaykh ʿAbdul Munʿam al-Zayn, who arrived in Dakar in 1969, almost a century after the establishment of the Lebanese community. There was no formal Shiʿi religious representation in Senegal until the founding of the Lebanese Islamic Institute in 1978. Shaykh al-Zayn's arrival came only shortly before the Lebanese Civil War (1975–1990) and Iranian Revolution (1979), two important events in the making of a global Shiʿi movement. Chapter 3 traces the shaykh's cosmopolitan upbringing: his childhood in Lebanon, religious training in Najaf, relationship with legendary Shiʿi leader Musa al-Sadr, and work founding the Islamic Social Institute of Dakar, which led to an identity shift in the Lebanese community.

Chapter 4 explicates how *transnational Islam* becomes *national Islam* and depicts how Shaykh al-Zayn influences his congregation in Dakar to "return" to patriotic Lebanese Shiʿi sentiments. It evaluates the success of the shaykh's work through examples of religious education, Arabic language instruction, and Lebanese understandings of the *marjaʿiyya,* the system of Shiʿi leadership. This chapter illustrates public expressions of piety, such as the increase in women wearing the veil and participation in religious charity events, and depicts the celebration of ʿAshura, Ramadan, and Mawlud holidays. Recent ties to Lebanon are analyzed, especially increased politicization of the Lebanese community due to the 2006 Lebanon War, suggesting that instead of becoming better Muslims, Lebanese in Senegal have become better Lebanese, further localizing their cosmopolitanism.

Part 2 begins in chapter 5 with an exploration of competition for Shiʿi influence in Senegal. Shaykh al-Zayn also established himself as the Senegalese Shiʿi leader equal in status to "caliphs" (heads) of Sufi orders. He built mosques and schools throughout Senegal to teach Africans about Shiʿi Islam. This chapter then outlines the spread of the Iranian Revolution to Africa and its influence on several Senegalese Sunni Muslim reformers. Concurrent Iranian influences also distributed Islamic books, brought Senegalese to Iran, and built a *hawza* (Shiʿi seminary) in Dakar. Yet resistance to foreign leadership led to the emergence of indigenous Senegalese Shiʿi organizations and NGOs, whose activities divided Senegalese converts in their loyalty to different religious leaders. This chapter locates Shiʿi Islam as an Islamic reformist movement among other Sunni movements in Senegal.

Chapter 6 recounts conversion stories of Senegalese Shiʿi men and women within the context of Senegalese and Western theories of conversion. Senegal's Shiʿa, some fluent in Arabic with university degrees from the Middle East, were initially inspired by the charisma of Iranian Ayatollah Khomeini or Lebanese Shaykh al-Zayn. They find the Shiʿi religious literature convincingly answers their questions about Islam that Senegal's Sufi leaders were unable to address. Shiʿi Islam enables converts to bypass the power of local religious authorities while remaining "good Muslims." Religion trumps ethnicity for Senegalese converts, and members of Senegal's myriad ethnic groups and religious orders come together in the common goal of propagating their new faith. Some even keep their feet in both Sunni and Shiʿi worlds.

Chapter 7 outlines the development of a *Senegalese* Shiʿi network. Senegalese Shiʿa spread religious knowledge in Wolof or other local languages, first to friends and family, and ultimately to a larger population through teaching, conferences, holiday celebrations, and media publicity. This chapter examines revisionist historical accounts of the spread of Islam to West Africa and describes the creation of schools and mosques. Growth of Shiʿi Islamic NGOs working in religious education through simultaneously promoting health care and other neighborhood development projects is especially notable in Senegal. Shiʿi converts establish autochthony through growing acceptance of their religious authority and Shiʿi Islam's authenticity. They tailor Shiʿi rituals, such as following the marjaʿiyya, the practice of taqiyya, the ʿAshura commemoration, and Shiʿi notions of temporary marriage, to a distinctly Senegalese context.

PART I

THE MAKING OF A LEBANESE COMMUNITY IN SENEGAL

Introduction to Part 1

If you find a fish in the sea, you find a Lebanese.

—Lebanese proverb

The Lebanese are like a bomb that exploded and fragmented all over the world.

—Lebanese informant, Dakar, 2003

MY FIRST RESEARCH trip to Lebanon corresponded coincidentally with "the First Conference for Lebanese Emigrant Businessmen and of Lebanese Descent" sponsored by the Ministry of Emigrants, June 5–9, 2000, at Hotel Phoenicia in Beirut. This conference was the first government attempt to encourage diasporic investment in Lebanon, especially important for rebuilding the country after the destructive civil war (1975–1990).[1] Presentations and ensuing discussion shed light on how Lebanese officials viewed Lebanese migrants and how different groups of migrants envisioned the Lebanese homeland. The conference organizer characteristically began with a quote from Michel Chiha, architect of Lebanon's constitution, who famously visualized a role for migrants within the Lebanese nation: "Lebanon without emigration cannot live; with too much emigration it can die."

The conference was perfectly timed, taking place only a few weeks after Israel had withdrawn from the south of Lebanon. There were numerous references to Lebanon's "victory," future Israeli withdrawal from the Golan, and opportune banter such as: "When Israelis realized the seriousness of your [conference participants] coming they fled. You came to change the wasteland [in the south of Lebanon from Israeli occupation] into a green land, darkness [from Israeli bombing of power stations] into light." The conference opened on June 5, symbolically transformed by its organizers into a historic date representing the difference between destruction (Israel invaded Lebanon on June 4–5, 1982) and construction (investment from the conference). There was much talk of the reconstruction of Lebanon, the role of the state, and other such encouragement for development, stressing that emigrants have been the main financers of rebuilding destroyed bridges and power stations. In this globalized world of communication, and with such grand regional changes, Lebanon's condition can no longer remain the same, officials urged. Speakers expressed hope that the conference would have an impact beyond the motherland. "You Lebanese businessmen scattered all over the world, this is your country," they declared. Discussion focused on topics of emigrants returning to Lebanon for tourism, the right to maintain Lebanese citizenship, and laws facilitating emigrants' rights to ownership, work, and investments while in Lebanon. Then Prime Minister Salim al-Hoss called for the setting up of emigrant Lebanese unions within general unions of doctors, lawyers, engineers, journalists, and businessmen in chambers of commerce. Participants talked of establishing a Lebanese lobby to promote Lebanese affairs around the world.

A small (five-man) delegation of Muslim and Christian businessmen from Dakar proudly represented their community. One of them requested from the minister of finance a Lebanese-Senegalese bank and offered that Lebanese in Senegal were willing to contribute their capital; as the Senegalese government was not licensing for the establishment of private banks, this investment would be possible only on the international level. The delegation from Dakar unabashedly pointed out in addressing the minister of finance that Lebanese of Africa appeared largely forgotten and forsaken by the Lebanese state. As proof, they were frustrated at the neglect they experienced when the ministry provided simultaneous translation of the conference in multiple languages for visiting emigrant delegations: English, Arabic, Spanish, and Portuguese, but not French, the predominant language of many Lebanese in West Africa. Although Arabic is Lebanon's official language, a special law regulates the use of French, considered a second language, for administrative purposes, and French is taught in many schools alongside Arabic and English. This omission is especially shocking considering the Ninth Francophonie Summit was even held in Lebanon in 2002, a point of great pride for Lebanese in Senegal, particularly since former Senegalese president Abdou Diouf was elected secretary general in Beirut.

I exited the conference room with the crowd of audience members and participants at the conclusion of the morning sessions. By chance, I noticed a mustached man standing near me in the hotel lobby, smoking a cigar, with a nametag that identified him as being from "West Africa." He approached me, rather flirtatiously, and invited me to the bank-sponsored business lunch that day. I accepted. Since I needed to be registered for the conference to attend meals, he acquired a nametag for me, which like his own associated me as being from "West Africa," where I had not yet been. He later explained that he could not identify with only one African country as he frequently travels back and forth throughout the region for business (much like Ong's [1999] "flexible citizens"). We entered the formal lunch, outside at the hotel pool, and I steered our way to a table of men wearing nametags that read "Senegal." These men happened to be influential leaders of the Lebanese community in Dakar.

*   *   *

I begin with this narrative to highlight Beirut (like Dakar) as a cosmopolitan city, reaching out to its similarly cosmopolitan emigrant communities around the world. As with all other cosmopolitanisms, there are limits to its Lebanese incarnation. In this example not all of Lebanon's "citizens of the world" were made to feel citizens at home due to language barriers. French was neglected over Spanish and Portuguese because Lebanese in Francophone Africa were perceived to be less affluent than those in Latin America. The need to recover from the long and bitter civil war with its "culture of sectarianism" (Makdisi 2000) did not give the allusion that difference was accommodated nor that Beirut had the potential to become once again "Paris of the Middle East." Nevertheless the conference followed Michel Chiha's ideology of tapping into the human capital of Lebanon's emigrants. It was fittingly held at Beirut's prominent Hotel Phoenicia, named after ancient Mediterranean sea traders, believed to be Lebanon's first migrants and cosmopolitans. Phoenicians established trade routes to Europe and Western Asia, and their ships circumnavigated Africa one thousand years before those of the Portuguese. A delegation of Lebanese from Senegal joined Lebanese businessmen from around the world for this monumental occasion. What could embody cosmopolitanism more than an entrepreneur identifying himself as from "West Africa," unable to claim only one African country as his place of residence?

While there are many others like this "West African," he does not epitomize Lebanese who are very much rooted in Senegal. Some, who consider their homes to be in Dakar, travel frequently between Lebanon and France or other European countries, occasionally the United States or Canada, and conduct business in the Arab Gulf, China, or elsewhere in West Africa. I met one man in Dakar who had worked in the diamond trade as far south as Congo. Many others, however, never left Senegal, even though they have family spread all over the world. One community leader would often brag that he has relatives living on every continent except Asia.

Lebanese in Senegal are thus a difficult community to define. They are not a homogenous group in terms of religion, social class, or period of immigration. Lebanese and Senegalese governments do not officially classify them as "Lebanese" or "Senegalese." They are a community defined as much by others as by themselves. Lebanese in Lebanon envision those in Senegal as having originated in Lebanon generations earlier, surviving by hard work in a foreign land. They hope that Lebanese in Senegal continue to hold strong affections for Lebanon and will financially invest in their homeland. Senegalese do not identify Lebanese in Senegal by national origin but group them as "Arabs," discernible by their white skin. This derogatory categorization is further marked by the perceived high socioeconomic status of Lebanese, of which many are envious. This identity raises questions of nationalism and inclusion, and whether an Arab community, born and socialized on African soil, can ever be considered "true" Senegalese or Lebanese.

Members of ethnic groups are often categorized by belonging to particular religious communities, speaking the same languages, and following certain social practices. Lebanese, in contrast, are characterized by religious pluralism. Sectarian difference in Lebanon has been exploited throughout history by foreign powers and remains in place today through division of political offices along religious lines as structured by the French-influenced constitution (Hanf 1993; Makdisi 2000; Salibi 1988). Yet in Senegal, distance from the homeland and the altered and multi-layered dynamics of transnational religious politics enabled the ethnic network of Lebanese to develop over time to become expansive and secular enough to include Christians and Muslims. There was not a second wave of immigration to Senegal during the Lebanese Civil War, as there was, for example, to Ivory Coast. This means that Lebanese in Senegal are primarily second-, third-, and now fourth-generation migrants, many of whom have never been to Lebanon. Ties with the motherland weakened over time. This makes Lebanese in Senegal an ideal case study in "integration" and religious change, where reactions to the 2006 Lebanon War were especially intriguing (see chapter 4).[2] Lebanese in Senegal can thus be differentiated from Lebanese in Lebanon (Khater 2001; Makdisi 2000), Ivory Coast (Bierwirth 1999; Peleikis 2003), the United States (Gualtieri 2009; Khater 2001; Walbridge 1997), Australia (Humphrey 1998), and other Lebanese immigrant communities marked by sectarian divisions.[3]

Cosmopolitanism has often been understood in relation to diasporas. Nussbaum's (1994) notion of a borderless cosmopolitan community has been critiqued as inadequate given large numbers of refugees and migrants fleeing violence and poverty. Clifford (1992) first noted class and circumstantial differences among travelers. Likewise, Hall envisions a "cosmopolitanism of the above" (global entrepreneurs) as separate from a very different "cosmopolitanism from below" of "people driven across borders, obliged to uproot themselves from home, place and family, living in transit camps or climbing on to the backs of lorries or leaky boats or the bottom of trains and airplanes, to get to somewhere else" (2008:346). Both cosmopolitans acquire the same skills of adaptation and innovation, but cosmopolitans from below *must* learn to live in two countries and speak a new language as a condition of survival—they have no choice but to become cosmopolitan.

Part 1 builds on these debates regarding the cosmopolitanism of migrant communities while examining the historical transformation from migrant community to ethnic group. Various religious denominations set aside specifics of religious histories and theologies and came together in spirituality and the practice of faith more broadly as Lebanese. Religious celebrations remained primary social events around which community life was organized. Vertovec and Cohen (2003) point out that travel and immigration led to greater acceptance of diversity, of *everyday* or *ordinary* cosmopolitanism. Yet migration studies scholars often neglect to research the influence of migrant communities on host populations, an omission that Part 2 of this book aims to correct through the related case study of Senegalese converts to Shiʿi Islam. This brings us back to Werbner, who says that these concepts "pose the question first, whether local, parochial, rooted, and culturally specific loyalties may coexist with translocal, transnational, transcendent, elitist, enlightened, universalist and modernist ones" (2008:14). It is precisely this coexistence that this book aims to illustrate.

Emigration, Africa, Imagination

Amrika was the generic term for any land—far, far away from the political strife and poverty-stricken Levantine villages of the late nineteenth and early twentieth centuries—to where Lebanese living under Ottoman rule and later French mandate dreamed of escaping. Lebanese intellectuals and politicians, aware from the very beginning that their country's greatest resource was the massive body of human resources abroad, developed an ideology of emigration. Michel Chiha, a Greek Catholic banker from Beirut and father of modern Lebanon's constitution, profoundly influenced political thinking in Lebanon. Chiha was quoted at the 2000 Ministry of Emigrants conference in Beirut. The former consular officer at the Lebanese embassy in Dakar, during an interview, also read me a passage from Chiha's writings:

> Among the earliest people, its [Lebanon's] inhabitants set out on the first available boat looking for distant adventure. One attempt after another, one initiative after another, drove them out to the open sea. They took the risks that came their way, passed through storms, landed on unknown shores after shipwrecks and met other people as we might discover another inhabited planet. With a view to making commercial exchanges, they took merchandise of their own fashioning with them, or objects wrought and decorated in beautiful colours, according to their taste. They brought back metals and raw materials. They spread knowledge of languages and news from afar. They were multilingual right from the beginning, and they have never ceased to be so. *They will be increasingly more so.*
>
> From this, relations, trade, entrepots, services, and later on the city and colony were born. Once incorporated into a new world which offered no outlet to the ocean, the Phoenicia of ancient times had no air to breathe. Lest they be walled in, men from these shores often departed *never to be seen again.*
>
> *The Lebanese will go on travelling more and more.* Perhaps it was for them that, after the ship, the aeroplane was invented. Their enterprises will spread out continually in time and space. (Chiha 1994 [1966]:137)

Linking Lebanese migration to ancient Phoenicians (thereby detaching Lebanese history from Arab history) became an ideological tool in constructing a specifically "Lebanese" (as opposed to Greater Syrian) nationality (Brand 2010; Gualtieri 2009; Kaufman 2004). This was evident in Michel Chiha's crafting of the 1926 constitution, which Hartman and Olsaretti (2003) analyze as the Maronite financial-mercantile elite's mirror image of itself, depicted through nationalist symbols of Lebanon's Phoenician/Mediterranean history and geography, Lebanon as a haven for minorities, and Lebanon as a land of opportunity. Nationalist movements were often at odds with local, regional identities, and Lebanism developed alongside other collective identities in the Middle East, such as Ottomanism, Syrianism, Arabism, and Islamism (El-Solh 2004; Kaufman 2004).

Chiha's ideology toward migrants is mirrored in the first book written on Lebanese of Africa, *The Lebanon in the World: Guide of the Lebano-Syrians Emigrants in Western and Equatorial Africa*.[4]

> In view of the Intelligence, the good education and the soft and conciliating character of the Lebanese immigrant, his integrity and decency in handling business, his good intention of a citizen always law and discipline abider, and besides, his indefectible respect for the belief and habits of others, without, however, counting his firmness and his forbearance as a man of patience, of abnegation, who does not refuse a sacrifice before the duty, in view of all these qualities and others, which are admitted with esteem and admiration by the natives of the countries where our immigrants live and work, in view of all this, the Lebanese immigrant enjoys, between all the Foreign people he frequents, an admirably enviable and happy respect and appreciation. (Saadeh 1952:236)

Not only is the Lebanese immigrant portrayed as being loved by his hosts, but he is also envisioned as having a deep love for the motherland.

> In all and any country visited by me, I found very brothers of a full and sincere affection, who hastened, with a heart overflowing with vitality, activity and love, to give evidence of their firm and undeniable attachment to their Mother-Country, their glorious and adorable Lebanon the quenchless nostalgia of which never leaves off invading and devouring, day and night, their hearts already broken for having been, some day, obliged to leave it, and to which they always delight in keeping fidelity, swearing, with the whole force of spirit, they never will forget their sacred engagements towards it. . . . The return to Lebanon is, for all them without distinction, the most rooted and sweet hope in their hearts; their dearest dream is to see again its enchanting beauties, the fairy-like abodes of its chaste "gazelles," and, finally, to spend the rest of life under its calm and perfumed shades! (Saadeh 1952:189–192)

Chapters 1 and 2 will explore how the French colonial administration in Dakar and later Senegalese postindependence national ideologies did not envision Lebanese in West Africa with an "admirably enviable and happy respect and appreciation." Weiss (2007) demonstrates how Lebanese travelers and immigrants internalized elements of colonial discourse, redeploying this racism toward black

Africans. Furthermore, Lebanese in Africa today do not consider Lebanon in such favorable terms.

Conflict in Lebanon

Lebanese arrived in Senegal from a politically tense and economically difficult climate in a religiously divided Lebanon. Modern sectarian tensions in Lebanon were not primordial identities but began in the mid-nineteenth century in the collision between European hegemony, Ottoman reforms, and local nationalisms (Makdisi 2000). The Ottoman Empire first conquered Lebanon in 1516–1517 under Sultan Selim I then returned to govern Lebanon in 1840 following a series of non-Ottoman rulers. During this time foreign powers manipulated differences in Lebanese religious communities to increase influence in the Ottoman Empire: France had close ties with Maronites; Russia supported Greek Orthodox, those Melchites belonging to the Byzantine Church and not in union with Rome; Austria-Hungary bonded with Greek Catholics in union with Rome; and Great Britain tried to gain influence among Druze, an offspring of Shiʿi Ismailis, historically persecuted as heretics by Sunni Muslims (Hanf 1993:57). Makdisi argues that European colonial imagination, emphasizing Christian salvation and Orientalist visions of Islamic despotism, invented Lebanon's "tribes" (2000:23). What began in the 1830s as a war between Maronites and Druze as a struggle for political, social, and economic dominance in Mount Lebanon soon developed into religious and confessional war. For Makdisi this was the foundational period of a sectarian culture that continued through the late Ottoman period and into the nationalist era. Sunnis and Shiʿa sided with Druze; Melchite communities sided with Maronites. This civil war reached its climax in 1860, with the massacre of thousands of Christians. Fearing a repetition of events, Christian communities looked to European powers for support. The Sanjak of Mount Lebanon emerged from the conflict, a new European-guaranteed Ottoman administrative system that restored stability and peace to the Mountain. Equilibrium lasted from 1861 until 1915, during which a Christian entity separate from the rest of Syria developed.

World War I marked a turning point in the historical and political development of Lebanon. The Allies defeated the Ottoman Empire, whose Arab territories were divided between Britain and France. Various sectarian communities were split regarding the future of Lebanon. Muslims and Druze favored Arab unity and followed Faisal, the ruler of Damascus, and his pan-Arabist lead. Those supporting Greater Syria were mostly secularly oriented intellectuals, backed only by a minority. Maronite Christians and Greek Catholics pushed for the establishment of Greater Lebanon separate from Syria and under French mandate. Greek Orthodox were split, fearing both Muslim rule and Maronite Catholic supremacy. One camp cooperated with Faisal and supported union with Syria; the other favored an independent Lebanon (Salibi 1988; Zamir 1985).

The French established modern Lebanon on September 1, 1920. With Michel Chiha's influence, a new French-approved constitution was drawn up in 1926 that transformed Greater Lebanon into the Lebanese Republic. This constitution formalized the idea of power-sharing based on the respective size of each religious group. Although Lebanon's first president was Greek Orthodox, after 1934 the custom (that continues today) was for a Maronite president, Sunni prime minister, and Shiʿi speaker of the house. World War II ended French mandate and Lebanon declared independence in 1943.

The 1943 National Pact, the unwritten agreement between Bishara al-Khuri, who became Lebanon's first Maronite president, and Riyad al-Sulh, first Sunni prime minister, was a compromise dividing political power in independent Lebanon with the aim of coexistence. At the heart of negotiations were Christian worries of being besieged by Muslim communities in Lebanon and surrounding Arab countries and Muslim fears of Western hegemony. In return for the Christian promise not to seek foreign (French) protection and to accept Lebanon's "Arab face," Muslims agreed to recognize the independence and legitimacy of the Lebanese state in its 1920 boundaries and to renounce ambitions of union with Syria. The pact reinforced the sectarian system of government begun under French mandate based on the confessional distribution of the 1932 census favoring Christians over Muslims.

Over the years, Lebanon's confessional demography shifted, with Muslims, especially Shiʿa, representing the majority. Yet the balance of power did not change as Lebanese leaders avoided conducting a new general census, afraid of political upheaval. Lebanese Muslims, particularly Shiʿa, have been among the poorest, most discriminated against, and most underrepresented in the Lebanese government. Tensions between religious confessions continued to grow, resulting in several months of civil war in 1958. Meanwhile Lebanon became more involved in the Israeli-Palestinian conflict, and fighting broke out in 1975 between Palestinians and Maronites, which turned into civil war. The ever-changing sectarian politics of the lengthy civil war are described in detail in a large and growing body of literature (see Picard 2002; Salibi 1988; Traboulsi 2007). Sectarian tensions were further exacerbated by kinship and clan politics (Khalaf 1971; 1977; Farsoun 1970). The Lebanese Civil War ended in 1990, costing 150,000 Lebanese lives since 1975 and leaving the country in ruins. The 1989 Taʾif Agreement concluding the war upgraded the Arabism of Lebanon from an "Arab face" to a full-fledged Arab country that would no longer be treated as a special case (El-Solh 2004), further marginalizing Maronites.

Immigration to West Africa

Different historical periods in Lebanon (Ottoman rule, French rule, independence, Israeli and Syrian dominance) contributed to various waves of migration.

Migrants began to leave Lebanon in the nineteenth century seeking better economic opportunities abroad to improve their local social rank (Taraf 1994; Khater 2001), fleeing the 1860 massacres (Hitti 1957; Makdisi 2000), and later avoiding conscription in the Ottoman army following the 1908 revolution in Ottoman Turkey. Lebanese migrated to all five continents, but first arrived in West Africa as early as the 1880s, and especially during the 1920s, via Marseilles, the transportation hub of the time. Emigrants planned to continue on to the Americas, where there had been previous Lebanese immigration (Abou 1998; Alfaro-Velcamp 2007; Gualtieri 2009; Hourani and Shehadi 1992; Karam 2007; Khater 2001; Lesser 1999). According to the tale today's Lebanese of Senegal tell, their ancestors boarded ships heading for the Americas, but they never reached their destination: ships docked at Dakar or elsewhere on the West African coast, and Lebanese found work as intermediaries in the peanut trade between French in cities and Senegalese peasants in rural areas.

The few remaining community elders who form the first generation of Lebanese migrants in West Africa recount narratives of accidental arrival. Adnan was shaving on the boat to the Americas from Marseille.[5] When the boat hit a wave he unintentionally removed part of his beard and then shaved off the remainder of his facial hair. When the ship docked, the French compared his bearded passport picture with his clean-shaven face. As he spoke only Arabic they were convinced he was a spy and imprisoned him. Upon his release from prison, Adnan was surprised to find himself among a black population and concluded that he could not possibly be in America. Other sources state West Africa was not a surprise destination. Health requirements for immigration to the United States were strict, and some Lebanese failed to make the cut because they suffered from trachoma. Additionally, many emigrants spent most of their money in Marseilles while waiting for transport and could no longer afford to complete the journey to the Americas. The solution to these difficulties was West Africa, where fares were cheap, health requirements lax, and French reports favorable (Boumedouha 1987:45–46; Crowder 1968:294).

Single areas of Lebanon sent emigrants to single areas in West Africa. "Thus in Senegal most Lebanese came from Tyre, in Mali from Bayt Shabab, in Accra from Tripoli in North Lebanon. In Calabar in Nigeria all the Lebanese came from the same village" (Crowder 1968:296). Immigration to West Africa depended on factors affecting both Lebanon and West Africa. Van der Laan (1992) divides Lebanese migration to Africa into three stages: the beginning of the century until 1914, when colonial powers heavily invested in West Africa; 1935–1938 as a result of rising produce prices; and the heavy wave of migration in the 1950s due to high prices for raw materials and new development projects. Labaki (1993) formed different divisions, with the first wave of travel to Africa occurring between the two world wars when Lebanon and parts of West Africa were under French mandate.

The second wave of immigration took place 1945–1960, before African independence. Migration slowed from 1960 to 1975, due to independence and accompanying politics of Africanization. After 1975 migration increased again, due to the Lebanese Civil War, in concurrence with activities in African receiving countries. Although stages of migration vary by scholar, importantly, factors in both sending and receiving countries determined the timing and destination of migrants.

Accurate statistics for the number of Lebanese in Senegal are unobtainable.[6] Labaki estimates the 1938 distribution of Lebanese in Senegal to include 1,000 in Dakar, 200 in Kaolack, 150 in Ziguinchor, and 100 in Diourbel, Louga, Thies, and Mbacke. They came from Kab Elias in the Beqaa valley and Qana, Zrariye, and Tyre in southern Lebanon. Those in Dakar worked mostly in imports and retail, and those in the interior worked in the peanut and sorghum trade. This same year Lebanese traders were reported to own 75 percent of commercial establishments in Dakar and 55 percent of those in the interior. Ten percent of buildings in Dakar and 50 percent in the interior belonged to Lebanese. They owned citrus groves and worked in floriculture, bakeries, print shops, and tanneries. Lebanese were wholesalers and retailers of cloth and hardware and dominated rice, sugar, biscuit, flour, canned tomatoes, oil, and soap sectors. They managed restaurants and hotels and worked in liberal professions as doctors and dentists. Lebanese contributed significantly to the construction of buildings in Senegal. In the 1960s, University of Dakar educated one hundred Lebanese students in medicine, dentistry, and technical sciences.

Van der Laan establishes 1920–1955 as the period of Lebanese internal migration from coastal cities to the West African interior, with the introduction of lorries for transportation of goods. By the end of the 1950s Lebanese began to withdraw from villages and return to cities. This occurred for a number of reasons: "(1) African emancipation in the rural areas; (2) government intervention in the produce trade; (3) a desire among the Lebanese for better housing and comfort; (4) the greater prosperity of the 1950s; (5) falling road transport costs; (6) the increasing use of private cars" (1992:545–546). In Senegal this was also due to President Senghor's 1961 nationalization of the groundnut industry, when he established cooperatives in towns and villages of the interior (chapter 2). This meant that most Europeans and Lebanese who had acted as local agents in the groundnut trade were deprived of jobs in buying centers and were forced to move to Dakar (Cruise O'Brien 1972:113).

By the 1970s, after nationalization and commercialization of agricultural products and the end of French colonialism, Lebanese in West Africa became involved in small and medium-sized firms in cities and larger villages. They worked primarily in the food industry, textiles, perfumes, plastics, print shops and paper production, leatherwork, soap, leasing, hotels, and services such as transportation and car rentals. The Filfili agro-industry was the largest and most success-

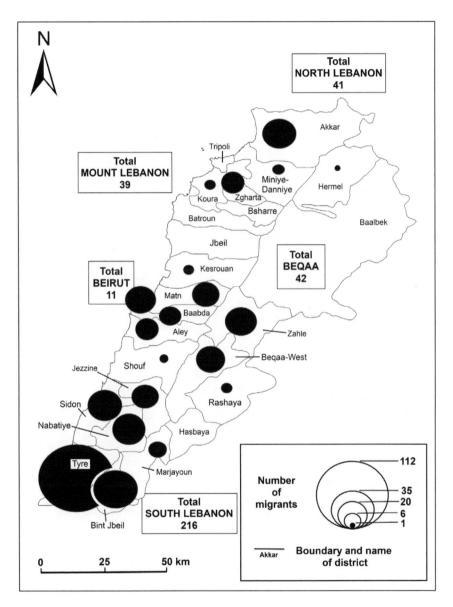

Distribution of heads of family of early migrants to Senegal by district of origin in Lebanon, 1946–1990. Map created by Adrianne Daggett and adapted from Taraf (1994:181). Source: consular civil status records from the Lebanese embassy in Dakar (sample size ⅕), authored by Florence Troin, Université de Tours. Printed with permission of Souha Tarraf.

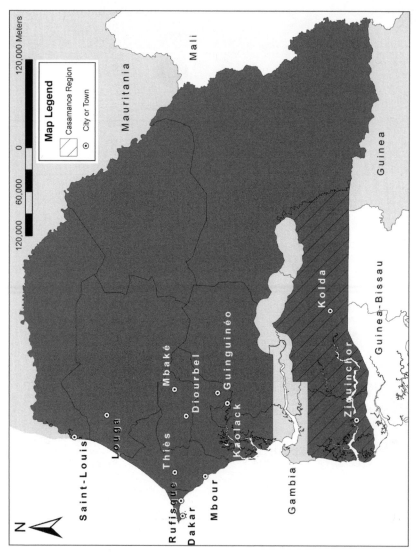

Cities and towns in Senegal with significant Lebanese population before independence (1960). Map created by Adri-anne Daggett.

Lebanese shop, Dakar, 2013.

ful of its kind (Labaki 1993:99–102. See Nadra Filfili's 1973 autobiography). Lebanese communities continued to grow, and by 1970 there were 20,000 Lebanese in Senegal, and 26,000 in 1985, when Ivory Coast surpassed Senegal with 60,000 Lebanese (mostly from the Lebanese Civil War), Sierra Leone was a close third with 25,000, and Nigeria ranked fourth with 16,000 Lebanese residents (Labaki 1993:94–96).

According to the former consulate officer at the Lebanese embassy in Dakar, there were approximately 25,000–30,000 Lebanese in Senegal in 2002. However, the former director general of the Ministry of Emigrants in Beirut informed me that there were 30,000 Lebanese in Senegal in the past, but they numbered approximately 15,000 in 2000. The higher number from within Senegal demonstrates efforts at emphasizing importance and identity as a Lebanese emigrant community. Likewise, the lower number is symbolic of the Lebanese government's deflating the importance of, and likewise the flow of resources to, the community. This discrepancy in numbers is also due to difficulty in estimating the population as there is now a substantial three-generation gap separating many Lebanese in Senegal from origins in Lebanon. The Lebanese community itself played a role in preventing recent waves of immigration by not inviting conationals and by influ-

Lebanese fast food restaurant, Dakar, 2013.

encing Senegalese authorities to restrict entrance visas for Lebanese during the civil war. The community envisioned that war refugees would bring with them tensions and political divisions of Lebanon, which would affect in a negative way the unity and coexistence that developed over time in Senegal. This also meant that there was no recent influx of Lebanese migrants to Senegal to reinforce Lebanese culture.

Lebanese community leaders in Dakar estimated in 2002 that 90 percent of Lebanese in Senegal were Shiʿi Muslim, with a couple hundred Sunni Muslims. Whereas Maronites once formed a majority of Lebanese Christians in Senegal, and Lebanese Christians comprised nearly half of Senegal's Lebanese population, in 2002 there were approximately 1,200 Lebanese Christians with a Greek Orthodox majority, 400–500 Maronite Catholics, and a few Protestants and Greek Catholics (see Leichtman 2013).[7] The consulate officer placed 95–97 percent of Lebanese in Dakar, heavily concentrated near the city center. The second largest concentration of Lebanese was in Kaolack, where one resident counted 400–450 Lebanese in 2002. A few Lebanese families remain in Mbacke, Diourbel, Rufisque, Thies, Mbour, Kolda, Ziguinchor, Saint-Louis, and other regions. Kaolack retains an ac-

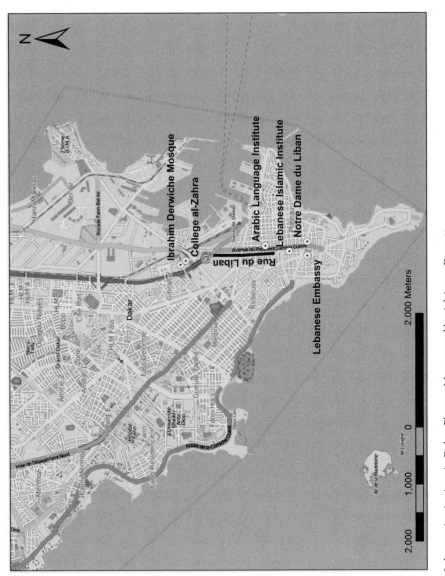

Lebanese institutions in Dakar Plateau. Map created by Adrianne Daggett.

tive Lebanese club, Amicale Liban Senegal, but other regional centers and villages no longer have functioning Lebanese institutions, and many never did.

Migrants who left West Africa returned to Lebanon or resided in Europe (especially France and England, former colonial powers) or North America. There was also a considerable amount of interregional migration throughout West Africa. Labaki envisions the first wave of Lebanese migration as temporary migration, with the intention to return to Lebanon to retire and reinstate children in country of origin. However, because of the Lebanese Civil War the nature of migration changed, and Labaki describes a triangular migration from Lebanon to West Africa to Western Europe or North America (1993:110). Among the population of Lebanese currently residing in Senegal, this process can be seen instead through generations, as it is now third and fourth generations who are leaving, with first and second (for the most part) remaining. Lebanese merchants are struggling today with a stagnant economy and increased Senegalese competition.

The first part of this book will examine different political categories constructed to govern Lebanese in Senegal and community responses, which led to the transition from immigrant group to ethnic group. I will focus on changes in religious identity, which took place over three stages: during the establishment of the Lebanese community in Senegal under French colonialism (1880s to 1960), from Senegalese independence until the latest war between Israel and Lebanon (1960 to 2006), and from the July 2006 Lebanon War until the present. Each historical period involves various configurations of ethnic, national, and religious expression shaped in different ways by the changing background of Lebanon and Senegal.

These issues of identity raise the question of how to label different groups. Obviously today's nation-states of Lebanon and Senegal are not composed of homogenous populations. However, to break down each nation into its respective ethnic and religious groups is confusing. Furthermore, when members of a group compare themselves to another, the "other," they assume an "us"/"them" system of categorization. Therefore I adopt, at times, a macro-perspective that regards "Lebanese of Lebanon" and "Senegalese" as single units, the "them." I refer to the ethnic community as "Lebanese of Senegal" while focusing on how different religious groups came to regard themselves this way. This term is problematic, as not all community members consider themselves as such, but I will highlight variations in status, identity, and orientation of successive generations of Lebanese in Senegal. When discussing Senegalese conversion to Shiʿi Islam, Senegalese society is broken down into relevant ethnic and religious groups.

1 French Colonial Manipulation and Lebanese Survival

Cosmopolitanism is . . . not only a trope of modernity but also, and very specifically, of colonial modernity.

—Peter van der Veer, "Colonial Cosmopolitanism"

Cosmopolitanism is the Western engagement with the rest of the world and that engagement is a colonial one, which simultaneously transcends the national boundaries and is tied to them.

—Peter van der Veer, "Colonial Cosmopolitanism"

Some scholars have been skeptical of cosmopolitanism discourses invoked by the civilizing mission of imperialism (Clifford 1992; Hannerz 1990; Ong 2006). Van der Veer (2002), however, makes a strong case for examining cosmopolitanism in the colonial period (see also Kahn 2008; Kuehn 2012). As missionaries and colonial officers had a willingness to engage with the Other, van der Veer understands colonial cosmopolitanism to be a form of translation and conversion of the local into a ("provincialized") universal. Colonial modernity thus "disclaims its roots in a European past and claims a cosmopolitan openness to other civilizations. However, this is an openness to understanding with a desire to bring progress and improvement, a cosmopolitanism with a moral mission" (167). He critiques academic discussions of cosmopolitanism for lacking systematic attention to religion (although this is slowly starting to change).

This chapter will explore the French *mission civilisatrice* as one case study for van der Veer's model of colonial cosmopolitanism. Conklin (1997) regards *civilization* as a particularly French concept, invented in the eighteenth century. Republican France deemed itself civilized because the metropole learned mastery over geography, climate, and disease in order to create new internal and external markets, and overcame oppression and superstition to form a democratic and rational government before other nations. Inhabitants of the non-European world were envisioned as barbarians in need of civilizing precisely because they were perceived to have failed on these same accounts. Wilder (2005) examines

French policy as *colonial humanism,* which enabled a cultural racism that was simultaneously universalizing and particularizing. French colonial discourses and policies—in particular approaches toward Lebanese migration and Islam in West Africa—can be analyzed as a form of translation and conversion of one conceptual framework into another that is more powerful and thus more universal. The Comaroffs (1991) have referred to this process as the *colonization of consciousness.* Linked to colonial cosmopolitanism is the question of autochthony, another basic principle of colonial policy, evident above all in the French *politique des races.*

On a more local but still cosmopolitan level, a subtheme of this chapter will consider how Lebanese in Senegal are a community defined as much by others as by self-definition. Whereas in Lebanon religion was the dominant identifier, in Senegal, race and country of origin became the community's distinguishing factors and served as the unifying characteristic of migrants. Lebanese in Senegal are conscious that their Lebaneseness is removed by geographical and generational distance from Lebanon, yet they are labeled "of Lebanon" by others. Being Lebanese is not a positive characteristic as defined by French and Senegalese administrators and businessmen. This chapter aims to further contextualize and historicize the development of Lebanese communal identity over several distinct periods in Senegal.

Van der Veer has been critical of what he interprets to be a Kantian view of universal, enlightened religion that is a source of morality and thus of cosmopolitanism, located in the interior life of the individual and not in social institutions. According to this Enlightenment view, religious people can thus be cosmopolitans if they are progressive liberals with private, and thereby secular, religious worldviews. Lebanese in Senegal have grappled with various ways of being pious cosmopolitans. Their religious traditions and practices have transformed over time and generation—not in an embracing of Western modernity and the privatization of religion, but in reaction to power politics and colonial manipulation. The following chapters examine how and why the Lebanese community has struggled to ignore sectarian tensions among Christian and Muslim denominations in Lebanon, yet maintain unique ethnic and religious identities in Senegal. I begin by exploring the impact of French colonial policy on the dissolution of Lebanese differences.

Academic scholarship on French colonialism in Africa highlights French Islamic policy and "divide and rule" strategies. The literature mentions but does not elaborate on the anti-Lebanese stance of the French (with the exception of Cruise O'Brien 1972). This chapter focuses on the period of French colonization in Senegal and chapter 2 on its aftermath. My goal is not to recount the entire history of French colonialism in West Africa (see Cohen 2003 [1980]; Conklin 1997; Cooper 1996; Crowder 1968; Harrison 1988; Robinson 2000) but to reconstruct from the works of these authors and from colonial correspondence in the Archives Nationales de la République du Sénégal a relevant account of French policy and attitudes concerning Islam in general and the Lebanese community in particular. Even before Lebanon and Senegal were nation-states, competition between secular, religious, and political forces was being negotiated in a colonial cosmopolitan context.

Lebanese or Syrian, Muslim or Christian?

There has been confusion regarding the historical origins of the Lebanese community of Senegal. Before the end of World War I, the Ottoman Province of Syria contained all of present-day Lebanon and Syria. Emigrants from this province were called "Syrians" without distinction, yet most were from Lebanon proper. After the Ottoman Empire's 1918 collapse, the former Province of Syria was divided by France in 1920 into two administrative units: Syria and Lebanon. After the French Mandate's establishment, immigrants became technically and legally Lebanese; nonetheless, the names *Syriens* and *Libano-Syriens* continued to be used in French West Africa as late as the 1950s in administrative reports and newspapers (Boumedouha 1987; van der Laan 1975). The community today identifies itself and is referred to by Senegalese exclusively as "Lebanese."

Although French colonial documents commonly referred to Africa's Levantine population collectively as "Libano-Syriens," they did, at times, distinguish between the two groups. I acknowledge that drawing too many conclusions from a limited selection of documents is problematic. However, additional evidence for this historical period is lacking. The archival data (with its colonial biases) presents the first generation of Lebanese migrants to Senegal as having arrived with the same sectarian differences that were prevalent in Lebanon. It is significant that such confessional differences continued to be recognized by the first generation in these early years, as well as enforced by French colonial officials. It is therefore worth quoting at length from a 1945 French report describing the "situation of Libano-Syriens."

> A distinction is made between Lebanese and Syrians, and between Christians and Muslims. Lebanese are generally Francophiles. The Libano-Syrien population consists of approximately 2,200 individuals . . . Three organizations exist: Comité Libanais de Dakar (Dakar Lebanese Committee), Comité Corporatif Libanais (Lebanese Corporations Committee), Comité d'Adhésion et de Bienfaisance (Social Services/Civic Committee).[1] Rivaling and competing with one another, they illustrate the obvious division of the Libano-Syrien community. . . .
>
> Lebanese do not like to be called Syrian, and most often refer to the French legacy in Lebanon. On the whole, they remain true to their origins and are extremely happy that Lebanon and Syria have become two distinct sovereign States. . . .
>
> They are proud that Lebanon became independent but consider French protection a compelling necessity. They dislike and fear Syrians, from whom they are separated by a different culture and by Islam. They are afraid of being dominated by them. . . .

Christians, including Orthodox, are Francophiles. The memory of distant crusades is still vivid in Lebanon. In contrast to Christian fears of an Arab government, Muslims are advocating pan-Arabism and what it represents. Their opinion toward France is therefore not very favorable. . . .With the independence of Syria and Lebanon, the hope of the youth is to be more highly regarded and not considered European. . . .

In short, "Christian" means attachment to France and "Muslim" detachment from France. With regard to their personal status, Christians are mainly afraid of being considered nonnationals. While both communities agree on the opening of a Lebanese consulate in Dakar, headed by a non-French West African Lebanese consul, Christians favor a Christian consul, Muslims a Muslim, Lebanese a Lebanese, and Syrians a Syrian. . . .[2]

To conclude, we must remember what distinguishes Lebanese from Syrians: Past, Culture, Religion. (Diégane Sene's Archive Collection/ANS:1945)

This report provides insight into French colonial views of Libano-Syrien communities in Afrique Occidentale Française (AOF). For French administrators, religion and national origin were indicative of political preferences, and were of utmost importance in a period of world wars, European competition for colonial expansion, and struggles to hold on to colonies despite protests by the colonized. French colonial documents in Senegal's National Archives suggest that the first generation of Lebanese immigrants was religiously divided. Archival evidence stresses that the first generation of Lebanese Maronites in Senegal endeavored to maintain sectarian distinctions in order to gain preferential treatment from the French, the custom for Maronites at that time in Lebanon (Salibi 1988). For example, the French noted in colonial correspondence regarding Lebanese Christians in Senegal:

Their [Lebanese Christian] arguments are always the same: they say that they are not Syrians, that Maronites belong to France, that Lebanon had better not get involved in an alliance in which it will represent an insignificant minority before a mass of Muslims who pose a threat to it.

They take up their old "clichés": the Crusades, their friendship for France, the schools created by the French, the religion that they have protected in Lebanon. (ANS 21G8(1):31 Mai 1945)

When asked, Lebanese Christians focus on the difference of religions and affirm their will to distance themselves from Syrians and Muslims whose sectarianism and extortions they fear. They attribute to the aforementioned the complete responsibility for a matter in which they claim to have no part. (ANS 21G8(1):18 Juin 1945)[3]

Furthermore, French colonial archives describe how the first generation of Lebanese migrants to Senegal differentiated between Maronite and Orthodox Christians. This distinction can be understood in the context of colonial competition between French and British in West Africa, in particular in Senegambia. Whereas the French established Roman Catholic missions in Senegal, envisioning Catholicism as an instrument for spreading French influence culturally and politically, Protestant missionaries came to British-controlled Gambia. The French noted regarding Lebanese Christians:

> One of them was saying these past days that Maronites have been even more clearly won over by France than Orthodox Christians, who would have a more marked penchant for the English. In any case, Orthodox Christians here have had to entirely hide their sentiments since their actions would not give rise to this interpretation. . . .
>
> In summary, Lebanese Christians whose rites are closest to those of the Roman Church seem to use their religion to prove that they are not our enemies, while others speak less often, and all appear to want to attribute complete responsibility to Syrians, whom they are not. (ANS 21G8(1):31 Mai 1945)

These quotes imply that the same ties between European colonial powers and different religious confessions in Lebanon also held true in another continent and colonial situation. However, although the French had a marked penchant for Maronites, and distrusted Arab Muslims whom they saw as a threat, they did not cater to Lebanese Christians in Senegal as they had in Lebanon.

This is highlighted in an interesting story recounted in this same document. A young woman by the family name of Nasrallah wanted to marry a man by the name of Saba Némé. The couple approached the French priest, Father Février, of Ziguinchor in the south of Senegal to perform the service. The priest (described as sectarian and intransigent) refused because the couple was Orthodox, and without the permission of the pope, the Catholic Church could not perform ceremonies for non-Catholics. The solution was a blow to the French. A British pastor from Bathurst "accepted without the slightest hesitation to marry these young people."[4] The ceremony took place in Ziguinchor. The French colonial officer who penned the document critiqued: "I do not know if the difference which exists between Protestantism and Orthodoxy is less important than that between Orthodoxy and Catholicism, and if it was easier for the English to marry these young people. In any event, Lebanese here praised this Pastor extensively and manifested the fear that Orthodox of Ziguinchor would not have a proper religious burial if they should die" (ANS 21G8(1):31 Mai 1945).

This story illustrates how the French distinguished between Catholics and Orthodox and exploited Lebanese sectarian differences in colonial rivalries in West Africa. Whereas Maronites stressed Catholicism as a unifying factor with the French, Orthodox were comfortable with either a Catholic priest or a Protestant pastor performing religious rites in the absence of a representative of the Orthodox Church.[5] It is significant that confessional differences continued to be recognized by the first generation in these early years. In 1953 the French counted

45 percent Muslims among the Libano-Syrien community with a Christian (Roman Catholic or Maronite) majority. Yet at other times the archives refer to this "primarily Muslim" community. Despite an occasional report about divisions in the community, in practice French administrators did not distinguish Muslim from Christian or Lebanese from Syrian, and in anti-Lebanese campaigns accused all Libano-Syriens of various crimes outlined below. They often thought of the entire community as Muslim, despite its significant Christian population, which corresponded to French fears of "Arab Islam" contaminating African Islam noir. In order to understand this anxiety we must take a step back in history.

Origins of French Colonialism in West Africa

French presence in West Africa began in 1637 with the establishment of trading posts in Saint-Louis at the mouth of River Senegal. Over the next two hundred years French competed with Dutch, English, and Portuguese in the trade of slaves, gold, gum, and animal hides. It was not until the early nineteenth century that French influence expanded into Senegal's interior with Louis Faidherbe's 1854 appointment as governor of Senegal. Robinson (2000:43) calls Faidherbe the "founder" or "father" of Senegal. His name appeared on schools and streets and his statue faced the governor-general's residence (later the presidency) in Dakar until the 1970s. Faidherbe began to change the image of the European from "master of water" to "master of land" (61), and the conquest of Senegal, in its present form, was completed by the mid-1890s.

French policymakers focused on the decade before World War I as a time of unrest in the Islamic World. The Persian Revolution (1906), deposition of Ottoman and Moroccan sultans (1908), radicalism of Egyptian nationalists, and first Italian Sanusiyya war (1911) fed European fears of Islam, which dated back to the Crusades (Harrison 1988). Fears were reflected in French colonial policy. By the early twentieth century French authorities were discussing and evaluating policies as a "Muslim Power," "by which they meant an imperial power with Muslim subjects" (Robinson 2000:75). They even secured *fatwas* (religious decrees) from leading authorities in Mecca stating that submission to European rule was acceptable for Muslims (76). Faidherbe refashioned French local military recruitment by changing dress to more "Algerian" and "Ottoman" styles and even allowing families to accompany soldiers. He "sponsored" pilgrimages to Mecca for friends of the colonial regime (80).

In 1902 the capital of the Federation of French West Africa was transferred to Dakar from Saint-Louis in the north. Dakar's first governor-general was Ernest Roume (1902–1908), who, according to Robinson, made two notable contributions. First he organized the Muslim Affairs service in 1905–1906, naming Robert Arnaud, an Algerian Islamicist, its head. Arnaud established the bureau's basic procedures, including a system for tracking Muslim teachers, scholars, and mystics now under French control. Roume laid foundations for the work of Paul Marty, Arnaud's successor, who published volumes on Islam in French West Africa that have become an important reference. French dual understanding of *maraboutage* developed during this period as well.[6] In Mauritania *marabouts* were seen as influential leaders and "peace-loving scholars" (Harrison 1988:41), whose support was crucial to French domination. In Senegal, however, marabouts were considered "idle scroungers" (41), and French referred to the "parasitic nature of his existence" (42). This was also a period of anticlericalism in France, and Harrison writes that French compared marabouts to French village priests, both of whom they envisioned as exploiting masses of believers by using Arabic or Latin to keep them ignorant while encouraging reverence for these religious men.

Senegal's Sufi Orders

Islam first arrived in West Africa in the eleventh century, when merchants opened up trade routes that led to the spread of Islam to isolated societies.[7] Clerics introduced Islam to the masses, whose conversion took place through both military conquest and peaceful persuasion. The religion spread most rapidly in Senegal through Sufi orders during the colonial period. Marabouts gained immense following as a result of French treatment of Senegalese and were often outspoken against the oppression of colonial rule. Islam served as a cultural ideology, preventing Senegalese "assimilation" into French ways. French officials responded by exiling certain Islamic leaders and training their own "marabouts" to work with the colonial administration.

The Tijaniyya order in particular gave new life to revolutionary impulses in West Africa. Although not all Tijaniyya branches were involved in resisting French expansion in Senegal, France's greatest opponents were almost all Tijani. French administrators feared the passion that Tijani marabouts could arouse in followers (Klein 1968:65–66). The Qadiriyya order, the oldest in Senegal, was less influential. Coulon (1981:52) considered the conservative Qadiriyya to be too closely associated with ruling classes to support marabouts' calls for change. Murids focused on gaining control of rural villages, and the slogan "God Alone Is King" was directed against Wolof chiefs who ruled for the French (Searing 2002). This threatened Wolof aristocrats and provoked French intervention.

The Qadiriyya order, one of the first to appear in West Africa (Behrman 1970), originated with ʿAbd al-Qadir al-Jilani, who taught in Baghdad until his death in 1166. The order came to Senegal via the Kunta lineage, an Arab-Berber clan in Mauritania (Batran 1979). Bou Kunta (d. 1914) founded the Senegalese order in the village of Ndiassane. Shaykh Ahmad al-Tijani (d. 1815), who was born in southern Algeria but gained a following in Fez, Morocco, founded the Tijaniyya. Al-Hajj ʿUmar Tall spread the order to West Africa. The primary representatives of the Tijaniyya in Senegal were al-Hajj Malik Sy (d. 1922) in Tivaouane and al-

Hajj ʿAbdallah Niass (d. 1922) and his son Ibrahim Niass (d. 1975) in Kaolack. The Tijaniyya's success was not limited to Senegal, and the order has many followers in The Gambia, Nigeria, and elsewhere, becoming likely the largest single Muslim organization in Africa (Cruise O'Brien 1988; Triaud and Robinson 2000). Niass's branch of Tijaniyya, called "the Community of Grace" or "the Community of the Divine Flood" (Hill 2012; Seesemann 2011) is referred to as "reformed Tijaniyya" because of its concern for teaching the Arabic language and Islamic sciences, as well as its pan-Islamic orientation (Cruise O'Brien 1988).

Brenner (1984) describes three elements in West African Islam: the Sufi or mystical, the literate-intellectual, and the nonliterate intellectual. Students of Islam spend many years devoted to studying the Qurʾan in Arabic, which is not their mother tongue. Initial Qurʾanic studies involve rote memorization without translation. Only advanced students gain an understanding of the Qurʾan when they reach the level of "books," when they study Arabic and the meaning of texts. The role of marabouts is to "purify" or "simplify" the basic teachings of Islam to make them more accessible to nonliterate Muslims. A component of Tijani Islam is working for the marabout in household chores and farming the land. Brenner describes the teacher becoming a substitute parent and the student learning humility toward God from exhibiting deference and respect to parents and teachers. The Tijaniyya has stricter requirements concerning Islamic rituals, and their *wird* (litany of prayers) is more complex than that of the Qadiriyya and Muridiyya.

The most famous of Senegal's Sufi orders—and the most organized (Cruise O'Brien 1971)—is the Muridiyya, meaning "those who seek after God." The only uniquely Senegalese order, the Muridiyya was founded by Shaykh Amadou Bamba Mbacke (d. 1927), who was originally a Qadir. The order originated in the aftermath of the battle of Dekkile in 1886, the final defeat of Wolof armies by the French. Cruise O'Brien notes that peasants and commoners were more ready to become Muslims than nobility, warriors, and their clients. The resulting insecurity and breakdown of the traditional order created a need for renewed stability and change, a gap quickly filled by Amadou Bamba (Babou 2007; Creevey 1979; Glover 2007). Murids are most closely linked to the Wolof ethnic group, and their capital, Tuba, was established in 1888 (Guèye 2002).

Venerated today as an ancestor of Senegalese nationalism and Negritude, Bamba never preached holy war or other hostility against Europeans (Coulon 1981). Bamba was also the first black marabout to gain white followers. He demanded his followers observe the five pillars of Islam and, for his more learned disciples, a life of meditation, self-instruction, and personal austerity. There was a wird specific to the Murid order, which today includes primarily Bamba's poems, believed to bring protection in the next world to all who recite them. The most original teaching of Bamba was his emphasis on the value of work in the service of a shaykh. His famous phrase "work as if you would never die and pray as if you

Table 1.1. Senegalese Religious Affiliation (in percentages)

Tijan	48.9%
Murid	31.9%
Qadir	8.7%
Layenne	0.63%
Other Muslim	5.5%
Catholic	3.7%
Protestant	0.07%
Other Christian	0.13%
Other	0.41%

Source: 2002 census.

were to die tomorrow" (Creevey 1979:281) allowed agricultural labor to substitute for religious instruction for followers who had no desire to learn. Called *les marabouts de l'arachide* (groundnut marabouts) by Copans (1980), Murids adapted to needs of the time, and agricultural labor enabled a new way of life for those in Wolof country who had lost their previous occupations (Cruise O'Brien 1971). This is exemplified by the ritual of *jebbalu*, the vow of obedience pronounced by Murid *talibes* (disciples) to their marabout: "I place my soul and my life in your hands. Whatever you order I will do; Whatever you forbid I will refrain from" (Villalón 1995:119), an oft-cited phrase by scholars who exaggerate the submission and lack of agency of talibes (Soares 2007). Submission to a marabout provided talibes with not only spiritual comfort and a guarantee of salvation, but also material security and political protection. This was an attractive option for lower classes and slaves who hoped to use Islam to escape the dominant Senegalese caste system (Cruise O'Brien 1971).

Development of *Politique des Races*

William Ponty (1908–1915) succeeded Roume and developed ethnic particularism (*politique des races*), a central theme of colonial administration in West Africa until World War II. This directive was about ensuring Africans' right to progress on their own terms and reinforcing French commitment to respect African customs. Ponty declared the right of Africans to be governed by leaders drawn from their own people (Conklin 1997). Through this proclamation of the republican principle of ethnic self-determination, Ponty set about to erode the alliance of marabouts and community chiefs by ensuring that Muslims were not placed as chiefs over non-Muslim peoples, as not to encourage the extension of Muslim clericalism over "fetishists." He distrusted all African chiefs and envisaged eliminating canton and province chiefs through transferring their administrative duties to village chiefs under direct supervision by French administrators. Conklin suggests that Ponty misunderstood how African society functioned; the concept of village chief was more French invention than African reality.

Ethnic particularism was also applied to Islam. "Although the marabouts were generally regarded as posing the greatest threat to French rule, French administrators drew some comfort from their belief that local West African Islam was not as dangerous as, for example, the Islam of North Africa" (Harrison 1988:51). Reform of the legal system followed politique des races aiming to prevent Muslim *qadis* from ruling over non-Muslim communities, which often contributed to the spread of Islam (Conklin 1997). A 1912 decree determined that jurisdiction would no longer be arbitrarily applied according to place of birth but would equitably reflect an individual's ethnic, religious, and cultural identity. While the French were most concerned with who owned the land, in particular Senegalese Muslims led by marabouts, they were also concerned with who might threaten their control over the land, which involved Lebanese as well.

Colonial cosmopolitanism enabled French administrators to comparatively draw on experiences in other world regions. The colonial notion of "Black Islam" as "inferior to"—or rather less threatening than—"Arab Islam" was a policy that directly affected French treatment of Lebanese. This idea originated with Arnaud, who was sent on a mission to investigate the state of Islam throughout the West African colonies and draw up a manual of Muslim policy for French AOF administrators. He published *Précis de politique musulmane* in 1906, the first French document to differentiate between French colonial understanding of Islam in Algeria and the development of a specifically West African perception, known as "Islam noir." This manual, however, focused exclusively on Mauritania. In 1912, his final year as chief advisor on Muslim affairs, Arnaud broadened his argument to apply to all West Africa. He was clearly influenced by Ponty's idea of politique des races. He saw the African Muslim as a novice to Islam. "The African Muslim, we learn on the first page, 'is still like a child who has just learnt his catechism'" (Harrison 1988:96). The French envisioned Islam in Senegal as a "form of bastardized Islam, a mixture of religion and ridiculous superstitions, a superficial religion in which the marabouts and the pseudo-marabouts who abound in this country are the carriers of malicious rumours, maintain the credulous people in sentiments of hatred against us and work towards the brutalization of the race by superstitious practices" (46–47).

Islam noir was further developed by Marty, who served in AOF from 1912 to 1921. An administrator born in Algeria with an impressive military career in colonial North Africa, Marty was attached to the Colonial Ministry to advise the lieutenant general on Muslim Affairs in Dakar. "Blacks, he claimed, could only pronounce fifteen of the thirty-eight letters of the Arabic alphabet with the result that 'If truly as the purists maintain Allah can only understand Arabic—and well pronounced Arabic at that—the prayers of the Senegalese marabouts certainly do not rise up to his throne'" (Harrison 1988:108). Furthermore, he believed the Murid Sufi order was heavily influenced by indigenous pre-Islamic customs and traditions:

> The black mentality is completely incapable of bearing the metaphysical concepts of the Oriental semites and the ecstatic digressions of the Soufis. These scenes are nothing other than an act of common prayer, soon followed by dances, choreographed mimes and bamboulas of which the Blacks are so fond. . . . As Islam distances itself from its cradle . . . as races and conditions change, it becomes increasingly deformed. Islamic confessions, be they Malaysian or Chinese, Berber or Negro, are no more than vulgar *contrefaçons* of the religion and state of the sublime Coran. (Harrison 1988:116)

Marty argued that Murids should not be assimilated in French minds to Islam of the Arab world; therefore West African Muslims were immune from pan-Islamism. Marty thus believed in a fundamentally different nature of "Arab" and "African" Islam. African Islam was docile, from the French point of view a harmless religion. Politique des races was embedded not only in racist notions of African culture, but also in a conception of West African autochthony as fundamentally pre-Islamic and incapable of conforming to outside religious traditions. French colonial policy, in the aftermath of this discovery, became the following:

> Our black countries are scarcely Islamised and are not in the least up to date with the current events in the Orient. Since the beginning of the war our policy has been to maintain the Blacks in this happy state of mind and we have abstained from all communications that might change this state of affairs. (Harrison 1988:128)

> Islam in Africa should not be assimilated to Arab Islam for it was strongly coloured by the indigenous pre-Islamic culture and traditions of the various ethnic groups. The French should not encourage Islam through the use of Arabic or Qur'anic law, and animist communities should be offered some sort of protection from Muslim intrusion. Within Muslim areas, where the French had nothing serious to fear from Islam, the French task was principally of forging alliances with Muslim leaders. (ibid. 136)

French colonial administrators sought to separate Arab migrants who practiced Islam (or even Christianity) from Africans in order to prevent their religious—and political—ideas from spreading to the native population. It became essential for the French to maintain a linguistic barrier between black Africa and the Arab world. Since the time of Faidherbe, however, Arabic had been used as the most convenient language for transactions between French and African rulers. As late as 1906 the language was also an important part of the curriculum at the French Ecole Normale in Saint-Louis. Over the next few years the colonial administration began to stress the importance of teaching French and the unsuitability of Arabic for Africans. In 1903 Roume established the education of France's African subjects as an official part of the civilizing mission. He firmly believed that Africans had to evolve within their own cultures rather than that of France, and the metropolitan curriculum therefore had to be "adapted" to specific needs of African peoples. According to Conklin (1997), Roume had promoted the use of French, not because of its superiority, but because there were too many African languages to master and West Africa needed a common mode of communication. French, by default, was the only such available language, and he envisioned as the objective of French language instruction to teach Africans to simultaneously love their country and France. Whereas Roume allowed a provision for instruction in Arabic in respect for local custom, Ponty expanded Roume's educational policy and established French as the official language of the Federation. He understood the spread of French as a means to counter Islam, "for experience has taught us that Muslims who know our language are less prejudiced" (Conklin 1997:132). Marty likewise argued that the exclusive use of French in schools would improve the level of education in Senegal. Local languages began to be transcribed in the Latin alphabet, thereby bypassing the use of Arabic.[8]

Ironically, as the French sought to divide and conquer Islam by racially classifying Muslim groups as religiously inferior and superior, they considered themselves to be "protectors of Islam": "France, great protector of Islam. This phrase, now confirmed, corresponds to a reality established over a long period of time. The history of our country abounds with examples of acts through which the French nation has consistently demonstrated its respect for the institutions and peoples to whom it has brought the benefits of its civilization" (ANS 19G6(17):1938). Harrison points out that France was a "'Muslim power' with not only a right but also a duty, so the theory ran, to direct the evolution of its Muslim subjects. In Black Africa this often meant that the French had a duty to 'purify' *Islam noir*—and the place to start this was in the *médersa*" (1988:65).

Marty viewed Qurʾanic schools as "a purely religious and purely mechanical education which has no effect on the intellectual development of the time . . . But one must acknowledge that this Coranic education system does not cause any political danger . . . and has no bad repercussion on public tranquility" (Harrison 1988:108). Faidherbe tried (yet failed) to promote French education in direct opposition to Qurʾanic schools. In response, the French established in Saint-Louis in 1908 the first *médersa* in Senegal. The French-controlled médersa system began in Algeria with a balance between teaching science and French and Islamic doctrine and law. The idea was to laicize Muslim education by replacing marabouts with a new generation of "open-minded, free-thinking Muslim teachers" (64). This was intended to diffuse the Islamic threat and give French control over Muslim leadership, while creating a liberal pro-French Islam in Africa (see Brenner 2001). Ware contends that French colonial meddling in West African education resulted in transforming the meaning of Qurʾanic schools from the precolonial period: they became instead "a place to affirm Muslim identity in a colonial world that inherently challenged it" (2009:37). Lebanese, however, were banned from attending médersas and entering Senegalese mosques.[9]

French Attempts to Contain Arab Islam

Not only were Lebanese in AOF prohibited from praying in public spaces and attending religious school, but they were also forbidden to live in popular Senegalese residential quarters. The French preferred that they live in a Lebanese ghetto in Dakar Plateau. One man was jailed for living in Medina, an African neighborhood in Dakar likely named after the holy Saudi Arabian city. He eventually put the title of his house under a Senegalese name in order to avoid more trouble with the French.[10] Lebanese in Senegal were denied access to news from Lebanon. Ponty restricted the use of Arabic in French colonies and attempted to exercise greater control over importation of Arabic publications, especially those that had taken an anti-French position on the Moroccan colony or glorified Arab revolt in Palestine. Wilder suggests that the French administration's "growing focus on surveillance, identification, emigration-immigration restriction, and censorship was directly linked to the fact that a new generation of deracinated natives . . . was in fact forming civic associations, formulating public opinion and fomenting political dissent" (2005:142). These very indices of public maturity were precisely those that, according to mission civilisatrice, Africans were supposedly not yet capable of creating.

Weiss (2007) and Arsan (2010) documented ties between Shiʿa in Lebanon and West Africa during the colonial period. Shiʿi institutions such as the ʿAmiliyya Islamic Benevolent Society's school, which opened in Beirut in 1929, and the Jaʿfariyya school, founded in Tyre in 1938, depended on funds from the Lebanese emigrant community in AOF. Weiss notes an inscription in the marble entrance of the Jaʿfariyya school: "In the name of God, most gracious, most merciful, God most exalted blessed us to build this structure in 1369 AH and it was named 'The Immigrant Building' in recognition from us thanks to our children in West Africa" (2007:52). Arsan (2010) highlights a June 1930 confiscation of three bags containing banned publications during a police inspection in Dakar of postal deliveries from the Middle East. These included copies of al-ʿIrfan, a Shiʿi publication to which many Lebanese in Senegal had subscribed, the first of its kind as a journal of politics, culture, and society (Chalabi 2002:168–174). Established in 1909, al-ʿIrfan became the Shi'i world's main journal until the 1950s and was published regularly until 1973. Arsan (2010) maintains that Lebanese in Dakar sought to participate in reformist undertakings of al-'Irfan writers (see Chalabi 2002; Mervin 2000).

Concern about importation of Arabic publications was linked to increasing numbers of Arab immigrants; the Libano-Syrien population in West Africa quickly exceeded that of the Europeans. The minister of colonies wrote in 1923: "More-over, the call to foreigners such as Syrians would constitute a real threat. It would mean permitting these collaborators to play a political role in the Colony, which we must not allow, as we must also avoid the establishment—through the creation of a propagandist newspaper—of a point of contact between Eastern Islam and Islam in French West Africa" (ANS 19G24(108):1923). In 1936 the French seized 503 Arabic periodicals and advised that a further 2,040 were "dubious." In 1937, 124 were seized and 1,056 proclaimed "dubious." In 1938 these numbers increased to 384 and 4,730 respectively (Harrison 1988:192–193). The majority of banned Arabic language journals came from Lebanon/Syria or the United States, Brazil, and Argentina, countries with a high rate of Levantine immigration (ANS 19G24(108): 1922). Images were also banned, and in 1911 the French seized engravings depicting an Ottoman fleet outside Constantinople as "subversive" propaganda (Harrison 1988:52). In their place Ponty commissioned from Paris color engravings of portraits of French heroes and French factory interiors.

Lebanese at this time were very much in touch with the motherland. They not only were involved in the flow of literature between Lebanon and West Africa and supported the reformist Shi'i movement in Lebanon, but they also followed other regional political events with fervor. The French began to monitor Lebanese activities in AOF in 1933, with the organization in Dakar of a ceremony to commemorate King Faisal's death. Faisal, with British support, established an Arab government in Damascus in 1918. However, the French, who had finally secured their mandate in Lebanon, ousted him in 1920 by proclaiming the creation of the State of Greater Lebanon. Faisal was then appointed king of Iraq (1921–1933) under British supervision. In Damascus, Faisal became the symbol for Arab nationalism after the fall of the Ottoman Empire, and supporters continued to be inspired during his reign in Iraq (see Salibi 1988:48). The colonial administration followed the commemoration of Faisal's death in West Africa with concern. "Nonetheless, it is a demonstration of pan-Arabism, cadet of pan-Islamicism, which has just occurred in French West Africa for the first time through instigation of Libano-Syriens." Furthermore, "The fact that nearly the entire population of Libano-Syriens participated in this ceremony proves to us that the majority of Syrian emigrants in French West Africa harbor a nationalist sentiment." And to top it off: "Finally, even more serious, you will note that more than a dozen natives of Dakar took part in this pan-Islamic demonstration. That is a large number, if one takes into account the fact that most of these natives do not speak Eastern Arabic and were consequentially incapable of understanding given speeches. Their attendance at this ceremony is proof that instigators of the nationalist movement have already found among our natives of French West Africa a number of sympathizers" (ANS 19G1(1):1933). Such events were cause for French to take action against Lebanese.[11]

Anti-Lebanese Activities in AOF

When French colonists first lured Lebanese to Senegal to work as intermediaries in the peanut trade it was at the height of French economic expansion and prosperity in West Africa. The French did not look upon Lebanese immigration with disfavor during this period, nor did they disapprove of the natural inclination of Lebanese to integrate in Senegal. The economic depression of the 1930s, combined with nationalist sentiments spreading through the Arab world, led to a change in French views of Lebanese. Rita Cruise O'Brien attributes this shift in French policy to the fall in world price of groundnuts between 1929 and 1931 (1972:51). Capital no longer circulated freely in Africa, and credit became more difficult for traders to obtain. French in AOF became economically wary of those Lebanese traders who skillfully competed with their economic control.

> The Lebanese had a number of advantages over their European competitors, the main one being the comparative lowness of their costs. Coming from an environment much harsher than that of West Africa and fearing to return empty-handed, they were able to, and did, live in conditions that were often more wretched than that of the poorest African in the town where they worked. They were prepared to live in mud-huts, where the European required a European-style house. They were content with much lower profit margins on sales than their rivals. They spent little on themselves, at least in the initial stages of their enterprises, re-investing every bit of profit they could. Their overheads were small. They sent for members of their family to work for them in return for just their food, lodging and clothing and the longer-term prospect of establishing themselves on their own. . . . Furthermore, they had a similar approach to trading as the African, being prepared to bargain for everything, whereas the European came from a predominantly fixed-price economy. (Crowder 1968:295)

Lebanese, as the closest competitor of French colonial businessmen, became an obvious scapegoat, and the French embarked on an anti-Lebanese campaign.[12] They tried to devalue the role of Lebanese with statements such as the following by the president of Dakar's Chamber of Commerce in 1935: "In order to provide (the civilizing mission) one must oneself have a sufficient degree of civilization. Outside the Libano-Syrian elite—there are a number of Syrians in Senegal who have descended to a level not very far from the natives among whom they live" (Cruise O'Brien 1972:52).[13] The anti-Lebanese campaign mounted during the 1930s was at first ignored by the administration and major companies, who permitted unchecked immigration and had given Lebanese their start in Senegal.

Members of Syndicat Coopératif Economique du Sénégal cooperated on publicizing anti-Lebanese propaganda, especially in the monthly *France-Afrique Noire*. This publication was described as the "organ of the defense of French interests in French West Africa" (ibid. 53), and its purpose was to alert its readers to the danger of "Libano-Syrian invasion." Propaganda targeted sympathizers in metropolitan France, aiming to restrict Lebanese immigration, but despite this goal campaign efforts remained confined to a French audience inside Senegal.

From the 1930s on, the French began complete surveillance of Libano-Syrien activities. The archives report on individual Lebanese suspected of dispersing banned literature, conspiring against the French, or being too political or pan-Islamic (ANS 21G23(17)). The French introduced stricter immigration controls on Lebanese and Syrian populations in 1938. "The effectiveness of the controls—immigrants were required to make a larger money payment and to provide extra documentation—can be seen in the dramatic drop in arrivals from the Levant: 1,936 in 1937 to 979 in 1938. In both years over a thousand were deported" (Harrison 1988:193). French colonists also followed with fear the reaction of Lebanese in AOF to Lebanon and Syria's independence in 1945. They record: "In Black Africa, where the Arabic language and Muslim religion constitute so many cultural and spiritual affinities between Negros and Arabs, the presence of such a large number of Libano-Syriens harboring nationalist pride, enjoying an unbounded hospitality and possessing powerful financial means would be without doubt a grave danger to which an expedient solution must be found, considering that it was with discrete jubilation that Levantines welcomed different events that led in Syria to the ousting of the French by England" (ANS 21G8(1):14 Juin 1945). Whereas the French attempted to separate Lebanese from Senegalese, thereby inhibiting Lebanese integration in Senegal, they recognized that the Arabic language and Muslim religion formed a bond between the two. Nonetheless, their obsession with Islam was a religious concern paired with fear of nationalist Muslim rebellion against the French.

Rita Cruise O'Brien divides French society in AOF into four classes: an upper class or social elite, middle class, lower-middle class, and unstable proletariat. She contends that social interaction and clubs were concentrated within each of these divisions. The lower-middle and working classes were pejoratively called *petit blanc* by local whites and Africans who competed with them for jobs and accused them of harboring racist sentiments. It was this group that engaged in a second anti-Lebanese campaign beginning in 1947 with the publication of *Les Echos Africains* created by Maurice Voisin (see Boumedouha 1987; Sene 1997).[14]

Considered the Dakar version of the French satirical *Canard Enchaîné*, this weekly newspaper called itself "the defender of Franco-African fraternity and *la presence française*" (Cruise O'Brien 1972:74). *Les Echos Africains* had an average circulation of between 8,000 and 12,000. The paper was widely read and discussed, especially for its local gossip, and aimed to protect French presence by protesting activities of the Lebanese, colonial administration, and large companies. While the paper claimed not to be anti-African, it did take a stance against local leaders considered to be anti-French. Voisin encouraged the formation of anti-Lebanese organizations such as Association des Amis du P'tit Jules (Voisin's nickname) and Organization de Défense Française. These organizations recruited Africans to protest against what they saw as the Lebanese contribution to unemployment, exorbitant profits, and usury. Whereas the French administration did take a strong position against these mass-hate meetings, it could not stop the publication of *Les Echos*, despite imprisoning Voisin on various occasions for his attacks on administration members.

Voisin viciously attacked Libano-Syriens as a whole, even though he classified them into three categories: "The Undesirable Lebanese, the Excess Lebanese, and the Desirable Lebanese" (Diégane Sene's Archive Collection/ANS:7 Août 1947).[15] Occasionally he clarified that he was only against "the Undesirable Lebanese, that is, those who are condemned for black-marketing, illegal pricing practices, currency and gold trafficking, assaults and injuries, fights, false declarations and production of false food stamps, must be deported" (Diégane Sene's Archive Collection/ANS:8 Août 1947). It is worth citing examples of Voisin's accusations against Lebanese at length.

> It is true that most shops shut down for illicit pricing practices are Lebanese. Shops closed by decision of Administrator of Dakar are a clear indication of this.
>
> It is true that Africans cannot find places in schools, while there are many Lebanese and Syrian children in these same schools.
>
> It is true that the quasi-totality of Lebanese and Syrians do not employ African workers.
>
> It is true that some Lebanese and Syrians have rented land from old Lebus at ridiculously low prices to make millions a year by building on these lots . . .[16]
>
> We are not and will never be against a particular race.
> We want the invasion of Lebanese and Syrians in AOF to stop. We want the deportation of all Lebanese who have been sentenced (even lightly).
>
> All Africans are supporting us. (Diégane Sene's Archive Collection/ANS:14 Décembre 1953)

Voisin called for the French to take action against the Lebanese with the following declarations:

1. The land to the Africans, the road for Libano-Syriens.
2. We want deportation of all Libano-Syriens condemned for illegal pricing practices.
3. The association Défense de l'Afrique de l'Ouest is not a political organization.

> 4. Libano-Syrien usurers must be expelled from rural areas and local trade given back at last to Africans.
> 5. We want Libano-Syrien merchants to be expelled from Medina area.[17]
> 6. We want Lebanese to hire African workers.
> 7. African land must no longer be rented at very low prices by Libano-Syriens.

and

> It takes a certain audacity to do that, especially since the Lebanese representative at the UN had the "cheek" to ask the French to leave Tunisia and Morocco.
>
> We are Lebanon's "cash-cow," since Lebanese in AOF feed 200,000–300,000 Lebanese back in Lebanon. (Diégane Sene's Archive Collection/ANS:21 Décembre 1953).

Voisin even compared Lebanese to Hitler and Germans in the January 20, 1954, issue of *Les Echos d'Afrique Noire*. He was especially enflamed by the Arab League and 1955 Bandung conference, in which Lebanon and Syria took part, taking a stance against French presence in North and West Africa.

Voisin's written assaults against Lebanese were repeated frequently throughout his correspondence with the colonial administration, publications in *Les Echos,* and calls to action of organizations he formed. However, each accusation was worded slightly differently from others, and lists of demands for the French administration varied considerably. This shows that despite the strong language used, efforts were not well organized and lacked success. Senegalese politicians such as Leopold Sedar Senghor and Mamadou Dia took positions against Voisin and defended Lebanese presence in Senegal. Even French journalist Albert-Henry wrote an article in *La Croix du Sud* of July 3–9, 1954, defending Lebanese and ridiculing the French.

> The French merchant gives a bad name to Lebanese who take advantage of the lack of understanding and innocence of the native.
>
> Excuse-me! . . . Are Lebanese really so strong that where we are victims, they are perpetrators?
>
> Let's be serious! And let's not be afraid to face the plain truth. Which settler has not taken advantage, to some extent, of the native *in the past*? (Diégane Sene's Archive Collection/ANS:1954)

In sum, France's Lebanese phobia was on a number of levels. On the religious level, the French had a fear of Islam in general, and in particular that Lebanese "Arab Islam" would contaminate African Islam noir, which they were trying to mold to their own needs. Politically, the French feared an outburst of pan-Arabism and pan-Islamism that would unite Arabs and Africans and undermine their authority in West Africa. These fears can be seen by French colonial actions banning publications in Arabic and surveilling Lebanese activities. Finally, on an economic level, the French were fully aware of the Lebanese ability to compete with them and win their market share in West Africa. As a result of these concerns, French administrators aimed to both prevent Lebanese from integrating with Senegalese and impede their contact with Lebanon. They chose not to differentiate between Lebanese in Senegal, nor did they give preferential treatment to Christians. They classified all Lebanese, even Christians, as the Arab Islamic economically and politically powerful enemy. It was thus the French who first envisioned Lebanese in Senegal as one homogenous group, regardless of sectarian differences.

Lebanese Fight Back Using Transnational Ties

Ironically, anti-Lebanese campaigns failed to sever ties between Lebanese immigrants in AOF and Lebanon, but served instead to strengthen these bonds. Lebanese in Senegal organized various protests. They closed their shops for one hour on May 16, 1947. They formed a Comité de Défense des Intérêts Africains on December 31, 1953, to call for Africans to unite with Lebanese to protest the French racism of *"Mauvoisin"* (Diégane Sene's Archive Collection/ANS:17 Décembre 1953).[18] The Lebanese community even asked the high commissioner general in Dakar to guarantee protection of their diplomatic representatives, afraid that the acts of violence Voisin threatened might materialize. The Lebanese consulate general wrote letters to the high commissioner governor general of AOF protesting treatment of Lebanese, especially after one *affaire de sucre* where Lebanese merchants were accused of trafficking sugar and were interrogated by police, beaten, and became "victims of unjust and illegal matters," some hospitalized as a result (Diégane Sene's Archive Collection/ANS:21 Mai 1947). Another example of French mistreatment of Lebanese that generated outrage was a 1947 order that all passengers disembark from ships in the following order: Europeans, Indigenous People, Lebanese.

Such efforts were heard around the world, and journalists from Lebanon began to request entrance visas to AOF for a short stay to write reports (Diégane Sene's Archive Collection/ANS:1946). The Lebanese newspaper *Beyrouth* published an article with information provided by their Dakar correspondent entitled "Our Arab settlers in Dakar demonstrate and declare a general strike. French flog Lebanese with ruthless blows in Dakar," May 28, 1947. *Al-Hayat,* a Beirut newspaper labeled by the French as "nationalist Shi'i Lebanese," went so far as to threaten protests against French in Beirut if they failed to stop attacks against Lebanese in AOF.

> There are dozens of French commercial firms in Lebanon, just as there are hundreds of such firms in Arab countries. Have the French ever heard that Arabs were planning in the near future to close down these shops and throw the French into the sea? Have they ever been called "yellow face"?

Will parents of migrants who are in Lebanon and elsewhere remain passive? We inform French consular officers in Lebanon that the campaign against our migrants is beginning to provoke a strong reaction in Lebanon. Organizations are being set up in Egypt and in this country to fight back by attacking French firms and civilians. We can prove the truth of what has been said. . . . If we really want to avoid a new crisis, our common interests must compel the Government in Paris to intervene directly to end such campaigns. (Diégane Sene's Archive Collection/ANS:15 Juillet 1947)

Christians in Lebanon also came forward in their publication *Al-Amal:*

Les Phalanges Libanaises have received alarming news as well as press clippings containing articles that were derogatory against Lebanese in Africa.[19]

Les Phalanges have not failed to fulfill their duty. They made contact with appropriate administrative offices. It was shown that complaints were justified and that a premeditated and insidious plan was in action with the goal of persecuting Lebanese migrants in Senegal. These actions are in any case contrary to humanitarian principles, to engagements that were made, and to the respect due to friendship and reciprocal interests. (Diégane Sene's Archive Collection/ANS:18 Juillet 1947)

Le Réveil published a letter to Voisin from Pierre Gemayel, head of the Kata'ib "national movement of Lebanon." Voisin responded to Gemayel, "you are telling me—'you are too violent'—Sir, I am the Editor in Chief of a satirical newspaper. What cannot be written in a serious newspaper, I can write. By the way, you know very well that similar newspapers in Lebanon have attacked France" (Diégane Sene's Archive Collection/ANS:7 Août 1947). The Syrian publication *Al-Ba'th* also published articles about the mistreatment of Lebanese and Syrians in AOF.

Sene (1997) argues that instead of helping the situation, this reaction in the Lebanese and Syrian Arabic press served only to amplify the problem. He accuses the Lebanese press of stooping to the same level as Voisin with evocative titles such as "If our emigrants in Africa have become 'Yellow,' it is because they have shed their red blood in this black continent" (55, citing *Al-Hayat* of July 15, 1947). While this transcontinental newspaper dialogue did not reduce Voisin's attacks against Lebanese in Senegal, it did strengthen ties between Lebanese migrants and the motherland.

Beginnings of Lebanese Unity

An influential publication of colonial propaganda entitled "The End of the French in Black Africa" (Paillard 1935) described at length how Lebanese would displace the French in West Africa. Later colonial documents continued to depict Lebanese as a French "problem" (Mangoné 1958; Charbonneau 1959). Imagery in newspapers and magazines can serve as a useful tool for illustrating various perceptions of migrant communities (Chavez 2001). Trees are a common national symbol for both Lebanon and Senegal, and the relationship of these trees became a metaphor for Lebanese integration (or lack thereof) in West Africa. Lebanon's national cedar tree is a member of the pine family, with clusters of needlelike leaves. The Cedars of Lebanon were mentioned in the Old Testament, making the ancient tree the pride of the country, even though only a few original groves remain today. The baobab tree is the national symbol of Senegal, a thick-trunked member of the bombax family, characterized by stunted rootlike branches. As the story goes, a displeased deity plucked the tree in anger and thrust it back into the ground upside down. *Voix d'Afrique* (October 4–17, 1976) featured a cover image of a large cedar hovering over the westernmost part of the African map, its roots attached to the side of the continent and rooted in its interior. This image, of the cedar uprooting the baobab, represents French views of Lebanese as a threat to their hold on West Africa.

As a result of French policy, Lebanese in Senegal began to envision themselves as a united community, despite religious baggage originally brought from Lebanon. Colonial archives document beginnings of Lebanese consolidation against French discrimination:

> Libano-Syriens, irrespective of their faith, can no longer hide hostile sentiments towards France. Radio programs in Arabic broadcasting from London recounting in detail events of the Levant have only served to provoke a negative reaction towards France in Lebanese circles. (ANS 21G8(1):6 Juin 1945)

> In Libano-Syrien circles there is much emotion over events taking place in their country. They fear repressive measures by the French administration and are careful not to circulate negative propaganda about us. Quite to the contrary, Syrians, Lebanese, Maronites, or Muslims—all proclaim attachment to France and remain silent as to origins of the current movement in the Middle East. (ANS 21G8(1):25 Janvier 1945)

During World War II Lebanese united to protest French policies. The French did not consider Lebanese equal to Europeans and denied them the same war rations of food and milk. Lebanese also resisted mandatory military service in the French army. "Moreover, this measure has quieted traditional quarrels between Muslims and Christians who now are all prepared to protest against the possibility of being incorporated into the army" (ibid.). Lebanese Muslims supported Germany, whereas Catholics sided with Italy. As far as the French were concerned, both countries were enemies, and Lebanese chose to support the Axis they thought would be victorious and the one most likely to promise independence to Arab states (ANS 21G8(1):25 Juin 1945).

This chapter has outlined the development of French colonial policy concerning Islam and Lebanese migration in West Africa. French administrators

Cover of French missionary magazine *Voix d'Afrique* 24, October 4–17, 1976, depicting a Lebanese cedar tree taking root in West Africa. The cover story is entitled "The Lebanese in Africa: Parasites or Agents of Development?"

recruited Lebanese as economic intermediaries then later opposed their immigration. Archival data have illustrated that French perception and treatment of Lebanese as a threat resulted in Lebanese unity against the French. French officers not only engaged with the Other in West Africa, but also actively envisioned themselves as a "Muslim power." Resulting administrative policies thereby converted the local into a "universal" that met colonial needs in other imperial contexts. Marty developed Islam noir through comparing Islam in North and West Africa, albeit in racist and hierarchical terms. French administrators built médersas in the name of colonial modernity, demonstrating their openness to Muslim civilization but expecting in return to create a local Muslim leadership supportive of the French civilizing mission. French colonists thus desired to translate policy into local forms of religious knowledge and leadership, with a desired outcome of eventual retranslation of African subjectivities into the colonial cosmopolitan moral mission. The French never strayed from their conviction that progress and improvement could develop only in an Africa open to superior European Christian ways. The French also continually adapted colonial policy on Lebanese migration in response to events taking place in their Levantine Empire. Efforts to stem the tide of transregional communication recognized and sought to control cosmopolitan empathies with independence movements elsewhere.

Politique des races was the ultimate response to these varied cosmopolitanisms. Not only did this policy aim to divide and conquer indigenous African ethnic and religious communities by ensuring that Muslims do not rule over non-Muslims, but in conceiving of West African autochthony as fundamentally pre-Islamic and incapable of conforming to foreign religious traditions, it sought to segregate Islam noir from Arab Islam. French colonial cosmopolitan universalism had a lasting effect, resulting in local reactions to policies that were likewise multiply translated. Lebanese internalized French perceptions and treatment of their community and began to unite as an ethnic group. The médersa served as a catalyst for alternative forms of Senegalese—and Lebanese—Islamic education. Ongoing struggles for religious authority and authenticity continued to position themselves against the French model. Cosmopolitanism and autochthony were thus paired in opposition to one another in multiple modes of translation and retranslation in the colonial period.

The French were the first to classify Lebanese Muslims and Christians as a single group. By implication over time Lebanese grew together in response to the colonial power. This chapter uses colonial archives as historical documentation for what Lebanese themselves articulated to me about their history. Kamil, in our first interview, noted that the French government tried to separate Lebanese from "natives," but this policy backfired and Lebanese learned Senegalese languages and adjusted to village life. Kamil, a Maronite Catholic, was the first to inform me of the French prohibition of Lebanese prayer in local mosques to prevent their "complete integration" into Senegalese society. Abbas, a Lebanese Sunni Muslim, likewise defensively remarked that Senegalese should not object to Lebanese absence from Friday prayer as they were historically forbidden from entering Senegalese mosques during colonial times. Farid, a Lebanese elder who first arrived in Kaolack in 1957, recalled how he used to speak Arabic in private with a Senegalese man, afraid of being expelled by the French for breaking the law. Rashid proudly remembered attending mosque in Ziguinchor in 1959 with a Senegalese police escort in order to demonstrate the end of colonialism. He continues to pray in Senegalese mosques today. Lebanese blame the French for maintaining a Lebanese ghetto in Dakar and not only forbidding Lebanese integration with Senegalese but also keeping Lebanese at a distance from the colonial power. The following chapter will examine this integration debate and Lebanese efforts to come to terms with contradictions of cosmopolitanism when their survival in postindependence Senegal necessitated strategies for claims to autochthony.

2 Senegalese Independence and the Question of Belonging

Everyone must be mixed in their own way.
—Leopold Sedar Senghor, 1975

SENEGAL GAINED INDEPENDENCE from France on June 20, 1960. As Senegalese administrators grappled with which aspects of colonial cosmopolitanism to maintain, Lebanese grew more uncertain of their place in postcolonial Africa. Becoming socially and politically invisible was key to Lebanese economic success. Clandestine patron-client relationships suited both Lebanese, vulnerable economic actors in need of such collaboration, and Senegalese politicians who benefited from Lebanese financial support, which they preferred not to publicize. This chapter will outline Senegal's postindependence ideology and political economy, focusing on repercussions for the economic, political, and social integration of the Lebanese community.

Senghor, Negritude, and Senegalese Nationalism

Leopold Sedar Senghor, Senegal's first president and one of Africa's greatest poets, was as key a figure in crafting postcolonial nationalism in Senegal as Michel Chiha was in Lebanon. Senghor defined Negritude as "the sum total of the qualities possessed by all black men everywhere. . . . The manner of self-expression of the black character, the black world, black civilization" (Vaillant 1990:244).[1] A universal black cosmopolitanism, Negritude, according to Diagne (2011), is a product of Africa and its diaspora, the Harlem Renaissance, and writers and artists such as Jean-Paul Sartre, Henri Bergson, Lucien Levy-Bruhl, Karl Marx and Friedrich Engels, and Pablo Picasso. These cosmopolitan linkages enabled by the imperial order brought together Francophone Africans, representatives of the broader African diaspora, other colonized populations, and the internationalist Left. Negritude engaged issues raised by French colonial humanism about the relationship between race, culture, nationality, and citizenship. Wilder suggests that "black colonial critics claimed membership in Greater France by trying, in various ways, to articulate citizenship with a distinct Negro-African (national) culture" (2005:161). For Senghor, "Negritude therefore is not a *racism*. . . . In truth, *Negritude is a Humanism*" (Senghor as cited by Wilder 2005:250).

Senghor envisioned an Africa that could preserve and develop characteristics of Negritude as the continent worked toward industrialization. For him, "cultural independence . . . is the sine qua non of all other independences, especially political independence" (quoted in Wilder 2005:179). Senghor accepted that it was no longer possible to speak of pure African culture, and envisioned all *nègres* as biologically *métis*. For him, *métissage,* cross-breeding, or synthesis, not separation, was the path to development. He looked to métissage for both personal identity—bringing together racial self-discovery and universal humanity—as well as national economic development, and "hoped to reconcile primordial Africanity with Western modernity and to secure a place for Negro-Africans within the imperial nation-state" (Wilder 2005:232). In so doing, Senghor "inverts the logic of colonial humanism by linking a rejection of cultural assimilation to a demand for political assimilation" (236). This alternative political formation would be neither strictly national nor colonial. Vaillant writes: "Indeed he had stated then that for the African there was no question of whether or not to assimilate. . . . It was rather a question of whether or not the African would assimilate French influence actively, as an animal transforms the food it eats into the tissue that it needs to grow in its own form, or whether the African would allow himself to be passively absorbed into French culture" (1990:264).[2]

Senghor called for a new generation of educated African elites to study their own cultural tradition alongside that of the Europeans with the slogan: "It is about assimilating, not being assimilated" (as quoted in Wilder 2005:237). Senghor, therefore, was not interested "in constructing Africa as the superior mirror opposite of modern Europe" but aimed to determine "'what the black man contributes' to European and universal civilization" (249). Through hybridity his goal was to displace the opposition of Western over African culture. Yet Wilder accuses Negritude as having enabled enduring postcolonial dependency relations between France and its former territories.

This chapter will focus on Lebanese "assimilation" in Senegal. I begin with a discussion of Senghor's vision of Negritude in order to underscore how assimilation was a concern for Senegalese from French colonial times. Diagne writes of Negritude's perpetual struggle against ontological exile, where "one does not have a home when one is black" when living in a world where "Being is white and speaks white" (2011:26, citing Sartre). Senghor believed that "Africanity, because it is exiled from itself and dispersed, will constitute itself as francophone and thus demand to be received by the language which naturally speaks universality. This encounter between Africanity and the French language will manifest itself as impossibility and will take place by means of the very fact of its impossibility" (Diagne 2011:27). As such, Senghor attempted to reconfigure universalism as African humanism, where its very universality was a function of its particularity.

In spite of this search for identity, Senghor defined his political goal, during an important policy statement in 1959, as the creation of an African socialism that was to be the political and social equivalent of métissage.

> The ideal society was to be African, in that it would remain true to the culture of Negritude, and socialist, in that it was to borrow the most advanced technological and organizational forms from the West. It was up to the African to choose the most useful discoveries of Western technology and culture, adapt them, and introduce them into a Senegalese context. That Western forms might be incompatible with African ones, or that the import of Western technology and forms of organization might set in motion changes that would shake African society to its foundations, does not seem to have troubled Senghor at this time. (Vaillant 1990:267–268)

Senghor realized, after Senegal gained independence, that racist implications of Negritude were too strong for his political slogan. He began to use the term Africanity, without renouncing Negritude, to denote the African world's values and culture. "This word focused attention on a common geographical location and a shared history as the source of a common culture, rather than on the race of the people who had created it" (Vaillant 1990:288). Negritude was primarily a cultural concept, not a political one, and not particularly useful in promoting loyalty to a new nation-state comprised of French advisors and businessmen, Lebanese traders, Sufi marabouts, and various rural and urban notables and bureaucrats with their own interests.

Scholars of Negritude have neglected to analyze Senghor's view of the Arab world and of Arabs residing in Senegal. Senghor acknowledged: "Thus, alongside African civilization, with its negro-African and Arab-Berber facets, we teach, on an equal footing, each of the great civilizations: European civilization, American civilization, the Chinese, Indian, Christian, Islamic, Judaic civilizations, etc." (Senghor 1980:74). Senghor's concept of Africanity included these Arabo-Berber elements. He wrote: "I often define Africanité as the 'complementary symbiosis of the values of Arabité and the values of Negritude'" (Senghor 1977:105). Senghor (1993:181) defined Arabité as a civilization expressed by biological ethnotype. He openly expressed his admiration for Arabs, likening Negritude to Arabité in constituting equal obstacles for Euramerica, and was convinced of the necessity of Arab-African cooperation. Nevertheless, he insisted that Arabité and Negritude should remain two separate issues:

> We believe that you first need not confuse Arabité and Negritude. There is Arabité, which must be defended and promoted by Arabs. They do it, and do it

well. The Arab league organizes, on a regular basis, conferences, where Arabs discuss their cultural policy. It is also our duty, we Negro-Africans and Negroes of the Diaspora, to defend Negritude by first defining it. . . . And this was also as it should be because, if Black civilization, Black culture, in sum, Negritude, must be defined, then it is the internal business of Negroes. We will not resolve the cultural problem of Arab-African cooperation if we do not raise those issues in a straightforward manner. (Senghor 1980:275–276)[3]

Senghor blamed Europeans for disseminating among Africans racist ideas about Arabs, such that they were all slave traders who scorned blacks. He positively acknowledged Senegal's Arab population: "The African people share a sense of solidarity, whether they are Arab-Berber or Negro-African. Senegal is an example of this. In our country we have 20,000 Lebanese-Syrians, of which half have obtained Senegalese nationality. Above all we have 150,000 Mauritanians, who own small shops all the way into the villages. Twenty percent of the Senegalese population is foreign. Yet, there has never been any racial conflict, even less an ethnic cleansing" (Senghor 1980:272–273). The Lebanese people, Senghor declared, were the most democratic people in the Arab world, and he favorably envisioned the integration of Arabs in Senegal (288). Likewise he asserted "the biggest favor we could do for our Lebanese friends is to refuse that the Lebanese in Senegal divide themselves into Christians and Muslims" (290). Counter to the French politique des races, Senghor favored integration over division, and his exclusively black concept of Negritude was translated into a more cosmopolitan Africanity inclusive of Arabs (and European colonial heritage) to reflect Senegal's reality. He recognized Arab-Berber culture and ethnicity as an autochthonous facet of African civilization. This abstract vision, however, was not so easily implemented on the ground.

Independent Senegal's Political Economy

Senegal's transition from colonial to African administration was relatively smooth. This began in 1957 when an African territorial government led by Mamadou Dia shared administrative authority with the French colonial governor and ended in 1960 with administrative reforms. Politics in independent Senegal was an elite activity based on patron-client relationships and clan politics, reflecting Senegal's pluralistic society and changing class structures. Senegalese political elite were Western-educated intellectuals who collaborated with French politicians, yet relied on the support of traditional notables and religious leaders to provide them with votes (Gellar, Charlick, and Jones 1980). Nevertheless, Senegalese postcolonial politics exhibited relative continuity and stability. Senegal was a one-party state until 1976, when opposition parties were permitted to function legally. The same political party, Union Progressiste Sénégalaise (UPS), governed the country from 1959 until 2000, changing its name to Parti Socialiste (PS) in 1976. The opposition did not gain power until 2000, schemed to retain power in the contested 2012 elections, but finally conceded in what was heralded a victory for Senegalese democracy.

Senegal's economic system had been dictated by France's needs, leading to challenges for Senegal's self-sufficiency. Caswell (1984) notes that at independence 80 percent of Senegal's exports were peanuts, and the peanut trade employed 87 percent of the Senegalese population, including many Lebanese. Prime Minister Mamadou Dia led Senegalese officials in the implementation of a new development strategy that stressed institution building, rural development, and structural transformation of the countryside over immediate economic growth and rapid industrialization. The cooperative movement was to implement African socialism and serve as the economic foundation for peasant democracy (Gellar 1987). Its explicit goal was to displace private moneylenders and crop purchasers (Gersovitz and Waterbury 1987). Lebanese were positioned beneath export-import houses as traders, who purchased groundnuts for bagging and transportation from smaller merchants in contact with growers (Tignor 1987). In addition to marginalizing Lebanese, Dia's economic nationalism and socialist policies threatened the French business community, Senegalese private sector, and local merchant class, including marabouts. Strong opposition led to his downfall in 1962.

Senegal's development policies changed significantly under Senghor's sole leadership. Senegal's first president stressed close collaboration between the state and the French business community in economic planning, created a market for French capital, and returned focus to the peanut crop. In 1966, Senghor aimed to make Dia's cooperative service more effective and less corrupt by establishing Office National de Coopération et d'Assistance au Développement (ONCAD). Fatton writes: "Far from alleviating the peasants' debts, ONCAD contributed not only to their increase but also to their stricter collection. . . . In fact, the state replaced the old colonial houses and Lebanese middlemen as the central source of peasant subjection and affliction" (1987:57–59). ONCAD also played a significant political role in consolidating the rural power of marabouts, who were granted special privileges that contributed to the expansion of their material—and spiritual—control over talibes, positioning them as economic competitors with Lebanese (Fatton 1987).

Senghor accelerated the economy's Africanization and reestablished the prime minister post in 1970. Senegalese took more important roles in the private sector and pressured foreign firms to hire African employees. In addition to working in the groundnut trade, Lebanese held a share in the urban textile market and imported ready-made and specialty garments from Europe, competing with French wholesalers of locally manufactured goods. By the late 1970s Dakar's major Lebanese textile importers began to retreat from the trade, unable to compete with

Senegalese illegal importation of unregulated ready-made goods (Boone 1992). A series of severe droughts in the 1960s and 1970s led to diversification of the economy away from peanuts toward tomatoes, sugar cane, rice, millet, cotton, fruits, vegetables, fishing, and livestock production. By the end of the 1970s, Senegal was finally moving away from neocolonial dependency on France, but at a cost of dependency on large volumes of foreign aid. Boone highlights Senegal's "distinctive combination of overall political stability and rural economic decline" (2003:138).

Lebanese Economic Integration

The Africanization of Senegal's economy proceeded very slowly at first. French, as well as Lebanese, were uneasy about Dia's nationalist and socialist sentiments and favored his departure, hoping Senghor would be more conciliatory toward their communities. Senegal's political and social crises in the late 1960s resulted in businessmen demanding certain sectors of the economy, such as those dominated by Lebanese, be reserved exclusively for Senegalese, with full governmental support for the African private sector's development. Ironically, Lebanese had an easier time integrating economically in Senegal under French colonialism.

Despite Senghor's cosmopolitan vision of Africanity's ability to assimilate African and Arab-Berber facets, as an ethno-racial minority and economically powerful group, Lebanese encountered hostility from the Senegalese population. An article entitled "Lebanese in Africa: Parasites or Agents of Development?" reports survey results on Senegalese and Ivoirian views of Lebanese. The overwhelmingly negative responses revolved around recurring topics resembling earlier French grievances against Lebanese. "They are just parasites, non-producers, whose purely commercial occupations no longer have any economic or social basis; they gain wealth at the expense of nationals by depriving them of a job or rigging the game of commerce and employment; they are too exclusively 'seekers of profit' and it is merely in appearance that they are integrated into African society" (Thibault 1976:14). The journalist further insisted that "employing only family members, the Lebanese pose an obstacle to the Africanization of the work force and consistently sabotage national efforts to improve employment rates" (13).

Senghor aimed to please both Senegalese and foreign businessmen and announced in December 1968: "There is no question of removing foreigners from their activities, but to give the Senegalese their place in the country. There is no question of driving out these foreign friends, ... [we] should cooperate with them and they should help us to build our nation" (cited in Boumedouha 1987:217). Prime Minister (later President) Abdou Diouf remarked in 1970 that "Senegalization" was not an easy task and should not be viewed as a struggle against foreigners who "have their place in the development of the country" (cited in Boumedouha

1987:222). Yet Senghor responded to mounting pressure against foreign businesses by creating in 1969 Société Nationale d'Études et de Promotion Industrielle (SONEPI) to provide credit and training to assist in the development of small and medium-sized Senegalese companies. That same year Senegalese businessmen replaced French control of Dakar's Chamber of Commerce. Lebanese felt threatened by these developments and formed an economic group of their own in September 1969, Groupement Professionnel des Commerçants et Industriels Libanais du Sénégal (GPLS). The group's main concern was the protection of Lebanese interests in Senegal; their first activity secured a fair distribution of import-export licenses. According to new laws of African socialism, foreign companies were required to Africanize their personnel. Lebanese began to employ more Africans, and those with financial capabilities moved into new fields of investment.[4] Lebanese merchants exhibit continued economic flexibility today and can quickly restructure businesses or switch products.

Despite Africanization and transformations in Lebanese businesses, Lebanese continued to be viewed as "parasites"—lawful or illegal. The cover issue of *Jeune Afrique Economie* on June 14–27, 1999, was entitled "The Cedar in the Shadow of the Baobab." Successful Lebanese businessmen were examined as scapegoats in West Africa, but the article suggested they were not innocent scapegoats. Lebanese were involved in foreign currency black market, drug and weapons trade, prostitution, corruption, trafficking, and fraud (Castéran, Kra, and Weiss 1999:14). The cedar tree was not depicted as uprooting the baobab, as in the earlier French publication described in the previous chapter, but as hiding in its shadow, where anonymity permits illicit activities.

Lebanese countered such accusations by proof of their good deeds. A lawyer cited to me statistics (from 2003) that demonstrated the Lebanese community was a better employer than the Senegalese government: Lebanese employed approximately 69,000 people, whereas the government employed only 60,000.[5] In interviews Lebanese envisioned themselves as hard-working and successful. Although Senegalese resented them for owning prominent national businesses, Lebanese argued that nobody is preventing Senegalese from doing the same. Lebanese highlight active involvement in charity work and financing mosques, schools, and hospitals. Occasionally the government would request large financial contributions from wealthy Lebanese to assist in certain projects. Boumedouha (1992) states that contributions increased considerably after 1975, the start of the Lebanese Civil War, when Lebanese had little choice but to invest more in Senegal. Lebanese publicly donated to important causes that won them necessary appreciation and strengthened the protectionist system. For example, they contributed in 1979 to building the Tivaouane Tijani mosque and financed the construction of a dispensary named after Philippe Maguilen Senghor, the former president's son killed in a car accident in 1981. They helped resettle Senegalese expelled from Nigeria in 1983 and donated significant sums in response to President Diouf's appeal to help rural communities affected by the 1984 drought (Boumedouha 1992:227). In sum, Boumedouha notes:

> the system of protection adopted by the French administration in their dealings with the Lebanese during the colonial period was maintained, if not strengthened, by the Senegalese authorities after independence. Similarly, Lebanese traders came to play an identical role toward the Senegalese ruling elite as they had in the past under the French. In this arrangement, the Senegalese provided the political contacts and the Lebanese brought in their trading experience and capital as well as international contacts. As one important Lebanese businessman put it: "Senegalese big men find our assistance crucial in the pursuit of their own economic enrichment." (1992:221)

Lebanese economic success was linked to involvement in politics.

Lebanese Political Integration

Lebanese sensed that change was going to occur well before independence. They worked to establish good relations with Senegal's nationalist parties, especially Senghor's Bloc Démocratique Sénégalais (BDS). They helped fund parties and lent politicians trucks to campaign in the countryside. Certain Lebanese were also active party members. At independence they were "rewarded" with Senegalese citizenship, and the community was assured continued protection (Boumedouha 1992).

The Bourgi family was particularly involved in Senegalese politics. Abdou Karim Bourgi, who came to Senegal in 1927, first met Senghor in Kaolack in 1947, the year he created BDS (Boumedouha 1987). He took an active role in the development and promotion of Senghor's party, and as a result was nearly expelled by the French in 1953. Mahmud Bourgi, a relative who headed Comité d'Adhésion et de Bienfaisance Libano-Syrien, supported Senghor's opponent Lamine Gueye. This split resulted in prominent family members who supported the losing party migrating to France, including Robert Bourgi, Jacques Chirac's advisor, and his brother Albert Bourgi, professor of public law and outspoken critic of democratization in Africa. Abdou Karim Bourgi was the first Lebanese to be offered Senegalese citizenship for "exceptional services rendered to Senegal" (Boumedouha 1987:188). After his father's death in 1977, Ramez Bourgi reaffirmed his loyalty to the ruling socialist party (PS) and to Senghor. Before the 1983 presidential elections, he became vice-president of Comité de Soutien à l'action du President Abdou Diouf (COSAPAD), an organization which drew financial support for Diouf's re-election.[6] He ran for mayor of Dakar that same year, but lost to Mamadou Diop in what was thought to be a rigged election where Bourgi had the advantage. Lebanese are proud that two streets in Dakar have been renamed after the Bourgis. The French colonial Rue Grammont was changed after independence to Rue Abdou

Karim Bourgi; Rue des Essarts became Rue Ramez Bourgi after his death in 1983 from poor health aggravated by campaign failure (Boumedouha 1987:254–255).

The Bourgi family was an exception among Lebanese, who are generally not politically active. Some fear being too much in the Senegalese public eye, citing past racist incidents against them, while others regret that such opportunities are not made readily available to them. Jamila, Senegal's only Lebanese female politician, explained that she entered politics because she grew up poor, lived in the Medina neighborhood outside of Dakar's Lebanese ghetto, and had nothing to lose. She illustrated her passion for grassroots politics with anecdotes. She once attended a meeting of rural Senegalese women, where she spoke last. They debated in French the need for cell phones and computers. This Lebanese activist accentuated that she does not speak *toubab* (Wolof for "French") and argued emphatically in Wolof that Senegal's development does not depend on computers. More important, she maintained, is how to feed our families, how to cultivate our grain, and how it took the West one hundred years to develop. Senegal should make use of Western technology but must slowly develop the country. Jamila's intervention received a round of applause, and she liberated women from speaking formally in French. She also recounted a meeting she attended of educated men discussing Mao, Marx, and other theorists. She was embarrassed to contribute because she had never completed her education, but spoke anyway about how Marx could not help Senegalese put food on tables and raise children. Again, those present applauded her words and offered her a chair as a sign of respect. She refused, emphasizing that she was not better than others and would sit on the floor with them.

Jamila had become a politician after police blockaded her neighborhood in 1998. Four hundred businessmen, unable to sell goods, congregated in protest, and she offered her assistance. They first blamed Lebanese for their troubles, but she helped them organize. She wrote letters to the prefecture and called a deputy she knew for support. When the problem was resolved the businessmen for whom she had advocated insisted that she become a politician. Jamila showed me photos of her political activism. She dressed in the Senegalese flag during a march commemorating the tragic sinking of the Joola ferryboat and carried the sign "united in victory, united in pain."[7] She had worn this same outfit a few months earlier for the celebratory march after Senegal beat France in the 2002 World Cup, the surprising victory referred to in the slogan. Other photos depicted her wearing a yellow and red *boubou,* her political party's colors. Lebanese women do not wear African dress, and, indeed, Jamila was the only Lebanese visible in her photos of politically active citizens.

Samir Abourizk, a member of Senegal's socialist party, founded a new political party called Democratie Citoyenne on July 17, 2000, with (unfulfilled) plans to run against Abdoulaye Wade in the 2007 presidential elections. A Lebanese informant once remarked that Abourizk had to be either courageous or crazy to form a political party, as he was not only Lebanese but also Christian. Lebanese are active in the Senegalese Chamber of Commerce, an economic organization with political clout, and certain influential Lebanese serve as special legal advisors to government bodies. Kamil recited the Arabic proverb, "behind every great man is a woman," which he changed to "behind every African man is a Lebanese."

Nevertheless, a feature article in *L'Express* noted Lebanese absence in Senegalese politics:

> Until now, only rarely have Lebanese ventured into the shaky ground of politics, with the exceptions of Kazem Sharara, ex-advisor to President Diouf, Fares Attyé, ex-socialist activist, Samir Abourizk, currently a municipal counselor in Rufisque, or even the late Ramez Bourgi. Truthfully, they do not feel welcome in this sphere. "Not a single high administrator, deputy or minister is of Lebanese descent. Among 60 advisors, President Abdoulaye Wade has not bothered to choose a single Lebanese. . . . Yet, our community includes talented people who, just like the Corsicans in France, feel they should have representation at the State level," commented Samir Jarmache, vice-president of Alliance. (Gyldèn 2002)

Lebanese politicians are few in number, yet the community has remained politically influential. Many voted in presidential elections, split among various political parties. Upon Abdoulaye Wade's election in 2000, a delegation of influential Lebanese men met with the new president to discuss issues important to their community. Lebanese, like many Senegalese, became disillusioned with President Wade's unrealized promises during his twelve-year rule.

Wade attended the 2002 Francophonie conference in Beirut. The Lebanese consulate officer in Dakar considered this to be a golden opportunity for the Lebanese government to thank Africa for its hospitality of Lebanese, demonstrate its readiness to receive African delegations, and express interest in furthering diplomatic relations. Lebanese from Senegal held a reception for the Senegalese delegation in Lebanon, sponsoring a dinner and covering transportation expenses for fifty Senegalese officials. One hundred (mostly second-generation) Lebanese of Senegal attended the conference, proud that Abdou Diouf, Senegal's past president, was elected secretary general of the Francophonie. Despite claims that Lebanese are not politically integrated enough, they do hold significant political clout in Senegal.

Lebanese Cultural Integration

The French colonial position regarding Lebanese in Africa was well documented in colonial correspondence and newspapers, in contrast to the quiet postindependence marriage of convenience between Lebanese and Senegalese politicians. Senegalese popular opinion on the Lebanese community was, however, widely expressed. Senegal has a free press and myriad newspapers, which many Lebanese and Senegalese avidly read. Media publicity can often be purchased: Lebanese hire journalists to positively portray certain events, whereas other journalists publish attacks on Lebanese individuals in exchange for bribes for their silence. Daily interaction with certain sectors of Senegalese society, informal conversations, and other sources (Mancabou 1998–1999; Gavron and Ndiaye 1999) confirm that media perspectives coincide with views of many Senegalese in Dakar.

Dominant Senegalese discourse accuses Lebanese of not sufficiently integrating into Senegalese society after French departure. Linked to friction between forces of cosmopolitanism and autochthony, this sphere of cultural integration forms the backdrop for all minority communities in Senegal and is a point of contention between Senegalese and Lebanese. My goal in this chapter is not to come to a conclusion regarding the state of Lebanese integration in Senegal, as certain informants hoped or feared. I will lay out contrasting perspectives on sociocultural integration and evaluate their interconnectedness with economics and politics. Lebanese economic success was symbolized by the shadow of the baobab enabling illicit activities. In the realm of cultural integration, Lebanese were also perceived as continuing to maintain Lebanese identity underneath appearances of adapting to Senegal.

In one magazine article, Lebanese youth—particularly in Dakar—were cited as an annoyance.[8]

> Believing themselves to be invincible, this youth, this new "savage horde," wearing skin-tight t-shirts, saddling mechanical pure-bloods (Honda, Yamaha, . . .) and emboldened by knowledge of martial arts (karate) often act like utter vandals. Some of them belong to families whose honorable reputation in the country dates back three centuries. Many were born here and speak national languages. They are not, then, foreigners, even if their integration into Senegalese society is purely superficial. But as soon as they take on macho and arrogant attitudes, their victims immediately remember that they are foreigners after all. (Thibault 1976:13)

This quotation highlights notions of autochthony as understood through birthright and national language. Lebanese are born in Senegal and fluent in local languages, yet the author argues in no uncertain terms that Lebanese dress and behavior is what marks them as outsiders. He alludes to social class though the example of motorcycles, a status symbol owned by many Lebanese but fewer Senegalese, which enables greater mobility in bypassing Dakar's frequent traffic jams.

The centrality of racial difference, while conspicuously absent from the article cited above, is more obvious in another newspaper article that compares Senegal's Lebanese and Guinean communities. The opposition of these two communities, and conclusion that Guineans (unlike Lebanese) integrated beautifully in Senegal, is very telling.[9]

Two communities, two different worlds. The first has integrated itself remarkably well into its host culture, to the point of attaining osmosis with the native population. The second lives in isolation, retracted into itself, as if in a state of siege it has buckled its suitcase and is prepared to flee at the slightest sign of danger. The first chose long ago to live its *sénégalité* without shame, to share the pain and joy of Senegalese, to live among them. The second has chosen to ignore them, deride them, hold them in contempt. The first community has always accepted to be the target of Senegalese, stoically bearing insults and frustrations and has thus ultimately managed to meld into Senegalese society. The second community has opted rather to take out its frustrations on Senegalese and to entertain with them a rapport based exclusively on money. (Ndiaye 1997)

Comparing Lebanese to an African migrant group over another Arab community (Moroccan or Mauritanian) highlights the complexity of cultural assimilation in Senegal. Guineans are perceived as the model for immigrant integration because they come from a neighboring African culture in addition to having racial similarities. They also provide Senegal with unskilled labor, often in selling fruit or charcoal, and their earnings do not surpass those of many Senegalese. I discussed this article with the editor of *Le Temoin,* proud of his newspaper for publishing provocative feature stories, often in tabloid fashion. He acknowledged that although many Senegalese consider Lebanese to be racist, they are in fact jealous of Lebanese economic success and unaware that today's Senegalese upper class has financial means that surpass the average Lebanese. He defended the journalist's comparison of Lebanese to Guineans by summarizing for me Senegalese stereotypes of various ethnic groups.[10]

There are, of course, exceptions to the views depicted above. One journalist called for more recognition of what Lebanese have given Senegal: "the athletic talent, the creation of commercial and agricultural enterprises. . . . What more could we ask than what they have already given?" (Guèye n.d.) Senegalese credit Lebanese for being integrated in one very important aspect of Senegalese life: sports. Zeina Saheli is a champion swimmer; Abdalah Sakheli is a soccer player and past president of Union Sportive Goréene; Ali Saheli created the soccer club l'Ecole de la Renaissance; Nage Kabaz is a three-time champion of the racecar rally *6 heures de Dakar;* and Samir Fawaz is a national kung fu hero, who won multiple championships in France and trained to compete in Taiwan ("Les Sénégalo-Libanais"). Fares Attye coached the Senegalese judo team, leading them in international competitions, and Said Fakhry was elected president of the Senegalese Football Federation in 2003.[11] I observed Lebanese and Senegalese boys playing soccer together in the streets. Zeina Saheli's father, a grocer, beamed with pride when speaking of his daughter having represented Senegal at the 2000 Australian Summer Olympics. Senegalese politicians and academics even suggested that the 2002 World Cup marked a positive change in Lebanese integration when Lebanese and Senegalese rallied together on the streets of Dakar in support of the Senegalese soccer team.

Race and Racism

Lebanese in Senegal have an ambivalent racial status. Perceived not only as "Arab" but also as "white" by the African population, they were not welcome in French "white only" social clubs during colonial times. Treated as a scapegoat for many of Senegal's ills, Lebanese are caught in between black and white, Senegalese and French, and, as middlemen, are often considered a race of their own—Lebanese. Migrant communities are often confronted with *racialization,* defined by Omi and Winant as the process whereby racial meaning is imputed onto "a previously racially unclassified relationship, social practice or group" (1986:64). Akyeampong (2006) discusses, in the case of Lebanese in Ghana, why it was conceptually difficult to envision a nonblack citizen in West Africa during the period of decolonization. Understood through the legacy of colonial legal institutions and pan-Africanism (in particular African American framing of Africa as the place of blacks), Akyeampong proposes that Lebanese in Ghana displaced European colonizers as targets of local hostility.

Senegal offers a unique situation for Lebanese, whose racial status and economic success is what set the community apart and was not a basis for its integration. These factors also contributed to the coming together of Lebanese Muslims and Christians. It is difficult to separate racial discrimination, based on skin color, from social class discrimination, based on economic success, from religious discrimination, based on not belonging to Senegal's economically and politically influential Sufi orders. Lebanese are identified in Senegal as a wealthy elite community, yet the Lebanese community itself is divided along lines of social class. Poor Lebanese depend on the community's charity. Those who can afford to visit Lebanon quickly realize that the social status and standard of living they secured for themselves in Dakar could never be reproduced in Beirut (Leichtman 2005).

Senegalese discourse regularly refers to Lebanese as racist. Lebanese, in turn, claim they do not discriminate against Senegalese, but Senegalese discriminate against them. Whereas they first blame French colonialism for lack of integration in purposefully attempting to isolate Lebanese from Senegalese, they also fault Senegalese for enforcing a Lebanese ghetto during independence. The derogatory Wolof word for "Arab" is *naar* (Arabic for "fire"). As the story was told to me, an Arab group came down from the north to conquer Senegal and set a village on fire, thereby creating the negative association of Arab with fire. These were likely Mauritanians, but the term *naar* has been applied to all Arab populations residing in Senegal, distinguished only by adjectives: Naar Fes are Moroccans, Naar Ganaar are Mauritanians, and Naar Beirut are Lebanese. Lebanese consider this classification to be racist. One Lebanese trader, upset by this term, explained that his father was a Naar, he is less Naar, and the third generation is certainly not Naar at all! My Lebanese neighbor was wearing a T-shirt one day with the logo "Nigger L's" on the front. He explained to me that "L" stood for Lebanese, and this was his friend's popular one-man rap group, where he sang songs in a mixture of Wolof and French.

Differing views of race manifest in violence. Lebanese became the target of hate crimes and theft of commodities—often flaunted by Lebanese of greater economic means—desired by Senegalese who cannot afford them. One such incident, which occurred during my first visit to Dakar, exposed the fragile ground on which Lebanese tread regarding coexistence. A Lebanese man, attacked on his way to work by five Senegalese men, fired his gun in self-defense. His attackers fled, but one was injured in the hip. The police, siding with Lebanese, ordered hospitals to turn over new patients with hip wounds. The attacker was found and Lebanese community leaders thanked police for handling the case in a just and effective manner. I heard stories of taxi drivers slapping elderly veiled Lebanese women for not having correct change. A Lebanese woman's purse was stolen while she was waiting for her husband in her car; when her husband tried to stop the robbery, he was knifed in the leg. Some Lebanese keep guns in their cars or shops or are trained in karate or kung fu for self-defense, and many Lebanese homes maintain dogs as a deterrent against intruders.

Lebanese often compared their community in Africa to the situation of Lebanese in South America (considered a "white" continent), where Lebanese were perceived as more integrated and as having no need for the (forgotten) Arabic language; Lebanese retained some degree of Arabic in Senegal in order to keep open the option of returning to Lebanon. Examples of white flight after centuries of black/white coexistence were frequently cited, in particular the cases of Mozambique and Zimbabwe. The Lebanese Maronite priest brought to my attention how in the United States Lebanese of three generations are considered American (Ralph Nader, for example), whereas Lebanese of Senegal will always be identified as Lebanese because of their skin color. A Lebanese Christian woman once proclaimed that there are no problems between Lebanese Muslims and Christians in Senegal "because we are all foreigners here."

Lebanese Civil Society

On May 6, 1996, a Senegalese maid was found dead in the bathroom of her Lebanese employer's home. Without proof of fault, this incident sparked anti-Lebanese violence, resulting in the creation of Alliance with an objective of "promoting and protecting the Lebanese community (of origin or nationality) residing in Senegal for the creation of a Senegalese society both plural and integrated." According to its president (in 2003), Alliance had approximately three hundred members, primarily Lebanese but also Senegalese. This secular, apolitical, and independent organization aimed to make Lebanese better known and understood in Senegalese society. Led by Lebanese elite, Alliance was comprised of predominately professionals and influential businessmen in Dakar.

The inaugural issue of the newsletter *Alliance Info* questioned how African integration was progressing while integration of Senegal's Lebanese community was not. Authors cited "racism," "xenophobia," and a "regime of political semi-apartheid" in outlining how despite the Lebanese community's undeniable economic integration, Lebanese were absent from Senegalese moral, political, legal, cultural, and institutional life: notably the National Assembly, political parties, government and administrative positions, army, and police force. The essay highlighted the community's development from a first generation of illiterate immigrants from disadvantaged regions of Lebanon to a second and third generation of "Afro-Libanais" educated in Senegal. "What distinguishes Afro-Libanais from beginning-of-the-century migrants is that not only was this country no longer a land of immigration for them, but they shared with their compatriots the same strategic questions of how to construct the nation today."[12]

Alliance's leaders theoretically differentiated *integration* from *assimilation*. They argued in interviews that Lebanese could integrate without losing their identity, and that Senegalese often confused *integration* and *assimilation*. Hakim, a Lebanese journalist, stated, "I am clearly for integration but I refuse the idea of assimilation." Alliance's president defined *assimilation* as losing one's ethnicity and becoming like Senegalese, whereas *integration* meant "living as a citizen and having the same rights (*droits*) and duties (*devoirs*) as a citizen." Lebanese, however, have "more duties," such as voting, paying taxes, and respecting man and the law, "than rights," conceptualized as the ability to live as one wishes without distinguishing between Senegalese of Lebanese origin and Senegalese of Senegalese origin. He quoted a French proverb, "for two weights there are two measures," to refer to the double standard in Senegal where one law is often applied differently to whites and blacks. The Senegalese public, not the state and administration, makes this distinction.

Lebanese used different metaphors to distinguish *integration* from *assimilation*. For one Alliance board member, *assimilation* was to mime the other, whereas *integration* was to merge together without losing one's identity—like tea, he told me, when you add sugar it becomes agreeable but remains tea. For another, *integration* referred to participating in the life of a nation while maintaining one's originality or specificity; *assimilation* was to cut ties with Lebanese roots and resemble Senegalese. Lebanese in Senegal could work, live, help the development of the country, and participate in its sports without erasing all that is Lebanese. The founder of Alliance commented that Lebanese had a historical presence in Senegal and were therefore much more integrated than a "Chinatown." He argued that the problem originated in the lack of an indigenous African notion of "nation."

Instead there was the concept of *telescopage*, forcing one ethnic group into another. Africans who studied in Europe experienced ideals of pedagogy and tolerance, he told me, but were unable to integrate these ideas into their own country. Hakim envisioned the integration debate as a problem of social class, originating with postcolonial Senegalese competition with Lebanese in transportation and commerce. An Alliance lawyer declared, "for me an integrated person is a person who works for the good of this country and its development with the commitment to live and die here." He defined *committed* as someone who has vowed to do his best for his country Senegal.

Thus *integration* for Alliance did not mean intermarriage and a "mix of colors," but the Lebanese right to be an ethnic group like other ethnic groups in Senegal. This multidimensionality of integration—racial, economic, political, and cultural—enabled Lebanese to be integrated in Senegal in certain spheres, while maintaining community and ethnic distinctiveness. Lebanese did not envision the cedar tree as uprooting the baobab or existing in its shadow but as being grafted together into one tree. The symbol of Alliance was such a graft, one united tree equally composed of half Lebanese cedar and half Senegalese baobab.

Alliance, however, did not last, collapsing shortly after I met with their leadership in 2003. Some former members later created a new Lebanese-Senegalese Association of Health Professionals. Kamil took over the lease of Alliance's centrally located office near Dakar's Place de l'Independence and stresses that his work continues to embody the mission of Alliance.

Kamil's father, a Maronite Christian, came to Senegal in 1920 from the north of Lebanon to escape the misery remaining in the region from the Ottoman period. His father returned to Lebanon in 1932 to marry Kamil's mother, from a neighboring village. Kamil was born in Dakar in 1938, a middle child among four brothers and two sisters. When he was one year old his father sent him to Lebanon with his mother and siblings to avoid World War II, as the French were recruiting soldiers in Senegal. Kamil and his family returned to Senegal in 1948, but he had difficulties adjusting. The school he had attended in Lebanon followed the Arabic curriculum, but Senegalese schools used the French curriculum. Kamil was later educated at Université Cheikh Anta Diop in Dakar, which at the time was a French-run university.

When I first met Kamil he worked in an import-export store that sold a variety of goods including kitchenware imported from Europe, cosmetics, clothing, Senegalese artwork, and African cloth. His store was larger than the average Lebanese shop, and he hired a number of employees, Lebanese, Senegalese, and métis (those of mixed Lebanese and Senegalese origin). He has since experimented with variations on his business, such as downsizing, dividing merchandise among employees to manage separately, and opening an art gallery. Kamil owns an apartment above his former store, which his father began to build and he completed.

" ALLIANCE INFO "

POUR UNE SOCIETE SENEGALAISE PLURIELLE ET INTEGREE

Alliance graft of Lebanese cedar and Senegalese baobab trees. Author's collection.

He moved his activities to the Alliance office, where he holds meetings to assist Senegalese with their business endeavors and collaborates in extensive charity work throughout Senegal. He serves as economic advisor to several foreign embassies, and now also works in interfaith activities. He is a member of the Senegalese Chamber of Commerce and influential in the Maronite church. He married in the 1990s and has no children of his own, although he treats his nieces, nephews, and many other Lebanese youth in the community as his own offspring. Kamil cares deeply for Senegal and is very attached to Lebanon as well, visiting often.

Marriage

As one journalist writes, "It is not enough to merely take on Senegalese nationality, speak Wolof, construct buildings, set up businesses and be buried under Senegalese soil in order to truly become Senegalese" (Sow 1998). Marriage is the Senegalese solution to integration and the greatest point of contention between Lebanese and Senegalese. According to Professor Mbodj, then a historian at Université Cheikh Anta Diop, "the essential objective of the marriage ritual is not to create an alliance between husband and wife, nor even an alliance between two families. Its objective is to mask hostility by proclaiming the creation of an alliance, to affirm an accord in order to avoid a clash, to substitute peace for war. . . . Marriage is above all a means of resolving conflicts between takers and givers of women" (Diop 1997). The promulgation of a 1967 law facilitated naturalization to those who married Senegalese, aimed at encouraging Lebanese intermarriage. Such marriages, however, proved difficult, as Mamadou Dia wrote in his memoires:

> My third marriage was to a Lebanese Muslim schoolteacher, named Salam Mourad. It was, in my mind, a political marriage whose purpose was to mark symbolically the fraternity between African and Arab Muslims.
> My wife, unfortunately, did not share this view. I was forced to recognize that she was attracted above all to my position as head of government and had been seduced by promises—made unbeknownst to me by a friend—of beautiful villas in Fann and Alexandrie. After a year of marriage, these promises had still not been fulfilled; our household was in utter turmoil and our alliance crumbled. (Dia 1985:240)

Lebanese consider the marriage question to be a false problem, as underscored in one lawyer's provocative words: "Integration is not done below your belt." Another Lebanese man pointed out: "We are not alone in preferring to marry among ourselves. The Toucouleurs also prefer this type of marriage. Most Senegalese would refuse to marry their daughter to a 'naar.'" Lebanese frequently told me that Senegalese could not ask Lebanese to intermarry when they themselves do not engage in this practice. One man declared that you can nationalize a bank or a company, but not a woman, and love should come naturally at the individual—not national—level. Although intermarriage between Lebanese and Senegalese is rare, Lebanese men are more likely to marry Senegalese women than Lebanese women are Senegalese men. Lebanese explain that unlike Senegalese Muslims they do not practice polygamy, which was never accepted in Lebanon.[13] For them, this is a question of culture and not of racism, and they argue that such marriages rarely last.

Many Lebanese men returned to villages of origin in Lebanon to find brides or were married to cousins elsewhere in Africa. Those who found spouses in Senegal preferred women of the same religious background and from the same geographical region in Lebanon (Taraf 1994). Nur and Hala were the youngest two sisters of a tight-knit Lebanese Shiʻi family, the only women in the family who did not wear the veil. Nur was born in Mbacke, where her family used to live, but Hala, the youngest by ten years, was born in Dakar. The sisters lived with their parents in a modest apartment in a building with all Lebanese residents. Their older three sisters were married with children, two living in Dakar and one in southern Lebanon. Life was not easy. Their father had a stroke, could no longer work, and needed lots of care, and money was tight. The sisters were very different but remained spirited despite life's challenges. Nur rode her scooter to work running a small grocery shop that sold imported Lebanese, European, and African goods for her Lebanese boss. She always joked with the two Senegalese employees and her (mostly but not exclusively Lebanese) customers, constantly code-switching between Wolof, Lebanese Arabic, and French. Hala was finishing high school when I first met her, working in a shop selling imported games and children's toys after school to help the family. She was a romantic, full of dreams for the future, and very spiritual, always reading books in French about religion and science. As Nur was in her mid-thirties and her marriage was long overdue, her mother sent her to visit Lebanon for the first time, hoping that a one-month stay in her village of origin would result in her finding a husband (without success). Hala searched for love over the Internet, corresponding with a Lebanese man in Benin. She met his parents during a visit to Lebanon, but he became jealous and possessive and tried to monitor her activities even though they had never met. Her mother finally ended the relationship by calling his father in Lebanon and declaring that she would disown her daughter if his son were to marry her. Nur has since married a French man and moved to Marseilles. Hala eventually married a man from Lebanon, who first tried his luck farming chickens in Senegal, but later moved his wife and their son to his village in southern Lebanon. She informed me in an e-mail update that she now wears the veil. Marriages with Shiʻa from southern Lebanon often reinforce the religiosity of Lebanese from Senegal.

Many Lebanese women in Africa, however, do not marry Lebanese men from Lebanon, choosing to marry instead Lebanese from Africa or Europe. One woman explained that the mentality is different and women have more freedom in Senegal than in Lebanon's conservative villages. In general, I was told, Lebanese prefer to marry other Lebanese, and a Lebanese Muslim would marry a Lebanese Christian over a Muslim of another Arab nationality. An unmarried woman in her thirties complained that most women marry someone of their same social class because of family preferences, and love marriages are rare. A Lebanese Muslim man, who married a devout Senegalese woman, objected to his family accepting the American Christian women his brothers married but not his Senegalese wife. He claimed his marriage alienated him from the Lebanese community. Another Lebanese Muslim man dated a French Christian woman (with a child from a previous failed marriage). He wanted to marry her, but when he introduced her to his family for their approval, they sent their son to Abidjan to break up his relationship and arranged for him to marry his seventeen-year-old cousin from Ivory Coast. Other marriages were between childhood sweethearts who grew up together in Senegal.

Biological Métissage

Although Lebanese consider marriage to be a cultural issue, intermarriage for Senegalese is a form of political and economic integration. Senghor promoted cultural métissage in Negritude and Africanity, yet biological métissage is more complicated. Children of mixed marriages have a marginal position in Senegalese society and are viewed as neither Lebanese nor Senegalese. Khuri observed nearly fifty years ago: "In Guinea, Senegal and Sierra Leone, Africans tend to consider the bulk of the mulattoes as Lebanese, whereas the Lebanese consider them as Africans; but the mulattoes identify themselves as citizens of the country in which they live. . . . Since the Lebanese do not confer on them any tribal rights and duties, the mulattoes cling to their African nationality. One mulatto meaningfully summed up this position by saying, 'I am Lebanese by tribe and Sierra Leonean by nationality'" (1968:97–98).

This search for belonging has continued in contemporary Senegal. Tony is a rare example of a métis who took a leadership role in the Lebanese community as past president of Alliance. Articulate about his mixed racial and religious upbringing, he described how courageous his parents' marriage was in the 1940s when intermarriage was not accepted in Senegal. Tony labeled his father as "white, foreigner, Catholic" and his mother as "black, Muslim." His Lebanese father died when Tony was twelve, leaving his Senegalese mother to raise ten children on her own as neither set of grandparents accepted their intermarriage. He argued that Lebanese should not always dismiss mixed marriages as a problem of different cultures.

> When, exceptionally, by a twist of fate, a Senegalese man and a Lebanese woman fall in love, things must take place normally. People should not intervene by saying "it's fine, but there are too many hurdles like cultural differences." The difference of cultures cannot always constitute an impeding factor; it can also be an enriching one. When my father married my mother, they were coming from different cultural and educational backgrounds; while they were illiterate, they managed to deal successfully with their differences. It is impossible to convince me that today in 2003 a Senegalese man and a Lebanese woman, or a Lebanese man and a Senegalese woman cannot live together because they are culturally different.

Tony married a métisse woman, his sister married a Lebanese man, and his other siblings selected Senegalese spouses. Even though many of his siblings chose Islam, Tony stayed Catholic in order to "remain true to the memory" of his father. He described the difficulties faced by children of mixed marriages in his position:

> It was very difficult, first on a personal level, because of numerous questions and multiple choices one has to face. If you are not careful you fall on one side or another. It is precisely the problem of *métis*. . . . They don't know if they are white or black. . . . There are a rare few who think of themselves as bi-racial, that is, belonging to both sides. In my case . . . I always felt comfortable in Lebanese as well as Senegalese environments.

Tony eventually left Dakar and returned to the village of his parents, where he modernized their property, which he uses as a base to develop his native community. He is building a school and tourist facilities, as well as bringing medical equipment to the countryside, which has earned him an honorary position as village head.

The majority of métis identify more strongly with their Senegalese roots. Pape worked for Kamil, who made an effort to employ those with mixed backgrounds. Pape was born and raised in Dakar, with a Lebanese Christian father from northern Lebanon and a mother who herself was a Mauritanian/Toucouleur mix. He told me he is proud to be Senegalese and married a Senegalese wife, although he gave his daughter an Arabic name. Pape never learned about Lebanon and did not feel part of the Lebanese community. His brother, however, visited relatives in Lebanon and now resides in France. In his opinion, métis are more attractive and have more opportunities because they have two cultures and countries to choose from. Other métis felt marginalized by the Lebanese community, but claimed that Senegalese forget they are Lebanese. Likewise, ʿAli, the mayor of a small village, did not want to be considered an *homme dechiré*, torn between two cultures, so he opted for Senegalese over Lebanese nationality. A Lebanese intellectual once told me that biological métissage is imposed on a person, but cultural métissage—the true métissage—is chosen. For him, like Senghor and other proponents of cosmopolitanism, one does not have to be a product of mixed marriage or marry a Senegalese in order to participate in various cultures and traditions.

Grafting the Cedar and Baobab: Lebanese Visions of Integration

During French colonial times Lebanese simultaneously adapted to Senegal while being prevented from fully integrating. They quickly gained fluency in local languages in the regions in which they worked—Wolof was most widespread, but some also spoke Pular and Mandinka. Lebanese from rural areas even claimed to speak local languages better than Senegalese in Dakar since they did not mix French words with Wolof. Lebanese adopted Senegalese culinary traditions, familiarized themselves with Senegalese ways and customs, respected national and religious holidays, and developed joking relationships with Senegalese and local forms of business bargaining. Lebanese considered themselves to be "pioneers" of the land, bringing infrastructure to rural areas whose brutal conditions were not braved by Europeans. Later they helped build and financially develop Dakar. Lebanese commiserated with Senegalese under French colonialism and supported Senegalese efforts for independence. They continued to invest in Senegal, keeping businesses open during the devaluation of the CFA franc in the 1990s when many French companies departed. Lebanese therefore resented that Senegalese public opinion was often more negative toward the Lebanese community than the French.

Lebanese were labeled *Libano-Syriens* by French and *Naar-Beirut* by Senegalese. Whereas the first generation of migrants also viewed themselves as "Lebanese," many Lebanese in Senegal today self-identify as hybrids.[14] They prefer the terms *Senegalese of Lebanese origin* or *Afro-Libanais,* a hyphenated identity adapted by leaders of Alliance from African Americans in the United States. They are culturally cosmopolitan with their own version of Senghor's African humanism. One informant emphatically explained:

> I had the chance to be interviewed by French television and to say that we [Lebanese in Senegal] are no longer Lebanese. . . . A Lebanese is defined by territory, culture, language, specific character. Today I ask the following question: are the grandchildren of those who migrated more than 100 years ago identical to their migrant ancestors? With education, literacy, discovery of the Other, one can't say that they are Lebanese. Today more of us are francophone Senegalese; when I say francophone it is in the sense that we studied modern knowledge in the French language. But we are of Semitic origin. That is what I cling to. I say that I have Semitic origins because I am Arab and Arabs are Semites. I am of Senegalese nationality because Senegal is my country. My life is here; my father, my family is buried here and I express myself in French from which I took a portion of my culture.

Lebanese of Senegal thus envision themselves as Senegalese yet distinct from Senegalese and as Lebanese but not like those in Lebanon. Abu-Lughod's term *halfies* refers to "people whose national or cultural identity is mixed by virtue of migration, overseas education, or parentage" (1991:137). Afro-Libanais divide their cultural influences not into halves, however, but into thirds: part Senegalese (or African), part French (or European), and part Lebanese (or Middle Eastern). They maintain that through these three civilizations Lebanese of Senegal have become ideologically richer than Lebanese of Lebanon and that their way of thinking, *mentalité,* is different. A businessman identified himself to me not as 33 percent Senegalese, French, and Lebanese, but as 100 percent from each culture. He personified these different identities as if his mother were Senegal, his father France, and his grandparents Lebanon. He explained that Senegal is his motherland, since he was born there. France educated him and gave him the means to become an intellectual. His French identity includes knowledge of science, basic values of human rights, and the enjoyment of French cuisine. However, his roots are in Lebanon. He defined Lebanese values as poetry, folklore, and oral tradition, which he learned from childhood stories his father told. Culinary traditions are another example of this cultural métissage. One lawyer generalized that for Lebanese in Senegal Saturday is always *kibbe* day (Lebanese specialty of ground lamb and cracked wheat), while Sunday is *ceb-u-jen* day (Senegalese national dish of rice boiled in a thick sauce of fish and vegetables). Such cosmopolitan self-identification, typical of many, demonstrates the cultural hold of not one or two but multiple "nations" on Lebanese of Senegal.

Yet many Lebanese in Senegal are losing fluency in Arabic in favor of French and Wolof. While some families continue to speak Arabic, this tendency has dwindled as second and third generations are no longer comfortable speaking the language, and many are not literate in Arabic. Lebanese of Senegal have developed a pigeon dialect of French, Arabic, and Wolof. The Arabic Language Institute, built in 1998 by a prominent Lebanese industrialist, offers modern classroom facilities for language acquisition. Its creation embodies the community's effort, after more than a century in Senegal, to hold on to its roots. Lebanese in Senegal keep Lebanese culture alive by reading books and newspapers from Lebanon in Arabic (the older generations), listening to Lebanese music, corresponding with relatives in Lebanon, and, most of all, watching Arabic satellite television.

Lebanese institutions have taken to performing their integration in Senegal. I was invited to attend the end-of-year celebration of the preschool run by the Lebanese Maronite Church, Notre Dame du Liban.[15] The children's playground was transformed into a stage facing two large tents hovering over rows of folding plastic chairs for the audience, decorated with Senegalese, Lebanese, and French flags fluttering in the breeze. The program began with the Senegalese national hymn, followed by songs, dances, and skits performed by young students. The audience was comprised of Lebanese and Senegalese parents sitting together, and dances were even choreographed to reflect integration. Lebanese and Senegalese children were paired as dance partners, and one skit mocked "a difficult husband" starring a Senegalese boy with a Lebanese girl playing his wife. Dances were stereotypically ethnic: Lebanese girls performed the Arab belly dance dressed in traditional outfits. Senegalese students performed what the program labeled Diola dance, Senegalese dance, and Antilles dance, with Lebanese boys as background dancers.

Some Lebanese in Senegal work passionately to promote Senegalese culture. Kamil finances various Senegalese ethnic celebrations by designing African cloth for these occasions, helping to film and record performances, and requiring his employees to attend these cultural events. He also sends Senegalese ethnic music and dance troupes to Lebanon to expose each culture to one another. Another man from Dakar began in 2000 an association in Beirut called L'Alliance des Libanais du Sénégal. The organization works to strengthen ties between Lebanon and Senegal. It assists with integrating Lebanese from Senegal who return to Lebanon, many residing in the city of Tyre, known as "little West Africa" and featuring a prominent promenade named "Senegal" by the sea.

Lebanese enjoy recounting travel accounts of surprising Senegalese abroad with their knowledge of Wolof or Pular. I once dined with a Lebanese family in the south of Senegal and as the father entertained me with such stories, his daughter mouthed along the words as these tales were often retold. His wife had once traveled to Morocco, where she purchased toothpicks and kola nuts from a Peul merchant. He overcharged her, but she was able to negotiate the correct amount of change after conversing with him in Pular. In another account, a cousin in France encountered a Senegalese man and addressed him in Wolof. The man looked around the room and could not find another black man. He approached a man from Martinique, thinking it was he who had spoken Wolof, until the Lebanese man clarified "I am your white brother."

Significance of Multiple Passports

The question of nationality is another highly politicized issue. Many Lebanese have multiple passports representing various identities and opportunities. Guarnizo defines *citizenship* "as an exclusive institution regulating national membership" and *nationality* as "a homogeneous monoculture characterized by an unambiguous ethnic identity" (1998:47). Smith differentiates dual citizenship from dual nationality in that "the latter does not include voting rights in the country of origin but normally enables an immigrant to hold two passports, the advantages of which are related to the holding of property and freer movement in and out of both host country and country of origin" (1997:n5). I use *citizenship* to refer to the Senegalese passport carried by many Lebanese and *nationality* to refer to all other passports.

Ong argues that passports have become "less and less attestations of citizenship, let alone of loyalty to a protective nation-state, than of claims to participate in labor markets" (1999:2). Her concept *flexible citizenship* concerns mostly business*men* who benefit economically from different nation-state regimes while relocating their families to "safe havens" in the West. Citizenship, however, can be flexible in other ways, not always concerning economics. For Lebanese in Senegal security, benefits, and ideologies play equally important roles. They have various combinations of nationalities including Senegalese, Lebanese, French, Australian, American, Canadian, British, Dominican, Gambian, Guinean, Ivoirian, Liberian, Moroccan, and Sierra Leonean. I will discuss benefits of having the three most common nationalities: Senegalese, Lebanese, and French.[16]

For some, obtaining Senegalese citizenship was a necessity. During the colonial period a large number of Lebanese had both Lebanese and French nation-

Lebanese performing dabka dance for schoolchildren, Dakar. Author's collection.

ality. With independence, many obtained Senegalese citizenship without revoking other nationalities. This reaffirmed Lebanese commitment to the new nation at a time of uncertainty and enabled them to keep jobs during nationalization of businesses. Some applied for citizenship in response to Senegalese suspicion that Lebanese continued to identify with and send remittances to Lebanon. By the late 1960s and early 1970s the Senegalese government began to exert pressure on Lebanese with Senegalese citizenship to revoke their original nationalities, but few complied. The Senegalese government was concerned that some Lebanese had returned to Lebanon, owing the state or local companies large sums of money (Boumedouha 1987:251–253).

The 1980s brought a change of law (Article 16) to the Senegalese *Code de la Nationalité* due to unemployment crisis. Responding to perceptions of Lebanese monopoly in certain professional sectors, the Ministry of Justice extended the waiting period for those who applied for Senegalese citizenship to ten years. This forced all newly naturalized citizens to renounce their original nationality and required a long wait to enter liberal professions, including law and public services. Whereas Article 16 hindered acquiring Senegalese citizenship, Article 7 gave immediate citizenship to foreign women who married Senegalese men. This law was promulgated to encourage marriages between Lebanese women and Senegalese men, with little success. In practice, the prohibition of dual nationality is not enforced; even Senghor had Senegalese and French nationality.

For others, Senegalese citizenship demonstrates the importance of being Senegalese. Some Lebanese prefer to have only Senegalese citizenship as a symbol of where their strongest loyalty lies. This was the case for Nadir, a founding member of Alliance who owns two fisheries and is frequently called upon to consult for the Senegalese government. He was a member of a delegation sent to Israel to celebrate the renewal of bilateral ties between the two countries. This led to a misunderstanding at the Israeli embassy, whose consular officer was afraid that Nadir's attendance would be problematic when he returned to Lebanon. He assured the Israelis that he is Senegalese and would never live in Lebanon.

I heard various versions of how and why Lebanese began to obtain Senegalese citizenship. Farid, who owns a grocery store chain in Dakar, informed me that Lebanese held French and Lebanese nationality until Senegal's independence, after which they felt threatened. Apartheid in South Africa and Mandela's efforts to bridge the gap between black and white encouraged Lebanese to also take the nationality of the country in which they were born. The director of the Islamic Institute told me an alternative account. He linked Lebanese acquisition of Senegalese citizenship to the Pasqua law in France, which was introduced in 1986 and revised in 1993. The tightening of immigration controls affected many Senegalese who had the right to French citizenship from colonial times, but were only recently inspired to claim it. Lebanese saw parallels to their situation in Senegal, where they had resided longer than Senegalese in France. The cosmopolitan outlook of Lebanese in Senegal simultaneously incorporates the Middle East, Africa, and Europe. Yet many Lebanese resent that despite having Senegalese citizenship they are treated as foreigners.

When I asked a family to describe benefits of having Lebanese nationality, they laughed and told me there are none but they are proud to be Lebanese. They were hopeful that after Lebanon fully recovers from the long and destructive Civil War the government might then offer nationals concrete benefits. Having Lebanese nationality implies cultural and ideological ties to the motherland, facilitates travel to Lebanon, and enables "return" migration (many Lebanese were born in Senegal). Some left Senegal to try their luck in Lebanon, others returned to Senegal after living a few unhappy years in Lebanon, and still others would never "return" to Lebanon but like to have the option available.

Lebanon never had a law prohibiting dual nationality, but Lebanon's nationality law is "sexist," in the words of the Lebanese consulate officer in Senegal. If a Lebanese woman marries a foreigner, her husband and their children cannot acquire Lebanese nationality. Yet a Lebanese man can pass on his nationality to a foreign wife and children. This law particularly outraged Rim, who owned a home decoration store and raised three sons. Her husband had revoked his Lebanese nationality out of love for and loyalty to Senegalese sports, and she was unable to pass her nationality on to her children. The consulate officer presented a petition to the president of Lebanon in order to regain Lebanese nationality for five hundred families who had revoked their nationality of origin due to Senegalese laws. Shaykh al-Zayn similarly worked to acquire Lebanese nationality for métis.

French (or other Western) nationality is often seen as a benefit and safeguard for Lebanese in Africa. This increases in importance as the economic and security situation in Senegal becomes more uncertain and civil war eliminated Lebanon as a safety net. Many Lebanese lived in Senegal under French colonialism, where children of French nationals could become French before their eighteenth birthday. Some Lebanese children born in Senegal were sent to boarding schools in Lebanon but were brought back to Senegal in time to claim French citizenship. Lebanese with French nationality are eligible for French medical care, health insurance, unemployment, maternity, and retirement benefits. French nationality is especially beneficial to Lebanese students from Senegal, who receive state scholarships to study in French universities and have better chances in the job market than immigrants without French citizenship. The negative aspect of being French, however, was the obligation to join the army. Farid's father did not apply for French citizenship for his son because he could not risk Farid being drafted into the French army during the Algerian War (1954–1962), which he did not support. He had another strategy for European protection for his children. His wife was half-Egyptian and half-British, and Farid had the right of abode in Britain through his mother's British citizenship.[17]

Lebanese in Senegal are proud of being French and frequently attend social events organized by the French embassy. Habib, a doctor, is a member of the Conseil Supérieur des Français de l'Etranger and has been twice elected to represent French in West Africa, each time serving a six-year mandate and responsible for Senegal, Guinea Conakry, Guinea Bissau, Cape Verde, Sierra Leone, and The Gambia.[18] He recalled a plaque he once saw in Paris commemorating Thomas Paine, a revolutionary, author, and one of the founding fathers of the United States. The plaque (dated 1795) read: "Here he lived: English by origin, American by adoption, French by decree." Habib made a parallel between Paine's identity and his own: Lebanese by origin, French by decree, and Senegalese by adoption.

The various cosmopolitan identities of Lebanese in Senegal are thus formally represented in multiple passports. The Lebanese community does not conform to Smith's (1997) "classic model" of citizenship. Second- and third-generation Lebanese extend Smith's "postnational membership" model beyond binational loyalties, providing an additional case study of Ong's (1999) "flexible citizenship." The colonial legacy enables Lebanese to obtain French protection without ever living in Europe. This (often) tertiary nationality is desirable when Lebanese and Senegalese nationalities fail to provide protection, benefits, and economic security. Faist (2000) argues that racism prevents "full and formal membership" in a nation. Immigrants seek multiple citizenships in order to secure jobs and ensure safety. Multiple passports facilitate departure from Africa in the event of political instability where a European passport safeguards against an insecure future.

Table 2.1. Senegalese Ethnic Groups by Census Categories

Census reports	Possible responses
Wolof (41.8%):	Wolof
	Lébou
Haalpulaaren (27%):	Toucouleur
	Peul
	Pular
	Fula
	Laobé
Sereer (14.8%):	Sereer
Diola (4.1%):	Diola
Manding (4.5%):	Malinké
	Manding
	Socé

Source: 2002 census; categories adapted from Villalón 1995:48.

Lebanese as a Senegalese Ethnic Group?

Senegalese society is divided into multiple ethnic and linguistic groups, depending on how one counts. The 2002 census specified thirty possible responses for indigenous ethnic groups. The largest Senegalese ethnic groups are collapsed into five major categories in Table 2.1.

Of these, three main groups—Wolof, Sereer, and Haalpulaaren (Pular speakers) —comprise over 80 percent of Senegal's population. The largest ethnic group is the Wolof, and Wolof has become Senegal's dominant national language (in addition to French). Historically constituting the bulk of the Walo, Jolof, Cayor, and Baol states between the Senegal and Gambia rivers, the Wolof have dominated Senegal both culturally and economically (Diop 1981; Cruise O'Brien 1998). The Haalpulaaren form the second most important ethnic grouping in Senegal, although they are more a linguistic appellation than a true ethnicity. This group includes the Peul or Fulbe, traditionally pastoral nomadic cattle herders, and the Toucouleur, settled agriculturalists, who have maintained their distinct ethnic identity. In response to the recent threat of Wolofization, Pular speakers have preferred to use the label Haalpulaaren, uniting the various ethnicities as a numerically larger force. Senegal's third-largest ethnic group, the Sereer, constitute the majority population in the states Sine and Saloum, as well as a significant minority in Baol. Villalón (1995) contends that ethnic divisions are far less likely to become politically significant in Senegal than elsewhere in Africa. Ethnicity in Senegal has never become the primary mode of political organization; nevertheless social cleavages remain important.

Table 2.2. Speakers of Principal Senegalese Languages
as Either a First or Second Language (in percentages)

Wolof	72.2
Pular	26.6
Sereer	12.7

Source: 2002 census.
Note: The census does not account for third or more spoken
languages, and actual speakers of these languages are some-
what higher. Scholars estimate that 90 percent of the Senegalese
population understands Wolof.

Caste cuts across ethnicity among most Senegalese groups and remains a more significant barrier to marriage than either religion or ethnicity. Although theoretically incompatible with both the notion in Islam of the equality of Muslims and Western modernity, caste systems are a central factor in Senegalese society, at times blurring with ethnicity (Dilley 2004; Diop 1981; Irvine 1974; Wright 1989). Lebanese are well aware of differences in Senegalese ethnicities and castes, and speak local languages of regions in which they reside. In a quest for autochthony, the community is working to officially change its former French colonial designation "Libano-Syriens" to the more indigenous category "Senegalese of Lebanese origin." Alliance worked with the Senegalese government to achieve this status and for Lebanese to formally become a Senegalese ethnic group. I was surprised, upon visiting the Musée de la Femme on Goree Island in 2000, to find this sign in the museum's first exhibition room:[19]

Elements of Human Geography: Wolof, Pulaar, Mandinka, Sereer, Soninke, Joola, Mankaan, Balant, Maure, Metisse, Cap-Verdienne, Lybano-Syrienne [*sic*].

In Senegal a dozen ethnic groups with varying degrees of importance share national space. Even if the mixing with people coming from Europe is apparent on the coast due to the installation of colonial commercial centers (Dakar, St.-Louis, Rufisque, Goree), each Senegalese ethnic group still recognizes its traditional homeland in the interior of the country.

In spite of the development of cities, especially of the capital Dakar, the increasing mobility of the population, national integration and rural exodus, each citizen recognizes his or her own original "biotope." According to the national statistics, (1988), the female population in Senegal represents about 52% of the total population.

For reasons linked to history and geography of African communities (not only in Senegal), the Lebanese-Syrians also have a notable presence in the country.

Despite this introduction, the museum exhibition displayed only artifacts of and information on African ethnic groups. I found one new museum addition when I returned in 2003. The final exhibition room then portrayed examples from Senegal's religions, with half a small wall dedicated to Islam and half to Christianity. There was now a photo with a short biography of Marie Rahmi, "*Senegalaise d'origine Libanaise*," included in the Christianity display. Her biography read:

- Born February 12, 1912 in Lebanon
- Came to Senegal in 1918
- Student at the *Institution de l'Immaculée Conception*—Dakar
- Co-founder of the *Association Notre Dame du Liban* in Dakar (charitable)
- Received membership at the *Congrégation de la Très Sainte Vierge Marie* in 1927
- Died on January 29, 2001 in Australia

It was curious that the only representative of the "Lebanese-Syrian" ethnic group chosen by the museum was a Lebanese Christian woman born in Lebanon who died in Australia. Nevertheless, this was an important symbol of acceptance of the Lebanese community, at least by select Senegalese bureaucrats.

* * *

Tensions surrounding the integration debate in Senegal evoke Barth's (1969) contention that ethnic groups are socially constructed and exist only in contrast to other groups (not in isolation). Ethnic identity is influenced from both sides of the boundary. Lebanese achieved their identity oftentimes in response to outside ascriptions. Economic and political realities further encouraged the Lebanese community to unite as an ethnic group in the face of uncertainty. They began to envision themselves as others defined them and adjusted their discourses and practices to conform to their categorization. The process of ascription or categorization of migrant communities is particularly dependent upon relative power relations (Jenkins 1986).

French authorities were the first to enforce Lebanese distinctiveness, the initial obstacle faced by Lebanese in Senegal as a group. French administrators did not give priority to Lebanese Maronites in Senegal as they had in Lebanon. Instead, they treated Lebanese as a bloc of "Muslims" who threatened French interests in West Africa. The French responded with an anti-Lebanese campaign and a policy of segregating Lebanese from Senegalese in order to prevent the spread of pan-Islamism and pan-Arabism. Lebanese religious practices were prohibited from externally conforming to those of the Senegalese; instead Lebanese sectarian divisions were internally accommodated as the community united in opposition to French policy. Paradoxically, colonialism determined the destination of migrants, established economic hierarchies, and encouraged notions of race and racism (Mamdani 1996; Stoler 1997). Yet French nationality also provided Lebanese an escape from discrimination in postcolonial Senegal.

Independence raised additional questions of Lebanese belonging. The community continued to unite in the face of new insecurities, Senghor and Dia's Africanization policies, and Senegal's neocolonial challenges. The nationalization of the peanut industry forced Lebanese migration to cities to take over positions once dominated by the French. Lebanese were thus seen as replacing the colonial power and became Senegal's scapegoats due to their white skin and economic success. Lebanese profit derived from flexibility in adapting businesses to Senegal's changing needs and the ability to differentiate themselves from both French and Senegalese. Accused of racism for not intermarrying and thereby integrating, Lebanese continued to be viewed as one united minority, despite Muslim-Christian religious divisions shared with the host society.

Lebanese were caught in between the cosmopolitan ideologies of Leopold Sedar Senghor's Arabity and Michel Chiha's national idolatry of migrants. Yet they were excluded from Senegalese society as the economic, racial, and religious Other. Senegalese notions of autochthony were linked to race, narrower in practice than their articulation in Negritude. Lebanese were told that intermarriage was their only path to belonging, yet biological métissage was not accepted in Senegal. Lebanese developed two strategies for survival. On the one hand they clung to cosmopolitan linkages—the Arabic language, international business ties, French education, multiple passports. On the other hand they renegotiated the integration debate in an effort for formal recognition as a Senegalese ethnic group, attempting to claim autochthony. Meanwhile in Lebanon, the primary form of identification was religious difference, not ethnicity. Shiʿi identity further differentiated Lebanese from Senegalese Sufi Muslims and connected them to their homeland. Having set the scene for the development of an emergent "secular" Lebanese ethnicity, the following two chapters will examine how religious identities began to strain community cohesiveness. Historical events continued to shape Lebanese subjectivities with the infiltration of global Shiʿi Islamic politics in Senegal, in particular the 2006 Lebanon War.

3 Shi°i Islam Comes to Town
A Biography of Shaykh al-Zayn

SHAYKH °ABDUL MUN°AM al-Zayn is an imposing figure in his long gray robes, white turban, and gray beard. He is a charismatic man, and when he speaks, people listen.[1] He demands respect not only because he is a shaykh, and the first Shi°i Islamic leader in Senegal, but also because he is one of the few highly educated men among the Lebanese community in Dakar. Here, knowledge is something to be shared, and Shaykh al-Zayn is not a man short of words. He lectures at more than four hundred occasions a year—weekly at Friday prayer, every evening during the month of Ramadan, and twice daily during the ten days of the Shi°i commemoration of °Ashura. On Tuesdays and Thursdays he teaches religious classes for men, on Saturdays he teaches Qur°an classes for women, and he speaks at memorial ceremonies and various other community events. He lectures about religion, politics, history, moral issues, and daily struggles the community might face. For example, his theme for Ramadan 2002 compared the Qur°an, Torah, and Bible. He has encouraged the community to live life to the fullest, be unafraid of death, seek knowledge and education, and quit smoking. He has used such occasions to talk about dangers of the Internet, which contains good sites about religion, but also bad sites about sex, which children should be forbidden from accessing. He has chided the community for gossiping too much, and once gave a lecture against abortion. By chance, a woman pregnant with an unplanned child, thinking of aborting, attended the shaykh's lecture and decided to keep the baby. Such is the power of a shaykh.

Early Years: Family, Education, Migration

°Abdul Mun°am al-Zayn was born in 1945 to °Ali al-Zayn, a Shi°i shaykh, and Fatima Karim, a Sunni Muslim, in a small town in the south of Lebanon between Tyre and Bint Jbeil.[2] When he was two years old, his family moved to Qamatiyya, a Shi°i Muslim village neighboring a Christian community. His father taught him Qur°an before he began formal schooling at age six. °Abdul Mun°am studied in two primary schools: one secular and one Maronite Catholic, Madrasa al-Qamatiyya and Madrasa al-Nahda. After receiving his primary school degree in 1956 he moved to Beirut, where he attended a branch of the prestigious Sunni Muslim al-Azhar University of Cairo. He graduated in 1961 from this college, which taught him according to Hanafi tradition, Sunni Islam's most widespread legal school. An influential Senegalese Sunni Muslim leader once told me that it was precisely this training that allowed Shaykh al-Zayn to succeed in Senegal. With a cosmopolitan and interfaith educational background from secular, Catholic, and Sunni Muslim institutions, he then began his formal Shiʿi education.

Traditionally, a shaykh trained in one or more of the Shiʿi holy cities, such as Najaf in Iraq or Qom in Iran. Because Saddam Hussein severely oppressed Iraqi Shiʿa, however, many Lebanese Shiʿa remained in Lebanon for clerical studies, although this may once again begin to change. ʿAbdul Munʿam's father had studied in Lebanon, but he wished for his son the opportunity to be educated in Najaf. At first ʿAbdul Munʿam did not want to become a shaykh. He liked math and science in school and wanted to complete his education in those fields, but he did not want to displease his father. In 1961 ʿAbdul Munʿam moved to Iraq, where he attended university in Najaf until 1969. There he studied Qurʾan and *hadith* (Prophetic traditions), as well as *fiqh* (Islamic jurisprudence), theology, logic, philosophy, Qurʾanic commentaries, and medicine. He learned to appreciate religious studies in Najaf. During this time he returned to Lebanon to marry at age eighteen.

Shiʿi Islam follows a hierarchy of clerical leadership based on superiority of learning (see chapter 4). Ayatollah Sayyid Muhsin al-Hakim was a *marjaʿ*, reference point for emulation, when ʿAbdul Munʿam began his studies in Najaf. His successor, and the marjaʿ under whom ʿAbdul Munʿam studied, was Ayatollah Sayyid Abu al-Qasim al-Khuʾi. He also studied under other *ʿulama* (clergy). When al-Khuʾi died in 1992, Ayatollah Sayyid ʿAli al-Sistani became a marjaʿ, and ʿAbdul Munʿam currently follows his teachings, even though they have never met. He is Ayatollah al-Sistani's *wakil* (authorized representative). The relationship between a marjaʿ and a shaykh is complex, where a marjaʿ can patronize a shaykh and provide him with financial backing, and a shaykh can represent a marjaʿ and reinforce his positions in sermons. In a complementary fashion, a shaykh also elevates his own rank through recognizing the position of a marjaʿ.

ʿAbdul Munʿam, now Shaykh al-Zayn, was sent at age twenty-five to lead the Lebanese Shiʿi community of Dakar. He first traveled to Africa in 1969 and did not plan to go to Senegal. He received his *baccalauréat* from Beirut in English, and at first had wanted to go to Nigeria, an Anglophone country. Two years earlier, Musa al-Sadr, the legendary leader of Lebanon's oppressed Shiʿa, traveled throughout Africa to gain support for his Movement of the Deprived (Harakat al-Mahrumin), which aimed to help poor people in Lebanon. Representatives of the Lebanese community in Dakar, the oldest Lebanese community in Africa, asked him to establish Africa's first Shiʿi religious center. Later these representatives traveled to Lebanon to remind Musa al-Sadr of their need. In turn al-Sadr journeyed to Najaf to find the right man for the job. There he met ʿAbdul Munʿam, whose family he had known previously, and appointed him to go to Dakar.[3] When

ʿAbdul Munʿam protested that Senegal was a Francophone country and he knew no French, al-Sadr promised that he could conduct affairs in Arabic.

* * *

Born in Iran in 1928, Musa al-Sadr studied under great Shiʿi savants in Qom and Najaf. In 1959 he moved to Lebanon, where he replaced his cousin ʿAbd al-Husayn Sharaf al-Din, who died in 1957, as Tyre's senior Shiʿi authority. Musa al-Sadr fought for economic and political equality for Lebanon's underprivileged Shiʿa. His influence reduced the power of traditional Shiʿi elites and inspired Shiʿa to speak out through religion and not accept deprivation (Halawi 1992; Norton 1987; 1994). Ajami writes that Lebanese Christians compared al-Sadr to Christ and dubbed him "Rasputin of Lebanon" (1986:27). Musa al-Sadr, "at once a saint and hero; even more an imam" (Mervin 2002:286), was also a *sayyid*, descendant of Prophet Muhammad; furthermore his unexplained disappearance in Libya gave him similar status to the Mahdi, the twelfth Shiʿi Imam believed to live in oc-cultation. While al-Sadr never became marjaʿ, Mervin considers him among the great Shiʿi reformers.

Musa al-Sadr has a strong following among Lebanese in Senegal, where he visited twice and is remembered for encouraging religious harmony. I spoke about his first visit in 1967 with Shada, whose daughter attested that her mother would cry tears of reverence whenever speaking of Imam al-Sadr. Shada explained that Christians loved him even more than Muslims. At the time of his visit she resided in Mbacke, where she maintained the imam had his best reception in Senegal, something he himself even claimed. According to her, Muslims had prepared for him one dish and Christians another. He chose to eat from the Christian plate to prove that there is no difference between Muslim and Christian—all are Leba-nese. This story suggests that that al-Sadr brought Shiʿi Islam to Senegal *while* re-inforcing a nonsectarian Lebanese ethnic identity. He represented the Shiʿi fac-tion in Lebanon and visited Senegal in search of money and support for his cause, but remained a symbol of the Lebanese nation and was appreciated by Muslims and Christians alike. The Shiʿi Islam he was building in Lebanon and around the world was one of unity, not division.

Al-Sadr's visit is also remembered by Senegalese marabouts. Kaolack is head-quarters of the Tijani branch founded by Shaykh Ibrahim Niass (1900–1975). In 2003 I visited Niass's grandson Shaykh Hasan Cisse (1945–2008), who then led Me-dina Baye, "the City of the Father" (Hill 2007; Seesemann 2011). Cisse informed me that his grandfather invited al-Sadr to lead prayer during his visit to Kaolack. Some Tijanis criticized Niass for offering a Shiʿi Muslim this sacred role. His re-sponse was that al-Sadr was a scholar and descendant of the Prophet and it was therefore an honor to welcome him to the Tijaniyya center. Kaolack was also home to the second largest Lebanese population in Senegal, and al-Sadr visited the Ami-

Visit of Musa al-Sadr (wearing turban) to Lebanese Social Club in Kaolack, Senegal, 1967.
Lebanese embassy in Senegal website.

cale Liban Sénégal, a Lebanese social club. His photo is memorialized on the wall
alongside the club's other prominent visitors, including Lebanese presidents and
Senegalese politicians.

* * *

Shaykh al-Zayn's arrival in Senegal was linked to Musa al-Sadr's legendary
visit. It was no coincidence that West Africa received its first Lebanese Islamic
leader during a period of revitalization of Shi'i religiosity and Shi'i sectarian identity in Lebanon. Power shifted since the 1960s from Shi'i political bosses from influential families (zu'ama) to new political forces in Lebanon. Amal was founded
by Musa al-Sadr in the early 1970s as the militia branch of Movement of the Deprived, and Hizbullah broke off from Amal in 1982. The Lebanese Civil War, Israeli
invasions of 1978 and 1982, 1978 disappearance of Musa al-Sadr in Libya, and 1979
Iranian Revolution provided the heightened political context for a more effective
Shi'i national discourse in Lebanon (Deeb 2006; Norton 1987; Shaery-Eisenlohr
2008)—and in the diaspora.

In Senegal, Shaykh al-Zayn gained his Lebanese following from his ability to
draw from al-Sadr's *baraka* (spiritual power), his command of authority, and his
shaykhly family genealogy. His interreligious background enabled him to estab-

lish himself in Senegal's religio-political landscape through his eventual mastery of Sufi signs and power politics (chapter 5). It was not easy for Shaykh al-Zayn to adapt to living in Africa. He did not know the languages or cultures. Lebanese there were not accustomed to following a religious leader or paying religious taxes needed to carry out his work. All Muslims are expected to pay *zakat*, 2.5 percent of assets. In addition, Shaykh al-Zayn receives and spends the Shiʿi *khums* tax of one-fifth of one's wealth under Ayatollah al-Sistani's supervision. Al-Sistani gives al-Zayn religious legitimacy to spend in Senegal as he sees fit for scholarly and charitable activities one-half of this religious tax, which he collects from the Lebanese community; the other half goes directly to al-Sistani.[4] If money received is not a religious tax, for example charity or donations, Shaykh al-Zayn has full authority and does not need the Ayatollah's advice or permission on how to spend funds.

At first the shaykh planned to stay only a year or two in Senegal, but the years passed as quickly as his work developed. He obtained Senegalese citizenship in 1979 but kept his Lebanese passport and returns frequently to Lebanon. Of his five children, his son and youngest daughter lived with him in Senegal. His oldest three daughters are married in Lebanon.

Religious Coexistence among Lebanese in Senegal

The situation Musa al-Sadr encountered in Senegal was not unique. Lebanese, both Muslims and Christians, informed me that they believed in "spirituality without boundaries" and respected all religious institutions, Muslim and Christian, Lebanese and Senegalese, alike. I often heard the phrase "religion is for everyone" and assertions that faith is essential, not the religion to which one belongs. Some Christians went to the shaykh for advice, and Muslims sought a priest's expertise. During one of our interviews Shaykh al-Zayn pointed to a portrait hanging in his office, painted by the daughter of a priest in Lebanon, based on a photo taken of Shaykh al-Zayn by her father. Shada, who recalled Musa al-Sadr's visit, was from one of two Lebanese Shiʿi families living among seventeen Lebanese Christian families in Mbacke. Her daughter was once very sick, and doctors were unable to help her. I was told that she recovered only after one of their Christian neighbors took her to Mbacke's church and lit a candle for the Virgin Mary. Even after moving to Dakar, this veiled Muslim woman and her daughter would go to church to pray for recovery. The daughter also remembered how their Christian neighbor in Mbacke would pray next to her father on his prayer mat. Lebanese Muslims and Christians in Senegal are comfortable praying side by side and entering one another's religious institution in times of spiritual need.

Hasan's family, comprised of both Christians and Muslims, is another example. His great-grandmother's name (on his mother's side) was Sara ʿAbdul-

Masih (servant of Jesus the Messiah). His great-grandmother's name on his father's side was Sara ʿAbdul-Husayn (servant of Shiʿi Imam Husayn). Hasan has
two brothers in North America named Muhammad and Saladin (classic Muslim
names) who hold influential positions in Protestant churches (despite their semi-
Catholic upbringing).[5] Hasan's parents, however, were both Shiʿa. He was raised
in Mbour, a costal town in Senegal south of Dakar, where his family lived among
Lebanese Christians. Following birth practices of other Lebanese in Mbour, Hasan
and his siblings were baptized. Peer pressure to identify with other Lebanese and lack
of Lebanese Muslim institutions led to some Lebanese Muslims practicing Christian rituals. Hasan attended church with Lebanese in Mbour, where he studied
catechism (but did not take communion). He has since moved to Dakar due to
postindependence nationalization of industry, as did many other Lebanese living in Senegal's towns and villages. Today he frequents the Lebanese Islamic Institute for Friday prayer and holidays. He joked that he has become so dedicated
a Muslim in order to make up for his years at church as a child. Religious fluidity
is not uncommon among Lebanese in Senegal, particularly among those who currently live or used to reside outside Dakar.

Despite restrictions during French colonial times, some Lebanese do participate in Senegalese religious life. Muhammad Barud best exemplifies the Lebanese
Shiʿi relationship with Sufi marabouts.[6] Barud's father first came to Senegal in the
1910s. Born in Tyre, Barud traveled to Senegal in 1954 at age seventeen. He worked
with his father in Dakar's textile industry and became a public figure in Senegal
at age twenty. ʿAbdul ʿAziz Sy (1904–1997), then caliph of the Tivaouane branch of
the Tijaniyya order, was a friend of Barud's father and other Lebanese public figures. This was a natural connection, Barud told me, because they were both Muslims who spoke Arabic and the Tijaniyya had North African origins. Sy adopted
Barud as his spiritual son, proclaiming that even though Barud was not black,
in his heart he considered him to be his birth son. Sy named him Muhammad
Barud Sy, and he is addressed as such in all official invitations. Barud informed
me that Lamine Gueye, the first Senegalese deputy in Europe, also regarded him
as a son. Gueye introduced Barud to many Senegalese politicians; Sy connected
him to Senegal's religious leaders.

Caliph Sy was invited by King Hasan II of Morocco to represent Senegal
at the inauguration of the Hasan II mosque in Casablanca on August 30, 1993.
He was unable to attend as the inauguration was planned for *Mawlud*, Prophet
Muhammad's birthday, when Sy annually conducted the ceremony in Tivaouane.
He therefore replied, "My son Muhammad Barud will represent me accompanied
by his younger brother Mansur."[7] The Moroccan king sent two first-class Royal
Air Maroc tickets, and Barud and Mansur were given a presidential car and tele-
vised reception. Representing the Senegalese Tijani caliph in Morocco was a big

honor for Lebanese. The Lebanese ambassador in Dakar reported this event to the Lebanese Assembly in Beirut. Then Prime Minister Hariri sent the minister of emigrants to Senegal to decorate Barud on behalf of the Lebanese president.

Not a day passed without Barud visiting Sy or Sy inquiring after Barud. Barud traveled with Sy in his entourage of doctors and sons, and every fifteen days Sy dined at Barud's mother's house. Barud accompanied Sy to Ivory Coast to request a donation from President Houphouët-Boigny for the mosque they were then building in Tivaouane. He and Sy visited together the tomb of Ahmad al-Tijani, founder of the Tijaniyya order, in Fez, Morocco. Barud gave examples of Sy's generosity. He was often given cash donations in sealed envelopes, which he placed in his pocket unopened. When the poor came to him for financial assistance he passed out the envelopes, not knowing how much money they contained. He did not discriminate by religion or skin color and never denied a request, performing the service himself, or at the very least giving his best attempt. According to Barud, upon Sy's death in 1997 he left an estate of only 30,000 CFA (US$60). More importantly, Barud proclaimed, he had inherited the honor of a man loved by all.

Barud considers himself to be Muslim, not Shiʿi Muslim, and declared that there is no difference in Muslim schools of thought. All Muslims believe in one God, one Prophet Muhammad, one Qurʾan, and the kaʿba (sacred enclosure) in Mecca. Muslims pray the same prayers and celebrate the same holidays. In Senegalese mosques Barud prays in the Senegalese Sunni manner and does not prostrate using the Shiʿi clay tablet; yet he prays according to Shiʿi custom in the Lebanese Islamic Institute. Barud attends all religious ceremonies in Senegal and is also friendly with Murid marabouts. He showed me pictures in which he was sitting next to the Murid caliph during *magal,* the annual Murid pilgrimage to Tuba. Barud's charity work helps the poor, blind, and unemployed. He distributes medicine to the sick and cloth from his store so women and children could have new clothing for Islamic holidays. His office is postered with awards, recognitions, and countless photos with Senegalese religious leaders and political figures. Barud was decorated by Senegalese presidents Senghor in 1975 and 1980 and Diouf in 1983, 1989, and 1992. Among numerous honors were decorations from the Ivorian ambassador and the Senegalese Red Cross, and an award for world peace from Japan and UNESCO.[8] He was named Baye Defal Yalla by the Senegalese, which means "father of the poor" in Wolof. Because of his recognition by Senegalese religious leaders and generous charity work, Senegalese consider Barud to be the model for Lebanese integration in Senegal, despite his marrying a Lebanese wife. Yet his discourse of one united Islam did not prevent his influence in the development of the Lebanese Islamic Institute. It was Barud who requested that Musa al-Sadr send a Lebanese shaykh to conduct religious ceremonies for Shiʿa in Dakar. Today he is an influential member of Shaykh al-Zayn's office, and his sister founded the women's charity al-Huda.[9]

Lebanese Christians were more numerous than Muslims in the Senegalese countryside and developed strong social, political, and economic relationships with Senegalese marabouts. Lebanese Christian communities in Mbacke and Diourbel had the strongest relations with Murid leaders. Historically, if Lebanese struggled financially they would approach marabouts who had money and power to assist them. It was common for Lebanese to display photos of Sufi leaders in shops. This was as much to demonstrate their friendship with marabouts as to lure Sufi talibes as customers. Lebanese Christians often tell stories about encounters with marabouts. One woman recounted that her father, from Diourbel, once found a large bunch of grapes and offered one to Amadou Bamba, founder of the Murid order, who remarked that the young boy would grow up to be successful. Shaykh al-Zayn would ask Lebanese Christians from Mbacke to lead him and a delegation of Lebanese Muslims to the neighboring holy Murid city of Tuba. Such visits occurred during particularly highly publicized affairs involving the murder of a Lebanese man or Lebanese involvement in illegal business practices. The shaykh would approach marabouts requesting their intervention in order to improve relations with the Lebanese community.

Some Lebanese Shiʿa, such as public figures like Barud, publicly considered themselves "Muslim," declaring that there is no difference between Sunni and Shiʿi Islam. Yet other Lebanese preferred to differentiate themselves by insisting on the superiority of their knowledge about Islam and religious practices. Being Shiʿi distinguished them from the Senegalese Sufi Muslim majority.

Bringing Lebanese Muslims "Back to Islam"

Before Shaykh al-Zayn arrived in Senegal, the Lebanese embassy had chosen six religious men who had made the pilgrimage to Mecca to conduct weddings and divorces for Lebanese Muslims. These businessmen were not formally educated in religion. One of these men was Shaykh Ayub, who is remembered fondly by many in the community and whose son continues some of his activities.[10] Born in 1904 in Abbasiyya in southern Lebanon, Ayub came to Senegal in 1928. He first lived in a small village near Mbacke for ten years, then moved to Dakar. He eventually left the city center in 1965 for the Pikine suburb, where he was one of only a few Lebanese. In 1994 he returned to Lebanon, where he died in 2000. Never formally educated, he taught himself how to read the Arabic alphabet. A businessman who sold wood, glass, mirrors, and hardware, Shaykh Ayub was popularly known as "the miracle man." He made charms free of charge from Qurʾanic verses and herbs, and never asked anything in return from those he "healed." His son criticized Senegalese marabouts for the income they generated through *gris-gris* production. Shaykh Ayub learned his trade in Lebanon, and his son considered him to be the only Lebanese Muslim in Senegal to practice "traditional medicine." He treated everybody: Lebanese, Senegalese, French, Muslims, Christians, Jews—

however, according to his son, he was unable to cure atheists, as amulets work only for those who believe in God. Shaykh Ayub left his son instructions for how to treat certain ailments.

Shaykh Ayub's son highlighted some tricks of his trade. He photocopies his father's handwritten Qurʾanic verses, writes the name of the concerned individual on the photocopy, burns incense to perfume the document, and covers the paper with scotch tape to protect it from water. The talisman is then ready to wear. Qurʾanic verses, he informed me, can cure women possessed by the devil. For example, he gave his neighbor a charm to protect her and help with insomnia, as she felt the presence of *jinn* (spirits) each night that had intercourse with her and caused her pain afterward. Talismans are thought to work on women with fertility problems, those with headaches, backaches, and knee aches, those suffering from fear, and those in beginning stages of cancer. Whereas some Lebanese went to Shaykh Ayub for protection or healing, others frequent Senegalese fortune-tellers to get fertility charms or to put a curse on women having affairs with their husbands. Others read fortunes or futures into coffee grounds and pin charms to babies' clothing as protection from the evil eye.[11] Many Lebanese Shiʿa ceased these practices since Shaykh al-Zayn's arrival.

The shaykh writes in the introduction to his first book in 1973:[12]

> The idea to write this book was born after my arrival in Senegal. The religious situation of the Lebanese community was disastrous with regard to a great void in religious culture and jurisprudence. This culminated in a lack of religious learning and spiritual practices, where prayer, the most important, was not at all satisfactory. Young people rarely approached religious circles and did not worry about legal obligations. . . . The majority of parents were not interested in these problems. Others were at too great a distance to learn religious laws and rules of practice so symbols could be put to action and not only words. (El-Zein 2001:3–4)

Through courtesy calls to family homes, discussions took place between the young shaykh and the Lebanese community on societal problems, such as economic concerns, lack of ties to the motherland, and difficulties adapting to Senegal. Shaykh al-Zayn slowly succeeded in making the community more aware of religious affairs and obligations.

The shaykh brought formal Islamic education to the Lebanese community of Senegal, teaching Qurʾan, hadith, and fiqh. He likens daily activities to that of a judge: community members approach him for religious advice and he mediates disputes, even between Lebanese in Senegal and family members in Lebanon. If community members want to get married or divorced, disagree over inheritance rights, or conduct business that involves buying, selling, and dividing up shares, they must make an appointment with the shaykh. He deals with issues such as sending children to school and choosing a doctor for medical treatment.

The shaykh additionally considers political concerns of the Lebanese community. Presidential elections in Senegal are an uncertain time for Lebanese. During Senegal's 2000 elections, Shaykh al-Zayn, along with the Maronite Catholic priest, met with the Lebanese community and instructed them not to react to provocations before the elections. When Lebanese were forced to leave Liberia in the 1990s, Shaykh al-Zayn organized the community in Senegal to raise money to assist them.

Such issues are not always clear-cut. Lebanese marriages are between two families, not two individuals, often resulting in difficulties. Furthermore, a Muslim wedding can occur only between Muslims, regardless of Sunni or Shiʿi denomination. If a Muslim desires to marry a non-Muslim at the Islamic Institute, the non-Muslim must convert to Islam. Shaykh al-Zayn has conducted several hundred Muslim-Christian marriages, where the bride is usually a Lebanese Muslim and the groom is a Senegalese, European, or Lebanese Christian who converted to Islam. In Islam, children inherit the father's religion, so Muslim women are encouraged to marry Muslims. Divorce is discouraged, and when community members come to the shaykh for advice on dissolving marriages, he pushes the family to resolve problems, requiring the couple to continue to live together for a few months to be certain that divorce is the only solution.

Shaykh al-Zayn encourages Lebanese to follow the five pillars of Islam: profession of faith, prayer, almsgiving, fasting during Ramadan, and pilgrimage to Mecca. Every year he organizes a trip that goes from Dakar first to Lebanon and then to Mecca, using a Lebanese travel service that arranges for transportation, lodging, and food. The trip lasts two weeks and ranges from thirty to fifty men and women. Beforehand, the shaykh teaches a class on *hajj*. He simulates the kaʿba out of cardboard in order to practice pilgrimage rituals so he can catch mistakes in advance. It is significant that pilgrimage to Mecca, an Islamic requirement of those who are able, is combined with a trip to Lebanon, linking the holy Saudi Arabian city to a return to the Lebanese homeland and a strengthening of national (and Shiʿi) identity. Some Lebanese combine the pilgrimage to Mecca and Lebanon with trips to Iran to visit tombs of Shiʿi scholars.

A shaykh is not only a teacher, counselor, and judge, but is also a scholar. Shaykh al-Zayn has written several books on Islam that he sells to the community. Books are written in Arabic and translated or transliterated into French for many Lebanese in Senegal illiterate in Arabic. Subjects range from a collection of prayers to two volumes on the family of the Prophet, a book on Islamic law and doctrine, more specialized books on the meaning of Ramadan, and the history of Karbala, where Imam Husayn was martyred. In 2013, he published two more books, one addressing Islamic dimensions of astronomy and temporal references and the second on medicine—including chapters on drugs, sexual deviants, suicide, abortion, smoking, and women's rights in Islam. He is working on a new book comparing the Ten Commandments in Islam, Judaism, and Christianity, and also plans to write his autobiography.

Shaykh al-Zayn's charisma leaves a lasting impression. It is less the holiness of holidays that brings community members to attend his late-night Ramadan lectures than the shaykh's ability to inspire and hold his audience with powerful messages, impassioned tones, and dramatic pauses. His patience is enduring: one Lebanese woman spends hours with him every week so he can teach her proper Muslim values to back up her decision to start wearing the veil. Some Lebanese shopkeepers revere him enough to place his photo in shops, alongside other Lebanese shaykhs such as Musa al-Sadr, and images of Senegalese marabouts.[13] Yet the shaykh's following, like that of all charismatic individuals, has limits. He attracts Lebanese youth in Senegal and many successful businessmen. Those least likely to attend his lectures and follow religious commands are the Lebanese community's Western-educated professionals. They respect Shaykh al-Zayn as a man of enormous power, and would never disapprove of him publicly, but scorn the fact that men use religion to gain wealth and the Lebanese community in Senegal made Shaykh al-Zayn a wealthy man.[14] One does come across the occasional devout Shiʿi businessman who has faith in God but not in organized religion.

The Islamic Social Institute

At first Shaykh al-Zayn worked from home, where it took him years to learn the ways of Senegal, establish himself among local religious leaders, and encourage Lebanese to pay religious taxes so he could carry out his work. In 1973 he was finally able to buy the first piece of land of what would become in 1978 the Institution Islamique Sociale. The Islamic Social Institute is a multipurpose organization that has been granted NGO status. The shaykh stresses the institute is an *Islamic* institution, not a *Shiʿi* institution. The Arabic language and Qurʾan, he argues, are neither Sunni nor Shiʿi, but Muslim. Whereas ʿAbdul Munʿam al-Zayn is a Shiʿi shaykh, the institute's vice president is Sunni Muslim, and the shaykh addresses Sunnis in the community as "our Sunni brothers." Many Sunnis attend Friday prayer at the Lebanese mosque because of Shaykh al-Zayn's influence and his *khutba* (Friday sermon) is conducted entirely in Arabic; imams at other mosques preach in Wolof interspersed with Arabic. There are Senegalese, Moroccans, Mauritanians, Algerians, and Lebanese Sunnis, among others, who attend Friday prayer with the Lebanese Shiʿi community.[15]

The Islamic Institute consists of a large formal lecture hall on the ground floor in black and white tile, with separate entrances for men and women. On the first floor is the mosque, a rectangular room with green carpeting decorated with a motif of red arches and geometric designs. There is a small room attached to the mosque where women pray; this door is opened during prayer and closed afterward. Not many women attend Friday prayer, which is not considered a sacra-

Shaykh al-Zayn, Islamic Institute mosque, Dakar, 2000.

ment for women. I attended the shaykh's sermons regularly and at most women numbered a dozen. During major holidays the larger room is divided in half for each sex.

Administrative offices are found on the first and second floors for the director, the committee of thirty-six men, elected every four years, responsible for financial concerns of institute activities, a young shaykh in training, and al-Huda, the Muslim women's charity organization. The third floor houses Shaykh al-Zayn's office, lined with bookcases filled with books: collections of Shiʿi and Sunni law, Qurʾanic *tafsir* (commentary), Islamic history, *tarjamat* (Islamic biographies) of kings and other rulers, books on Christianity and Judaism, and books he himself published, which he sells to community members.[16] Near his office is a comfortable air-conditioned salon with plush chairs and sofas, green furniture and carpeting, a red rug, large chandeliers, and black Islamic decorations on the wall. In this room he holds religious classes for men and women. Attached to the building is a clinic, which treats the poor free of charge and helps those in need travel to France, Europe, or Lebanon for specialized medical treatment. The shaykh and his family reside in the institute's upper levels.

In addition to the Islamic Institute, Shaykh al-Zayn founded in 1979 a primary and secondary school in Dakar, College al-Zahra, that offers courses on Islam and the Arabic language, in addition to the regular Senegalese curriculum.[17] The

A coed class at College al-Zahra, Dakar, 2003. A photo of Shaykh al-Zayn decorates the back of each classroom.

school is a mix of religious denominations: various Senegalese Sufi orders, Shiʿa, and even some Christians attend the "shaykh's school," as it is called. There is a mosque located next to the school led by a Senegalese Shiʿi imam. The student population is approximately 20 percent Lebanese and 80 percent African.

The Islamic Institute in Senegal is the first of its kind in Africa. Shaykh al-Zayn has traveled to other West African countries such as Ivory Coast, Liberia, and Guinea to help found similar institutions, but pointedly remarked that elsewhere Islamic institutes are exclusively for the Lebanese community, whereas in Senegal the institute is open to all Muslims. The shaykh stressed that he has little contact today with these other institutions, which have developed independently of his original influence. He noted that there are no formal religious relations between the Islamic Institute and Shiʿi institutions in Lebanon; he follows instead the marjaʿiyya in Najaf. Nonetheless the central location of the Islamic Institute in downtown Dakar stands as a testimony to the shaykh's dedication to the Lebanese community and commitment to Islam.

In 1993 Shaykh al-Zayn opened a branch of the Islamic Institute in Kaolack. This institute (which closed in 2013) consisted of a small lecture hall, but no mosque, and included living quarters on the top floor for a Senegalese Shiʿi shaykh who gave sermons. The Senegalese shaykh began his post in 2000, and before his arrival Lebanese Shiʿa without formal Islamic training would intermittently lead the Lebanese Kaolack community in religious needs. The institute was created because the Lebanese community of Kaolack was diminishing and Shiʿa no longer had anywhere to congregate.[18] In the past Shaykh al-Zayn would frequently visit this community, but his visits became less frequent. With the influx of Shiʿi wives from the south of Lebanon, Lebanese in Kaolack wanted a place where they could celebrate religious holidays and send children to study Arabic. As Kaolack is one of two centers of Tijani Islam in Senegal, there is no shortage of mosques or Arabic schools there. Yet Shiʿa with renewed ties to Lebanon preferred a Lebanese-run institute, even one led by a Senegalese Shiʿi shaykh.

Shaykh al-Zayn does occasionally need to keep his opposition from within the Lebanese community in Dakar in check. One example of his power is illustrated by the following narrative, taken from my field notes, summarizing one of the shaykh's nightly lectures during the first ten days of Muharram in 2003. Chapter 4 will provide a more in-depth description of the ʿAshura commemoration.

> Hala met me at my apartment. We then picked up her sister Nur and a few of their neighbors and took a taxi to the Islamic Institute. We were there a few minutes early and watched men and women enter the *husayniyya*.[19] When Shaykh al-Zayn entered the room, men rose out of respect. A Senegalese shaykh read a short prayer, the *fatiha,* and then Shaykh al-Zayn took the floor. He began with a story of a man who was very bad to his wife, demanding that she cook for him, but he was not satisfied with what she prepared. He ordered her to let him sleep, but he was not happy in his room. He insisted on sleeping in the salon, but it was too hot so he ended up on the roof. This story was full of examples of how this man derided his wife when all she wanted was to please him.
>
> The shaykh then made a parallel between this story and a man in his congregation who told Shaykh al-Zayn that he did not attend his sermons because he disapproved of the banner of the horse and other figures illustrating the story of Karbala.[20] The shaykh sternly remarked that if this man had a problem with the shaykh and refused to come to mosque that was one thing, but to use the banner as a pretext for his lack of attendance was wrong. His mockery of this man's rejection of him had the audience laughing.
>
> The shaykh then recounted the history of Kufa and its people.[21] A Senegalese shaykh, who had a beautiful voice, followed Shaykh al-Zayn's lecture with a moving recitation of the slaughter at Karbala, and how Zaynab and her son suffered from a terrible thirst.[22] Hala and Nur convulsed in sobs.

This sermon illustrates Shaykh al-Zayn's charisma. By beginning with an example the public could relate to, the shaykh was able to win his congregation's sympathy for his personal dispute.

Other Muslims in Senegal are not always open to or trusting of Shaykh al-Zayn's religious work. During a meeting with the shaykh during Ramadan 2002, he recounted experiences with those spying on him. The following summary is also taken from my field notes.

> A man, perhaps an Iraqi, once joined Shaykh al-Zayn's congregation with a tape recorder with which to capture his sermon. The Lebanese community protested this action. The shaykh responded by taking this stranger's tape recorder and placing it next to his microphone in order to publicly record his message. In another incident, someone from the Senegalese secret service recorded his lecture from a car parked in front of the Islamic Institute, using high-tech equipment. In a third event, a Senegalese man dressed as a beggar listened to the shaykh from outside the Institute's door. The shaykh knew he was not a beggar because a Senegalese minister came to greet the shaykh after the service. This man, pretending to be lame, immediately stood up to greet the minister. The shaykh asked the minister if he knew the man, and the minister responded that they had attended university together. The "beggar" worked for the secret service. The shaykh told me that anybody has the right to listen to what he has to say and he even recorded his own lectures for a period of time to be used as proof in the event that he was misquoted or accused of slander.

Shaykh al-Zayn's charisma thus enables him to respond openly and publicly to suggestions that his sermons may be politically or religiously incorrect. He frequently uses major religious holidays when he is guaranteed a large attendance at his institute as a forum for lectures to the Lebanese community not only on Islamic history, but also on proper Muslim behavior or Shiʻi politics. An example of a Friday prayer sermon demonstrates the shaykh's skill in maintaining strong influence over the Lebanese community through mixing the sacred and the secular.

Friday Prayer

Hirschkind (2006) emphasizes growing importance of cassette sermons in Egypt, and Schulz (2006; 2012) and Soares (2006) focus on broadcast media for spreading Islam in Mali. Cassettes and radio are important in heightening Islamic education in Senegal but not among Lebanese, who rely instead on face-to-face interactions with their shaykh. The khutba given on April 11, 2003, following the March 19 U.S.-led invasion of Iraq, illustrates Shaykh al-Zayn's style and command of knowledge, authority, and charisma. The shaykh begins, after the usual Islamic supplications, as follows: "Oppressive regimes meet their end even if this is at the hands of other oppressors in Baghdad on the same day the martyrdom occurred of the Eminent Imam, Pure Martyr, Master Muhammad Baqir al-Sadr (may God have mercy upon him). The issue of assassinating our scholars, whether by the current oppressive regime or by another regime in this world has been an ongoing issue from times of old." Continuing his sermon, Shaykh al-Zayn explains that

Muhammad Baqir al-Sadr was a great Shiʿi scholar in Najaf and talks about his intellectual accomplishments. He highlights one of the many crimes of Saddam Hussein's administration, that of imprisoning al-Sadr for protesting the regime's tampering with his book *Falsafatuna* (Our Philosophy) in order to omit its Islamic ideology and turn it into the philosophical basis for the Iraqi Baʿth Party. Al-Sadr was assassinated on orders from Saddam Hussein in 1980 for refusing to issue a fatwa declaring the Baʿth to be a legitimate Islamic party.

Shaykh al-Zayn then compares this event to one in the Qurʾan: Moses and his brother Aaron come before Pharaoh and ask him not to require the Egyptian people to worship him since he is a human being and not a god. Pharaoh could have killed the two men, but instead summons his advisors, who agree to call an assembly of magicians to test the truth of Moses and Aaron's claims. When they find that Moses's stick is indeed touched by a miracle from God, they prostrate and declare faith in God. Moses and Aaron live. Such a comparison makes the murder that Saddam Hussein committed even more barbaric as he did not follow Qurʾanic precedent.

The sermon portrays Shaykh al-Zayn's personal relationship with Muhammad Baqir al-Sadr as one of master-disciple and talks of his teacher's grand ideas of building an Islamic university to reform the *hawzat,* religious seminaries of Iraq, and modernize Islam.

> We live today in an era that is both amazing and remarkable; it is a highly advanced era. It is not an era of backwardness so that we are satisfied with giving and receiving instruction on matters relating only to ritual cleanliness and uncleanliness or valid and invalid business transactions. No. We are now wrestling with philosophies, highly advanced civilizations, and formidable scientific progress. We cannot present Islam in the simple old form. Of course this does not mean we are saying that we should bring a new Islam. No, no. Islam remains as it is, but we must understand it in the new style. . . . Islam is not a religion of ritual worship only, mosques only, pilgrimage only, or fasting only. Islam is a religion, a way of life, a system that is complete and comprehensive, beginning at the mosque and ending at the manufacturing plant. This is Islam.

The shaykh ends his sermon by tying his message to Lebanon. He recalls the loss of another Shiʿi scholar, Muhammad Baqir al-Sadr's paternal cousin Musa al-Sadr, who had first sent Shaykh al-Zayn to Senegal in 1969 and who disappeared in Libya in 1978. He concludes with a prayer asking God to alter this pitiful current condition of ours and to compensate us for what we have lost of illustrious and great scholars by giving us other scholars in the future, so that they will realize the hopes that have been lost with assassination of these scholars. He also asks God to return security, peace, and tranquility to Iraq and to all Muslim countries.

The khutba is one means of linking Islamic history and scriptures to the present and mixing the sacred with the secular. Shaykh al-Zayn's powerful sermon educates Lebanese in Senegal about their past and scholarly traditions of Shiʿi Islam while preaching a reformist view of Islam, calling for the religion to be applied to the modern day and age. Shaykh al-Zayn also expresses political views: his stance against the United States and Saddam Hussein as oppressors and pride that in Musa al-Sadr Lebanese had a Shiʿi scholar equal in greatness to those of Najaf. The flexibility of religion as highlighted by the shaykh makes Shiʿi Islam attractive to Lebanese Muslims in Senegal. Many attend sermons because they respect him as a man of knowledge, and community members are able to write anonymous questions about religious practice that are given to the shaykh and publicly addressed. Turnout at Friday prayer is considerably more sparse when Shaykh al-Zayn is out of town and replaced by the Lebanese director of the Arabic Language Institute or a Senegalese shaykh.[23]

Global Shiʿi Connections

Shaykh al-Zayn's religious activities and influence spread beyond Senegal. He has strong ties to Lebanon, most famously exemplified by his role in negotiating the French hostage crisis of the 1980s. Abdou Diouf, past president of Senegal, personally called upon Shaykh al-Zayn to help free French hostages taken by Hizbullah in Lebanon. Although the conflict did not concern Senegal, Shaykh al-Zayn agreed and personally saw to the hostages' release. From April 1987 until May 1988 he traveled between Paris, Beirut, and Tehran, voicing conditions for the release of hostages, such as freeing Lebanese and Iranian prisoners in France (see Péan 2001). One of his favorite stories is how French ministers came into his office and asked why Lebanese are all terrorists. To their horror, he informed them that the French engaged in the first act of piracy in the history of civil aviation by hijacking a Moroccan aircraft carrying five leaders of the FLN (Algerian National Liberation Front) on October 22, 1956.

The Lebanese shaykh maintains connections with leaders of transnational Shiʿi organizations such as the Imam al-Khuʾi Foundation and World Ahlul Bayt Islamic League in London. He works closely with Sayyid Murtada al-Kashmiri, Ayatollah al-Sistani's primary wakil. Sayyid al-Kashmiri informed me during an interview in London that he visited Senegal, which he considers to be Shaykh al-Zayn's territory.

Shaykh al-Zayn attends numerous international conferences and dialogues on Islam and published his papers and speeches in a book printed in Lebanon. He presented his scholarship at a conference in London connecting Shiʿi Islam to Global Islam, a conference in Tehran on Islamic Thought, and a conference on the Holy Qurʾan in Qom. He spoke during the triannual Islamic Summit Conference of the Organization of the Islamic Conference during its 1991 meeting in Dakar, the first time the international Muslim organization convened in sub-Saharan Africa.[24] He has also been involved in local politics. He met with Pope John Paul II during his visit to Dakar in 1992, when they discussed the position of Christianity vis-à-vis Islam and Israeli occupation of southern Lebanon. Shaykh al-Zayn's activism did not end there. He wrote a letter to the United Nations General Security Council deploring the situation in Iraq under Saddam Hussein, and participated in Muslim-Christian dialogue in Detroit, Michigan. Following 9/11, however, the shaykh complained that the United States government repeatedly denied his visa applications, which limited his activities, especially in North America. Chapter 5 will continue to outline Shaykh al-Zayn's work as it relates to Senegalese Muslims. Chapter 4 will first describe the shaykh's efforts to bring Shiʿi Islam—as well as Lebanese nationalist politics—to Lebanese in Senegal.

4 Bringing Lebanese "Back" to Shiʿi Islam

Perhaps real cosmopolitans . . . are never quite at home again, in the way real locals can be. Home is taken-for-grantedness, but after their perspectives have been irreversibly affected by the experience of the alien and the distant, cosmopolitans may not view either the seasons of the year or the minor rituals of everyday life as absolutely natural, obvious, and necessary.

—Ulf Hannerz, "Cosmopolitans and Locals in World Culture"

J'ai quitté mon pays, j'ai quitté ma maison
Ma vie ma triste vie, se traîne sans raison . . .

I left my country, I left my home
My life, my sad life, drags on without reason . . .

—Enrico Macias, *Adieu, mon pays*

Am na ma jabber	I have my wife
Am na ma doom	I have my children
Doutou ma dellou Beiruta	I will never return to Beirut

Kamil sang these two songs, one in French, the other in Wolof, as he drove us to Thies, where he was going on business and I was accompanying him to be introduced to the Lebanese community there. Kamil sang simultaneously of nostalgia for life in the homeland and of being settled in the Lebanese diaspora. A Lebanese man from Kolda expressed similar sentiments in reciting for me a line of poetry indicating his commitment to Senegal: "My country, even if it is unjust to me, I will love her." Cosmopolitan loyalty to both countries often leads to contradictions, especially when exacerbated by war.

The July 2006 Lebanon War was an important turning point for West African Lebanese. For the first time since their formation as a community, Lebanese in Senegal organized a demonstration in Dakar displaying solidarity with Lebanon. This protest illuminates dynamics between global forces and local responses, even if responses among Lebanese in Senegal did not mirror reactions in Lebanon. Hizbullah's effectiveness in winning international public opinion of both Sunni and Shiʿi Muslims in the war against Israel led to a surge in Lebanese diaspora identification, even among communities who had not been similarly affected by previous Lebanese wars. In analyzing Shaykh al-Zayn's role in bringing religious rituals and Lebanese national identity to Lebanese in Senegal, this chapter explores how community members maintain political ties to Lebanon even when they have never visited the "homeland." This sheds new light on the cosmopolitan relationship among religion, migration, and (trans)nationalism and highlights challenges for claims to autochthony.

On July 20, 2006, eight days after the start of the Lebanon war, three thousand Lebanese demonstrated in the area between Senegal's national television station and Dakar's Grand Mosque.[1] A token representation of those from outside the Lebanese community joined in the demonstration, including Karim Wade, the president's son; Mustafa Niass, former prime minister and leader of the opposition; and other Senegalese politicians, professors, religious leaders, and members of nongovernmental organizations. Those in attendance waved Lebanese and Hizbullah flags as well as signs in French, English, and Arabic supporting Lebanon and protesting Israeli attacks. Lebanese community leaders in Dakar, who had formed the committee Solidarité Liban 2006, gave public speeches denouncing the war and comparing it to Nazi destruction of the French village Oradour-sur-Glane in Normandy on June 10, 1944. They also cited as an example of their "hope and courage" the eventual victory of Nelson Mandela's struggles against apartheid in South Africa.[2] Such comparisons place the Lebanese struggle alongside other well-known cases of tragedy and human rights violations while providing examples familiar to a French-educated African audience.

The demonstration was followed by a march, led by Shaykh al-Zayn. The shaykh was fundamental in bringing Lebanese Shiʿa in Senegal "back to Islam" as well as (spiritually if not physically) back to Lebanon. Clerics, through their Islamic institutions, are particularly important in organizing minority or immigrant communities whose members live in close proximity to one another and who face challenges and discrimination from dominant society. Shaykhs in the diaspora serve not only as religious models for the community to emulate but also as representatives of country of origin.

How do religious leaders link congregations to country of origin and Islam to nationalism? Protesters marched with Shaykh al-Zayn past the Senegalese presidential palace and U.S. embassy. They ended at the Lebanese Islamic Institute, where there was a well-attended service including Syrian and Iranian ambassadors and other dignitaries. Although it is not unusual for heads of state to attend religious ceremonies, it was a clear political statement for two countries with their own goals in Lebanon to be present at such a public event showing solidarity with the Lebanese people.[3] I was told that the shaykh spoke more about politics at this occasion than usual and was full of praise for Sayyid Hasan Nasrallah, whereas

Demonstration against 2006 Lebanon War, Dakar, July 20, 2006. Protesters are carrying Lebanese, Hizbullah, and Senegalese flags. Reprinted with permission of *Agence de Presse Africaine*.

previously he had always been careful not to demonstrate attachment to Lebanese political parties.[4] What is even more remarkable is that many protesters who had been living in West Africa for two, three, or even four generations, and had never before marched in the streets of Dakar for a political agenda, had also never visited Lebanon. Although there were many demonstrations against Israel's actions in 2006, with the largest protests taking place in cities in North America, Europe, and the Middle East, I argue that something different was manifesting among Lebanese in Senegal. Taking a public stance against the war broke with the community's previously cautious public profile as a minority not fully accepted in Senegal and can be analyzed as a culmination of their emerging Lebanese identity.

National identity in the diaspora is not only linked to home country solidarity. During the protest, Lebanese also carried the Senegalese flag and signs saying "Merci Sénégal," thanking Senegal for its hospitality for over a century. They hung a banner with the image of the Lebanese national cedar tree on a *car rapide*, one of Dakar's primary vehicles for public transportation, characteristically blue and yellow, proclaiming in bold, black letters on the front of the large Renault van "*Al-hamdu lillah*" (praise God). The car rapide is a symbol of Senegal, reproduced

Public library created by Shaykh al-Zayn, located across the street from the Islamic Institute, Dakar, 2013. A poster of Hasan Nasrallah, secretary general of Hizbullah, is above the bookcase, next to a photo of Mecca. The television broadcasts Arabic-language news.

in children's toys and tourist souvenirs. Times of tension in Lebanon underscore for the Lebanese community the insecurity of their situation elsewhere, and they use these periods of political instability in their "homeland" to reaffirm commitment to their "host countries" and express gratitude for having been given the opportunity, now long ago, to settle in West Africa. Stressing loyalty to Senegal as well as to Lebanon was therefore necessary, and speakers exclaimed: "Long live Senegal! Long live Lebanon! Long live Senegalese–Lebanese solidarity!" Lebanese national identity exhibited by those in the diaspora can sometimes be a response to exclusion from national belonging in country of residence.

Religious rituals are one way of reinforcing belonging to the homeland while unintentionally representing the host society as *not home*. Louër reasons that "any inquiry about the transnational practices of [Shiʻi Islamic] movements implies an examination of their relation to religious authority" (2008:2). Through focusing on the work of Shaykh al-Zayn in Senegal, this chapter insists on the importance of the African example in adding another dimension to our understanding of the relationship between religion and nationalism in the Middle East. Area studies scholars often examine events in the region at the exclusion of related processes taking place in the diaspora.

I am using here a broader conception of religion than one focused solely on the sacred, religious rituals, individual piety, or religious authorities and institutions. I concentrate my analysis on interactions of all these components of religion, suggesting a new way to think about the globalization of religion through a more in-depth understanding of migration and politics. I first examine different theoretical understandings of nationalism. In highlighting the importance of Islamic institutions and authority in the diaspora, I then evaluate Shaykh al-Zayn's success in heightening religious and national awareness among the Lebanese community. I explore his efforts to institute formal religious education, encourage public expressions of piety, and introduce new religious rituals in commemorations of ʿAshura, Ramadan, and Mawlud. Finally, I describe other ties Lebanese in Senegal have with Lebanon. This enables me to emphasize links between religion and politics and how Lebanese Shiʿa have an understanding of the relationship between Shiʿi Islam and Lebanese nationalism different from Shiʿa in Lebanon.

Lebanese Diasporic (Trans)Nationalism

The case of the Lebanese diaspora in Senegal demonstrates that when "Islam" travels to another Islamic context, it is the *national* (exemplified through the *ethnic*), and not strictly the *religious,* that becomes the focus of migrant identity. Mandaville has argued the contrary (using case studies of the Muslim minority in England), that "'the religious' rather than 'the national' becomes the focus of political identity" (2001:109). The relationship between religion and nationalism has recently come to the forefront in scholarship on Lebanese Shiʿi politics, in which religion is an integral part of national ideology. Shaery-Eisenlohr (2008) asserts that it is when Lebanese Shiʿa face other Shiʿa that their vision of their community becomes most visible. She demonstrates how transnational relations between Iran and Lebanon have assisted in breaking the hegemony of Christian narratives of Lebanon as a nation and in placing historically marginalized Shiʿa at the center of Lebanese national politics and self-imagining.

Nationalism is a delicate process in Lebanon and becomes even more multifarious in the Lebanese diaspora. Wimmer and Glick Schiller (2002:306) understand the *nation* to be a people who share common origins and history as indicated by shared culture, language, and identity. It is also an "imagined political community" (Anderson 2006 [1983])—an ideological construction that forges a link between cultural groups and the state (without a necessarily associated feeling of solidarity). Yet Reinkowski (1997) argues that academic understandings of nationalism have failed to grasp the complexities of ethnic and national identities in Lebanon and the traditionally weak state, which has been monopolized by certain confessional groups. He distinguishes between a *Lebanese national identity*, a general mass sentiment and historical memory, and the diverse and competing *ethnonationalisms* of confessional groups, none of which could rally the support of a majority. National identity has come into existence through "the common experience of a state, the simultaneous experience of war and the failure of competing ideologies and nationalisms" (512). Most Lebanese born in Senegal have experienced Lebanon's wars and state bureaucracy only from afar, and identify with multiple Lebanese, Senegalese, and French histories, cultures, and languages.

Some have suggested the existence of *long-distance nationalism*, "a set of identity claims and practices that connect people living in various geographical locations to a specific territory that they see as their ancestral home" (Glick Schiller 2005:570). A complementary process to globalization and transnationalization, long-distance nationalism spans the globe and, "by utilizing modern global communications networks, crosses ethnonational boundaries with unprecedented ease" (Skrbiš 1999:xiii). Glick Schiller indicates that long-distance nationalists exhibit *active politics*, where actions may include "voting, demonstrating, lobbying, contributing money, creating works of art, fighting, killing, and dying" (2005:570). I agree with Humphrey (2004) that long-distance nationalism does not apply to the Lebanese diaspora, especially given that the 2006 protest in Dakar was the *first* demonstration in support of Lebanon by the community in Senegal.

The Lebanese example in Senegal also does not follow Guarnizo, Portes, and Haller's (2003) definition of political transmigrants as those who must necessarily be involved in home-country polities on a *regular* basis. Analysis of *political transnationalism* has been limited to migrant political activism in the host country around home country issues, which may include expatriate voting, electoral campaigns, running for political office, or pursuing foreign-policy goals (Bauböck 2003; Levitt 2008; Østergaard-Nielsen 2003). As I have argued elsewhere (Leichtman 2005), degrees of political interest in country of origin are more relevant than direct political involvement for communities no longer composed only of first-generation migrants. Although Lebanese in Senegal did protest the July 2006 attacks, this can be seen as symbolic solidarity with victims in Lebanon and is not representative of "active politics."

Humphrey defines the *Lebanese diaspora* as the "reconstitution of 'Lebaneseness' across generations at a very particular time historically" (2004:42), referring to the Lebanese Civil War. I maintain that in the case of Lebanese in Senegal, "Lebaneseness" has been increasing since the 1969 arrival of Shaykh al-Zayn and the 1979 Iranian Revolution and that it culminated in the protest against the 2006 Lebanon War, which revitalized diasporic identification. Instead of being an indicator of long-distance nationalism as regular engagement in home-country politics, the July 20, 2006, demonstration in Dakar is an example of *transnational collective action,* that is, "coordinated international campaigns on the part of networks of activists against international actors, other states, or international institutions" (Della Porta and Tarrow 2005:2–3).

Consequences of Lebanon's wars for its diaspora have not been fully explored (see Humphrey 1998 and Walbridge 1997). Hizbullah's actions mobilized the Lebanese diaspora, and transnational collective action led to Lebanese national identification. This sense of Lebaneseness became articulated through larger struggles of Hizbullah as representative of the country as a whole (Deeb 2008). This was a Lebanese Shiʿi national identity, although it was not religious per se.[5] However, unlike the distinct Shiʿi national stories in Lebanon of Hizbullah, Amal, and Sayyid Fadlallah, as carefully outlined by Shaery-Eisenlohr (2008), many Lebanese in Senegal do not identify with the specific political ideologies of these parties. Rather, Lebanese Shiʿa in Senegal create their own discourse of origins, illustrated through speeches by visiting Lebanese politicians from both Hizbullah and Amal, stories from Lebanese in Dakar who have "gone back," photos, videotapes, and images of Lebanese Shiʿi destruction and resistance as portrayed through Lebanese satellite television. This amalgamation of Lebanese Shiʿi identities, ritualized through religious commemorations, is different from the identities Shiʿa in Lebanon imagine and to which they refer.

Whereas the Maronite Church has historically been seen as a symbol of Lebanon, today, it can be argued, Shiʿa have become the new sign of Lebanese nationalism. Once the economic and political underdogs of Lebanon, Shiʿa have risen in both number and power to become the largest and most politically active religious denomination. Although many Lebanese of Senegal had never visited Lebanon, they began to take pride in their origins from southern Lebanon and in regional politics of Hizbullah against Israel. Such an interest, as a return to their Lebanese past, at a time when Shiʿa in Lebanon have broken with their past of underrepresentation, results in the creation of a new present. Shaykh al-Zayn's founding of the Islamic Institute in Dakar corresponded temporally with this important period for Shiʿi Muslims around the world.

In the past, Senegalese of Lebanese origin were confronted with religious differences only when they left Senegal. Ziyad, a second-generation Muslim born in Senegal, recounted how he studied in a Sunni school in Sidon, Lebanon. He visited a Shiʿi friend's family and was introduced as a Sunni, which took him by surprise. Other men who simply identified as Muslim in Senegal similarly learned they were Shiʿa during trips to Lebanon. Muhsin, a Lebanese university student in France, born and raised in Senegal, informed me that he learned the difference between Sunnis and Shiʿa from a French schoolteacher when he was twelve years old. His father raised him Muslim, not Shiʿi, and Muhsin grew up without awareness of different schools of Islamic thought. With the arrival of Shaykh al-Zayn, despite his claims to be running an *Islamic* institute, Lebanese in Senegal are learning how to be Shiʿi and what it means to be Shiʿi. Shiʿa not only prostrate on a *turba,* block of clay, and perform ablutions differently than Sunnis, but they are also defined by a long history of religious persecution that has, since the Iranian Revolution, led to a reclamation of Shiʿi rights. Dabashi (2011) therefore refers to Shiʿi Islam as a "religion of protest." Lived experiences of Lebanese Shiʿa in Senegal illustrate recent exposure to Shiʿi Islam and transforming subjectivities as a result of this newfound knowledge.

"Return" to Shiʿi Islam: Religious Education

Qurʾan Classes

On Tuesdays and Thursdays Shaykh al-Zayn teaches religious classes for men and on Saturdays he teaches Qurʾan classes for women. Men's attendance averages thirty people, comprised of mostly members of the Lebanese community, but Senegalese Shiʿa and an Iranian shaykh sometimes join discussions. I occasionally attended women's Saturday afternoon classes, along with thirty-five to forty-five Lebanese women of all ages. Taught in the Islamic Institute's salon, classes were educational but also an occasion for women to socialize in a socially accepted and meritorious venue (Osanloo 2009: ch. 3).

In a typical class, the shaykh entered the room and greeted those in attendance. Women took Qurʾans from the stack of books on the table in front of them. He led them to a passage, reading the classical Arabic, then explaining tafsir in the Lebanese dialect. Lessons lasted half an hour. Afterward the shaykh made a few announcements, such as plans for upcoming Islamic holidays or canceled classes when he was frequently out of town. The floor was then opened for ten minutes to questions about Islam and religious obligations, after which women greeted one another or lined up to talk to the shaykh individually.

Questions were asked directly or written anonymously and sent to the shaykh before the lesson. One woman wanted to know what to focus on during Ramadan, and the shaykh's response was Qurʾan and prayer. Another inquired about food restrictions, and the shaykh explained that food imported from another Muslim country is *halal* (permitted), but food from a Muslim who also sells alcohol is *haram* (forbidden), since the money he earns is dirty money even if he does not drink alcohol himself. Fish, abundant in Senegal, are haram if dead before leaving the ocean or fished using dynamite, but are halal if fished live from the sea and die in the air. He instructed women that if they make a mistake during prayer they should finish the prayer and then repeat it to correct the mistake. He often reiterated that it is better to study the Qurʾan than to pray or fast if one does not have religious knowledge. Another favorite topic of the shaykh was to discourage the community from smoking. He gave examples from fiqh how one can smoke only if one has permission from others. On an airplane one needs the pilot's permission to smoke and must obey a no-smoking sign.[6] He complained regularly about Lebanese men not following Islamic laws of commerce, hoping to influence women to correct family business practices. This, however, appeared to be in vain as women glanced at one another when he broached this topic as if to say "here he goes again . . ."

Another question addressed during a particular Saturday class was more controversial. When I attended Friday prayer the day before, one woman was seated behind other women and refused to move forward when beckoned to. The shaykh answered a question about women's mosque attendance and placement, explaining that it is not allowed for a woman to be in mosque during any stage of her menstrual cycle. The elderly should be seated in front, and children should sit behind adults. This question angered Ruqayya, an elderly *hajja* (an honorific title for those who made pilgrimage to Mecca), who invited me to her home for coffee after the lesson. She was upset that even though questions were supposed to be anonymous it was obvious whom this one concerned and she even deduced who had asked it. After all, we were only five or six women in mosque the day before. Ruqayya remarked that people gossip about nothing at all and it is better to address directly the offending woman than to bring the problem before the shaykh.

In addition to attending the shaykh's classes, Lebanese purchase books on Shi'i Islam from a Moroccan-run bookstore, which carries books on Sunni and Shi'i Islam in Arabic and French. Families often have in their homes *Nahj al-Balagha* (Peak of Eloquence), the collection of Imam 'Ali ibn Abi Talib's writings, and sometimes *Mafatih al-Jinan* (The Keys of Heaven), a collection of supplications compiled by Shaykh Abbas al-Qummi. Many purchased Shaykh al-Zayn's books directly from the Islamic Institute or in bookstores. One man living in the south of Senegal far from the Islamic Institute proudly informed me that he had taught himself how to pray from the shaykh's publications.

Arabic Language Instruction

The Arabic Language Institute run by the Lebanese Islamic Institute is open to all who want to learn Arabic. Amal, for example, enrolled after a visit to Lebanon when she filled out the trilingual (Arabic, English, French) customs form in French and was ridiculed by the inspector for being Lebanese yet unable to write in Arabic. The Arabic Language Institute instructs Lebanese and Senegalese students with language materials promoting Lebanese nationalism and Islam.[7] Course materials are produced in Dakar and printed at the Islamic Institute's printing press or imported from Lebanon. One book, *Um 'Amara,* printed in Saudi Arabia, tells stories of lives of members of the Prophet's family. Materials locally produced in Senegal give examples from both Senegal and Lebanon, such as a doctor from Lebanon choosing to vacation in Senegal, a beautiful country with a plethora of beaches. These booklets also have an Islamic emphasis, including quotes from the Qurʾan, a chapter on honoring one's parents, and descriptions of Muslim prophets. The children's grammar books from Lebanon are dated, written in the late 1970s and early 1980s, and are taught to adults. These books cater to both Muslims and Christians by imparting a strong nationalist message of the beauty of Lebanon, its cedar trees, respect for the Lebanese flag, and praise for Lebanese soldiers who defended their beloved country against the Israeli enemy. Politics and religion make their way even into what was intended to be a secular and not exclusively Lebanese educational context.

The Marjaʿiyya

I once asked Hakim, who owns a clothing store and rarely missed the shaykh's Ramadan lectures, to summarize for me a lesson I was unable to attend. He recounted that the shaykh had spoken about many topics not discussed in the Qurʾan, on which the marajiʿ (whom Hakim defined as those who write fatwas) have taken positions. The example the shaykh had cited the night before concerned recent Islamic regulations on travel during Ramadan. While it is true that travel has gotten easier—a short airplane flight rather than days on the back of a camel—the application of certain Islamic laws is not so simple. For example, various marajiʿ recommend that Muslims avoid fasting while traveling in order to drink water on airplanes to avoid dehydration. Hakim explained, according to what he had learned from Shaykh al-Zayn, that one chooses a marjaʿ like one picks a shirt, according to views of that particular marjaʿ.

Not every Lebanese Shiʿi in Senegal understands the system of marjaʿiyya, institution of highest-ranking Shiʿi leadership (Walbridge 2001). In Islam, the question of leadership began with the Prophet's death and problem of succession. Shiʿa determined that the Prophet's cousin and son-in-law ʿAli was his rightful successor, followed by his sons Hasan and Husayn. Twelver Shiʿa follow nine other descendants through the line of Husayn as Imams, leaders of the faithful. The succession of Imams ended with occultation of the twelfth Imam, expected to return alongside Jesus to rid the world of injustice. In Shiʿi theology *wilayat* is the authority invested in the Prophet and his family as representatives of God on earth.

When Safavids rose to power in Iran and established a Shiʿi state (1501–1736), Shiʿi ʿulama gained greater prominence. A group of ʿulama assumed the Imam's all-comprehensive authority as a just ruler, pending the twelfth Imam's return (Momen 1985; Takim 2006). Religious elite emerged in the eighteenth century who could practice *ijtihad*—religious decisions by independent interpretation of Islamic legal sources. One becomes *mujtahid*, qualified specialist, by being declared such by another mujtahid; often a teacher grants pupils authorization to exercise ijtihad on their own (Halm 1997). The institution of the marjaʿiyya materialized in order to integrate Shiʿi clerics and establish contemporary lines of authority (Walbridge 2001:4) as well as to become an alternative authority that could replace corrupt rulers of the time who failed to uphold justice (Sachedina 1988).

In Shiʿi Islam the religious leader who obtains the highest level of scholarship, enabling him to make legal decisions, is given the title *marjaʿ al-taqlid,* a source to emulate or follow. Shiʿi Muslims generally follow a living marjaʿ and have the right to determine the jurist's qualification to assume the Imam's comprehensive authority.[8] Those without specialized religious knowledge are expected to submit to a marjaʿ's interpretation of Islamic law in what is called *taqlid.* Khums constitutes the major source of revenue for a marjaʿ, spiritually imbued with charismatic representation of the Hidden Imam through a share that belongs to the Imam.

Throughout history both Sunni and other Shiʿi groups have challenged the authority of Shiʿi ʿulama and their learned hierarchy (Moussavi 1996). Another problem facing Shiʿa has been factionalism caused by recognition of multiple mujtahids as marjaʿ al-taqlid. This intensified with Ayatollah Khomeini's establishment of *wilayat al-faqih* (jurist's guardianship) in Iran, which other Shiʿa do not endorse. Hakim, who summarized Shaykh al-Zayn's sermon, had some idea what a marjaʿ does but claimed not to know who is "the current marjaʿ." He thought maybe he was Ayatollah ʿAli al-Sistani in Najaf, the religious scholar frequently mentioned by Shaykh al-Zayn. He understood that "the marjaʿ" should be followed as an example for times of prayer, when to fast during Ramadan, what to do if one makes a mistake during prayer, and other legal details of religion. He had not read books by marajiʿ nor did he know if they were available in Senegal, but he assumed the shaykh had them. In contrast to Hakim's understanding of the marjaʿiyya as embodied in a single marjaʿ, there are multiple marajiʿ at any given time, and a Shiʿi Muslim follows teachings of the marjaʿ of his or her personal choice.

I asked Nur which marjaʿ she followed. She responded that she did not know but would ask her father since he determines who the family follows. Her friend was listening to our conversation and asked Nur to explain what is a marjaʿ. Nur had just returned from her first visit to Lebanon and responded with her love for Sayyid Hasan Nasrallah, the secretary general of Hizbullah. She exclaimed that every morning she starts her day looking at his picture, and when he appears on television her mother jokes that the TV will explode because her daughter hugs it so hard. Nasrallah, however, does not have marjaʿ status.

Other Lebanese are knowledgeable about the marjaʿiyya. Haydar, literate in matters of Islam, explained to me that Sunnis have the al-Azhar shaykh in Cairo as their authority, and likewise Shiʿa can choose from various scholars learned enough to become the reference for all Shiʿa. He explained that Lebanese follow various marajiʿ. We were sitting in a bakery with a group of men who regularly meet there every Sunday morning. Haydar pointed to one of his friends who follows Sayyid Muhammad Husayn Fadlallah in Lebanon, another follows al-Sistani, but he himself had not yet chosen a marjaʿ.[9] The man who followed Fadlallah asked what Haydar was waiting for, as he had listened to Fadlallah's speeches on Arabic satellite TV and found him to be very knowledgeable. A fourth man did not have a marjaʿ because, he informed me, he did not care.

Imad, a thirty-year-old merchant with a penchant for racing motorcycles who regularly visits Lebanon, explained that he follows Ayatollah Sayyid Abu al-Qasim al-Khuʾi as his marjaʿ. He clarified that after al-Khuʾi's death, Ayatollah Muhammad Reza Golpaygani of Qom became marjaʿ and declared that one may not continue to follow a deceased marjaʿ. However, Sistani succeeded Golpaygani and reversed his ruling, decreeing that one may follow a deceased marjaʿ as long as there is nobody more learned than he. Imad returned to following al-Khuʾi, who, according to him, was the most educated marjaʿ. He informed me that most Lebanese in Senegal follow al-Khuʾi, although he agreed that many are not knowledgeable about the marjaʿiyya. Likewise a Lebanese woman told me that she, like many others, also follows al-Khuʾi because Shaykh al-Zayn was his former student in Najaf and spreads his ideas to the Lebanese community. She called Shaykh al-Zayn the marjaʿ of the Lebanese of Senegal. Her husband disagreed, questioning how he could be marjaʿ if the shaykh himself follows a marjaʿ, and his wife concluded that he must be marjaʿ since Lebanese in Senegal follow him and he declares when Ramadan should start. The shaykh does not have marjaʿ status, but is a wakil for Ayatollah al-Sistani. Others claimed that the majority of Lebanese Shiʿa in Senegal follow al-Sistani, al-Khuʾi's successor, because he is the marjaʿ chosen by Shaykh al-Zayn.

Imad pays khums to both Shaykh al-Zayn in Dakar and Fadlallah in Lebanon. While he emphasized that he did not follow Fadlallah as marjaʿ, as he was known primarily in Lebanon without a wider following, Fadlallah was accredited as al-Khuʾi's wakil. He complained that many Lebanese in Senegal do not pay khums, but spoke with great respect of one prominent, pious, and wealthy Lebanese businessman who built the Arabic Language Institute and a large elaborate mosque for Senegalese Muslims from his religious obligation to pay the Shiʿi tax.

Public Expressions of Piety

Some Lebanese attributed an increase in individual expressions of piety in their community to the shaykh's teachings. Drawing on Mahmood (2005), Deeb defines *public piety* as a bringing together of "the notion of piety meant to be seen with that of piety that is inextricably linked to the public good" (2006:34). Piety brought from one's personal space to the public visibly establishes an individual's membership in the religious community by serving as a public marker of religiosity. Since Shaykh al-Zayn's arrival in Senegal, men and women have learned to pray, fast during Ramadan, give charity, and participate in community service, and more women have begun to wear the veil. These changes in Senegal correspond to similar increases in religiosity throughout the Muslim world, often analyzed as reactions to the failure of postindependence promises of Western-style liberal progress and linked to advantages of Islamic dress for women who increasingly study or work in mixed-sex environments.

Praying, Fasting, and Other Pious Acts

Many Lebanese in Senegal have recently begun to pray regularly. I was visiting a young family one day in their home when their two-year-old son placed a napkin on the ground like a prayer mat and prostrated, saying something that resembled *allahu akbar*. His mimicking his parents' actions led to a discussion about the proper age at which a child should begin to pray. The father felt prayer should begin at the legal Islamic age of maturity: fifteen for boys, eight or nine for girls. The mother argued instead that her son should pray as soon as he was old enough to understand, since the earlier he is exposed to prayer the easier it would be to make it a habit. Her parents were not observant, and she began to pray in 1997, after deciding to become more pious. Her husband took up prayer even more recently, crediting Shaykh al-Zayn for teaching him about religion.

The observance of the month of Ramadan, abstaining from food, drink, cigarettes, and sexual intercourse from sunrise to sunset, is an individual activity and Lebanese in Senegal respect this Islamic obligation in various ways. Some fast and pray; others fast without praying. Those who drink alcohol regularly may refrain from drinking during the month of Ramadan. One woman explained that she prays, fasts, does not drink, but also does not veil. A Lebanese man in his late twenties informed me during Ramadan 2003 that he fasted for two days but then stopped because fasting is only worthwhile if one is pure, which would have to wait until he is married! In addition to being unable to abstain from sexual adventures during the holy month, he is also addicted to cigarettes, but claimed to have given up drinking during Ramadan for prayer.

Bashir, who has a high school education and sells sanitation supplies, proudly told me that he newly started to fast during Ramadan, but his wife Nadia laughed and clarified that in the beginning he fasted Monday through Friday and took the weekends off. He retorted that Lebanese Muslims have different levels of knowledge: for some prayer is enough, while others desire to read books and learn more about Islam. Bashir learned all he knows about Islam from two of Shaykh al-Zayn's books. When he decided to become more pious, his father, who is not observant, warned him not to become too closed-minded as a result of religion, but otherwise supported his decision. His parents own a large dog, as do many Lebanese, for protection and to deter thieves from entering their homes. Bashir pointed out that Islam forbids dogs as they are unclean and one cannot have a dog in the same area where one prays. He began to prohibit his parents from bringing their dog into his apartment, and as a result his parents referred to his living quarters as "Mecca." Everyone justifies religiosity in his or her own way.

Charity Associations

One religious transformation in Lebanon described by Deeb (2006) is the reinterpretation of the behavior of Sayyida Zaynab (Imam Husayn's sister) at Karbala, which led to public participation of Shiʿi women in Islamic community work. Women of all ages in the southern suburbs of Beirut became actively involved in community service, many beginning volunteer work as they became more religiously committed. Deeb's interlocutors referred to their service as *jihad*—personal struggles within oneself, struggles against poverty in the community, and the struggle of Lebanon's Islamic Resistance, which such volunteer work was seen as advancing. Likewise, Lebanese Shiʿi women in Senegal began their own charity association, al-Huda. Unlike the wide participation in charity activities of Lebanese women in Beirut, prominent middle-aged women, with few young participants, led the service organization based at Dakar's Islamic Institute. Women hold regular meetings and organize fundraising activities to help Senegalese and certain Lebanese in need. Activities are occasionally reported in Senegalese newspapers, and the most significant fundraising event is the annual Ramadan *iftar* (break-the-fast meal).

I attended iftars in 2002 and 2003, where funds were raised through pricey entrance tickets and raffle tickets for donated prizes. There were approximately three hundred people in attendance, including many wealthy Lebanese Muslims and community leaders, in addition to two dozen Lebanese Christians. An al-Huda board member welcomed guests in Arabic while waiters served dried fruit and vegetable soup to break the fast, after which the shaykh and Lebanese ambassador led the hungry crowd to the dinner buffet. The large spread of typical Lebanese cuisine disappeared very quickly. Members of al-Huda approached each dinner table selling envelopes containing either winning prize tickets or French proverbs. The women of al-Huda also organized an annual *kermesse* (carnival or fair), popular with families with young children. Game booths were set up and food could be purchased with tickets bought at the door; additional entertainment included music, singing and dancing, children belly dancing, and a raffle.

Although women run Lebanese religious charities, Lebanese men contribute money to various causes and are active in secular charities such as Lions Club International, a service organization with chapters around the world. I attended the annual fundraising dinner of the Dakar branch, which featured a buffet of Lebanese cuisine to feed a high-society audience with a few Senegalese and Moroccans interspersed in a predominantly Lebanese crowd. One table passed around a *narguila* (water pipe). Entertainment included dancing to Arabic and French music, with an occasional salsa or Lebanese *dabka* song. After dinner a chubby fifteen-year-old Lebanese girl beautifully performed the belly dance, a slightly older dance troupe wearing traditional Lebanese dress danced the dabka, and a man played the keyboard while his partner sang Lebanese songs, including a nationalistic Fairuz song about Lebanon's cedars. The evening ended, as usual, with a raffle, prizes donated by local Lebanese businesses, including complimentary haircuts, a new television set, a weekend at a fancy Dakar hotel, and round-trip tickets for two to Paris. The Lebanese community numerically and culturally dominated this event, sponsored by an international charity.

Lebanese men also give generously during Islamic holidays. It is customary during Tabaski (ʿId al-Adha) for every Senegalese head of household to purchase a sheep (or multiple sheep, one for each wife). They eat a portion of the meat themselves and distribute the remainder to the poor. Although Lebanese Muslims, unlike Senegalese, usually do not ritually slaughter sheep themselves, many purchase two or more sheep, one for their family, and others for charity.

The Maronite church has its own women's charity, Notre Dame du Liban, begun in 1969, which organizes two annual fundraisers: an Easter ball and a February sales exposition. Notre Dame du Liban is a member of the organization of Catholic women in Senegal, and, along with al-Huda, forms part of Fédération des Associations Féminines du Sénégal, a group of fifty-some organizations. Although al-Huda and Notre Dame are separate associations, members attend the other's activities and occasionally work together, especially during highly publicized events, to be represented as "Lebanese." Charities assist Senegalese orphanages, donate sewing machines, and contribute to women in prison. They answer calls by the Senegalese government to help with vaccines and schoolbooks, and assisted in the aftermath of the tragic sinking of the Joola ferryboat in 2002. Although Lebanese genuinely give charity to help the poor, their actions are often publicized and noted by Senegalese. Charity thus becomes a political statement, a sign of "integration," and necessary for the Lebanese community, seen enviously by many Senegalese as wealthy and successful, to "give back" to their host society.

To Veil or Not To Veil?

Although the *hijab* is required to enter certain institutions in Senegal, such as the Islamic Institute and College al-Zahra, many women in Senegal do not wear the veil, and there is little social pressure to do so.[10] The decision to veil is therefore seen by some as one of great moral strength. Shaykh al-Zayn meets individually with Shiʿi women who have newly veiled to encourage them in their resolve and educate them on other changes in their daily lives that must accompany this dress modification. Some women begin to veil when they marry or when their husband goes to Mecca, either at the husband's request or of their own will to begin a more pious way of life. Amal, a Lebanese friend in her mid-thirties who worked in a store selling fashion accessories, told me it was too soon for her to veil. Her veiled mother disagreed as the veil was obligatory for Muslim women. Amal divulged that when her mother first arrived in Senegal from Lebanon to marry her father she was already wearing the veil, but her father's family asked her to remove it since she was still young. Her mother therefore began to veil again in her forties.

Not all in Dakar's Lebanese community support an increase in women wearing the hijab. Nur and Hala's older sister expressed to me her desire to go back to work but feared some Lebanese businessmen would refuse to hire a veiled woman. Even though Senegal is a Muslim country the veil is sometimes seen as a deterrent to doing business with non-Muslims. Many Lebanese businesses prefer not to place a veiled woman in a position, even secretarial, where she will be seen by Europeans who would perceive the veil as "backward" or be offended by a woman refusing to shake their hands.

Many Lebanese women work, often in family-run businesses or for other acquaintances in the Lebanese community. One informant mentioned that some Shiʿi women set up shop because their husbands want to keep an eye on them. Placing them in a clothing store that they manage, even if it is not financially successful, is one way of keeping women occupied while men are at work. This is also a question of social class, as many Lebanese women are employed out of financial necessity. One successful young merchant emphasized that his wife does not *need* to work. If they had financial difficulties he would allow her to have a job, but for now business is good. A group of working Lebanese women in Kaolack, however, disagreed with this male point of view. They proudly explained that either their stores are in their names or they own a 50 percent share along with their husbands. They claimed that women control Lebanese commerce, and referred to Lebanese women as bold, hard workers, and go-getters. Lebanese women who do not work keep busy by raising children, preparing meals, visiting friends and family, working out in the gym, or frequenting Dakar's cafés and beaches.

There are more veiled women in Senegal today than in the past (among both Lebanese and Senegalese Muslims), yet some Lebanese Shiʿi women feel pressured *not* to veil. Nadia told me she would like to wear the veil one day. I asked why she did not begin now, and she explained it was because of the devil: if she lived in a society where everyone was veiled, she could more easily follow suit. However, sunning on the beach is a deterrent, especially on Sundays when most shops are closed. She also mentioned her mother-in-law would not support her choice and cited a friend who removed her veil after only two days because it was too difficult. She deemed it better not to veil than to begin to wear the veil without moral resolve to follow through with this decision. She was determined to start veiling when she made pilgrimage to Mecca. She was under the impression that this was what her husband wanted as he disapproved of how men looked at her when she walked down the street. Bashir, however, told me privately that he was not in favor of women wearing the veil, but he was also not against it. He approved of freedom of choice and stated he would not prevent his wife's decision, although he preferred that she did not veil, which would entail a restrictive lifestyle.

In contrast, Lebanese in Senegal are surprised when they travel to Lebanon to find that they are criticized for not veiling sooner and are shocked by the large number of veiled women in villages of origin. Nur, upon returning from Lebanon, told her friend that she must visit there one day. The friend replied that she had almost made the trip, but the need to veil in her village of origin deterred her from going. Nur agreed, mentioning that one relative in southern Lebanon asked her mother in Dakar how many daughters veiled. The relative retorted all but two was not enough; they should all veil. Nur, who did not wear the veil, refused to visit this relative in Lebanon.

I heard a similar story from Fuad, a biscuit and candy wholesaler from Dakar who visited his mother in Beirut, whom he labeled a "modern" (unveiled) woman. They went to Nabatiye, their town of origin, and were shopping in the market when an "extremist with a beard" approached Fuad. This man inquired whether the woman he was with was his mother, and if he could insist that she veil, as it was disrespectful for a woman of her age to be uncovered in public. Both mother and son were offended, but Fuad admitted that if his mother lived in Nabatiye and not Beirut she would be obliged to veil as religiosity is growing in southern Lebanon.

In addition, those Lebanese women who choose to veil in Senegal do not pin their scarves according to distinct styles of Hizbullah or Amal. Deeb (2006) and Peleikis (2003) discuss different meanings of veiling for Lebanese women, where various styles carry associations with particular age groups and trends, protect against social pressure to conform to increasing popularity of plastic surgery, and reflect political loyalties in Lebanon. In Senegal, veiling among Lebanese Shiʿa is as much a question of fashion, lifestyle, and acceptance by society as it is of religious obligation.

Religious Rituals

Lebanese Shiʿa are more actively participating as a community in religious rituals that have not historically been part of their social life. The Islamic Institute's celebration of ʿAshura, Ramadan, and Mawlud provide examples of how Shaykh al-Zayn enforces linkages to Lebanon through performance of Islamic holidays.

ʿAshura

The first ten days of the Islamic month of Muharram, which commemorate the martyrdom of Imam Husayn (Prophet Muhammad's grandson) at the battle of Karbala, represent a critical aspect of collective identity for Shiʿa around the world. ʿAshura is both the remembrance of a battle of righteousness against corruption and evil and a tribute to a key moment in Shiʿi history.[11] Lebanese in Senegal began to observe ʿAshura after Musa al-Sadr's 1967 visit. Dakar's Islamic Institute was founded in 1978 so Lebanese would have a *husayniyya*, a meeting place in which to commemorate ʿAshura, separate from the mosque; it was then that community-wide participation began in Senegal. This involves attending *majalis* (s. *majlis,* mourning gatherings) at which the history of the martyrdom of Husayn and his family is retold. The Islamic Institute holds afternoon sessions for

women, led by a *khatiba* (female preacher) brought annually from Lebanon to recount the story of the battle of Karbala, and evening sessions for both men and
women, led by a Senegalese shaykh trained in Lebanon, who has a beautiful voice.
Shaykh al-Zayn gives twice-daily sermons at both gatherings. Men who do not
need to be at work meet in a private home for daily afternoon sessions. The wom-
en's majlis at the Islamic Institute the morning of the tenth of Muharram is the
most heavily attended. Another large commemoration that day is hosted at a private home for men, children, and a few dozen women who help prepare caldrons
of *harisa*, the customary dish of grain and chicken, each stir of which with a large
wooden stick is thought to bring a blessing. Lebanese in Senegal commemorate
ʿAshura behind closed doors, and there is no public procession as takes place elsewhere in the Shiʿi world.[12]

I attended majalis at the Islamic Institute, where the lecture hall was filled
with three hundred to four hundred women and children dressed in black, the
color of mourning. Outfits ranged from the loosely fitting long-sleeved *abaya* to
tight-fitting pants or skirts and sweaters. The room was decorated with black wall
hangings illustrating the battle of Karbala and the martyrdom of Husayn, with
colorful Arabic script and solemn images. Each day, the khatiba narrated a different Muharram event in a style of lamentation, graphically yet poetically detail-
ing the suffering and killing of the Imam, his family, and army. Together with the
narration, the khatiba included sermons containing lessons to be learned from the
horrific events. Women came with boxes of pastries and bags of doughnuts and
biscuits flavored with anise and sesame seeds and passed around boxes of tissues
to those eating or crying. The audience was moved by the recitations, which at
times became emotional as the khatiba wailed in sorrow and women cried, some
passionately, dabbing their eyes, red with tears, and convulsing in sobs. Tears
shed for martyrs of Karbala are *mustahab* (religiously commendable) and may increase one's chances of entering paradise. During commemorations the audience
switched from pensively listening to sermons in quiet concentration to singing
along to a *nadba* (elegy) and beating their chests in rhythm. At one point an older
woman in front of me started to suffocate from crying. The women around me
sat her down, pulled off her veil, removed her glasses, splashed water on her face,
placed perfume under her nose, and gave her a drink of water. After a few minutes
she came to, quickly reassembled herself, and stood again in prayer. The majalis
concluded with the audience standing and facing the direction of Husayn's tomb
and reciting in unison *ziyarat al-husayn,* a supplicatory prayer for the Imam.

When the khatiba finished the day's narrative, Shaykh al-Zayn entered the husayniyya. As the largest event of the year bringing together Lebanese Shiʿi women,
the occasion was used not only to teach them about ʿAshura, but to instruct them
more generally on lessons and obligations of Islam. He lectured about courage and
standing up against odds, correcting wrongs of others vis-à-vis Islam, and set-

ting a good example. Education, obligatory for all Muslims, was stressed as central in the fight against ignorance. The shaykh emphasized the role of women as different from that of men as women raise and educate children. He encouraged them to become more active in the community, attend Friday prayer and Qurʾan classes, and volunteer for al-Huda, particularly those who did not work and had free time. Baskets were passed around to collect charity donations. Afterward, women filed out of the lecture hall greeting one another, surrounded by Senegalese disabled and those asking for charity hoping to benefit from their good graces.

* * *

The holiday is even more meaningful and difficult for Shiʿa today. Events that took place in Iraq throughout Shiʿi history parallel contemporary politics, and Lebanese link the tragedy that befell Husayn to persecution of Shiʿa in the present day. A banner hanging in the husayniyya with the proverb "Every day is ʿAshura, every land is Karbala [kul yawm ʿashura wa kul ard karbala]" recalled the slogan Ayatollah Khomeini used to mobilize followers during the Iranian Revolution.[13] In 2003 ʿAshura began only a few weeks before the U.S.-led war in Iraq. Lebanese women were brought to tears about continuing injustice in the world and suffering of the innocent. More symbolically, during the Dakar protests of the 2006 Lebanon War, some women dressed as they would for ʿAshura—all in black wearing a headband with the Arabic words ya Husayn. ʿAshura is the Shiʿi holiday that highlights their victimization in much of the world and reinforces the Shiʿi history of suffering. It is a solemn yet powerful event, where women conform to ʿAshura rituals, narratives, and history, and use its symbolism to protest present-day oppression. This cosmopolitan commemoration reminds Lebanese in Senegal of their origins, connects them with Lebanon through the arrival of the khatiba and the linking of the Karbala battle to recent wars in Lebanon, and ties them to Shiʿi Muslims in Iraq, Iran, and beyond.

Ramadan

The shaykh also speaks nightly during the month of Ramadan. He announces lectures in a written notice circulated to business communities in downtown Dakar and posted in the Arabic Language Institute and Islamic Institute. The bilingual French and Arabic invitation informs Dakar's population that Ramadan is a time of prayer, reading Qurʾan, and the gates of paradise opening; they should not forget in commercial activities that Ramadan is also a time of good deeds, study, and family. He invites the community to attend his mosque every evening at 8:45 PM for prayer and lectures, which would help them observe Ramadan and resist attractions such as drinking and nightclubs.

One Ramadan evening at the Islamic Institute was different from others, featuring visitors from Lebanon whose presentation was videotaped. After reciting a prayer, Shaykh al-Zayn introduced a man from the Sadr Foundation and a shaykh from the Amal political party. The former spoke about the foundation's history, the life of Musa al-Sadr, Israeli occupation of southern Lebanon, and the good works of charity the foundation carries out, such as providing vocational schools, orphanages, and other philanthropic institutions to less fortunate Lebanese Shiʿa. He listed a number of other organizations throughout Lebanon, insisting on the importance of donations. He mentioned that Ayatollah al-Sistani had recently decreed khums could be paid directly to charity organizations, and he encouraged the audience to give money to charities in Lebanon. He showed a short film on the Sadr Foundation. The film began with scenery from the south of Lebanon, where the institute is based, and the women next to me exclaimed nostalgically, "How beautiful is Lebanon!" Lebanese in Senegal often speak longingly of Lebanon's exquisiteness, the country's abundance of fruit and vegetables unavailable in West Africa, the wealth of historical landmarks, and the magnificence of the Mediterranean Sea.

When the film was over, Shaykh al-Zayn discussed a hadith on charity, highlighting that Muslim countries were more strongly based on giving charity than Christian countries, and how important the Sadr Foundation is for Lebanon. He concluded by mentioning the charity work he and the Lebanese community undertook in Senegal, specifically the scholarships of College al-Zahra, Arabic Language Institute, and 130 *madaris* (Islamic schools) he founded throughout the country for Senegalese villagers. He thanked the two men for their visit, and mentioned that Nabih Berri, Lebanese speaker of parliament and leader of the Amal party, would soon be coming to visit Senegal's Lebanese community. The floor was opened to questions, and one man remarked that Lebanese in Senegal are also poor and need money, and that they have their own problems with education. Ramadan thus served not only as a time of fasting to reach a closeness to God and reflect on those less fortunate but also to bring Lebanese in Senegal closer to Lebanon, unintentionally causing them to lament their own misfortunes in the diaspora.

Mawlud

Not all holidays at the Islamic Institute are solemn affairs. The celebration of *Mawlud*, Prophet Muhammad's birthday, was a festive occasion. The lecture hall was decorated in colorful balloons and signs with "Allah" and "Muhammad" written in tinsel or typical holiday greetings wishing *kul ʿam wa intum bi-khayr* and *ʿid mubarak*. Children stood at the entrance of the women's section holding brightly colored signs with these greetings, and women handed roses to each mother, compliments of the Arabic Language Institute.[14] The room was crowded with children;

Mawlud was the only mixed-sex event at the Islamic Institute where women out-numbered men. More Senegalese Muslims were also in attendance than usual. A prominent group of invitees sat at the front of the hall: the Lebanese ambassador, the Maronite Catholic priest, a government official representing Senegalese President Abdoulaye Wade, and an Iranian shaykh.

The evening began with a Senegalese girl chanting Qurʾanic verses. Shaykh al-Zayn then introduced the Maronite Catholic Lebanese ambassador, who spoke briefly about how the holiday represents freedom for Southern Lebanon from Israel. He invited the audience to his residence the following week to celebrate Lebanese independence.[15] A group of female students, one Lebanese girl among Senegalese classmates, sang a song, their performance followed by that of another school group, this time comprised of mostly Lebanese and a few Senegalese students. The director of the Arabic Language Institute then spoke about the need to learn Arabic. He praised his school's students and called upon a group of children to present bouquets of flowers to the Lebanese ambassador, Senegalese official, and Maronite priest. Another group of students stood with colored banners and sang a song. The Senegalese official was invited to speak, and began with a few Arabic greetings before switching to French.[16] He thanked everyone in attendance and raved about how *Sénégalo-Libanais* were well integrated in Senegal. Afterward a group of Lebanese men in their twenties and thirties performed a skit. The religious parody where one played the Prophet and others characterized his companions had the audience rolling in laughter. A Lebanese girl then recited a poem about her mother, and the evening ended with distribution of juice boxes, bottled water, and plates of Lebanese pastries, marble cake, macaroons, dough-nuts, cookies flavored with sesame seeds, and cakes scented with anise. Every child in attendance received a wrapped gift.

This combination of holidays is important. Merging the celebration of the Prophet's birthday with the independence of the south of Lebanon and Mother's Day connected a religious holiday, a secular national holiday, and a secular international celebration. The introduction of the formal commemoration of ʿAshura, Ramadan, and Mawlud in Senegal is an example of Shaykh al-Zayn's attempt to set up what Cohen (1969) referred to as a *ritual community*. The rise of Shiʿi nationalism in Lebanon became informally articulated in Senegal "in terms of religious ideologies, symbols, myths, attitudes, loyalties, ceremonial, and power structure" (141). Direct contact with Lebanon, through the visiting khatiba, leaders of Lebanon's Shiʿi political parties, the well-respected Sadr Foundation, and the Lebanese ambassador, transformed religious events into national ones. It is ironic that these rituals also helped to constitute Senegal as *not home* for the Lebanese. Furthermore, unlike the unity that resulted from this process for Cohen's example of Hausa migrants in Yoruba towns, in Dakar such ritualization served to distance Lebanese Christians from their Muslim compatriots (Leichtman 2013), as Lebanese Shiʿi politics were articulated alongside Islamic rituals.

Recent Ties to Lebanon

Some Lebanese Shiʿa in Senegal have learned from Shaykh al-Zayn how to be Shiʿi Muslims. Recent contact with Lebanon, on either Lebanese or Senegalese soil, reinforces the meaning of being Shiʿa. Many members of second and third generations have never been to Lebanon, but my research suggests that one need not frequent Lebanon in order to maintain Lebanese identity.

In addition to becoming practicing Muslims, many Lebanese of Senegal became more knowledgeable about Middle Eastern politics. Such interests have been spurred by recent availability of Lebanese satellite television in Senegal, in particular Hizbullah's channel, al-Manar. The channel consists of news programs followed by political propaganda, evoking images of the collaboration of Hizbullah, Hamas, Lebanon, and the Palestinians against Israel and the United States. Graphic photos projected a message of absolutism, that Hizbullah's goals of resistance are nonnegotiable, a message that at times contradicted the ethnic unity and religious coexistence of Lebanese in Senegal. Al-Manar flashed nationalist images across viewers' television screens of martyrs, men wearing explosives around their waists, people throwing stones, veiled women mourning, and dead Israeli soldiers. One image portrayed an outline of the map of Israel in the background with a man carrying the Palestinian flag in the foreground. Men flew from the sky on cables holding Hizbullah flags, Sayyid Hasan Nasrallah spoke for the Palestinian cause, and soldiers dressed in black uniforms marched over a painting of the American flag on the street. Chants of *allahu akbar* (God is great) or Qurʾan recitations sounded in the background. Visuals evoking Lebanese martyrdom, nature, and Islam were interspersed with these other messages: birds, flowers, a sunset, the ocean, the kaʿba, Jerusalem's al-Aqsa mosque. Religion for the Lebanese was suddenly and very visually linked to Middle Eastern politics.

Al-Manar brought Lebanon to Senegal, but Lebanese from Senegal were also brought to Lebanon. Rise in marriages between men in Senegal and women from villages in southern Lebanon (especially after the Lebanese Civil War) increased contact between the populations. The engagement ceremony of a Lebanese couple from Senegal was celebrated twice: first in the bride's family's village of origin in Lebanon (captured on videotape for the family in Senegal) and second in Dakar. Lebanese from the south of Lebanon who married in the diaspora had charity boxes at weddings to collect donations for villages of origin in Lebanon, in particular to provide food and supplies during Israeli occupation. Kamil acquired a video on the occupation during a visit to Lebanon shortly after Israeli withdrawal in 2000, which he circulated among Shiʿa in Senegal to update them on Lebanese politics. The community in Dakar also signed a petition in support of Lebanese efforts against Israel. When a Lebanese man born in Senegal died in Lebanon, the Shiʿi ceremony on the seventh day after his death was conducted by Shaykh al-Zayn at the Islamic Institute in Dakar, videotaped by his family in Senegal, and sent to relatives in Lebanon. Lebanese in Senegal shared experiences in Lebanon with those who had not been. They raved about Lebanese wonders, such as the Jeita Grotto, the largest natural cave in the Middle East. They also recounted negative experiences. One man from Kaolack had been interned in al-Khiam prison for ten years during a visit to Lebanon "for no apparent reason," he told me. The Israeli-run prison was closed in 1999 and taken over by Hizbullah in 2000, becoming a highly politicized tourist site.

Due to economic difficulties in Lebanon, some young men who recently arrived in Dakar open shops and restaurants with loans from Hizbullah, which they can pay back upon establishing themselves. Senegal has become a destination for Lebanese officials. Hizbullah deputies visit annually and speak at the Islamic Institute about the need for stronger political and economic relations between Lebanese in Africa and Lebanon. In March 2004, Nabih Berri, Lebanese speaker of parliament and leader of the Amal party, visited Senegal at the invitation of the president of the Senegalese National Assembly. This official diplomatic visit of Lebanon's highest-ranking Shiʿi politician was publicized in the Senegalese press: "According to the [Lebanese] ambassador, this visit is consistent with excellent relations that have traditionally existed between Senegal and Lebanon. It is an indication of strengthening bilateral cooperation between the two countries. Senegal has been home to a significant Lebanese community since the 19th century. The goal of the Lebanese speaker of parliament's visit is reasserting the will of both countries to maintain their cooperation. This is the first official visit in ten years of such a high Lebanese office-holder to Senegal" (Cissé 2004). In recognition of Berri's visit, Dakar's municipal council renamed Tolbiac Street, in a commercial sector lined with Lebanese shops, "Rue du Liban." This street naming "glorified more than one century of relations between Lebanon and our country. It attests to the perfect integration of the Lebanese community in all structures of economic, social, cultural, and, indeed, spiritual life in Senegal" (Tall 2004).[17] Berri used the occasion of his diplomatic visit to discuss Middle Eastern and Islamic politics with President Wade and to further encourage Shiʿi identity among Senegal's Lebanese, addressing the community at the Islamic Institute and a dinner hosted by the Lebanese ambassador and Dakar's wealthy and influential Lebanese.[18]

The test for how much ties had increased with Lebanon was the July 2006 Lebanon War. As Elizabeth Picard writes in her 2007 coedited volume on the war (which I found in Dakar's largest Lebanese-run bookstore), Hizbullah is both a national resistance body and transnational political organization.[19] Like Lebanese in diasporas all over the world, Lebanese in Senegal were deeply saddened and out-raged by the war and some had family members who were affected or had gone on vacation to Lebanon and were caught in the conflict. Unlike the Lebanese Civil War, which Lebanese in Senegal followed in a detached manner through the re-porting of French television, the round-the-clock reporting by al-Manar and the horrific images of death and destruction it displayed moved Lebanese in Senegal to action.

The July 20 march on the streets of Dakar received much coverage in Sene-galese newspapers. As one subtitle declared: "The conflict in the Middle East is exported to Africa."[20] Shaykh al-Zayn was quoted in another article: "As God said in the Qurʾan, 'the prayer of the oppressed is unstoppable, so we pray.' And this is why we are demanding of all mosques in Senegal to pray for the libera-tion of Lebanon, to pray for the martyrs, to devote tomorrow's sermons to this problem."[21] The Lebanese shaykh even addressed the Senegalese president during the march: "President Wade must ask all other presidents to turn up their noses [bouder] at the UN Security Council and to subsequently close the Israeli embassy in Senegal."[22] The director of the Department of Central and West Africa in the Israeli Ministry of Foreign Affairs responded: "I don't think this [Lebanese] com-munity should dictate to Senegal its foreign diplomacy."[23]

Lebanese efforts to target Dakar's Israeli embassy eventually lost ground, but this event was significant in marking how the Arab-Israeli conflict played out in Senegal for the first time through the leadership of Shaykh al-Zayn. Furthermore, on August 3, 2006, a silent vigil took place at Dakar's Independence Square, where Lebanese and some Senegalese lit hundreds of candles commemorating war vic-tims pictured on placards. Those in attendance signed their names in solidarity. Included was a large poster stating "Qana: No Comment" with the image of a blue Jewish star and sketch of a mutilated body. Commemorating the second Qana massacre was especially meaningful because many Lebanese in Senegal originated from the south of Lebanon, including the village of Qana.[24] Youth draped Senega-lese and Hizbullah flags over their backs, while others wore T-shirts of the Leba-nese flag with the image of a clenched fist next to the cedar tree commanding, "Résistons!" Some women dressed as they would for ʿAshura—all in black wear-ing a headband with the Arabic words ya Husayn. This symbolism, along with the sign evoking resistance, is important, as Lebanese in Senegal joined those in Lebanon in following the ideology of Hizbullah (and Khomeini) in not passively accepting their persecution as Shiʿa.[25]

When I returned to Senegal the following summer, "Résistons!" placards could still be found in homes and shops in addition to posters of Nasrallah with the Arabic saying anta al-nasr (you are the victory), a play on Nasrallah's name and the word for victory in Arabic. Although an occasional Lebanese individual in

Vigil in memory of the victims of the 2006 Lebanon War, Dakar, August 3, 2006. A Lebanese woman (holding candle) is dressed as she would during ʿAshura. Lebanese embassy in Senegal website.

Senegal could previously be found with a Hizbullah keychain or refrigerator magnet, such images of Lebanese Shiʿi resistance were never so numerous or prominently displayed in Dakar as during and after the 2006 war.

The war was not the only Lebanese political event commemorated in Senegal. Hizbullah and Amal deputies came to Dakar in May 2007 for the celebration of the liberation of the south of Lebanon (May 25, 2000). Although this reception takes place annually at the Lebanese ambassador's residence, this year it was hosted at the more spacious Sporting Club because a larger audience than usual was expected.[26] There were many speeches as well as a poet who performed readings about Hizbullah and Lebanon. Deputies spoke about Lebanon's latest tensions resulting from the siege of Nahr al-Barid Palestinian refugee camp near Tripoli, condemned attacks on the Lebanese army by al-Qaʾida–affiliated Fatah al-Islam organization, and declared that Lebanon would survive this latest conflict. Although the July 2006 march and August vigil were the only public Lebanese demonstrations in Dakar, the Islamic Institute and Maronite Mission held several private religious services over the previous four years commemorating "martyrs" of Lebanon, including Prime Minister Rafik Hariri, killed on February 14, 2005; Ji-

Lebanese woman signing name in solidarity with victims of 2006 Lebanon War, Dakar, August 3, 2006. Lebanese flag with image of clenched fist next to the cedar tree commands, "Resist!" Lebanese embassy in Senegal website.

bran Twayni, a parliamentarian assassinated in December 2005; and Pierre Jumayil, an anti-Syrian cabinet minister and Christian leader killed in November 2006. There were also more general commemorations for all Lebanese who died during the 2006 war and Nahr al-Barid struggle in June 2007.[27] Although Lebanese religious institutions in Senegal denounced violence in Lebanon and officially commemorated martyrs regardless of religion, the war led to a divide between Shiʿi Muslims and Christians. The latter were outraged at the destruction of Lebanon yet blamed Hizbullah for provoking Israeli attacks and feared Nasrallah's increasing power. When I conducted initial fieldwork in Senegal (between 2000 and 2004) I never heard such talk about Lebanese politics. This latest war in Lebanon further altered the delicate balance between religion and secular ethnicity among members of the Lebanese diaspora in Senegal. Although the war heightened sectarian tensions between Shiʿi Muslims and Christians in Senegal, Christians in Lebanon were split in two, with some joining the Hizbullah-led alliance along with many Shiʿi Muslims, and others joining the Hariri-led alliance with numerous Sunni Muslims (Norton 2007:152–153).

Back to Islam or Back to Lebanon?

How successful was Shaykh al-Zayn in bringing Lebanese Shiʿa "back to Islam"? The shaykh takes pride in the fact that Lebanese Muslims in Senegal are learning about their religion, and many have begun to pray, fast, pay religious taxes, wear the veil, volunteer in charity work, and leave drugs and alcohol behind. He preaches an Islam that adapts to the modern day and stresses religious tolerance, following Musa al-Sadr's efforts for a Lebanon for all Lebanese. The shaykh understood that inclusive, rather than exclusive, religious politics would be most successful in Senegal. He welcomed Sunni Muslims into his institution, and joined Christians in affairs concerning the Lebanese community as a whole. Yet Lebanese Shiʿa in Senegal are a piously imperfect community. Although the shaykh envisions his work to have made a significant difference, not every community member agrees that he has impacted the Shiʿi community as a whole.

Not all Muslims go to the Islamic Institute. Shaykh al-Zayn's greatest following is among businessmen with little formal education; he has less appeal among Senegal's Lebanese professionals with diplomas from Western universities. A woman not regularly present at the shaykh's lectures informed me that some attend because they need him to read prayers for them. A minority of Lebanese literate in Arabic prefer to pray at home. For example, when I was visiting Fuad, a Senegalese client entered his store and asked if he prayed. The Lebanese biscuit wholesaler replied that he prays in the morning. The client responded that he should pray five times a day for Senegal's future. Fuad cleverly retorted that he prays only once a day, but on carbon paper that produces five copies!

Others have no interest in attending the Islamic Institute. Some youth note this; in the words of Muhsin, on holiday from university in France to visit his family in Dakar, "God is dead!" Many Lebanese of his generation, especially those with a Western education, do not pray, fast during Ramadan, or observe other Islamic requirements, which they perceive not to be "modern." Muhsin informed me that this notion arises when Lebanese youth observe how Senegalese pray in the middle of the street (which in Dakar's commercial areas is polluted with rotting garbage) on a piece of cardboard or burlap sack, if not on a prayer rug. Such a sight disgusts certain Lebanese, who remark that Senegalese do not understand laws of Islamic purity, and it turns off these youth from prayer. While some Lebanese in their twenties and thirties who recently became more observant do populate the Islamic Institute alongside middle-aged and elderly, others prefer to maintain their lifestyles. One man refers to himself as a "modern Muslim," who drinks, goes dancing, and likes women. The shaykh strives to eliminate such sin, not always successfully.

Other Lebanese renounce the commemoration of ʿAshura. The former president of Alliance, a doctor, declared that he was born and raised Shiʿi but that does not guide his life, and he does not need to cry for Husayn 1,400 years after his death. He agreed, however, that it is important to remember that Husayn was killed at Karbala, just as Jews remember the Holocaust and French should be reminded occasionally that Catholics killed Protestants at St. Bartholemy. For him, Shiʿi identity is an unconscious factor. His Shiʿi origins are perhaps the reason why he feels injustice or has certain reactions, but he does not need to actively participate in reliving each year the martyrdom of Husayn. Jamila, the politician active in grassroots causes, felt that Shiʿa were "fanatics" in following ʿAli, and exaggerate when they mourn the death of Husayn by beating their chests and crying for ten days. She told me that when her mother died she cried, but not for ten days. She believes in God and has faith, but does not practice her religion, and if anyone asks, Jamila proclaims to be Muslim, not *Shiʿi* Muslim.

The community perceives illiteracy in Arabic as another obstacle to religiosity. Most of the first and second generation can speak the Lebanese dialect but cannot read or write standard Arabic. They are literate in French and fluent in Wolof, the languages they use for everyday transactions and interactions with Senegalese society. Whereas Shaykh al-Zayn conducts Friday sermons in standard Arabic, for him a religious necessity, all other lectures are delivered in the Lebanese dialect. The books he writes in Arabic are translated or transliterated into French for Lebanese in Senegal. Amal told me she believes in God and has faith but does not practice her religion because she does not understand Arabic; prayer is therefore meaningless to her. Bashir is ashamed of his illiteracy in Arabic and inability to read Qurʾan, which he refuses to read in French translation, believing the holy book to be impure in any language other than the language of Islam. The Arabic Language Institute has not had great success in increasing Arabic literacy in Senegal among French-educated Lebanese. This struggle with Arabic, the language of Islam and of their homeland, is a source of dishonor and humiliation for many, especially when confronted by those from Lebanon.

As a community, Senegal's Lebanese Shiʿa lack the religious knowledge, literacy in Arabic, and commitment to practicing their faith to enable Shaykh al-Zayn's goals of bringing Lebanese "back" to Islam to be fully realized. Their transformation, however, can be understood in another way. In creating a "ritual community" of Lebanese Muslims in Senegal, and through this ritual component stressing the wider meaning of belonging to a community of Shiʿa, Shaykh al-Zayn has succeeded in making them better Lebanese. I return to the question I raised earlier about what happens when religion migrates. The spiritual journey of Lebanese Shiʿa in Senegal can be interpreted as a "return migration" to Lebanon. This occasionally involves actual travel to the homeland but more often only an ideological return to their roots as the homeland migrates to Senegal. The shaykh's powerful sermons, lessons from Lebanese textbooks, visitors from Lebanon, marriages with women from southern Lebanon, and stories told by others who have gone "back" inform Lebanese who have never been to Lebanon about their country, implanting in them the ethno-religious pride of being Lebanese. Furthermore, satellite television has illustrated the shaykh's efforts more forcefully than he ever intended. The nationalist message of Hizbullah's channel informs Lebanese in Senegal of their history, rise to power, and current struggles, exemplified by the 2006 war. This leads to tensions in Senegal between Lebanese Shiʿa and Christians or Sunnis who do not sympathize with Shiʿi political endeavors. Frictions go beyond the shaykh's attempt to teach Shiʿi pride through religious accommodation in Senegal.

Exposure to cross-regional Shiʿi forces has resulted in Lebanese in Senegal more strongly identifying as *Lebanese* Shiʿa. Some are tied to Shiʿa around the world through affiliating with marajiʿ such as Ayatollah al-Sistani in Iraq or visiting Shiʿi shrines in Iran. The commemoration of ʿAshura in Senegal, part of a larger movement of Shiʿi revitalization inspired by the Iranian Revolution, reminds them of Shiʿi tragedies in Iraq of both the past and present day. Yet Lebanese in Senegal are connected with Lebanon through the arrival of the khatiba and Hizbullah's al-Manar channel, and the ʿAshura story has most recently been applied to the 2006 war in Lebanon. Despite empathy with Shiʿa around the world, Islamic holidays in Senegal are used to further Lebanese Shiʿi causes, such as giving charity to the Sadr Foundation and celebrating the independence of the south of Lebanon. Transnational Islam for Lebanese in Senegal is thus a Lebanese Shiʿi Islam. The Senegalese example suggests that when Islam travels to another Islamic context it is sometimes the national over the religious that becomes the focus of migrant identity. Such a finding diverges from the literature on (Sunni) Muslim minority communities in the West. The Senegalese case stresses the importance of research among Shiʿi minority groups, whose identity politics differ from Sunni Muslims, and south–south migrant communities, who construct networks and identities from what Tsing (1993) has called "out-of-the-way" places.

It is difficult to separate Lebanese religious and political transnationalisms. These boundaries are further blurred by the incorporation of Lebanese sectarian organizations such as Hizbullah in the Lebanese parliament and their transformation into political bodies that garner financial and ideological support from coreligionists in the diaspora, who are not (yet) permitted an absentee vote in home-country elections. How does the diaspora transform institutions of the polity and its conception of membership? This chapter has described the spread of the Arab-Israeli conflict to Senegal. Although researchers predict that transnational ties will weaken among children of migrants (in the West), I have demonstrated that this depends on global political contexts and levels of security and sentiments of where "home" is located for migrants and descendants in country of residence (Levitt and Glick Schiller 2004). This is the case for Lebanese in Senegal, who, while demonstrating against the war in Lebanon—showing political support outside of formal government ties and reaffirming their claim to be part of Lebanon—also felt obliged to demonstrate their autochthony and reinforce their loyalty to Senegal, where the future of their community is uncertain.

Expanding on Mandaville's reasoning, *traveling Islam* is not only "travel *within* Islam*" (2001:109) but also travel across time and space, spanning a community's past, present, and future and, especially in the case of Shiʿi Islam, is inextricably linked to national identity and a secular struggle for equality, human rights, and, at times, self-determination, in addition to power politics. For Lebanese Shiʿa in Senegal, being part of a community still matters, but this does not mean a sense of greater belonging to the all-encompassing Muslim umma, understood by some scholars as the Muslim diaspora-at-large (Mandaville 2001; Roy 2004; Sayyid 2000). The ideology of the umma disintegrates in the face of a Muslim minority's discourse of and responses to political marginalization by the Muslim majority host society. Lebanese Shiʿa in Senegal belong instead to a particular community with ethnic, religious, and national (albeit transnational) boundaries. This community, rooted in Dakar's Islamic Institute, is led by Shaykh al-Zayn, who is a representative of Lebanon. Despite Roy's (2004) insistence that Islamic religious debates in the diaspora are no longer monopolized by the learned ʿulama, I have demonstrated that Islamic authorities have not lost their influence. Shaykh al-Zayn facilitates religious and political ties with the homeland. Ties are fluid and redrawn over time and in response to global events. Hizbullah has become a transnational organization while remaining a symbol of Lebanese national resistance by reaching out to particular communities of Lebanese Shiʿa around the world. Transnational loyalties therefore predominate over other diasporic religious identities, bringing Lebanese in Senegal to action over the destruction of Lebanon and in a declaration of allegiance to the motherland.

Yet Hizbullah's specific political agenda became diluted in its transformation into a transnational resistance movement, just as al-Qaʾida's politics became lost in a global fragmented arena (Devji 2008). In Lebanon, the war brought about an increase in sectarian divisions. Certain Christians and Sunni Muslims were outraged at the destruction, yet blamed Hizbullah for provoking Israeli attacks and feared Nasrallah's increasing power. The war reemphasized the divergence of the Maronite vision of Lebanon from Hizbullah's nationalism, which pushed for an Islamic and Arab nation (Shaery-Eisenlohr 2008). Politics were heightened as well among Senegal's Lebanese Christians, who quietly objected to the increasing pro-Hizbullah sentiments of their Shiʿi neighbors. In response, some backed former general Michel Aoun, the Maronite member of parliament who leads Lebanon's Free Patriotic Movement and publicly aspires to be a *secular* Lebanese leader.[28] Despite his declared secular leanings, Aoun is a divisive figure, in particular resulting from his surprise alliance with Hizbullah in 2006 (and break with other Maronite politicians in the March 14 coalition). Lebanese in Senegal had noticeably become more politicized as a result of the 2006 war, and, for the first time, some even voted in the 2009 Lebanese general elections.[29]

On the one hand, the cosmopolitanism of Lebanese in Senegal was linked to a distinct *Lebanese* ethnic identity not fully detached from wider politics of sectarianism in Lebanon. On the other hand, this very cosmopolitanism enabled unity as a *secular* Lebanese ethnic group in order to claim in Senegal what McGovern (2013:67) has termed *fictive autochthony*, constructed from the community's long history and economic, political, and cultural contributions. The 2006 Lebanon War impinged on this harmony, indicative of difficulties faced by Lebanese religious institutions in the diaspora in continuing to embrace secularism and distance themselves from sectarian politics in Lebanon. Yet the war with Israel, while having arguably weakened the Lebanese nation-state, had conceivably strengthened national identity among Lebanese in the diaspora, who became more emotionally tied to the embattled homeland. Lebanese Shiʿa in Senegal were moved above all by the ethics of Hizbullah. Its Islamist politics aside, Hizbullah stepped up against Israel, taking charge of a failed state, to protect Lebanese human rights and provide humanitarian services to war victims. Despite the intertwining of Lebanese nationalism and Shiʿi Islam in Senegal, this aspect of Hizbullah's message has universal appeal. Lebanese Christians are also too small a minority for the community cohesion that has characterized Lebanese as an ethnic group not to persevere in Senegal. Shiʿi cosmopolitanism is thus distinct from yet also shaped by *national religion*—which remains inherently tied to state politics and, in the Lebanese case, sectarian nationalism (Leichtman 2013).

PART II

SENEGALESE CONVERSION TO SHIʿI ISLAM

5 The Vernacularizaton of Shiʿi Islam
Competition and Conflict

> Placing West Africa's past connections to the Mediterranean world and its
> Islamic legacy right at the center of our conception of Africa is crucial to
> overcome this microcosmic vision and broaden our horizon.
>
> —Mahir Şaul, "Islam and West African Anthropology"

IF WE EXPAND emphasis on the Mediterranean world to the Middle East as a
whole, Şaul's statement, which reflects Launay's (2004) insistence that the study
of Islam in Africa should not be viewed as the periphery to the Middle Eastern
core, can be taken as a starting point for examining the complex relationship between Senegal, Lebanon, and Iran. While on the rise, studies of Islam in Africa
remain secondary to scholarship on Islam in the Middle East and even Asia, and
anthropology continues to perceive of Islam as extrinsic to indigenous African
cultures. Anthropologists initially took little interest in Islam in Africa, seen as
insufficiently exotic by comparison with other, more "authentic" African beliefs,
such as "witchcraft" and "traditional" religion. They preferred instead to roman-
ticize the era before the spread of Islam, thereby ignoring Africa as part of Islamic
heritage. As a result, few studies have fully investigated religious linkages between
Africa and the Middle East.

Thus far this book has focused on the Lebanese community in Senegal. It is
my goal to move beyond a typical community study to write instead an ethnography of a religious movement. The following chapters will therefore focus on
the spread of Shiʿi ideas to West African Muslims and Senegalese "conversion"
to Shiʿi Islam. Local and global loyalties and identities intersect and are strategically manipulated in dissimilar ways for Lebanese migrants and Senegalese converts. The Lebanese model of cosmopolitanism embraces religious difference in
the formation of a "secular" Lebanese ethnic group, struggling to leave sectarian tensions in Lebanon. Exclusion from Senegalese society simultaneously led
to increasing political solidarity with Lebanon while enhancing efforts to estab-

lish "fictive" autochthony in Senegal. Cosmopolitanism plays out very differently for Senegalese converts, who choose to follow a foreign minority religion as the most "authentic" branch of Islam. In contrast to the growing awareness of "Senegalese of Lebanese origin" of Lebanese Shi'i politics, Senegalese Shi'a separate the religion from Middle Eastern politics in order to demonstrate that Shi'i Islam can be autochthonous to Senegalese religious life and contribute to the African public good. This chapter will contextualize the small but growing community of Senegalese Shi'a within the larger context of Sunni reformist movements in Senegal.

Shi'a in Senegal are connected to global religious networks through two major influences: Shaykh al-Zayn ties them to Lebanon, and indirectly to Iraq, and the Iranian embassy and nongovernmental organizations bring Iranian religious ideologies to Dakar.[1] As it has for Senegalese Shi'a, the Iranian Revolution has also inspired Senegalese Sunni Muslim reformists. Competition is emerging over who will shape the new Shi'i movement: Lebanon or Iran. Tension between Arab and Iranian schools of Shi'i thought results from political views: a majority of theologians in Iran follow Ayatollah Khomeini's notion of wilayat al-faqih. Khomeini's argument in favor of Islamic government denounced monarchies and gave religious judges the divine right to rule. Many Lebanese Shi'a do not support this view or the propagation of the Iranian Revolution. Senegalese Shi'a acknowledge that wilayat al-faqih is unlikely to develop in Senegal, yet some are in favor of the Iranian model, hoping one day to find their place in Senegal's political system, currently (and unofficially) dominated by Sufi marabouts.

Western scholarship often portrays Senegal's Sufi marabouts as all-knowing intermediaries between talibes and God, who have the role of purifying or simplifying basic Islamic teachings to make them more accessible to nonliterate Muslims. The ultimate social, political, and economic power granted to these marabouts and their occasional abuses of power led to Muslim reformists, both Sunni and Shi'i, contesting hierarchies of Sufi orders in Senegal. Disciples displeased with their marabout can pledge their vows to another. Choosing a branch of Islam from outside Senegal enables Senegalese to escape local adaptations and hierarchies of Islam. Throughout the Muslim world there is a tendency to return to earlier practices of Islam perceived as a solution to failures attributed to Western influence and innovations (bid'a) in recent Islamic practice. It is this desire for "true" knowledge about Islam in a return to scriptural sources that drove some Senegalese Muslims to read religious and legal books, visit Islamic scholars and clerics seeking "the truth" about their religion, and learn about other ways of being Muslim. Such movements in Africa are not a recent or foreign phenomenon but go back several generations to an older Sufi tradition of reform (Loimeier 2003).

Origins of reformist groups in Senegal can be traced to the gradual concentration in urban areas of students who returned from studying abroad in religious centers of the Middle East and North Africa. Referred to as *Arabisants*, these young

men were fluent in Arabic, well versed in textual Islam, and often unable to succeed in Senegal's Francophone modern sector. Many became Arabic teachers in
Senegal's secondary schools. They were also likely recruits for Islamic reformist
movements, and various associations of Arabisants formed as early as the 1930s.
Villalón (1995) writes that these groups are both potentially useful and threatening to the Senegalese state. Their critique of the maraboutic system served the
state in offsetting the power of marabouts, and their Islamic ties gained the secular
Senegalese government international aid. Yet assistance from "radical" religious
groups also challenged the state, as the following chapters explore.

Foreign Shiʿi Leaders, Senegalese Disciples

Early in his career Shaykh al-Zayn did not have access to a body of Lebanese who
were well educated in matters of Islam and connected with Senegalese religious
authorities. Instead he drew on the expertise of Senegalese who were knowledgeable and influential in local Islamic affairs. Barham Diop, Président des Ulémas
du Sénégal et du Maroc in Dakar, assisted Shaykh al-Zayn with public discourse.[2]
Diop used to live in Kaolack and served for twenty-five years as Shaykh Ibrahim
Niass's religious secretary. Diop traveled all over the world representing Niass in
this public position and became quickly known to Lebanese in Kaolack, whom he
easily befriended because of their commonality in speaking the Arabic language.
Diop was present during Musa al-Sadr's visit to Kaolack. He informed me that
al-Sadr paved the way for Shaykh al-Zayn, leaving instructions for him to meet
Niass to assist him in building educational institutions. Al-Sadr requested that
Lebanese contribute to building the Tijani Tivaouane mosque. After Shaykh al-
Zayn established himself in Senegal, he maintained contact with Diop, who would
occasionally pray in Shaykh al-Zayn's mosque even though the Shiʿi prayer was
different. Shaykh al-Zayn even planned to construct a large Islamic university in
Senegal, but this never materialized due to the aftermath of the Iranian Revolution and criticism of Shiʿi Islam. When Musa al-Sadr's sister, Rabab al-Sadr, visited Senegal after his disappearance in Libya, she offered Diop a watch with the
face of her brother that appeared and disappeared leaving the words "Why Libya?"

When Shaykh al-Zayn traveled, Diop or another Senegalese Sunni Muslim
would lead prayer and conduct funerals for Lebanese until a second Shiʿi shaykh
arrived from Lebanon. Some of these Senegalese men who assisted Shaykh al-Zayn
were among the first to learn about Shiʿi Islam; others such as Diop never left their
Sunni ways. Today the shaykh employs Senegalese Shiʿa as teachers in the Arabic
Language Institute and one Senegalese Shiʿi shaykh leads prayers during Islamic
holidays in the Islamic Institute. Some of these men are responsible for spreading
messages from Shaykh al-Zayn to other converts in their community. Others consult with the shaykh on religious issues. One man asked the shaykh's assistance in
fine-tuning points he argued on radio programs about Shiʿi Islam. He explains:

"I did not learn about Shiʿi Islam in Shiʿi schools. With the help of the [Shiʿi] literature, I was able to convert the knowledge I had acquired in other schools to broaden my [Islamic] culture to intervene with authority in [religious] debates. Once you contribute very effectively, the next step is to present your views to the shaykh. If there are points that must be rectified he lets you know. Sometimes he even asks us questions about legal issues." Another Senegalese Shiʿi, particularly well connected with the Senegalese government, was sent to negotiate Shaykh al-Zayn's diplomatic status and assist with other state bureaucracy.

Shaykh al-Zayn was not always successful in training Senegalese in the Shiʿi tradition. Diop recounted that an imam in a village near Thies who was friends with the shaykh sent his son to study in Lebanon for seven years. When the imam died his son led the village in prayer. After his fifth Friday sermon, the community demanded that he clarify what religion he represented as his sermons insulted Sunni Caliphs Abu Bakr, ʿUmar, and ʿUthman as well as Muhammad's wife ʿAisha. The community requested another imam when the son explained he criticized the Prophet's companions out of respect for ʿAli. I was likewise informed that some Senegalese parents withdrew children from College al-Zahra upon learning it was a Shiʿi school. Students were initially enrolled because parents believed foreign schools were more serious than Senegalese-run schools, but were uncomfortable grounding children in religious traditions other than their own.

Senegalese Shiʿa respect Shaykh al-Zayn, seek out his expertise, and appreciate the religious work he achieved in Senegal.

> We have relations with Shaykh al-Zayn because he is our imam; on Fridays we pray behind him. We often have meetings with him. He teaches us because he has much more knowledge than we do about Islam. So we come to him and discuss certain topics with him. If we have questions to clarify he answers them; he is easy to understand and he is very open and kind with us. That is the nature of our relationship with him. It is a fraternal relationship between shaykhs; it is also about someone who is there, who is a highly respected authority.

Senegalese Shiʿa also claim to have excellent relations with the Lebanese community.

> These are fraternal relations between one Muslim and another who live together in a country. Among us there are some who have Lebanese friends, very close friends. So these are interpersonal relationships on an individual level. We have no institutional or associational relationships with Lebanese. . . . We pray together, greet one another . . . but we have never collaborated to organize anything together because this community is much more interested in business and is not very activist.

They bring this separation of religious activities back to French colonial policy. "As you know the French always prevented Muslim unity. They decided that Lebanese settlement would not translate into their full integration into the native population; they successfully achieved goals by imposing many restrictions." Yet Senegalese converts state that French policy of the past is no excuse for Lebanese lack of religious knowledge in the present. Despite Shaykh al-Zayn training "Senegalese who were more interested in religion than the Lebanese community," converts complained that the shaykh's work remained limited to Lebanese, who brought him to Senegal and financed his institute. There was thus an "invisible barrier" between Lebanese and Senegalese Shiʿi communities. For these reasons Senegalese Shiʿa envision Shaykh al-Zayn's leadership of their movement to be only symbolic. His activities are also limited by the Senegalese government, with which he does not want relations to sour by accusations of spreading propaganda. Senegalese hope for the emergence of an African Shiʿi leader.

Other informants attributed the spread of Shiʿi Islam in Senegal to two main reasons. As early as 1971 books in Arabic, French, and English translation began to circulate in Senegal from Iran.[3] "Before the Iranian Revolution, the Shah had been doing what Saudi Arabia is now doing, acting like petty kings [*roitelets*] of the Middle East. He would send out numerous copies of the Qurʾan, Islamic books, and many other religious items to other countries to display his love of Islam. These practices were not inaugurated by the Islamic Revolution; they started much earlier." Second, despite allegations that he was not doing enough, the Lebanese shaykh began to teach Shiʿi Islam to Senegalese.

Shaykh al-Zayn's Relations with Senegalese Muslims

The Lebanese shaykh's growing knowledge of Senegal and charismatic appeal enabled him to actively expand his influence beyond the Lebanese community to Senegal's Sufi orders. He maintains cordial friendships and political relations with Sufi marabouts. The shaykh visits Senegalese religious organizations, and their leaders visit him. He attends with a small delegation of influential Lebanese Muslims annual Sufi religious events, such as the Murid *magal* that attracts pilgrims to Tuba from all over the world, and the *gamu* celebrating the Prophet Muhammad's birthday in the Tijani center Tivaouane. He is present with a larger Lebanese delegation at special occasions such as the funeral of ʿAbdul ʿAziz Sy, the Tijani caliph and close friend of Shaykh al-Zayn. The shaykh's photo can periodically be found in Senegalese newspapers as proof of his attendance at such locally important events, attesting his status as a public figure.

He also provides financial assistance to Senegalese Muslims and teaches them about Islam. Whereas the Islamic Institute and its affiliated institutions in Dakar cater to both Lebanese and Senegalese, the shaykh founded 5 mosques and approximately 130 madaris located outside of Dakar and led by Senegalese religious scholars whom he trained.[4] Madaris range from larger schools to simple one-room learning facilities, and teach Arabic and Qurʾan to Senegalese villagers. This charitable work, however, has missionary undertones to gain Shi'i Islam a Senegalese Sufi following.

The September–October 1994 issue of *Noor Al Islam*, a bilingual Arabic-English Shi'i magazine printed in Lebanon, focused on "Senegal: Efforts to Strengthen its Deeprooted Islam." The cover story describes Shaykh al-Zayn's work among Lebanese and Senegalese communities, highlighting the number of Senegalese students in his schools and the money he contributed to building mosques, schools, and wells in (sometimes Christian) villages in southern Senegal. "During the last 25 years, a number of Senegalis [*sic*] began to adopt the Ahl el-Beit (A.S.) doctrine.[5] Moreover all Muslims in Senegal respect Ahl el-Beit Imams (A.S.). There are few thousand that have adopted the Ahl el-Beit doctrine, but we should add about 25 thousand Lebanese immigrants who have been living in Senegal for decades" (Youssef 1994:8). This publication reveals that Shaykh al-Zayn is teaching *Shi'i* Islam.

A second round of publicity for Shaykh al-Zayn occurred more recently. Divisions among Muslims have a long and complicated history since the death of the Prophet Muhammad in 632 CE, beginning with conflict over his succession. Starting with Abu Bakr, Sunni Muslims followed a series of caliphs who were the selected or elected successors of the Prophet in political and military leadership. Shi'a vested leadership in Imams, who must be direct descendants of the Prophet and 'Ali, the first Imam. Both political leader and religious guide, the Imam was final authoritative interpreter of God's will as formulated in Islamic law. The title "caliph" was also used in precolonial West Africa, such as caliph of Sokoto. In Senegal, the title "caliph" continues to be passed down from father to son in maraboutic families. The Lebanese shaykh wanted to be recognized as leader of Senegal's Shi'a, and accepted the title Caliph Ahl al-Bayt, even though "caliph" has traditionally been used for Sunni Muslim leaders.

An article in *Le Soleil*, Senegal's national newspaper, described the 2002 gamu celebrations in Tivaouane:

> Among numerous delegations to the Gamu of Tivaouane, representatives from the Lebanese community distinguished themselves in particular because head of the delegation, Shaykh 'Abdul Mun'am al-Zayn, was about to receive the title of Khalifatou Ahlou Baïty Rassoul (Caliph of the family of the Prophet Muhammad –SAWS) in Senegal.[6] The title was conferred by three caliphs from the brotherhoods, Serign Muhammad Mansur Sy [Tijaniyya], Shaykh Salih Mbacke [Muridiyya] and Shaykh Bu Muhammad Kunta of Ndiassane [Qadiriyya]. (Tall 2002)

The shaykh proudly uses the title Caliph Ahl al-Bayt, which follows his signature on all written documents. Further publicity for the shaykh was found on the front page of the December 2, 2003, *Le Messager*, one of Senegal's myriad newspapers, which advertised "Shaykh ʿAbdul Munʿam al-Zayn, A Charitable Soul. The Shaykh Achieved 130 Schools and Clinics in Senegal." A follow-up article calls him "an atypical Shiʿi Shaykh in Senegal." Here, too, his title is cited: "Consequently, the General Caliph Ahl al-Bayt is not only the spiritual guide of the Lebanese community in Senegal but of all Ahl al-Bayt followers in Senegal, West Africa, North Africa, and beyond. It is important to mention that this is the first time that a general Caliph Ahl al-Bayt is appointed for Africa and Senegal" (Seck, Diop, and Aïdara 2003). This article declares Shaykh al-Zayn to be the spiritual leader of the Lebanese community in Senegal *and* all other Shiʿa in West and North Africa.[7] Yet when I discussed the meaning of this title with Senegal's *Islamologues,* scholars who study Islam or religious men who are also academics, they revealed to me that this title has no meaning, that it does not exist elsewhere, and that the Tijani, Murid, and Qadir caliphs never agree on anything. In fact, one Islamologue confirmed, the Lebanese shaykh created this title and asked Senegalese caliphs to sign to it.

Shaykh al-Zayn's charisma is thus linked not only to knowledge of Islam but also to political astuteness. He obtained a Sunni title for his Shiʿi leadership, raising his local status to become equal (in name) to leaders of Senegal's Sufi orders. The shaykh's success is due to his cosmopolitan skill in knowing when to highlight universal Islam over a more particular Shiʿi leaning. Such language has purpose. Zaman (2005:101) writes of a new cosmopolitan Islamic language whose "importance lies in the effort to make the discursive language of the ʿulama relevant to the contemporary world or, to put it differently, to express contemporary issues and concerns in that language." He argues that ʿulama have not been marginalized nor their authority eroded, but they have been challenged to adapt discourses to new contexts and new media.

Similarly Shaykh al-Zayn's strategy to unite Lebanese Sunni and Shiʿi Muslims in Senegal as a Lebanese ethnic group is to refer to his institute as *Islamic.* When dealing with Lebanon, where sectarian conflict is strong, he is clearly identified as a *Shiʿi* shaykh and strives to be recognized as such by the international Shiʿi community. With the Senegalese population, however, his Islamic politics are subtle. The *Messenger* articles describe Shiʿa, in the shaykh's words, as followers of the Prophet's family, and stress similarities between Sunni and Shiʿi Islam, which share fundamental principles of Islam: God, Qurʾan, Prophet Muhammad, prayer, Ramadan, and pilgrimage to Mecca. Such discourse avoids tensions between the shaykh, government, and wider Senegalese population. In minimizing differences of the two Islamic schools, the shaykh hopes to attract more Senegalese followers. Yet, in describing his charitable work in Senegal, and in understanding pains taken to establish himself (at least on paper) as leader of ahl al-bayt of not only Lebanon, but also Senegal (and West and North Africa) as a whole, the shaykh stresses the Shiʿi nature of his mission. This is further highlighted by exaggerated statistics: "The Shaykh estimates that the number of Shiʿi Muslims in the country is approximately between 120,000 and 130,000. According to him, most of them have been trained in schools he opened in Dakar's suburbs and in other regions of Senegal" (Aïdara 2003). From the few thousand Senegalese Shiʿa mentioned ten years earlier, suddenly this number exponentially increased. Shaykh al-Zayn's title and these figures make him more credible to the Senegalese Shiʿi community and heighten his and Senegal's importance in international Shiʿi religious networks. Nevertheless, the actual number of Shiʿa—those who self-identify as such—is unobtainable. He also faces increasing tensions from Senegalese Shiʿa who desire indigenous Senegalese, not foreign Arab, leadership of their community. The shaykh is only one cosmopolitan leader linking Muslims in Senegal to global Shiʿi Islam. Iran serves as a second source of Senegalese Shiʿi Islamic internationalism.

Exporting the Iranian Revolution

The 1979 Islamic Revolution in Iran reverberated around the world. Muhammad Reza Shah Pahlavi's regime was overthrown by a coalition of opposition forces dominated by Shiʿi Muslim reformists, led by Ayatollah Ruhollah Khomeini (1902–1989). Since Islamic revivalists had since the late nineteenth century (without success) been advocating movement away from Western-influenced secular regimes, the revolution gave renewed impetus to their struggle and triggered a rise in political Islamic activities throughout the Muslim world (Beeman 1995).

During the early 1980s Ayatollah Khomeini elaborated a philosophy aimed at exporting the revolution. He repeated themes in speeches that formed elements of an Islamic ideology meant to engage Sunni as well as Shiʿi Muslims in one universal language while, at the same time, speaking to Shiʿi Muslims in a particularistic Shiʿi terminology (Zonis and Brumberg 1987). The universal appeal of Khomeini's message derived from emotional content and not from any prescriptive message of how to construct an Islamic polity. The Organization of Islamic Propaganda (Sazman-e Tablighat-e Eslami) and Iranian embassies engaged in spreading Islamist propaganda.

Relations with Islamic groups abroad were managed by the International Department of the Revolutionary Guards. Yearly conferences held in Tehran called for establishment of a united Islamic Front and proposed forming a political movement to propagate the revolution's ideology. The 1980 conference was composed of what Halliday called "oppressed masses and Islamic liberation movements" (1986:103) from Iraq, the Arabian Peninsula, Oman, the Canary Islands, Lebanon, Morocco, and Moro (southern Philippines). The 1984 conference included representatives from Senegal, Nigeria, and Mali.[8] Additionally, Buchta (2001) describes the foundation of Tehran's Majmaʿ al-Taqrib (Ecumenical Society) in 1990, led by a mixed Sunni and Shiʿi board of directors from Iran and abroad, including Nigeria's Ibrahim Zakzaki.[9]

What is rarely discussed in scholarship on the Iranian Revolution is that Africa was also a target for propaganda. In the 1980s, Iran's foreign minister, Ali-Akbar Velayati, established embassies throughout Africa, some of which closed in the 1990s.[10] The Iranian government carries out a modest foreign aid program in Africa, and the international Iranian television station, Sahar, broadcasts in Swahili. *Sauti ya Umma,* a colorful magazine in Swahili, was first published in Iran by the Foundation of Islamic Thought in 1985 and is distributed in African countries where Swahili is spoken. Past magazine issues explained the revolution's main trends, as well as the Iran-Iraq War (1980–1988), the killing of (mostly Iranian) Muslims in Mecca during Hajj (July 31, 1987), Saddam Hussein's use of chemical weapons against Iraq's Kurdish population (March 1988), and American policies in the Middle East. The magazine concentrates on cultural relations between Iran and East Africa and Iran's role in the history and development of Islam (Balda 1993).

Iran made other symbolic efforts to gain black support. Fischer and Abedi (1990) note that one of the stamps issued by the Islamic Republic shows a black *muezzin* calling people to prayer—and to Islam. The face of Malcolm X appeals to African Americans to join the revolution and overthrow the oppression of white American capitalist imperialism. The image also evokes Bilal, the Prophet's black companion (believed to be a freed slave from Ethiopia), as an icon of the color-blindness of Islam. Hodgkin writes: "To many African reformists, Iran was also a symbol of how all this could be done by a non-Arab state, of how the 'Ajamis' could lead the Arabs in speaking to the world in the name of Islam" (1998:203–204).

At the outset, the Iranian Revolution was perceived by Shiʿi Muslims as a Shiʿi affair, yet Sunni Muslims also claimed it as an Islamic event, impressed by the collapse of a secular state in Iran. When the revolution did not succeed in uniting Muslims around the world, Sunnis, in time, reacted by viewing it as more Iranian and Shiʿi than Islamic. Nasr concludes, writing about Pakistan, India, and Afghanistan, "the more lasting impact of the Iranian Revolution in the region has not been promotion of Islamist activism, but deep division between Shiʿis and Sunnis, a sectarian discourse of power, and deepening of social cleavages in the region" (2002:348).

Nasr's statement, however, is less applicable to Africa. Keddie (1995) conducted a survey in the Muslim world, including two African countries, Nigeria and Senegal, with regard to revolutionary tendencies. She concluded that in order for an Islamist movement to succeed, a country must have oil revenues or profits (such as remittances), rapid modernization, migration from countryside to cities, growing income gaps, upper-class conspicuous consumption, and a secular or Westernizing government with widespread popular disillusionment. She found that Nigeria fit this model, but Senegal did not and does not have a major Islamist movement. Keddie remarked that Islamists tended to at first welcome the Iranian Revolution, but later became disillusioned. The problem was that few appreciated its specific Iranian conditions: namely that a leading cleric could lay down rulings in religion and politics that all believers had to follow. Islamist leaders outside of Iran tended to be laymen, and their real and ideological hold on respective populations could not approach that of Khomeini.

Revolutionary Responses in Senegal

Despite the odds outlined by Keddie, Senegalese have dabbled in Islamist endeavors. Kane (1998) mentions the revolution's role as a catalyst for political change in sub-Saharan Africa in his introduction to *Islam et islamismes au sud du Sahara*. Other authors have drawn similarities between the maraboutic system in Senegal and Ayatollahs in Iran. Niasse uses both titles interchangeably: "the Iranian marabout, or rather, the Ayatollah as they say in Tehran" (2003:48). Moreau asks: "Is it possible to imagine Senegalese or Malian marabouts playing a role similar to that of Iranian mullahs and ayatollahs against the Shah's regime?" (1982:290). Such a comparison is evident in Magassouba's (1985) provocative title *L'islam au Sénégal: Demain les mollahs?* (Islam in Senegal: Tomorrow the Mullahs?). He remarks that the Iranian Revolution had repercussions in Senegal and sparked much interest and commentary by the Senegalese Muslim community. He describes the beginning of the political career of al-Hajj Ahmad Khalifa Niass, nicknamed the "Ayatollah of Kaolack," who created an Islamic party called Hizboulahi (Party of God) in August 1979.[11] According to Magassouba, this was the first attempt to create an Islamic political party in Senegal, and perhaps in all of sub-Saharan Africa. Niass disseminated cassettes throughout Senegal and The Gambia with his call to overthrow Senghor, Senegal's first (Catholic) president, who worked toward a secular state. He set fire to the French flag and brought banners saying "Yesterday Iran, Today Senegal" to a press conference covering François Mitterand's 1982 visit to Senegal.

Niass was not the only Senegalese Muslim to be inspired by Iran. Al-Hajj Shaykh Muhammad Touré (d. 2005), leader of Union Culturelle Musulmane (UCM), Senegal's most important Islamic reform movement founded in 1953, criticized both French colonialism and the maraboutic system. He modeled his version of a Senegalese Islamic state after Khomeini's Iran. Touré was born in 1925 to a prominent religious family and studied in a traditional Qurʾanic school. He wrote of the Senegalese maraboutic system, which he rejected at the age of ten: "There was also a marabout who was thought of as a little god, to whom no one even dared asked questions; as well as the talibe who behaved like a lamb" (Loimeier 1998:156). Touré later studied in Mauritania and participated in a pilot program of Senegalese students in Algeria. However, Senghor, then an influential politician and representative at the French National Assembly, under pressure from the French administration in Algeria, decided that it was useless to learn Arabic and revoked their scholarships in 1952. Touré had already been trained by

Association des Ulémas Musulmans Algériens (AUMA) in how to modernize Islamic education and learned the religious sciences neglected in Senegal. He returned to Senegal, founded UCM (modeled after AUMA), and began to write prolifically about Islamic reform, protesting the initiation of a marabout-supported Franco-African community. After two visits to Saudi Arabia, he left UCM in 1979, disapproving of its collaboration with the Senegalese government, and founded the Ibadu Rahman and al-Falah movements, two Sunni reformist organizations (Loimeier 1998).

Shaykh Touré was also inspired by Iran and wrote two articles about his travels there (1982a; 1982b). Invited by Iranian authorities along with three hundred writers, journalists, and leaders of Islamic movements from forty-eight countries, Touré participated in the third anniversary of the Islamic Revolution (February 1–12, 1982) and saw for himself the revolution's realities. He attended various popular demonstrations at Behesht-e-Zahra cemetery, Martyr's Square, and the Sports Complex. Touré was moved by these demonstrations, for him a symbol not only of the mullahs' and ayatollahs' leadership, but of the Iranian people's will to defend the Islamic Republic, most notably women and children.[12] He witnessed how Western imitations were banned from Iranian lives, Islamic values were honored, and spiritual and temporal dualities converged in symbiosis toward one goal: the Creator. Iran's international invitees met the president, prime minister, minister of Islamic orientation, members of the Supreme Court, Qom's ayatollahs, and Khomeini himself. Touré was touched by their simplicity and humility. He noted: "It is not only a matter of liberating, restoring justice, and saving Iran and Iranians, but also of helping all oppressed people of all countries liberate themselves across geographic, national, or religious differences. Islam prescribes all Muslims to engage in this direction" (1982a:9). He asked: "Under the organization and hierarchy of Shiʿi Islam, are Ayatollahs the only ones who have direct influence and control over the masses? Without their blessing, civil politicians are ineffective." He hypothesized that it must be the notion of martyrdom in Shiʿi Islam that enabled such success, as there was no greater glory for a Muslim than to become a martyr for a great cause, that of Islam. Martyrs do not die, but live in happiness in Paradise. That, Touré believed, was how the Iranian people were able to be victorious without fear, discouragement, or disdain. If only Senegalese could follow their lead . . .

Sidi Lamine Niass and Wal Fadjri News

The brother of the Ayatollah of Kaolack, another Senegalese public figure, also has ties to Iran. Sidi Lamine Niass is the son of a prominent Tijani marabout, and, fluent in Arabic, studied Islamic law at Cairo's al-Azhar University from 1975 to 1979. Niass disapproves of the direction Senegal is heading, namely toward the West. He writes:

> What does it mean to "be a marabout" in Senegal in the early 1980s at a time when, discovering the Iranian Revolution with great horror, the Western world was doing all it could to intimidate the people of the Third World who might follow such an example? The "turbaned" man evokes as well the image of a dictatorship as the remains of an archaic feudal order. The fact that I have been trained in the Arabic tradition relegates me to the ranks of these "medieval beings," barely able to accomplish a superficial job, an "Arab's job," as it is called. (Niasse 2003:33)

Niass first visited Iran at the beginning of the revolution, with the goal of applying the revolution to Senegal. He later concluded that the West would never let an Islamic revolution occur in Senegal, and the best he could do was introduce Islam through the media, a more limited goal. He was imprisoned from November 2, 1979, to November 2, 1980.[13] In prison he met a journalist, and they discussed the need for a Muslim newspaper to compete with *Afrique Nouvelle,* a Senegalese newspaper begun by the Catholic Church in 1945. In his autobiographical account of the establishment of his media empire, Niass reflects: "My goals . . . are to restore, using *Wal Fadjri,* the place and importance the Muslim religion should have maintained in a society that has been Islamicized for centuries, but Islam's heritage has been neglected and its cultural references lost. On the side of the journalists, the demand for editorial freedom has been accommodated. This convergence between two ideals that have learned to respect one another has been the key to our success" (2003:47).

In 1983 Niass obtained 100,000 FF (5 million CFA) from an Iranian in Paris who worked for the Ministry of Islamic Orientation. He used this money to start *Wal Fadjri,* whose first biweekly edition appeared on January 13, 1984.[14] Niass connects his newspaper to Islam: "In fact, what have my essential concerns always been if not to show that Islam as a civilization admits and encourages the exercise of freedom, and especially freedom of expression? What is Islam if not the discourse of freedom? If journalism is the search for truth, then journalism is in synch with Islam" (2003:53).

Niass mentions Iran and the revolution more than ten times in his autobiography. He recounts an amusing anecdote about his first rendezvous with former Senegalese president Diouf, which demonstrates that he, like his brother, is also a political instigator. "I took the decision to dress like an Iranian, my head covered by a turban and wearing a full tunic, in the style of the Ayatollahs" (2003:56).[15] Diouf commented on his dress, but, to Niass's surprise, compared him to a Sudanese, not to an Iranian. "Maybe . . . the second comparison might have been an implicit accusation, if not a justification of their concerns regarding my pro-Iranian stance" (57). In the end, the president allowed for the establishment of the Islamic press, but reminded Niass that Senegal is a secular country and that he would not accept the infiltration of fundamentalism through the press. Niass retorted: "If you are threatening me, Mr. President, I ask you to be so kind as to act upon it. I have already been jailed twice. And to become a martyr is my highest aspiration. I therefore implore you, this time, to not let me go free" (57).

Wal Fadjri succeeded, at first as a biweekly radical Islamic magazine and since 1994 as a respectable liberal newspaper, although today it is becoming more mainstream. Readers acclaimed *Wal Fadjri* for providing the opposition's perspective to the government newspaper *Le Soleil.* Early editions were openly pro-Shiʿi.[16] For example, the first edition included an article by Sayyid Muhammad Baqir al-Sadr, an Iraqi scholar later murdered by Saddam Hussein, entitled "Detailed Economic Lines of Islamic Society." *Wal Fadjri* published long extracts from Khomeini's writings, a defense of Iran's position against Iraq in the Iran-Iraq War, and bitterly attacked Saudi Arabia and the Organization of the Islamic Conference. The magazine also concentrated on the Lebanese Civil War, drawing in Senegalese readers with enticing titles such as "Beirut: What the Press Does Not Say" (no. 1:28). Another article, "Efforts of Shiʿi Scholars" (no. 61:19–22), provided a general description of Shiʿi Islam, including the following statement: "Efforts of Shiʿi scholars did not aim to impose beliefs or the conversion of Sunnis because that would go against Islamic freedom of thought" (20). The article provided brief biographies and described intellectual accomplishments of reformers such as Jamal al-Din al-Afghani, Lebanon's Shiʿi authority ʿAbd al-Husayn Sharaf al-Din, and Iraqi scholar Kashif al-Ghita. The article explained tensions between Sunnis and Shiʿa.

> During the second half of this century, after the intrigues and plots of colonialists (whose policy was "divide and rule"), the Islamic state was threatened by dispersion and divisions, as well as by ignorance of true beliefs. One of the results of such a policy was the Sunni brothers of Saudi Arabia coming to think that Shiʿi Muslims were in defiance of Imam ʿAli, and had in their possession another book, that of Fatima, and considered the visit of Karbala and Najaf to be the true pilgrimage. On top of that, they also accused them of defiling the temple of God every year during the pilgrimage. (22)

The article concluded by discussing the work of these reformers toward a rapprochement between the two Muslim denominations. Kepel (2002) states that *Wal Fadjri*'s choice of topics led to the hostility of the Senegalese state and pro-Saudi networks toward *Wal Fadjri,* and at the same time clashed with marabouts' vested interests.

Niass represented himself in 2003 as openly pro-Iranian. Senegalese rumors, however, revealed that he also had pro-Iraqi sympathies, especially before the outbreak of the Iran-Iraq War, and early editions of *Wal Fadjri* focused heavily on the war. It is believed that he solicited Iraq as well as Iran for funding, and he even presented himself as a possible mediator between Iran and Iraq. I met with the Paris representative of the Imam al-Khuʾi Foundation (headquartered in London), who manages correspondence from Francophone Africans.[17] Before establishing Association Culturelle Imam al-Khuʾi in Paris in 1992, this Iraqi ran Association Ahl al-Bayt from 1981 to 1987 with ʿAbbas Ahmad al-Bostani. Association Ahl al-Bayt held prayer meetings every Thursday night, and this Iraqi confirmed that Sidi Lamine Niass was in attendance in the early 1980s. Niass did not always publicly present himself as pro-Iranian, but if one cannot be simultaneously pro-Iranian and pro-Iraqi, Niass has always been pro-Shiʿi.

Wal Fadjri was thus one of the earliest local establishments to expose Senegalese to Shiʿi Islam through its widely read articles. Sidi Lamine Niass, Ahmad Khalifa Niass, and Shaykh Muhammad Touré are three examples of Senegalese public figures inspired by the Iranian Revolution. Whether through forming political parties, Islamic reformist movements, or an "Islamic" press, their ideas were openly available to the Senegalese people.

The Iranian Embassy in Dakar

The Iranian embassy also played a subtle role in encouraging Shiʿi Islam in Dakar. Iran has a history of economic cooperation with Senegal from the time of Muhammad Reza Shah Pahlavi, but the embassy was closed in 1984 for encouraging Islamic propaganda:[18] "Senegalese authorities, according to these sources, have accused embassy staff of unlawful activities, in particular: circulating 'extremist propaganda' among Senegalese Muslim associations and among the Lebanese Muslim community in Senegal; financing Senegalese associations as well as newspapers; reinforcing their infrastructures and staff without authorization; and organizing visits to Mecca for Senegalese, despite repeated warnings" (Drame 1984).

President Diouf reopened the Iranian embassy in the early 1990s out of economic interests in phosphates and carpets. The embassy has been careful to stress only economic activities in Senegal; however, certain embassy events continue to promote Shiʿi Islam. It holds annual receptions for prominent Lebanese and Senegalese Muslims for the anniversary of the Islamic Revolution, in addition to purchasing full-page advertisements in Senegal's major newspapers publicizing the meaning of the revolution and Iran's subsequent evolution.[19] In 1992, a ten-person Senegalese delegation celebrated the anniversary of the revolution with an official visit to Iran, from February 1 to 11, commemorating the period from Khomeini's return from exile until the "victory" of the revolution. Diouf sent an official telegram on February 12 to Iranian president Rafsanjani in honor of the occasion, and apparently the diplomatic rupture had healed.

Other events enhanced ties between Senegal and Iran: a friendship pact between the Iranian Red Crescent and Senegal's Red Cross in 1990 and the visit of

Ayatollah Yazdi, president of the judiciary power, to Senegal in May 1991.[20] Raf-sanjani's presence at the Organization of the Islamic Conference (OIC) meeting in Dakar in 1991 was highly publicized, as was his visit to Tuba, the Murid pilgrimage site. In addition, the embassy sponsors an iftar during Jerusalem Day, the last Friday of Ramadan, as decreed by Ayatollah Khomeini to show solidarity with the Palestinian people.[21] Iran finances Senegalese intellectuals to attend Islamic conferences in Tehran. The Iranian cultural center organized a conference on June 3, 2009, at the University of Dakar for the twenty-year anniversary of Khomeini's death. In 2002, an Iranian shaykh built a Shiʿi seminary, Hawza al-Rasul al-Akram, in Dakar, where young boys (and now girls) are educated from Arabic texts by Senegalese shaykhs who studied Shiʿi theology in Iran or Lebanon. The hawza consists of a prayer room with Shiʿi wall-hangings proclaiming *al-salam alaykum ya Husayn ibn ʿAli* (May peace be upon you Husayn son of ʿAli), an office displaying photos of Ayatollahs Khomeini and Khamenei, and a classroom filled with wooden desks, Qurʾans, and Arabic grammar books. When I visited the school in 2003 there were plans to open a small library.

Senegalese President Wade visited Iran in 2003, 2006, and 2008, including a 2008 meeting with Supreme Leader of the Islamic Revolution, Ayatollah ʿAli Khamenei.[22] During this meeting, Wade was quoted as saying "we always set Iran as our example."[23] In 2007, Iranian Judiciary Chief Ayatollah Mahmud Hashemi Shahrudi visited Dakar to gain support for his proposal for the formation of a union of Islamic states and a Muslim countries' juridical council, and declared: "We believe it is our duty to expand ties with Islamic countries and use the capabilities and potentials of Muslim states to help the growth and spread of Islam."[24] President Ahmadinejad also attended the 2008 OIC conference in Dakar. These visits strengthened ties between Iran and Senegal, whose bilateral relations formed a strong part of a larger comprehensive policy on the part of Ahmadinejad's government to expand influence through diplomatic, economic, and military strategies in Africa and Latin America (Rubin 2008).

Not all Senegalese, however, welcomed Iran's renewed activities. *Le Témoin* published an article on August 3, 1993, accusing Iran of the following:

> We are witnessing in Senegal, for almost a decade now, a revival of small fundamentalist groups that are very closely associated with the Shiʿi community and its membership. . . . Having learned from the experience of the first period of deployment in Senegal, the Iranian authorities seem to have decided to play on the diversity of Senegalese Islam, but also to take advantage of the poverty of the Senegalese population, particularly the youth, by intervening in densely populated neighborhoods. . . . Given that the Shiʿi tradition does not recognize [Sufi] brotherhoods as legitimate units of the Muslim community's social and religious organization, we must question the true intentions of Iran's deployment in Senegal.

The article accuses Iranian authorities of playing the Murid card against the Tijani community. These charges resulted in a response from the Iranian embassy printed on September 7, 1993, denying such allegations with evidence to the contrary.[25]

The Iranian embassy has more contact with Senegalese than with Lebanese in Dakar, although occasionally an Iranian shaykh is present at Islamic Institute events. Shaykh al-Zayn claims he does not have good relations with the Iranian embassy. He describes his work in Senegal as being benevolent and educational, not political, in nature.[26] Since he does not promote the Iranian Revolution, he told me, the Iranian embassy criticized him and published their denunciation in an Iranian newspaper. Shaykh al-Zayn does, however, have contacts in Iran, as demonstrated by his involvement in the French hostage crisis in the 1980s. The *Le Témoin* journalist who wrote the article cited above also printed the reproduction of a letter in Arabic from the Ahl al-Bayt (AS) World Assembly in Tehran to a Senegalese Shiʿi in response to his request for money. The translation of the letter informed this man that "concerning financial aid, Shaykh Tahiri, during his last visit to Senegal, gave Mr. ʿAbdul Munʿam al-Zayn some assistance. This is why our availabilities do not permit us to do more." According to the journalist's sources, Shaykh al-Zayn received US$200,000 from the Iranian organization. Shaykh al-Zayn was also present at the Beirut airport to greet Iranian President Khatami during his 2003 visit to Lebanon.

The latest twist in political relations was the severing once again of diplomatic ties between Senegal and Iran in February 2011. Thirteen containers of Iranian weapons were found in Nigeria, which Senegalese authorities believed were destined via Banjul for antigovernment rebels in the southern separatist Casamance region. Iranian bullets were found to be the cause of death of Senegalese soldiers.[27] Two years later, Senegalese President Macky Sall reestablished diplomatic ties with Iran on February 6, 2013, when he met President Ahmadinejad at the OIC conference in Cairo. The Iranian embassy lost no time in resuming its annual commemorations of the death of Khomeini and the Day of Fatima. There is also a newly formed Association for Iranian-Senegalese Friendship. It remains to be seen how Iranian president Rouhani will prioritize relations with Africa.

Although the Iranian embassy was closed during this two-year period, and the Iranian cultural center kept a low profile, a Senegalese professor informed me that during this time four high schools in Dakar began offering Farsi as a language option. These programs, however, have not been extremely successful. English is a mandatory second language in Senegalese schools, and students can choose an additional language. Spanish is most popular, followed by Arabic, Portuguese, German, Russian, Italian, and then Farsi, with very few students currently choosing that option. Université Cheikh Anta Diop of Dakar also established a Department of Persian Language, Literature, and Civilization in 2003 in partnership with the Shahid Beheshti University in Iran.

Vernacular Shiʿi Islam in Senegal

The Senegalese public figures described above were influenced by Iran without leaving Sunni Islam. These earlier, more "radical" approaches to Islam in Senegal did not last. Villalón (1995) contends that those Arabisants who adhered to a reformist line remained limited to a small group of urban Muslims with little resonance among Senegal's majority. Although his later research focused on Murid and Tijani reformist groups with growing adherents (Villalón 1999; 2000; 2004; Kane and Villalón 1995), he maintains that new forms of Islam cannot transform Senegal's existing religious system. Hodgkin likewise writes: "The Iranian revolution . . . had an important influence especially among students, but on movements already in existence rather than on new movements. Iran was seen, naturally, as an example of how an Islamic movement could overthrow an oppressive government, form an Islamic state and refuse the dictates of the US and the West. . . . In the Sunni west of Africa this support for Khomeini did not lead to conversions to Shiʿism even among those who were setting up Iranian film shows and circulating Embassy literature" (1998:203–204).

Yet Iran's greatest influence in Senegal today, aside from programs of economic exchange, is a small but growing network of Senegalese converts to Shiʿi Islam, encouraged by the charisma and proselytizing efforts of Ayatollah Khomeini (in addition to that of Shaykh al-Zayn). Whereas Senegalese reformists have not yet mobilized the masses, they are not as marginalized or as powerless as Villalón, Hodgkin, and others have portrayed them to be. As the next two chapters will illustrate, the Iranian Revolution did lead to Senegalese conversion and efforts to form a new religious movement. Furthermore Shiʿi Muslim associations are not limited to urban areas and have developed in the Senegalese countryside as well as in Dakar.

Not all Senegalese converts came directly to Shiʿi Islam. Some were first influenced by Sunni Salafi movements. One informant explained the attraction:

> Since the time of our ancestors we grew up in an environment of Sufi movements. All of them have as their basis Maliki ritual, although a distinction is made between Maliki ritual and what we call Sufism. They have other schools, imams, guides, and references. So, the Salafis were telling us Sufis, you have weird rituals that are not consistent with the six fundamental books [the major Sunni hadith collections]. Sufis are not used to fighting back against those accusations, you know—we are not really warriors. Most of them face criticism without responding because they privilege paths of wisdom and peace. The attacks were numerous. We were very young, we did not answer back very convincingly. That is why many young people, young "Arabophones," or others even, young "Francophones" who were educated in French schools, paid attention to the debates. They saw that Sufis, our ancestors and guides, were unable to provide convincing answers to questions raised by these people about reli-

gious foundations, theories, and practices of selecting shaykhs, rationales of visiting and interacting with leaders and donating money. . . . Sufism did not give a precise answer . . . [which] motivated of a lot of young people at that time to leave the ranks of Sufism and join Salafi schools.

Not all of these youth, however, were ultimately satisfied with Salafi responses to these issues and continued to search for answers in other branches of Islam.

That is why, when the Shi'i discourse first emerged, it gave us the chance to explore another path to see whether we could obtain the same answer. And, indeed, it provided the definitive answer to everything we were looking for. Well, of course it required a big investment; there was a lot of research to be done. It was not at all easy to know everything. To know these movements, you need the right moment, the right documentation, while remaining very patient. That is why those who left these movements to join Shi'i Islam for the most part are exceptional people, people who do a lot of research, people who are much more independent [than the norm]. They do not live off others' donations and gifts; in general, they have jobs, get a salary; we are talking about people who are pretty well-off, who acquire their own books, who long for information in a more dynamic way. That is how Shi'i Islam took root here.

Kepel, in *Jihad,* argues that radical Islamic movements in Senegal hoped to use the Iranian Revolution as an example to "shake up the traditional Islam of the brotherhoods, whose rituals they found suffocating. At the same time they were eager to distance themselves from the modern European example, which they associated with colonialism and imperialism" (2002:130–131). He claims, however, that these movements failed because they aroused the hostility of the state, pro-Saudi networks, and marabouts, and were unsuccessful in offering alternatives to social integration or access to resources and property that talibes received from marabouts. "Radical movements of this type . . . eventually proved incapable of holding the allegiance of those young people whose enthusiasm they had at first aroused. . . . As time passed, a few of their leaders and intellectuals were absorbed by the Brotherhoods and joined the local Islamic establishments they had formerly condemned: others transformed their militant political enterprises into successful commercial ones" (131). Sidi Lamine Niass's *Wal Fadjri* news is an example of the latter—and the only African example given by Kepel. Kepel also argues that "terrorists" aimed to mobilize Muslim support and win them over to their cause, "to arouse emotional sympathy and enthusiasm and to galvanize with an example of victory won by violence" (2). He claims that Islamism won control of the direction of Islam in the 1970s: "It accomplished this by imposing its own values and marginalizing or dismissing other interpretations of the Muslim religion" (41–42).

Yet despite Kepel's claims, some Islamic movements have continued their initial enthusiasm in Senegal. Senegalese have endeavored to form a Shi'i network in

Senegal as an *alternative* to joining Sufi orders (and not necessarily to shake up or dismiss them). Shiʿi influence should not be judged on success in political awakening and calls for revolution, which is not the goal of Senegalese Shiʿa. Instead they portray themselves as leaders of an intellectual movement, and use their Islamic knowledge, of both Sunni and Shiʿi sources, as a weapon to educate—and modernize—the Senegalese population. Efforts to expand reformist Islam do not aim to create an Islamic state in Senegal. Through building schools, mosques, and Islamic associations they focus on bringing religious awareness, literacy in Arabic, and the ability to read Islamic texts so followers can achieve their own understanding of Islam, decreasing the influence of Sufi marabouts while attracting the allegiance of these students to other figures of religious authority. Such actions, in accord with Senegalese Shiʿi self-image, suggest the need to rethink the dominant framework for analyzing the success of the Iranian Revolution in other parts of the world as a violent movement aiming to overthrow the political status quo.

Senegalese Shiʿa approach the dissemination of reformist Islam differently than the forcefulness and violence depicted by Kepel and other scholars of Islamic reformist movements. Although converts are convinced that their way is the true way, they do not compel others to accept their views. Moreover they do not forbid Sufis from practicing or even learning about their own traditions in Shiʿi spaces. In fact, some Senegalese converts keep their feet in both Sunni and Shiʿi traditions. Shiʿi Islam is made more Senegalese (and more cosmopolitan) through ways in which various Islamic traditions converge. Indeed, converts believe that only by spreading religious tolerance and coexistence can Shiʿi Islam bring peace and economic development to Senegal. As one informant told me: "You know, Sunnis and Shiʿa share the same Qurʾan, Prophet, orientation, religion, and values; therefore what brings them together is much greater than what divides them, and what divides them has nothing to do with Islam. Everything that is essential unites them. The bonds of brotherhood between Shiʿa and Sunnis are powerful; but brothers can misunderstand one another in some cases. . . . Even two brothers may disagree on certain issues and have different opinions. But these for sure are not fundamental divergences but minor ones based on taste and feelings." Reaching beyond Sufi origins to foreign interpretations of Islam can lead to hostility for Senegalese converts within their own communities. Unlike claims of Islamic reformist movements elsewhere in the Muslim world, Senegalese conversion to Shiʿi Islam did not result in *cultural authenticity*, defined as "being true to one's community and faith" (Deeb 2006:20). Converts therefore work hard to adapt Shiʿi theology and ritual to distinctly Senegalese cultural practices.

Rosander (1997:1) juxtaposes African Islam with Islam in Africa, defining "African Islam" as "contextualized" or "localized" forms of Islam found in Sufi contexts, seen as culturally as well as religiously flexible and accommodating. "Islam in Africa" designates Islamist tendencies that aim to "purify" Islam from indigenous African ideas and Western influences. I question such a division, arguing that Shiʿi Islam is not purely an outside Islamic force, but has become vernacularized along its journey, adapting to local social, economic, and political climates.[28] In this context, vernacularization is the intellectual process by which Shiʿi Islam is adjusted and interpreted against Sufi ideology and Senegalese culture. These scholarly operations and the scriptural dimension of Shiʿi Islam subtract cultural and political Arab or Iranian elements from Islam, enabling it to become, as my informants have articulated, distinctly Senegalese.

The following chapters describe the development of a vernacular Senegalese Shiʿi Islam through examining how cosmopolitan Islam is incorporated into the particular Senegalese religious context of Sufi orders. Through choosing to associate with global Islamic ideologies, the meanings and functions of local Islam are rethought. Converts break (incompletely) with their religious and political past, inspired by ideas imported from abroad in the hope of inventing a new Senegalese future. Turner (1969) has adapted the term *communitas* to describe a common experience shared by a community, usually through the liminality involved in a rite of passage that brings all participants onto an equal level. In communitas, people are joined together through intense feelings of social belonging and stand together outside society. Senegalese Shiʿa congregate for religious holidays and rituals and engage in communal discourse about religious experiences as well as their occasional marginalization by other Muslims in Senegal. Working together to combat accusations that Shiʿi Islam as a foreign religious tradition cannot be Senegalese, they hope to transition from being envisioned as outside Senegalese society to establishing themselves as autochthons. Because of the political connotations of the term *movement* as described in social movement theory, I prefer Turner's development of the notion communitas to describe the community of Senegalese converts, especially as they are not choosing Shiʿi Islam to stage a political Islamic revolution.[29]

The universal discourse of Islam strategically orated by Ayatollah Khomeini and Shaykh al-Zayn imparted Shiʿi Islam with cosmopolitan appeal that attracted both Sunni and Shiʿi Muslims. As the language of Shiʿi Islam became more universal, the global religion lost specific political connotations in Iranian and Lebanese contexts. The vernacularization of Shiʿi Islam is the latest addition to a long tradition of religious and political debates in Senegal (Loimeier 2003). The redefinition in the 1990s of the relationship between the Senegalese state and Sufi orders, due to government functionaries' disenchantment with the established system, generational changes, and economic crisis, has opened up new spaces for alternative Islamic movements (Diouf and Leichtman 2009). Whereas both Sunni and Shiʿi reformist movements have formed externally to Sufi orders, Senegal is also experiencing the growth of influential new movements from within Sufi orders. These have blurred the presumed distinction between "Sufis" and "reformists," where neither group forms a homogenous movement in Senegal. It is this long tradition of religious pluralism that enables the emerging community of Shiʿa to carry out their activities amid a climate of coexistence in Dakar.

6 Migrating from One's Parents' Traditions

Narrating Conversion Experiences

> Before this century's waves of migration, interaction was minimal between
> different kinds of Muslims, who tended to live in fairly closed communities
> with limited knowledge of other understandings of Islam. Migration has forced
> Muslims to interact with one another and to become more aware of their
> religion's internal variety and vicissitudes.
>
> —Peter Mandaville, *Transnational Muslim Politics*

> People living in this expansive transregional setting frequently shift between
> very different indexes and ways of being Muslim during the course of their
> daily lives. In so doing, they forge intricate, intimate, and dynamic relations
> with other Muslims, not only from different places, ethnolinguistic groups,
> or confessional backgrounds, but also with very different life histories and
> personal experiences of this transregional space.
>
> —Magnus Marsden, "Muslim Cosmopolitans"

I MET JOSEPH AND his son Khomeini at one of the three conferences organized
by Senegalese Shiʿa during the first ten days of the Islamic month of Muharram
in January 2008, where various religious leaders and teachers publicly debated
the meaning of ʿAshura in a mixture of Wolof, Arabic, and French (see chapter 7
and Leichtman 2012).[1] Joseph attends all Shiʿi events in Dakar, and recently there
has been a proliferation of religious conferences and radio and television appearances explaining to Senegalese Sunni Muslims this unknown or misunderstood
minority branch of Islam. Joseph was born in 1950 in Saint-Louis, in the north of
Senegal. His Christian father of Serakole ethnicity converted to Qadiriyya Islam
to facilitate marrying his mother, as this was the religion of her uncles and brothers.[2] His father's Christian origins explained Joseph's Christian name, although
Joseph emphasized that before his discovery of Shiʿi Islam he considered himself to be simply Muslim and did not identify with any Sufi order. Joseph's father
was a civil servant and moved frequently with his family. Joseph was educated

in Senegal's French system and attended primary school in Saint-Louis and secondary school in Ziguinchor in the south. His family then moved to Diourbel in Senegal's central peanut basin, but he continued his schooling in Thies. He later studied law at Université Cheikh Anta Diop of Dakar, and upon his graduation worked as a civil servant like his father, first in the southern village of Kolda, where he lived during the Iranian Revolution. Joseph became Shiʿi around this time, and he elaborated on this memorable period in an emotional manner, vividly recalling every detail of Imam Khomeini's life, as if the revolution happened yesterday. Although he was then based in Kolda, he was hospitalized for three months in Dakar, where the following events took place.

In 1978 Joseph was reading documents about the Shiʿa, which portrayed them in a negative light. He would leave the hospital every day at 6:00 PM to go home to watch the news—there was only the national Radiodiffusion Télévision Sénégalaise (RTS) at the time.[3] When the news programs featured Ayatollah Ruhollah Musavi Khomeini, he heard from the imam a different discourse than what journalists broadcast about Shiʿa. When Khomeini was exiled to Paris, Joseph purchased all magazines featuring articles on Iran and the ayatollah that he could find in Senegal, from *L'Express, L'Humanité,* and *Paris Match,* and he even remembered names of journalists who wrote these articles that he could still quote by heart.

Joseph followed Khomeini's movements—his arrival in Paris in 1978, and the closing of Tehran's airport in an attempt to prevent his return from exile. *Le Monde* published a famous interview with the imam where he projected his politics, based on divine inspiration, Joseph specified. The journalist called Khomeini a mystic influenced by classic philosophy, and Joseph came to the conclusion that he must follow this imam. He bought all books on Shiʿi Islam (in French) available in Senegal, and was influenced by the work of French Islamicist Henry Corbin. As the Iranian embassy was not yet closed in Dakar, he went there for additional information and received the newspaper *Message de l'Islam,* which summarized Khomeini's ideas. Other texts that inspired Joseph were the testament of Khomeini; writings of Shiʿi Imams, in particular *Nahj al-Balagha* (Peak of Eloquence), the collection of sermons by Imam ʿAli ibn Abi Talib; volumes by Sayyid Muhammad Husayn Tabatabaʿi, Ayatollah Morteza Mottahari, and other clerics; and books on Islamic philosophy. He was able to obtain this literature either from the Iranian embassy in Dakar or through writing to the Association Ahl al-Bayt in Paris. Joseph claimed to be the first in Senegal to support Imam Khomeini at a time when the world was divided into Eastern and Western blocs, where the East supported Saddam Hussein. He described himself as an "ardent partisan" and "defender of Khomeini."

Joseph jumped back and forth in time recalling key events in Imam Khomeini's life, finally pausing at the end of May 1989, when the ayatollah was hospitalized in Tehran. Joseph's own life now became intermingled with that of Khomeini. That week it was very hot in Dakar, and Joseph had a dangerously high fever. He walked himself to the hospital, and the doctor was shocked that someone as sick as he was able to walk in that heat. The following week, on June 2, Joseph's wife gave birth to a son after trying to conceive for fifteen years. When she felt the pains of labor, Joseph rushed her to the hospital and spent the night there. The following morning he went home to sleep for a few hours, and when he awoke that afternoon he turned on the radio and learned that Khomeini had died that very day. He did not hesitate to name his son Khomeini—and this, he declared, was at a time when the imam was thought to be an assassin, a murderer, and not even a Muslim. Today, however, Joseph is known at the Iranian embassy as "the father of Khomeini."

How does one understand the Iranian Revolution in a Senegalese context? As I argue in these final two chapters, the revolution brought awareness of Shiʿi Islam to Senegal, which led to intellectual reforms, where education is a fundamental concept in African economic development. Ironically, Senegalese converts to Shiʿi Islam have taken the ultimate denunciation of the West—Iran's rejection of Muhammad Reza Shah's Westernization policies in a return to Islam—to translate Khomeini's vision into an alternative African modernity.[4] Like Donham (1999) has argued in the case of Ethiopia, revolutionary outcomes, or in the Senegalese case ideologies, sometimes only further what they are trying to oppose: the modernization of the state. Ethiopia was the only country in Africa to have a social revolution because it escaped European colonization (Donham 2002), and conversely, as Keddie (1995) and Kepel (2002) have suggested, the Iranian Revolution could never succeed in Senegal because of strong links to France. Yet Khomeini's ideologies have taken root in Senegal, through both French- and Arabic-language media, not as a political revolution but as a call for Islamic reform.

This chapter takes life history narratives of Senegalese converts and builds on theories of conversion through contextualizing converts' individual experiences within cosmopolitan encounters *and* Senegal's political economy. I define conversion as a change in religion over time, involving a transformation of one's religious culture resulting from multiple factors including social networks with other believers, a discovery of key religious texts, and a response to a particular location in both time and place. I explore how the search for power, autonomy, economic advancement, peace, and spiritual meaning influences religious imagination, even "conversion" from one branch of Islam to another.

I contend that certain Senegalese became aware of Shiʿi Islam at the moment when the Iranian Revolution became a topic of international importance, yet went beyond Western media coverage to engage intellectually with Shiʿi texts. Furthermore, I contest the dominant framework for evaluating the success of Shiʿi movements through the assumption that Shiʿi influences must necessarily be political and aim to replicate the Iranian Revolution. Central to my argument is an examination of how cosmopolitan Islam enables a particular Senegalese nationalism with claims to autochthony. Muslim populations throughout the Middle East and Asia experienced a resurgence of Islamic practice following the revolution. In Africa, some Sunni Muslims were also inspired to adopt Shiʻi Muslim ways. Grounded in local power struggles, competition for Islamic authority, and disillusionment with the Senegalese state, new ways of being Muslim offered new hopes for the future. Strategies of conversion reveal the political climate of the time and the intersection of local and global religion. Incorporating West African cases into discussions about conversion, Shiʻi Islam, and globalization highlights how Senegalese perceive that proselytizing, media technologies, and Muslim networking can lead to socioeconomic, cultural, and perhaps even political change.

Conversion to Modernities

Social scientists of the post–World War II period looked to Max Weber for an understanding of conversion and polarized religion between the "traditional" and the "rationalized" (see Hefner 1993). Horton (1971; 1975a; 1975b), in disagreeing with Weber, sparked a debate on African conversion with his "Intellectualist Theory" by insisting that "traditional religions" are not less rational than "world religions," just narrower in focus. This led to a famous dialogue with Fisher (1973; 1985) and others (Ifeka-Moller 1974; Ikenga-Metuh 1987), and Horton's theory continues to be debated today, especially by scholars examining conversion in Africa (Aguilar 1995; Comaroffs 1991; Gabbert 2001; Hamer 2002; Peel 2000; Ranger 1993b; Searing 2003). Horton has been critiqued for not defining *conversion*, ignoring the influence of colonialism, failing to recognize the religious dimension, and grounding his theory in simple local—national, premodern—modern dichotomies. Peel (2000) suggests that we cannot treat "traditional" religion as a purely indigenous cultural baseline and an entity wholly independent of Islam. Other scholars have moved away from these debates, describing conversion as a cultural passage in a quest for human belonging (Austin-Broos 2003); as an upwardly mobile step toward elite status (Gellner 2005); or as a clear political statement of dissent against identities constructed by the state (Viswanathan 1998).

Does converting to Islam entail different processes and motivations than converting from a "traditional religion" to a "world religion"? What about converting from one branch of Islam to another?[5] Senegalese were attracted to Shiʻi Islam in what can be called *intellectual conversion*. As described in Lofland and Skonovd's (1981) typologies, the convert becomes acquainted with alternative ideologies by individual, private investigation such as reading books, watching television, or other impersonal ways. Some individuals convert on their own in isolation from devotees of the respective religion, but the convert is likely to be socially involved with members of the new religion. There is little or no external social pressure to convert. The majority of Senegal's male Shiʿi leaders experienced this; chapter 7 will analyze "intellectual" aspects of conversion.

Senegalese converts regard the intellectual attraction of Shiʿi Islam differently from Horton's "Intellectualist Theory." In the same way literacy elsewhere and at other times has served as a time bomb of reform (Fisher 1973), and has enabled the forging of connections with congregations from afar (Ranger 1993b) or even within the same nation (Anderson 1983), Shiʿi texts provide alternative answers to questions about Islam. Augis (2002) argues that Muslims who make an intrafaith conversion are reading the Qurʾan for the first time as a result of participating in reformist organizations that advocate Qurʾanic literacy. Conversion is based on learning what converts consider to be the absolute textual truth. Shiʿi texts, however, are available only to a small elite group that has mastered the Arabic language and has funds to purchase this literature from abroad, beyond what is distributed free of charge by proselytizing agencies. Converts like Joseph, who are French-educated and illiterate in Arabic, are less common.[6] Ability to read Islamic texts and not to rely on their interpretation by a marabout or other intermediary separates converts from the more "traditional" Islamic practices of Sufi orders, especially the Muridiyya.

Asad (1996) laments that religious conversion needs explaining in ways that secular conversion to modern ways of being does not. Religious conversion can also be attributed to a conscious choice for a more "modern" way of life. Van der Veer (1996) argues that a solution to the eighteenth-century European situation of religious civil warfare was a call for religious tolerance and syncretism, but also an interiorization of belief and privatization of conversion. He critiques theories in which modernity implies secularism by suggesting that in fact conversion to Christianity, in the context of the interplay between Europe and the colonized world, is a conversion to modernity.[7] Yet many in the West have (mistakenly) perceived Islam to be incompatible with modernity, democracy, civil society, and pluralism (Esposito and Burgat 2003). Muslims may also deliberately resist the Western Modern. As Deeb (2006) demonstrates, a dual emphasis on both material and spiritual progress is necessary for "modern-ness," where spiritual progress is what distinguishes Muslim modernity from the perceived emptiness of modernity as manifested in the West, in addition to Western perceptions about Islam. Hefner (2005) stresses that there is no uniform Muslim modernity, nor a monolithic Muslim politics, which is my point of departure for the Senegalese Shiʿi case.

Modernity can be defined as a geography of imagination that creates progress through the projection and management of alterity and historicity, requiring an Other and an Elsewhere (Trouillot 2002). *Vernacular modernities* are attempts to reorder local society by using strategies that have produced wealth, power, or knowledge elsewhere in the world (Donham 1999). Anthropologists have critiqued what is often seen as a singular Western model of modernity (such as Harvey

1990) suggesting either the local appropriation of modernity in other places or "alternative" non-Western understandings of modernity (see Knauft 2002). Others suggest the term lost all analytical value with overuse and assumption of too many contradictory meanings (Deeb 2006; Donham 2002). I am interested here in considering new strategies as understood by Muslims in Africa for implementing social change. Becoming Shiʿa is one way certain Senegalese, especially those who are highly educated and relatively affluent, attempt to escape the colonial legacy, weakness of the Senegalese state, and growing structural inequalities in their country through adopting while adapting a religious model that for them has been successful elsewhere in combating the West.

French colonialism led to the acceptance in Senegal that the West was the universal example for all that is modern. Today the French educational system has not led to success for all Senegalese, and competition from reformist Islamic schools is growing (Brenner 2001; Ware 2009). With the exception of a few converts such as Joseph, who read religious texts in French translation, it was through fluency in Arabic brought by this turn toward reformist Islamic education that Senegalese Muslims discovered spiritual and material opportunities of Shiʿi Islam. This was encouraged through Iranian and Lebanese efforts at building schools and disseminating literature on Shiʿi Islam, and by Senegalese activists inspired by Khomeini and the Iranian Revolution.

In Senegal, there was already an accepted practice of converting from a "traditional" African religion to Islam and Christianity, or from one interpretation of Islam to another, which was essential in the formation of Shiʿi networks. Conversion to Islam, and the knowledge that came with it, was a means of achieving higher status at a younger age (Mark 1978); challenging elders' authority (Searing 2003); and gaining access to new resources for predicting, explaining, and controlling events in a world penetrated by external social forces (Simmons 1979). In sum, conversion radically altered local configurations of power, kinship, wealth, and inheritance. Conversion to another form of Islam, like conversion to Christianity (Comaroffs 1991; Donham 1999; Hefner 1993; Keane 2002; Meyer 1999; van der Veer 1996), is about assuming new identities in situations of historical and social change that undermine old systems of status. The decision to convert is embedded in the individual convert's struggle to fit into a changing society, and the search for one's place outside of (and even within) one's traditions. Asad (1993) stresses the relationship of religion to power, and religious power in Senegal entails having economic resources and some influence on the political system.

The Iranian Revolution and Senegalese Conversion to Shiʿi Islam

I began this chapter with the vignette of Joseph to focus my analysis of conversion away from deterritorialized accounts of individual spirituality that dominate the literature on religious experience. Ongoing efforts in social theory have struggled to address the relationship between the individual and society in relation to religious transformations. I will turn now to conversion stories of other Senegalese Shiʿi converts, as described to me in interviews. My primary concern in these vignettes is to draw attention to ways in which converts articulate not only individual religious experiences, but also social contexts in which they discovered Shiʿi Islam. Despite efforts of the Iranian embassy and Lebanese shaykh to bring them to Shiʿi Islam, many Senegalese came to the religion on their own. Furthermore I am interested in these last two chapters in the very ambitious and nationalist goals they project for Senegal, which converts envision that the dissemination of Shiʿi Islam will achieve. Their discourse reflects a growing reality among Senegalese Muslims that the religio-political status quo is not working and that change is inevitable.

Converts are from all ethnic groups in Senegal and initially from various Sufi orders (with some Christians). Although the majority of movement leaders were Tijani before becoming Shiʿa, others were Murid or Qadiri. Some first made a Salafist detour; others converted directly to Shiʿi Islam. Converts are from all over Senegal, ranging from Dakar's urban areas, its suburbs, and Saint-Louis, to regional hubs such as Kaolack, to the villages of the Futa and Casamance. Some converts were well-off and had means to study in the Middle East or North America; others lacked financial means, but through dedication to their studies and the right networks received scholarships to study abroad or in Senegal's Lebanese-run Islamic schools. The majority of converts were fluent in Arabic; a minority were French-educated and did not have a firm command of Arabic. They discovered Shiʿi Islam both in Senegal and in travels to other countries. They work in foreign embassies, the Senegalese government, and NGOs, and are bankers, businessmen, artists, journalists, teachers, scholars, students, shaykhs, and laymen and laywomen. Senegalese Shiʿi leaders are an elite community of highly educated intellectuals who frequently speak standard Arabic among themselves and share a minority religion that others do not understand and often do not even know exists in Senegal. They are struggling to legitimate Islam for themselves by forming religious networks, based on their knowledge of Shiʿi legal texts and direct ties to marajiʿ. Senegalese converts partially depend on the Lebanese shaykh and prominent Lebanese merchants to help finance their institutions and activities. In addition to their own income-generating activities, they also hope for more tangible rewards for their faith from Iran than merely the propagation of the Islamic Revolution.

I am frequently asked how many Senegalese have converted to Shiʿi Islam, and such an estimate is even more difficult to determine than the population of Lebanese in Senegal. In 2003 a Senegalese shaykh once guessed that there were anywhere from a few thousand to possibly 25,000, or 1 percent of Senegal's population. Another Shiʿi activist estimated that year that his community did not surpass 1,000 members. These figures differ substantially from the 130,000 quoted by Shaykh al-Zayn in chapter 5. A decade later, a Senegalese shaykh told me in an interview in 2014 that there are millions of students who have been taught by the schools run by his organization—all of whom will be Shiʿa in several generations. "Shiʿi Islam is irreversible in West Africa now," he exclaimed. A convert once emphasized that the quality, not quantity, of Senegalese Shiʿa is what interests community leaders. "Only God knows how many we are," he told me. A distinction can be made between those Senegalese who self-identify as Shiʿa and those who are identified as such by others, a point to which I will return.

Converting to an "Active Islam"

Cherif informed me that he always wanted to be close to the Islamic religion in Iran.[8] He was drawn by Imam Khomeini's charisma, and even though he was only sixteen or seventeen years old during the time of the revolution he avidly watched events unfold on television. Khomeini claimed to be a descendant of the Prophet, which, according to many Senegalese, gave him Islamic authenticity.[9] For Cherif, the reaction of the rest of the world to the kidnapping of the fifty-two American hostages in Tehran (1979–1981) demonstrated Khomeini's power in causing widespread fear and anxiety. Khomeini's deftness in political Islam caused Cherif to exclaim, "*Voilà un musulman!*" Before becoming Shiʿi he was obsessed with Ayatollah Khomeini but was also enamored with music, especially that of Bob Marley. He went to mosque and afterward listened to reggae. Bob Marley's death in 1981 led to a rupture in Cherif's hobby, and eventually he began to read and became interested in the Qurʾan. His return to Islam coincided with the 1982 attacks against Americans in Beirut. He and other youth were pleased to see that a small country like Lebanon could be victorious over great powers like the United States, France, Italy, and Israel and bring them to their knees. Again he exclaimed, "*Voilà l'Islam!*" and told me, "You understand that here was an active Islam that could do some good for humanity. The Islam that remains in place only to conduct marriages, say greetings, and drink tea, that is not really Islam." Cherif claimed to be the first in Senegal to organize a celebration for the anniversary of the Iranian Revolution.

Cherif was born in Dakar in 1963. His father, a career officer in the French army from 1947 to 1963, served in Indonesia, Vietnam, and Algeria, although none of his sons were interested in completing their military service. After he was liberated from the army, Cherif's father worked for a company assembling and selling French cars. A rambunctious child, Cherif began his studies at two and a half years of age at the corner religious school. He entered a Franco-Arabic school at age seven, and in 1972 enrolled in the school of Fédération des Associations Islamiques du Sénégal, a state-controlled reformist association. After receiving his *baccalauréat* in 1981 he took classes at the Islamic Institute of Dakar, where he continued Arabic lessons.[10] In 1985 he began to study French and Arabic at Université Cheikh Anta Diop. He finished three years of university but was unable to complete his degree because he needed to work. That same year, at the age of twenty-two, he began working part-time as a librarian at the Senegalese-Turkish school, operated by Turkey's Fethullah Gülen revivalist movement. There he discovered books on Shi'i Islam, but was told by a librarian that Shi'a were heretics and the books were not useful. Such comments only sparked his imagination more, he told me, because man is always curious about what is forbidden to him. The library closed at 6:00 PM, but he often stayed until ten or eleven o'clock at night engaging in "extraordinary" conversations with friends discussing Shi'i ideas. After discovering these Shi'i books, he approached the Iranian embassy to ask for additional information. Cherif considers Shi'i Islam to be an intellectual movement, not a warrior movement.[11] He explained to me that in Senegal poverty often means illiteracy, but the Qur'an states that one should read and promotes education.

Cherif is well traveled in The Gambia, Mauritania, Guinea, Sierra Leone, Ghana, Nigeria, and Kenya. He has also been to France, Dubai, United Arab Emirates, Saudi Arabia, Morocco, and many times to Iran. In every country he visits he talks about Shi'i Islam with people he encounters. In Iran he had the opportunity to attend seminars to continue his studies. However, his family was in Senegal and he was unable to leave them for long. Iranians provided him with books; eventually he taught himself enough about Shi'i Islam that during a subsequent visit to Iran he was awarded shaykh status and given a turban to wear, a great honor that inspires awe and respect for his religious knowledge.

Cherif married in 1986 and gave his five children Arabic names. His youngest three children have distinctively Shi'i names: Muhammad Baqir (the fifth Imam), Fatima Zahra (the Prophet's daughter and Imam 'Ali's wife), and Narjis Zaynab (mother of Imam al-Mahdi, the twelfth Imam).[12] In 1997 he began teaching these new religious ideas to his family. Two of his brothers work paving roads, two others are small businessmen, another buys and sells fish, and another brother is a woodcarver. All became Shi'a, along with Cherif's wife. His parents also converted to Shi'i Islam from Cherif's influence, as has his sister, although his siblings' spouses retained their memberships in Sufi orders. His brothers allowed him to educate their children; as a result his nieces and nephews are being brought up in the Shi'i tradition. Cherif plans to continue to work in Islamic education by writing books about human development, women's and children's rights, poverty, and unemployment to instruct the Senegalese public about Islam. He founded the Ali Yacine Centre Islamique de Recherches et d'Informations (described in chapter 7).

Other Conversion Accounts

Assan also discovered Shi'i Islam as a result of the Iranian Revolution. Raised Tijani and educated at al-Azhar University in Cairo in the philosophy of the Qur'an, Assan was first exposed to Sunni Islam and became a jurist, but worked as an economist in Dakar. Like Joseph, he followed the media's portrayal of Khomeini and was disgusted at how he was demonized by Western and Senegalese journalists and how Shi'a were accused of being blasphemous.

> The Iranian Revolution drew the whole world's attention. I followed the events, how they unfolded, but I paid particular attention to the ways in which events were interpreted; commentary in the Western media, and how identical commentary, style, and formulas were mimicked in the Senegalese press. I questioned what was going on and tried to understand the image of Khomeini conveyed by television. I saw the image and its very essence was Islamic: his grace, clairvoyance, serenity, and so on. Everything that Islam represents was reflected in the image of Imam Khomeini shown on television and in photos reproduced by newspapers.
>
> But the written commentary was awfully distorted. It gave a totally false image of a bloodthirsty Imam Khomeini. That made me more critical and pushed me to explore internal dynamics of the Iranian Revolution, to collect more information and retrieve from here another version. The Western version was not satisfactory to me, the one that said that even if he was not the enemy he was the adversary because he was setting up an alternative political system to the capitalist one in order to compete with the West.

Instead of believing what the media portrayed about Khomeini, Assan came up with his own reality. "I finally realized that [Shi'i Islam] is Islam in its primordial form; authentic, sincere, and loyal." He saw the Iranian Revolution, which in his view restored dignity to Islam and belief to Muslims, as the only successful revolution since the time of Muhammad. He became Shi'i in 1987 in his late twenties, at a time when there were numerous conferences and debates in Dakar about Shi'i thought. He was of that generation of judgmental students who discovered Shi'i Islam because of Khomeini, and who became Shi'i because it offered "solutions to all the issues I have been grappling with and could not find answers to anywhere else. I found there [in Shi'i Islam] adequate answers to satisfy my thirst." Assan is convinced that Senegalese are slowly starting to see that Khomeini was right in his revolution as a means to protest the West, and that the conflict between Saddam Hussein and George W. Bush opened the world to becoming even more favorable toward Shi'i Islam.

Assan attended a number of religious conferences in London, Morocco, Canada, and many other countries. He hopes that by bringing new Islamic ideas to Senegal he will be helping the development of his country. "That is my philosophy. My ambition is to spread Islamic knowledge in Senegal, to help more effectively in the development of the country while preserving at the same time its coherence and national unity. This is important because you cannot work in a conflictive environment. It is not possible; people must eat and drink. For that, they have to live in a pacified and peaceful environment to be then able to think and use their brains."

Assan stressed that even though many Senegalese Shiʿa were influenced by the Iranian Revolution,

> our community is not a political movement; we are not interested in political matters, neither are we defining our positions. We are simply paying attention to Islam's teachings on different issues, the line of conduct we think is relevant to different situations. We are always trying to find the best approach to overcoming obstacles. This could certainly help politicians think more clearly and reach the best possible decision. . . . The Prophet tells us that we have to teach the ignorant. . . . The first step of teaching is to get him to accept to listen, and then to accept the truth. If this means being political, then we are political, but not in the way others think we are, by demanding an Islamic state. Such a demand does not make sense. Let me repeat it: it makes no sense to proclaim that Senegal must be an Islamic state. That is not the issue. People live as sincere Muslims, truthful, others live as sincere Christians, truthful, and we all live in harmony. We are all brothers.

Gibril, a Toucouleur born in Dakar, likewise discovered Shiʿi Islam because of the Iranian Revolution, while studying abroad in the late 1970s.

> At the time I was studying in Tunisia. I was not planning to leave the country but I left to visit France. I saw Iranian students preparing for the arrival of Imam Khomeini. That was in 1979. I asked what they were doing and was told that they were welcoming their shaykh. Well, it wasn't until I returned to Tunisia from France to go back to school when I learned that an imam named Khomeini had come to settle in France.[13] On our side, we were emotionally involved while trying hard to form an opinion. Who is this Imam Khomeini? There was a group strongly critical of him. I asked myself why. So now we wanted to find out the difference between this old man and other religious old men. That motivated us to dig even deeper: What is it? First of all, who is Imam Khomeini? On which grounds is he standing? And then we learned that he was Shiʿi. But what is Shiʿi Islam? Well, I returned home ten years later, after the [Iran-Iraq] war . . . , and books were now available to people; books that dealt with legal issues instead of just political ones. The legal approach provided a better context for the knowledge we had already acquired. These books provided us with knowledge that we now estimate to be much broader, much more global, a general knowledge of Islam.

Gibril became Shiʿi in 1988 and homeschools his children in the Shiʿi tradition, in addition to teaching his eldest son to be an artist like his father.

Ibrahima was also drawn to Shiʿi Islam through Iranian efforts. Born in 1960 in Kaolack, he studied Arabic and Qurʾan at a Tijani school and later attended secondary school in Thies. He was a student at Université Cheikh Anta Diop when he was introduced to Shiʿi Islam in 1987 through magazines from Iran that he found in the Arabic department. He was part of the group of thirty-five students who founded Dakar's university mosque, ten of whom were Shiʿa, including the mosque's first imam. Upon graduating he travelled to Sierra Leone where he studied *shariʿa* (Islamic law) from 1989 to 1990 in a Lebanese- and Iranian-run hawza. He additionally studied in various Shiʿi institutes in The Gambia, Guinea Bissau, and Mali. In 1991 he received an Iranian scholarship to study in Qom for two years, where he earned the title "shaykh" and became Khamenei's wakil. He directed an Islamic school in the Parcelles suburb of Dakar for ten years, although he was afraid to openly wear his turban due to strong Wahhabi influence in the area. In 2002 he was chosen to head the branch of Shaykh al-Zayn's Islamic Institute in Kaolack (until it closed in 2013). He performed holiday celebrations for Lebanese and taught classes for Senegalese on the Arabic language, Qurʾan, and fiqh. He was working on influencing Senegalese in Kaolack to become Shiʿa.

Conversion experiences such as those described above are not unique. All around the world Khomeini stood at the center of the Iranian Revolution, and he alone brought together the masses, giving them identity, unity, and purpose. This was the argument of Abrahamian's provocative book *Khomeinism,* by which he referred to a variant of "Third World" populism in which a middle-class movement used radical rhetoric to mobilize lower classes. Abrahamian (1993) argues that Khomeini in fact broke with Shiʿi tradition in employing a borrowed rhetoric of vast public appeal that centered not on theological issues but on real socioeconomic and political grievances and entailed the struggle of nation-states to come to terms with modernity. Khomeini can thus be seen as a pragmatic reformer, not a "fundamentalist." Khomeini's popularity caused scholars such as Casanova (1994) to take notice of how religion in the 1980s "went public" and became "deprivatized," and how religious traditions once considered marginal and irrelevant in the modern world assumed public roles.

The Iranian Revolution was symbolically important to many because Islamic reformist opposition forces overthrew a Western-influenced secular regime. Foucault even interpreted the revolution as a protest against the political rationality of the modern era (Jahanbegloo 2004:ix; see also Afary and Anderson 2005). The Iranian Revolution led to a surge in scholarship on Islamic resistance trends in other Muslim countries, often encouraged by events in Iran. Hunter's brief examination of Iran's influence in the "Third World," including Africa, focuses on "finding an audience" for its "revolutionary Islamic ideology" and on Iran's self-image as the "champion of the oppressed" (1990:167). Keddie (1995:189) declares:

"The Iranian revolution . . . helped spread a militant and revolutionary version of Shiʿism and of the Muharram celebrations." Keddie later writes, "The political aspects of the religio-political movement identified with the leader of the Iranian Revolution and Islamic Republic, Ruhollah Khomeini, have in recent years been more influential than have been its religious aspects" (2002:6). Likewise, Nasr (2002) explores how in Asia the revolution served to mobilize minority against majority, and concludes that the lasting impact of the revolution was a deep division between Shiʿa and Sunnis, sectarian discourse, and deepening social cleavages. With the exception of a brief mention by Bayat and Baktiari (2002) that revolutionary developments in Iran contributed to an increased mood of religiosity in Egypt, most scholarship focuses on the political and revolutionary impact of the revolution and not on the spread of Shiʿi Islam.

Shiʿi converts are rendering Khomeini's Islamic Revolution in Iran into a nonviolent philosophy of an authenticated Islam that will bring progress to Senegal through knowledge and not through confrontation. Cosmopolitan Shiʿi Islam is thus denationalized from its Iranian (and Lebanese and Iraqi) context. Revolutionary language and ideology are translated to be more compatible with Senegalese political culture through creation of "a new religious consciousness and practice from various familiar and familiarized cultural resources and traditions" (Larson 1997:979). Chapter 7 will explore how Shiʿi ritual practices are transformed into a Senegalese understanding and application. Furthermore, the former colonial struggle is itself converted into a postcolonial one of Islam (an anti-Western Islam, not an accommodationist one) versus the West. In appealing to those holding Islamic power and resources, converts arm themselves with books, knowledge, and financial means to empower themselves in Senegal's Islamic debates, which enables them to remake Shiʿi Islam into something meaningful to other Senegalese who are concerned, on a national scale, with peace and economic development.

Shaykh al-Zayn and Senegalese Conversion

The Iranian Revolution, while prevalent in Senegalese conversion accounts, was not the only event that drew Senegalese to Shiʿi Islam. The Lebanese shaykh's efforts, as described in the previous chapter, also extended to Senegalese. Shaykh al-Zayn actively worked to recruit capable Senegalese Muslims to his religious institutions. For example Ousmane, along with several other thirteen-year-old students from a Tijani-run religious school in Thies, was given a scholarship to study at College al-Zahra in Dakar. Surrounded by Shiʿa at the Lebanese school, Ousmane learned about the religion and adopted its beliefs. He was then sent to Lebanon on another scholarship to complete his studies at an Islamic school in Tyre. He also studied under Ayatollah Muhammad Husayn Fadlallah in Beirut. In 2000, Ousmane returned to Senegal a shaykh and began teaching at the Arabic Language Institute and assisting Shaykh al-Zayn with holiday prayers. The following conversion accounts illustrate additional examples of Shaykh al-Zayn's influence in bringing Senegalese to Shiʿi Islam.

Converting to a "Peaceful Islam"

Ismaïl is a public figure in the south of Senegal. When we walked together along the streets of Ziguinchor, men who passed us greeted him with respect. Ismaïl was born in 1945 in a small Casamance village to a family of religious scholars. He recounted how his Muslim paternal great-uncle was village chief in Guinea Bissau and his Christian maternal grandfather also headed a nearby village. The two men befriended one another, and the maternal grandfather offered the neighboring chief his daughter's hand in marriage, explaining that although she was Christian she neither drank alcohol nor ate pork and frequently remained alone in contemplation. His paternal grandfather responded, "That is a great honor, but I am old and do not want to marry a virgin. My nephew is a good man who has learned the holy Qurʾan by heart. Would you bless their marriage?" Ismaïl's mother thus married his father, converted to Islam, and gave birth to a large number of children, many of whom did not survive.

Ismaïl learned Qurʾan from his parents for six years and later studied Arabic grammar and religious sciences under his uncle in Ziguinchor. He returned to his village in 1968 to care for his mother and remained there for ten years, working unsuccessfully as a merchant. He became Shiʿi when Shaykh al-Zayn inaugurated a religious school in Ziguinchor. Because of his eloquence, the local Lebanese community asked Ismaïl to interpret the shaykh's Arabic speech into Creole. When Shaykh al-Zayn arrived they gathered in the school and he delivered a sermon. Ismaïl began to interpret sentence by sentence but the shaykh requested that he wait until the conclusion of the sermon. Despite the difficulty of this task, Ismaïl said he managed to translate every word and even replicated the shaykh's movements. Shaykh al-Zayn listened to Ismaïl's interpretation and embraced him when he finished, inquiring with a smile whether he was in possession of an inner tape recorder.

During the shaykh's second visit to Ziguinchor he invited Ismaïl to have dinner with him and encouraged him to seek the path of righteousness. Ismaïl agreed and later took the ferryboat to Dakar on December 2, 1993, in order to visit Shaykh al-Zayn's Islamic Institute. He accepted the Shiʿi doctrine on that very day and began to call on people to perform good deeds. He regarded others as brethren in humanity and faith and abided by God's Holy Book and the Prophetic traditions. Shaykh al-Zayn provided him with books, and Ismaïl began to believe, with the help of the shaykh, that Imam ʿAli was the closest of the Imams and caliphs to the Prophet. Nevertheless, Ismaïl respects Sunnis and never insults or disagrees with them.

Ismaïl dedicated his life to education after becoming Shiʿi. He opened a school in Ziguinchor in 1998, College Imam ʿAli Reda (the eighth Shiʿi Imam), in which he teaches Qurʾan, Arabic, grammar, and jurisprudence. His sons also teach at the school, which consists of two classrooms built in front of their house. He holds regular majalis in his home, where he conducts religious ceremonies and delivers lectures on Islam. Although our interview was conducted in Arabic, he speaks to his followers in Wolof and Creole. The main goal of his school is

> to strengthen Islam and support humanity, make peace prevail and achieve equality among human beings, and stop seditions that result from ignorance. Once man knows and believes in God and the Day of Judgment, he will never dare to commit bad deeds and will never hurt others. My goal is to free the world of hatred and enmity. God knows what is better for all of us. He knew our future and destiny long before we were born. Nobody can escape or change God's fate. Man should believe that his own interest should stem from interests of others. That is exactly what I try to convince my students. When all Muslims and mankind truly believe in God, the whole world will live in peace and manage to coexist.

Since 1982 rebels in the southern Casamance region of Senegal have been waging an independence campaign against the central government in Dakar. The Movement of Democratic Forces in the Casamance (MFDC) instigated attacks from neighboring Guinea Bissau. Ismaïl recounted his family's tragedies—his brother, a teacher, was killed by rebels, his house was bombed, and many ʿulama were killed. More than any other region in Senegal, the Casamance has been dominated by Christians but retained "traditional religion." Ismaïl explained that the war in the Casamance gave Islam a chance to succeed because people lived in fear. He and other Senegalese Shiʿi leaders trust the spread of Islam can help bring peace to the region.

> Our movement in Casamance is helpless and weak. Yet we implore God the Almighty to grant us peace as we want to be believers. We pray to God day and night to find peace everywhere. We want peace to prevail not only in Senegal but also in the whole world. When a person is killed anywhere, the whole world should feel sorry for him regardless of his religion. A Christian once visited me after hearing my sermons on the radio and exclaimed that if all Muslims spoke in the same manner then good and peace would prevail everywhere.

Ismaïl has never traveled to the Middle East and is less learned about Shiʿi Islam than coreligionists. He admitted to being "weak in Shiʿi Islam" but proudly told me he is learning, often by discussing religion with a Lebanese métis man in Ziguinchor.

Ismaïl is an example of a Shiʿi leader who does not work in Dakar. Although many Senegalese Shiʿa are elite intellectuals from various Senegalese ethnic groups who have the opportunity to travel internationally and have access to resources, they do not work only in urban areas. Richard Werbner's notion of *cosmopolitan ethnicity* is applicable here for tensions it displays: "It is urban yet rural; at once inward- and outward-looking, it builds inter-ethnic alliances from intra-ethnic ones and constructs difference while transcending it. Being a cosmopolitan does not mean turning one's back on the countryside, abandoning rural allies or rejecting ethnic bonds" (2002:732).[14] Interethnic cooperation and mutuality is key to understanding the postcolonial development of cosmopolitan ethnicity described by Werbner in Botswana, which also arises out of a broader process of minoritization: "making minorities who, in terms of consciousness, identification and labeling, are actively differentiated from a majority and each other yet, in some ways, also transcend their differences" (732).

Werbner's notion, which resonates with my case study of Senegalese Shiʿa, contradicts Ferguson's (1999) earlier elaboration of a more dualist cosmopolitanism in another southern African context with contrasting "localist" and "cosmopolitan" cultural modes. Ferguson suggests that localist Zambian copper migrants demonstrated a strong sense of allegiance to their rural "home" community, displaying a strong ethnic or regional identity, whereby cosmopolitan style marked the distance certain workers maintained from "home," often rejecting rural ties and embracing Western-dominated mass culture. Ferguson thus defines cosmopolitanism specifically through demands and pressures of localism (and not in relation to international mobility or cultural affinities to "the West"). "It is less about being at home in the world than it is about seeking worldliness at home" (212), he writes, and goes so far as to suggest that cosmopolitans cannot be "at home" at home since they are unable to be bound by claims of the local. In the Senegalese context the desire to migrate abroad, not merely to Dakar, is so compelling, and foreign-acquired wealth such a status symbol, that cosmopolitans enjoy nothing more than to return to communities of origin, urban or rural, to share with family, friends, and community members their newfound knowledge and rank. This encourages others from "local" communities to join their network and convert.

Converting to an Islam of Opportunities Abroad

Youssou was shaykh of the largest Shiʿi mosque in Senegal and the only Senegalese Shiʿi institution in a central location. Like Ismaïl he wore the outfit of a Shiʿi cleric: gray or black robes over a white shirt and white turban.[15] Other Senegalese Shiʿa dressed in boubous, Western business suits, or button-down shirts and slacks. Al-Hajj Ibrahim Derwiche, a prominent Lebanese industrialist, built a large Shiʿi mosque next to Shaykh al-Zayn's al-Zahra school and Dakar's main intercity bus station. The mosque is impressive, with high ceilings and a decorated plaster dome, and attracts crowds of Senegalese Muslims during Friday prayer.

Friday sermons are orated in Wolof to a mixed group of Murid, Tijani, and Qadiri Muslims, with a Shiʿi minority. Youssou also taught classes in the mosque,
and later in a three-room school also built by Derwiche. Senegalese Shiʿa pray in
this mosque in addition to Shaykh al-Zayn's mosque.

I first met with Youssou following Friday prayer, which he invited me to attend. He explained that the *adhan* (call to prayer) is the Shiʿi adhan, which includes references to ʿAli along with the Prophet Muhammad. Although Shiʿi doctrines are applied in the mosque, Youssou stressed that he lectured on universal
Muslim themes.

> If you address Shiʿa only, Sunnis will find a Sunni mosque. That is why over
> 2,000 Sunnis pray here on Fridays along with some 150 Shiʿa.[16] They all pray
> together. Each of them finds what he is after. The sermon is not just for Shiʿa
> or Sunnis—it is for all Muslims. During Ramadan, for example, sermons focus
> on issues related to fasting. During hajj season they center on hajj issues and so
> on. You pick a topic related to all and apply it to both Sunnis and Shiʿa.

Youssou's choice of Islamic discourse was nonconfrontational, and, according
to him, Sunnis in his congregation did not object to having a Shiʿi imam. During Muharram both Sunnis and Shiʿa spend the day at the mosque and listen to a
special sermon about events of the battle of Karbala. Youssou informed me that
Sunnis are also deeply touched by these events.

Youssou first learned about Shiʿi Islam from a Lebanese "brother," a coffee
seller in the Futa where Youssou was born. He studied with this man's son and
made no distinction then between Sunni or Shiʿi. The boys learned Qurʾan, fiqh,
Maliki jurisprudence, and other areas of religious knowledge from Youssou's father and his father's colleague. Youssou then left the Futa for Dakar in pursuit of
books and knowledge. His uncle in Dakar sent Youssou to study for four years
under a Sunni scholar who taught him Qurʾan and shariʿa.

Upon completing these lessons Youssou wanted to travel abroad—to Saudi
Arabia, Kuwait, Morocco, Lebanon, or any other Arab country. Youssou approached
his brother, who directed a school and had relations with Saudi Arabia, hoping he
would have connections to send Youssou abroad. His brother advised him to first
complete his primary and secondary degrees in Arabic in Dakar. Upon completing this education Youssou still longed for a scholarship to study in Saudi Arabia.
He had another uncle who had first introduced him to the Lebanese coffee trader
in the Futa and who requested that this man help Youssou travel. The Lebanese
trader gave Youssou Shiʿi books and corrected Youssou's knowledge, heard from
others, about Shiʿi Islam. Youssou became Shiʿi in 1982, convinced that ʿAli should
have succeeded the Prophet Muhammad. The Lebanese trader informed Youssou
about a Lebanese shaykh in Dakar who sent students to Iran, and asked Youssou
where he wanted to travel. Youssou had no preference as long as he could study

Interior view of Ibrahim Derwiche mosque, Dakar, 2013.

abroad. His Lebanese mentor took Youssou before Shaykh al-Zayn. The shaykh told Youssou to obtain a passport, but first Youssou enrolled in the shaykh's courses at the Islamic Institute. Youssou studied under Shaykh al-Zayn for four years and met many Lebanese Shiᶜa who helped him follow the Shiᶜi path. Although he completed his studies in Senegal, with books from Lebanon and France, his dream of traveling abroad was also achieved: he visited Iran several times, in addition to Egypt, Morocco, and Tunisia.

Once Senegalese learned more about its ideas, they accepted Shiᶜi Islam. Youssou remarked that it was hard to know exactly when Shiᶜi Islam began in Senegal. "Determining that is difficult as many would appear saying they were Shiᶜa but did not think others were Shiᶜa so they were discreet. At first, Shiᶜa were practicing rituals at home, not being public about it. Most Senegalese Shiᶜa were Sunnis first, then followed the Shiᶜi sect with a backdrop of rampant unemployment. Now it is senseless to hide being Shiᶜi in a country of Islam, religious freedom, democracy, and human rights, where one does not infringe on freedoms of others." Youssou's wife and sons are Shiᶜa, as are some of his brothers and their children. Many of his friends also converted due to his influence, and he boasted that some even became scholars.

Travel and Conversion

Although some converts like Youssou, Joseph, Cherif, and Ismaïl first discovered Shiʿi Islam in Senegal, others such as Assan and Gibril were exposed to Shiʿi debates through studies in Egypt and Tunisia. Thus another theme in conversion stories is the experience of travel (or desire to travel) to other Muslim—and even non-Muslim—countries. The following account is very telling in this regard.

Mamadou was born into a prestigious religious family of the Qadiriyya order. His father was an important marabout and gave his children a proper religious education. Mamadou studied Arabic and Qurʾan at an early age. He was able to learn about Shiʿi Islam only by leaving Senegal and his family's strong religious traditions. He went to Algeria to continue his education and eventually ended up in Burkina Faso as an Arabic teacher. One of his students was reading a book by Muhammad al-Tijani al-Samawi called *Thuma Ihtadaytu* (Then I Was Guided) about the Tunisian author's discovery of Shiʿi Islam. Mamadou told his student, who was given the book by an Iranian school in Ouagadougou, that Shiʿa do not believe in God, a common stereotype. Nevertheless Mamadou started to read the book and could not stop. He had finished al-Samawi's book before the next day, when he shared it with the director of the Arabic school, who also read it and discussed it with him. The most striking part of the book for them was when a group of Africans went before Ayatollah Sayyid Abu al-Qasim al-Khuʾi, a great Iranian religious scholar who taught in Najaf, Iraq. Ayatollah al-Khuʾi asked the Africans which religious leader they followed, and their response was Malik, founder of the Maliki school of law during the first century of Islam. The Shiʿi leader questioned how they could follow a man who is dead. Al-Khuʾi explained that Shiʿa no longer follow Jaʿfar, founder of the Shiʿi branch of Islamic law, but they follow al-Khuʾi.[17] Senegalese like Mamadou were convinced by this argument. After reading the book Mamadou went to the Shiʿi bookstore in Ouagadougou to learn more and immediately converted in 1990.

When Mamadou later returned to Senegal, he searched for other Senegalese who, like him, had discovered Shiʿi Islam. These men formed an Islamic association that aims to teach other Senegalese the truth about Shiʿi Islam. As the son of an influential Qadiri marabout, Mamadou is an asset for Shaykh al-Zayn. When important Lebanese religious leaders visit Senegal, Shaykh al-Zayn organizes a tour of Senegal's Sufi centers. The shaykh relies on Senegalese Shiʿa with local connections in Sufi orders to serve as go-betweens, and Mamadou frequently escorts Lebanese on official visits to Tivaouane and Ndiassane, Sufi centers nearest to Dakar, whose leaders are closest to Shaykh al-Zayn.

Mamadou's itinerary is an illustration of the link between Arabic literacy, travel, and religious conversion. This is not a new phenomenon. Circulation of religious ideas, Islamic clerics, and commodities across the Sahara into the Sahel and across the Indian Ocean into East Africa existed historically, long before this present moment (Austen 2010; Eickelman and Piscatori 1990; Ho 2006; Robinson 2004; Simpson and Kresse 2008). As Mandaville (2001), Marsden (2008), Roy (2004), and others have noted, migration, Islamic learning, and new media technologies further encouraged Muslims to interact with one another and to become more aware of their religion's internal diversity.

While a majority of Senegal's converts discovered Shiʿi Islam through studies in the Middle East, Abdou became Shiʿi in Canada. Born in 1969 to a Tijani family in Dakar, Abdou studied at a French Catholic school and never received a formal Islamic education in Senegal. He lived in Washington, D.C., for a few years when his father worked for the World Bank, then studied in Montreal. Abdou discovered the Shiʿi school of thought in 1988 at age nineteen by reading books on Islam alone in McGill University's library. He was first drawn to the spiritual message of Shiʿi Islam and the notion of the Imamate and later became convinced by philosophical arguments and uses of logic and reason of Shiʿi scholars. Although Abdou never had an Arabic education, he can read books on Shiʿi Islam in Arabic, French, and English. It took two years after his conversion before he met other Shiʿa in Canada. After living in Montreal for seven years, Abdou returned to Senegal in 1995. He was part of a vibrant group of Iranian, Iraqi, Pakistani, Lebanese, and other Shiʿa in Montreal, where he was the only Senegalese, but it took him five years to find a community of Shiʿa in Dakar. He explained that many Shiʿa in Senegal lived their conviction alone because they became Shiʿi independently, did not have the means to organize, and were therefore not visible like Sufi orders. He considered Shiʿa to be among Senegal's intellectuals as they spend their free time reading and studying. He called Shiʿi Islam an "acquired religion," not an "inherited religion" like most other religions.

Variations on a Scale of Shiʿi Belief

Not every Senegalese who comes in contact with Shiʿi Islam feels as strongly about the religion as those whose conversion stories I narrated. Abdou described three attitudes toward Shiʿi Islam in Senegal. First are those who chose to follow Shiʿi Islam. Second are "sympathizers," those who do not consider themselves Shiʿa but attend Shiʿi gatherings. According to Abdou, although sympathizers philosophically accept Shiʿi Islam, they continue to practice as Sunni Muslims. Finally are opponents of Shiʿi Islam who never read books about the religion and accept stereotypes that Shiʿa consider ʿAli, not Muhammad, to be the prophet. Ignorance, Abdou tells me, is the reason why people are opposed to Shiʿi Islam, but once opponents listen to its ideas, they, too, will "cross the border" from the Sunni to Shiʿi school of thought.

Sympathizers correspond with Lofland and Skonovd's (1981) third typology of *experimental conversion,* where the potential convert gives the process a try and genuine conversion may come later. The prospective convert participates in group activities and learns to act like a convert. There are low degrees of social pressure, and the process takes place over a prolonged period, where belief arises out of participation. Not all sympathizers convert, however. Cherif sent me to visit his friend in Michigan, from whom I learned religious identities are not so clear-cut. Although Cherif considered his friend to be Shiʿi, the friend claimed not to be Shiʿi at all. He informed me that he once attended the Lebanese Shiʿi mosque in Dakar but did not know enough Arabic to follow the khutba and was under the impression that Shiʿa assumed more knowledge of Islam than Sunnis. Cherif's friend, in fact, belongs to the Murid organization of Michigan, proclaiming the Sufi order to be easier to follow than Shiʿi gatherings. He commented that in Senegal people are Shiʿa only when in the company of other Shiʿa, although he considered his friend Cherif to be "a true believer in Shiʿi Islam."

I visited another of Cherif's friends in the Senegalese community of Harlem, New York. This man considered himself to be part Sunni and part Shiʿi. He performs ablutions and prays with his arms down like Shiʿa, and even attends a Pakistani Shiʿi mosque during Muharram, but otherwise prays regularly with Sunni Muslims at the Malcolm Shabazz mosque in Harlem. He remarked that Shiʿa work harder than Murids to proselytize, and Shiʿi books are therefore easier to obtain than Sunni books. He provided me with the address of ʿAbbas Ahmad al-Bostani, whose Association Ahl al-Bayt in Paris distributed books free of charge. Al-Bostani has since moved to Montreal, and Shiʿa in Senegal regularly refer to his website (www.bostani.com).

These accounts raise the question of who is Shiʿi. Cummings critiques those who envision conversion to Islam as "a fundamental change in beliefs, an act of replacement perfect and complete when all pre-Islamic beliefs disappear in favor of Islamic tenets" (2001:559). According to Cummings, this rigid notion of conversion allowed scholars to distinguish "true" Muslims from those who emptily perform Islamic rituals while retaining original beliefs. Such a division is not that simple, and he calls instead for a reconceptualization of the process of religious conversion based on local perceptions. Peel (2000) further elucidates this emphasis on social identification by insisting that the only workable definition of *conversion* is the process by which people come to regard themselves, and be regarded by others, as members of particular religious groups. My goal here is not to compartmentalize people into rigid categories but to understand the processes by which they undergo identity change, which I describe using their own words.

The interlude following this chapter examines the life history of ʿUmar, a self-proclaimed convert to Shiʿi Islam who remains a well-respected Tijani scholar.

Shi'i cosmopolitanism therefore does not necessarily lead to a complete break with Sufi roots. Yet Shi'i converts continue to share many moral and social values with Sunni counterparts, and therefore conversion does not obscure Senegalese values, nor does it lead to "discontinuity" (Engelke 2004), "rupture," or "complete break with the past" (Meyer 1998). In maintaining their *Sénégalité,* converts continue to be part of and even influence Senegalese national culture through organizing religious events and efforts to contribute to economic development, yet they bypass local religious power structures in order to build their own.

Women, Wives, Conversion

The question of who is Shi'i pertains to women as well. Senegalese men dominate the Shi'i network, and my initial fieldwork found female converts to be wives or family members of male converts with little knowledge about the religion. In Senegal a woman customarily adopts her husband's religion. Over the past decade, however, an increasing number of female students attended Shi'i events, which have become more public and more widespread since my initial foray into this topic. This section is therefore indicative of my early research, and additional fieldwork is necessary to make definitive conclusions. In 2003 I interviewed two particularly passionate women who came upon Shi'i Islam independent of their families. Whereas many Senegalese men described an intellectual conversion experience, the women whose conversion accounts I summarize below follow Lofland and Skonovd's (1981) mystical mode of conversion. This is characterized by high intensity and trauma with little or no social pressure upon the convert, likely to be alone at the time of the event. While the critical period of conversion is brief, a period of stress preceding conversion may date back some time.

A Transformative Dream

For Fatou, who grew up in a village in southern Senegal and was twenty-one years old at the time of our first interview, becoming Shi'i was a sudden spiritual awakening.

> I was eleven in 1993 and my mother had just died. I saw Fatoumata [Fatima] al-Zahra in a vision, the daughter of Prophet Muhammad (PSL).[18] She told me to keep following this path because it will lead to happiness. I loved to pray and read Qur'an. At that time I did not wear the veil; I was in the 5th year of secondary school. I was reading Qur'an in translation—in general in Senegal the Qur'an is only taught in Arabic; the translation is not taught. I looked at Surat al-Nur [The Light, Sura 24] and Surat al-Ahzab [The Confederates, Sura 33], and saw that the Qur'an says that women should wear the veil. This surprised me and I asked my uncle whether it was true. He replied yes, it is true, but here in Senegal we have customs according to which younger women do not have to wear the veil. It is only when she turns fifty or seventy that she starts wearing her scarf. Whereas normally in Islam it is the young girl who should wear

the veil and once she turns fifty or sixty the veil will no longer be required of her. In Senegal it is totally the opposite and so I put on the veil right away and did not ask any questions.

After Fatou's dream she began to wear the veil against the will of her family. Even though her family disapproved, Fatou sensed others treated her with more deference: men gave up their seats for her on buses and called her *soxna-si*, a Wolof title of respect. She suffered from bad headaches when she was younger and experimented with many medicines to no avail. She found the headaches ceased when she covered her head. She even wraps a scarf around her head when she sleeps and has not had a headache since she began to veil.

Fatou credits one of her schoolteachers for educating her about Shiʿi Islam. He studied in Dakar and became a disciple of Cherif before his first teaching post in the Casamance. Fatou recounts, "I immersed myself in Shiʿi Islam; I tried to discover what it is. Later, I discovered teachings of Imam Khomeini and the strong woman that Fatoumata al-Zahra was." What her teacher, who later became her husband, taught her about the religion corresponded to what she saw in her dream.

Life was not all rosy for Fatou. After her mother's death extended family did not want to care for her and forced her to marry her teacher. It was an unhappy marriage resulting in a daughter when Fatou was fifteen years old and a son when she was eighteen. A painful divorce gave her ex-husband full custody of her children. Fatou left the village to live with her father in Dakar but struggled to earn an income while commuting long distances. During this period her faith never faltered.

> Imam ʿAli said that as your faith becomes stronger challenges become more and more difficult. . . . Imagine a young woman who is trying to preserve her dignity and honor without a penny. There are other girls in my situation, or under even worse conditions, but they do not hesitate to embark on something else, that is to sell their bodies. I want to stay clean. Maybe my luck will come some day, but it is hard. I practice Shiʿi Islam full-time and defend my ideas. . . . You know there is no worse punishment for a mother than to take away her children, show that she is poor, without a source of income, burden her with that. It is very hard.

Yet Fatou came to understand that Shiʿi Islam affords women more rights than Senegalese Sufi Islam.[19]

> Women are allowed to study, expand their knowledge, conduct research. In Shiʿi Islam women are allowed to express themselves before an assembly and they will be heard. In Shiʿi Islam women are allowed to go out, take care of their business, without at the same time being tightly controlled. But in Sufi Islam it is completely the opposite. In Shiʿi Islam, the woman has a right to own prop-

erty; you are not forced, if you have a husband, to join your property together, that is to say what belongs to you will belong to him. All that does not exist in Sufi Islam. . . . You act with responsibility, conscience, awareness of cause and consequence, so that if I do this that is what will happen to me. That is what I like about Shiʿi Islam.

Fatou envisions that Shiʿi Islam will become a spiritual, not political, revolution in Senegal and prays that the religion will bring more rights to Senegalese women.

I don't think there will be a revolution because the typical Senegalese is naturally fearful—he does not like violence. But I do think of a revolution of attitudes, of ideals, the transformation of perspectives, for example, acceptance of the other. This is what makes Shiʿi Islam exceptional—it accepts the other and his or her difference; to understand the other, you have to accept his or her singularity, to be able to integrate him or her completely. To change things, it is necessary for men and women to reach out to one another and work side by side to make this world work.

Fatou was thus attracted to Shiʿi Islam's cosmopolitanism. She completed a distance-learning program in accounting from France, which enabled her to land a good business job in Dakar. She eventually married a Shiʿi man in the United States after a lengthy Skype courtship.

When Prayers Are Answered

Khady was born into a Tijani family of Wolof ethnicity in Dakar. When she was young, she identified not only as Tijani, but also as Murid and Qadiri. She felt she belonged to all Sufi orders, and when asked what faith she followed she replied "universal" Muslim. When she married, her husband did not pray and influenced her to become less religious. Khady taught at a Catholic school in the late 1970s and used to dress fashionably in miniskirts. Colleagues did not know if she was Muslim or Christian. She credited a 1989 vacation in Canada for changing her life. She was shocked by the appearance of transvestites in a nightclub, of which she did not approve. A few days later she visited the Sainte-Anne waterfalls and meditated while experiencing "God's miracles." At the waterfalls she began to feel a strong faith and awe for this God who created such beautiful nature. This was also the year of the Rushdie affair. Her sister-in-law in Canada found Khady reading the Qurʾan in English translation and asked if she was reading *The Satanic Verses.*

Khady no longer wanted to frequent nightclubs or dance to Youssou N'dour's *mbalax* music. Only the Qurʾan made her happy. She claimed to even prefer reading the Qurʾan to eating. She became chaste and no longer wore short dresses, although she continued to wear European dresses that covered her knees. She had always liked scarves, she told me.

When Khady returned from vacation she registered for Qur'anic classes, which was where she met Cherif, Assan, and Gibril. They would meet after work to discuss religion. The men with whom she studied never distinguished between Sunni and Shi'i Islam. Gibril convinced her to wear long sleeves and veil. Her first response was "Never!" but little by little her sleeves and skirts lengthened and she wore her scarves to cover her head. Eventually her style of dress completely transformed and she never wore the clothing purchased in Canada. She recounted, however, that she once saw a Shi'i Muslim wearing the Iranian *chador* in Senegal, to which she was opposed, arguing that one should not change one's people's ways. She dresses only in Senegalese clothing and wears Senegalese veils.[20] Friends were shocked at her altered style and began to visit her to see how she changed. They did not understand that her new mode of dress was by conviction alone and that nobody forced this transformation upon her. People judged her and criticized her, although a few admired her. Khady did not have a support network of other women.

Khady began to listen to the radio and attend religious conferences, where she quietly sat in the back of the room. At that time other veiled women in Senegal belonged to the Sunni Ibadu Rahman movement and wanted to recruit additional female followers. Khady befriended a woman in this movement whose husband was a migrant worker who lived most of the year abroad. She spent a lot of time with Khady and eventually informed her that everyone thought she was Shi'i. Khady had never heard of Shi'i Islam and inquired about the religion when people gossiped about her. Every time she prayed she asked God that if Shi'i Islam is good to guide her in its path, but if it is not good to divert her from its ways.

One day Khady decided to become Tijani to end the gossip about her beliefs and made an appointment with a marabout to get his authorization. As her parents were Tijani, if she formally accepted the wird she thought everyone would stop calling her Shi'i. However, before she saw the marabout another Senegalese Shi'i lent her a book about Shi'i ethics and proper behavior and gave her an address in France where she could write to obtain additional information.

Another day Khady's friend met her at the school where she worked. It was 5 PM and time to pray. Her friend brought her to a post office where other Ibadus worked, and they prayed together. That was Tuesday or Wednesday. On Thursday or Friday Khady's Ibadu friend invited her to a conference that afternoon. Radio Dunya announced the conference, whose theme was "the world of the devil," presented by an Arabic professor. The radio talked of Sunni healers, and Khady attended since the topic interested her. Men and women sat separately and this was the first time she experienced segregation at a public lecture. She felt deceived as instead of learning about the world of demons, she heard critiques of Shi'i Islam and specifically of Imam Khomeini. Khady loved Khomeini without ever having met him, calling her love for him a platonic love for the religion of God. She admired him because he supported the veil, which caused her many problems at first. She hung his photo in her room and concluded that maybe this was why others thought she was Shiʿi. She decided to leave the conference because she did not hear anything that would help advance her religious beliefs, which caused a ruckus and served as proof to others that she was Shiʿi.

On Monday or Tuesday her friend came to visit, bringing her again to the post office to pray. A man she did not know told her that she had deviated from the true path through Khomeini. This angered Khady, and she told the man that a dog always barks when it is afraid. She had not yet read the books she ordered from Paris, but warned this man that she would now study Shiʿi Islam and he should pray that she finds the right path. A dog who barks must be afraid of Shiʿi Islam, she concluded, and we must step up to grasp what is above us, as it is higher than us. She accused her friend of having set her up, allowing people to discuss her private life. Their friendship ended there.

Khady began to read books about Shiʿi Islam, which Gibril also explained to her. She wanted to choose Shiʿi Islam but was afraid. At the same time her father died and she did not want to betray his Tijani beliefs. She once again decided to accept the Tijani wird to put an end to her struggle. A friend offered to drive her to see Caliph ʿAbdul ʿAziz Sy. Her friend's husband, however, informed her that she could not become Tijani if she is a universal Muslim; becoming Tijani would no longer enable her to accept other branches of Islam. This man advised her to take six months to reflect before accepting the Tijani wird. She agreed because she only wanted to become Tijani so as not to betray her parents' religion and to put an end to the Shiʿi gossip. For six months she prayed and listened to a cassette to learn the history of the Tijani order. During her prayer she recited invocations and told God that she is a universal Muslim but everyone calls her a Shiʿi. She asked God to choose for her between Shiʿi and Tijani Islam and guide her toward the right path.

One night in 1993 Khady's prayers were answered. One of the Shiʿi men with whom she studied taught her how to request what is best from God in a guidance supplication called *istikhara,* using the Qurʾan to provide a response. According to her consultation the Qurʾan's letters produced favorable results. She wrote down an invocation, grasped her chaplet, and began to pray: "God, by Your miracles of nature, if Shiʿi Islam is good show me immediately." It was the dry season in Senegal and as she prayed to end her confusion a heavy rain began to fall. She was thus convinced, in a mystical moment, to openly identify as Shiʿi and no longer be afraid. She went to Shaykh al-Zayn's office the following day to inform him that she is proud to be Shiʿi. She told her Ibadu friend of her ultimate decision. Her husband also admired her determination. She began to attend the Lebanese mosque for Friday prayers. She decided to go to Mecca and learned from Shaykh al-Zayn how Shiʿa perform the pilgrimage. She made hajj with her two faiths. She did not want to exclude Sunni practices, but in addition she followed what the shaykh had instructed her to do. Shiʿi Islam strengthened her faith in the Prophet and his family. She read many Shiʿi books, prayers, and invocations, all in French. She felt happy and free from the earlier pressure she experienced.

One day her male Shiʿi friends came to Khady's home with their wives and wanted to create a Shiʿi women's association. The wives, she told me, became Shiʿi but did not know the religion well. As Khady was the most educated Senegalese woman in Shiʿi Islam, they approached her to be the association's president. When she agreed to lead the association with the permission of her husband (who was not Shiʿi), she scheduled a meeting at her house, but nobody came. The women lived scattered in Dakar's remote suburbs, so a second women's meeting was organized in the more centrally located suburb of Parcelles. Khady made a list of participants and went to the minister of the interior to obtain paperwork to register as an official association. She decided that association members would have to wear the hijab, and Khady's sister began to veil that very day. Khady approached Shaykh al-Zayn about an appropriate name for the association, and he suggested Jamaʿat Um al-Muʿminin Khadija al-Kubra (the Association of the Mother of Believers Khadija the Eldest). This was in 1999 or 2000, before the men's association, Ansar Muhammad, was formed (see chapter 7). The women's group had many aspirations: to teach people about Shiʿi Islam, perform communal domestic tasks that engaged in family economics, and open a Qurʾanic school, a kindergarten, and a women's cooperative that would teach sewing and cooking. The women, however, never paid dues and stopped attending meetings, and the initiative lost momentum. Despite the failure of the Shiʿi women's association, Khady performs her own benevolent deeds. For example, she prepared a prayer book in French translation and transliteration for people going to Mecca that includes both Sunni and Shiʿi prayers.

* * *

How does an individual construct a religious identity in a world fraught with contradictory local and global forces? This chapter outlined the trajectory of Shiʿi Islam among Senegalese converts. Although the Lebanese community had been living in Dakar for over a century, it was not until the Iranian Revolution became an international debate when Imam Khomeini relocated to Paris in 1978 that Senegalese began discovering Shiʿi Islam. This moment of crisis, when the Ayatollah was exiled from both Iran and Iraq, also turned him into a Western subject. His popularity in Western media spread beyond Europe and the United States to former colonies, including Senegal. Yet conversion to Shiʿi Islam was deeper than Western fascination with the Iranian Revolution; some Senegalese took an intellectual approach to religious change. Islam and the Arabic language enabled them to go beyond the French press to the source, and through accessing Shiʿi religious texts they were also able to interact with other Shiᶜa, including the Lebanese shaykh, and be part of a cosmopolitan Islamic movement. The Arabic language became another territory for Senegalese converts: they could resist the Western conception of Islam and experience Iranian Shiᶜi Islam, even without leaving Senegal.

Yet Senegalese converts portray Shiᶜi Islam as a peaceful intellectual movement denationalized and depoliticized from its Iranian context. In fact, the banner hanging in front of Université Cheikh Anta Diop's Dakar conference center advertising the Iranian cultural center's 2009 conference on the twentieth anniversary of Khomeini's death proclaimed in the imam's words: "Before it was a socio-political revolution, your great Islamic revolution had a moral and spiritual character." Senegalese Shiᶜa are not aiming to transform Senegal into a theocracy, but are trying to merge their appreciation of Shiᶜi Islam with Senegal's secular democracy. Through knowledge of Senegalese hierarchies of power, converts create a new religious identity that enables them to negotiate their position in Senegal by cutting themselves loose from its social, political, and economic constraints. The influence of Islamic orders, while not formalized in the Senegalese political system, is ubiquitous, and Senegalese endeavored to form a Shiᶜi network in Senegal as an alternative to joining Sufi orders (and not necessarily to shake up or dismiss them). Pan-Islamism (or pan-Shiᶜism) is a way to remain a "good" Muslim and Senegalese citizen while escaping Senegalese adaptation of Islam and its Arab variants. Converts can revolutionize local concepts of nationalism through following Khomeini's teachings without adopting the Islamic Revolution. They universalize Shiᶜi humanitarianism and work toward education, economic development, interethnic cooperation, and peace in the Casamance to benefit all Senegalese.

Senegalese Shiᶜa were convinced first by Iranian revolutionary ideologies and second by Shiᶜi Islam. Although not all Senegalese converts recount experiences that include the Iranian Revolution, the predominance of their admiration for Khomeini cannot be ignored. Choosing Shiᶜi Islam is not simply a matter of religion, and individual conversion experiences cannot be understood in isolation or decontextualized from the history of Senegal. The Senegalese Peul ethnic group refers to converts as *perðo mbotu*.[21] This is translated as "migrating from the cloth that ties the baby to its mother's back," that is, straying from one's parents' tradition. This means that in addition to being exposed to new ideas, the convert must also be ready to leave the native religion. Whereas opportunity or circumstance led them to Shiᶜi texts, media representations, or encounters with Lebanese or Iranian Shiᶜa at home or abroad, the sociopolitical context of Senegal and distaste for the dominant maraboutic tradition is what encouraged conversion.

This Pular discourse enables a broader thinking of processes of conversion and modernity. One can be both Shiᶜi *and* Senegalese if one embraces nationalism and cosmopolitanism, travel and translation, globalization and assimilation, Sunni and Shiʿi Islam. In Senegal the relationship between the national state and colonization, the postcolonial state, and attempts at postnationalism must be considered. Converts are attracted to foreign religions while cognizant of the political-economic context of their nation *and* conscious of global forces. This (trans)national conversion pushes theories of religious change to a new level as converts simultaneously search for their place both outside and inside their traditions. Chapter 7 will bring this discussion of conversion back to strategies for demonstrating autochthony.

Interlude

ʿUmar: Converting to an "Intellectual Islam"

ʿUMAR INVITED ME to his home in the outskirts of Dakar. We sat on mattresses on a floor covered with Middle Eastern–style carpets, what he referred to as a traditional Shiʿi salon. ʿUmar took his time narrating to me his experiences in a careful and thoughtful manner. He informed me that this was the first time he told the story of how he became Shiʿi; usually people ask him to explain complex theological and juridical questions. Our interview took place over two full days. Men and women from a wedding celebration outside occasionally entered the salon to pray. This account is an attempt to preserve ʿUmar's distinct style, albeit through double translation (Gibril served as an excellent Pular-to-French interpreter) and with minor editing.

ʿUmar is from a well-respected religious family from the Futa, a semidesert region in the north that he proudly proclaimed to be Senegal's Islamic capital. ʿUmar's grandfather was a prominent Tijani scholar, and ʿUmar's father, who had a good grasp of the Qurʾan and founded the Futa's first religious school, was locally renowned for performing a miracle. The village chief once visited ʿUmar's father in defiance and discouraged him from fostering new converts. The chief threatened ʿUmar's father, requiring him to write the Qurʾan from memory in one day or he would be killed. ʿUmar's father began writing at sunrise, pausing only to lead afternoon prayer. The chief, however, died before the second half of the prayer. Islamic hadiths forbid man from reading the Qurʾan in one day because it is too much for him to handle, recommending instead a minimum of three days to digest the holy book. ʿUmar's father had written half the Qurʾan in half a day; if the chief had lived he would have finished his transcription in one day.

Born in 1952 to this esteemed Tijani family, ʿUmar studied at various Sunni schools. Since his childhood he was known as "imam" as he became village imam at age thirteen. At age sixteen he was nominated to become imam in a second large mosque, replacing an influential shaykh. His father wanted him to continue his studies in Kuwait, but ʿUmar had eye problems, later treated in Dakar. In the Futa he worked small jobs as a night guard. When his father died, ʿUmar left his family some of the money he earned and chose to buy books with the remainder of his savings. He did not find his parents to be well informed in the direction he was seeking and departed in search of other knowledge.

In 1973, when he was eighteen years old, ʿUmar went to Dakar. He lived in a house with two big rooms that he shared with a friend of his father's. He liked Arabic music and bought a radio. With his cassette player, tea, and books he never got bored after work. His father's friend stayed up with him every night until midnight to listen to Arabic singers such as ʿAbdul Halim Hafiz and Um Kalthum. By chance, an Iraqi diplomat lived on the same street and was happy to hear the Arabic music. The diplomat never saw ʿUmar, who worked as a night guard and taught classes during the day when he was not catching up on sleep. One day ʿUmar did not go to work and encountered the Iraqi when he stepped outside to get some fresh air. The diplomat asked ʿUmar to summarize the newspaper he was carrying as he did not read French. He asked if ʿUmar was the one who lived in the house that played Arabic music.

The year was 1975 or 1976. Shaykh al-Zayn had just opened an Arabic language school and recruited the Iraqi diplomat as a teacher.[1] One day a young man mistakenly came to ʿUmar's house inquiring whether an Arab who supervised the Arabic classes lived there. ʿUmar did not know the Iraqi well but took the young Senegalese man to knock on his door. They were well received, and the Iraqi invited this boy along with ʿUmar to take classes. ʿUmar politely responded that he had no need for Arabic classes as he was already a *grand maître* who taught Arabic. The Iraqi was convinced that ʿUmar would benefit from additional classes.

There was a Tijani book—the *mukhtasar* (concise handbook of legal treatises) of Khalil—and it was believed that if one learned this last book of Maliki jurisprudence, one's lessons would be complete. ʿUmar gave this book to the Iraqi to demonstrate his knowledge. The Iraqi spent a long time studying one page, but did not succeed in understanding the book. ʿUmar realized that Arabs may not be strong in jurisprudence but were stronger than him in Arabic, and thus decided to enroll in Shaykh al-Zayn's Arabic school. He was placed by the school's director in the class for first-year students, but quickly passed out of the first, second, and third levels. When the director examined ʿUmar he found his level of Arabic to be higher than that offered by the school. The diplomat was eventually sent back to Iraq, but before he left Senegal he told ʿUmar that "Muslims like him" should continue their studies. ʿUmar stayed in the third level to perfect his grasp of the language. Every time the Arabic teacher taught a lesson ʿUmar intervened to correct the teacher. It was brought to Shaykh al-Zayn's attention that a student was disrupting the school by disagreeing with the teachers.

One day Shaykh al-Zayn took over for ʿUmar's teacher. He brought a Qurʾan to class and chose to teach the fatiha. ʿUmar responded correctly to all the shaykh's questions, and the shaykh smiled. Another Lebanese teacher taught the class and decided that ʿUmar could respond well in writing but could not speak Arabic eloquently. Another teacher came and then a fourth, and ʿUmar defeated them all with his responses and questions. The director of the school was convinced that

ʿUmar was a scholar and gave him some books to summarize. ʿUmar completed this assignment in only two days. The director then concluded that ʿUmar had reached a level in Arabic that would enable him to study abroad.

ʿUmar encountered a former teacher who inquired about his activities. He informed the teacher that he was studying Arabic at the Lebanese institute. The teacher warned him that Lebanese are Shiʿa and that ʿUmar should be careful because they are bad people, although strong and powerful. This was the first time he heard the word Shiʿa, in 1976.

In 1978, having studied with the Lebanese for several years, ʿUmar took his first trip abroad. The Lebanese sent him on a scholarship to study in Iran, where he wanted to understand more about Shiʿi Islam and why people said it was bad. He spent five years in Iran, arriving before the Islamic Revolution and staying until 1984, during the Iran-Iraq war. He told me many fascinating stories about the war. When he first arrived he had two questions in mind: What is Shiʿi Islam? Why is it not good? An Iraqi author of a book he read owned a bookstore in Iran. The bookseller commented that ʿUmar chose only books that criticized Shiʿi Islam. He began to set aside for ʿUmar Sunni books that described Shiʿi Islam's divergence from Sunni Islam.

ʿUmar came across a delicate subject in these readings: Sunnis say Archangel Gabriel erred in giving his message to ʿAli instead of Muhammad. How could he err? In the Qurʾan it says God created angels who could never sin in what God tells them to do. Angels were formed with the purpose of carrying out God's orders. It is people who lie. ʿUmar consulted a Shiʿi expert on this matter, which was how he became Shiʿi. He discovered through his studies that Shiʿi texts did not describe ʿAli as a prophet.[2] Those who made this claim were manipulating the story through contradicting Shiʿa and the Qurʾan. ʿUmar conducted comparative research and found Shiʿi jurisprudence to be more valuable than Sunni laws. For example, he told me, Shiʿa have a prayer for chasing away an enemy. A special prayer is recited before one is killed by one's enemy. Another prayer is for those drowning but not yet dead. Shiʿi Islam also treats the issue of family planning more clearly than Sunni Islam. ʿUmar had never come across this level of detail through his solid background in Sunni jurisprudence. He was thus convinced that Shiʿi jurisprudence was more progressive and evolved with time. When Senegalese later attacked him for being Shiʿi he used examples such as these to defend himself, justifying his responses using Sunni books. Senegalese Sunnis were often surprised that this Shiʿi Muslim knew their texts better than they did.

ʿUmar illustrated through various anecdotes his leaving the ways of his influential Tijani shaykhly family in order to become Shiʿi. There was once a great scholar who managed his community's legal affairs but did not have time to teach his children. When he died the community assumed that his children were educated like their father. The eldest son was asked to continue his father's work in all manners of jurisdiction, a request he was unable to refuse. He instructed community members to return to his home the following day with their questions. He immediately left the village and came back forty years later full of knowledge. When people asked why he left he responded that before he was under the shadow of his father but now he obtained his own knowledge.

A second anecdote was also about the death of a respected shaykh. This time the community approached his older brother, thinking he was also instructed in Islam. This man read from an important book of the Tijani tradition. When people approached him he placed the book behind him and taught them. When they departed he put the book back in front of him and became again a student. ʿUmar explained once more that one must avoid being in the shadow of a great scholar and that inheriting books of another does not automatically make one knowledgeable. Everyone must study for himself, and this is why he left the tradition of his father.

However ʿUmar does not renounce Tijani Islam but builds upon the notion of *njebbel,* the vow of obedience to a marabout. Even though ʿUmar is now Shiʿi, Tijanis also consider him a respectable scholar. Caliph Mansur Sy (1997–2012) nominated him as *muqaddam* (authorized Sufi representative) even though ʿUmar simultaneously serves as wakil for Iranian Ayatollah Khamenei. His Islamic knowledge enables him to go beyond the requirement within the Tijani order that talibes not follow any other doctrine. Tijanis approach ʿUmar before going to see the grand caliph. ʿUmar stopped wearing the Shiʿi turban when he was made muqaddam. Nock's (1933:7) concept of *adhesion* refers to the possibility of participating in religious groups and rituals without assuming a new way of life, of adopting "new worships as useful supplements and not as substitutes." Baum (1990) also contends that conversion in Africa need not involve the renunciation of one's former religious system.

ʿUmar's fame began to spread. In the 1980s his brother returned to Senegal on holiday from studying in Germany and organized a debate with many scholars at Université Cheikh Anta Diop in Dakar. Senegalese students came from all over the world, ʿUmar came from Tehran, and others attended from local Islamic schools, including Wahhabis. Students criticized ʿUmar for performing ablutions in a different manner. One discussion debated why it is permitted to pray on a straw mat. Shiʿa do not need to pray with the turba on a straw mat, although many Sunnis do not distinguish between natural and synthetic prayer mats. Two students who studied in Libya inquired about the significance of the Qurʾanic verse "God chose Mary the mother of Jesus to purify as a woman of the world." ʿUmar responded that Mary was chosen to be queen of women of this world, but Fatima was chosen to be queen of women in Paradise. The importance of this conference, held during university vacation, was for students who returned home from abroad to bring debates back to their universities. Someone studying in Germany

School mosque doubles as a classroom, Dakar suburbs, 2004.

had heard of ʿUmar's knowledgeable responses and requested his books. ʿUmar was also invited to Mauritania to address questions of a Sunni shaykh about Shiʿi Islam.

From 1987 to 1990 ʿUmar served as imam of the Ibrahim Derwiche mosque. He left the mosque when its congregation requested that it become a grand mosque.[3] This could not take place legally according to both Sunni and Shiʿi jurisprudence because the four corners of the mosque were located less than four kilometers away from another grand mosque. In fact there was not even one kilometer's distance between the Ibrahim Derwiche mosque and Shaykh al-Zayn's mosque. This would be problematic if one imam prayed before the other. ʿUmar criticized the congregation for wanting the prestige of many mosques in a small area, which does not follow Islamic law. Following a big disagreement he left the mosque, telling me that God will judge us for applying things we know are not valid. ʿUmar did not work for two years.

Yet when ʿUmar began to wear the turban in Iran—he was the first Senegalese to earn this honor—he also accepted the responsibility of carrying out the work of Islam. The work of God includes helping Muslims build mosques and schools and serving ahl al-bayt, a rich Shiʿi tradition but one that is not accepted in Senegal, he told me. In 1992 he moved to a suburb located 20 kilometers outside of Dakar, which at the time consisted of fields in need of cultivation. The path he chose for himself was to educate children, and he built an Islamic school, which his nine children attend. His goal is to contribute to the growth of ahl al-bayt as a foundation of knowledge, and he hopes his endeavors will eventually succeed in removing the curtains dividing Tijani and Shiʿi Islam.

7 The Creation of a *Senegalese* Shiʿi Islam

> I think if you understand your history as always a history of movement,
> migration, conquest, translation, if you don't have some originary conception
> of your own culture as really, always the same—throbbing away there unchanged
> since the tribal past—you could become a cosmopolitan at home. . . . But this
> is a different kind of cosmopolitanism from the one which is available to those
> who've travelled to live permanently in different places, out of choice or as a
> matter of expanding one's experience.
>
> —Stuart Hall, in conversation with Pnina Werbner

CONVERTS LIKE ʿUMAR were introduced to religious books through personal relations to Lebanese and Iranian Islamic leaders and religious communities both inside and outside Senegal. This was key in locating Shiʿi Islam in Senegal at precisely a time when more and more Senegalese were becoming literate in Arabic. Senegalese were able to imagine themselves as part of a global Shiʿi community, and publications received from Iran, Iraq, and Lebanon (sometimes via Europe) helped them feel closer to those who shared their newfound religion, despite cultural differences and geographic distance. Islam—and the Arabic language—enabled Senegalese to interact with other Shiʿa and become part of a global cosmopolitan religious tradition.

The increasing availability of books and Middle Eastern–style education are essential to challenging existing Islamic authority in Senegal, established through *local* Sufi knowledge and Qurʾanic schools. This final chapter explores the making of a vernacular cosmopolitan Shiʿi Islam. How do Senegalese Shiʿa, who have chosen to be a religious minority, construct an Islamic identity separate from that of Senegal's ubiquitous Sufi orders, which are often perceived to be synonymous with Senegalese national identity? How is Shiʿi Islamic knowledge transmitted in West Africa? Senegalese followers are convinced of Shiʿi Islam's authenticity as well as spiritual advantages of joining this new movement through the construction of religious schools and mosques; the building of NGOs to promote Shiʿi Islam's material benefits; the revision of Islamic history; the propagation of public conferences and media programs; and the adaptation of Shiʿi beliefs and rituals to the Senegalese context. Employed together, this variety of complementary discourses and practices forms a strategy for transforming religious authority in Senegal.

In examining genealogy and mobility across the Indian Ocean, Ho coined the term *resolute localism,* which recognizes how designations of "foreign" or "local" are relativized by history and framed in hierarchy, and can become valorized over time from "despised-foreign to valued-local status" (2006:68). Cosmopolitanism creates new religious traditions, the most successful of which flexibly enable a mix of rituals that simultaneously encompasses the reality of a global Muslim network and the particularity of the Senegalese context. Unlike the more rigid demarcation between Salafi and Sufi traditions of other Islamist reformist movements (for example the 2012 conflict in northern Mali), Senegalese Shi'a integrate Sufi Muslims into their institutions.

Whereas national borders and local customs do not circumscribe Senegalese religious lives, Senegalese do not necessarily envision their new Shi'i identity as a complete break with their Sufi roots. Drawing on Bakhtin's *hybrid utterances,* Hill (2012) develops a notion of *hybrid cosmopolitanism.* This model is useful for understanding Senegalese Shi'i practices, where hybrid cosmopolitans "refract symbolic and material resources of multiple universalizing regimes through particular projects" (65). Hill argues that contrasting ways of being cosmopolitan act synergistically, and participation in (largely anti-cosmopolitan) neoliberal and other global networks is refracted through cosmopolitan Islamic centers for their own purposes. For Hill, to be cosmopolitan is to command repertoires of behaviors and ways of speaking, be attuned to particular customs and expectations, engage in culturally transcendent activities, and manage potential contradictions and turn them to advantage. I will similarly examine Senegalese mastery of Shi'i discourse and ritual through converts' ability to transform globalization from unfamiliar foreign practices into local development projects and claims for autochthony.

Senegalese converts to Shi'i Islam have consulted scriptural texts as a result of their appreciation of Ayatollah Khomeini. The Iranian Revolution was *the* historical event that encouraged them to go back further in history to the schism between Sunnis and Shi'a and to refer to textual sources from the century following the Prophet's death. Asad (1986) refers to Islam as a *discursive tradition,* linking religious discourses to established histories of interpretation, debate, and authorization, which highlight traditions of the past. Tradition, for Asad, establishes orthodoxy and orthopraxy in a given historical and material context: "A tradition consists essentially of discourses that seek to instruct practitioners regarding the correct form and purpose of a given practice that, precisely because it is established, has a history" (14). I open up Asad's (1986) definition to include discursive traditions that are not (yet) established historically, along the lines of Hobsbawm and Ranger's (1992) *The Invention of Tradition.* I am suggesting not that Shi'i Islam is invented, but that its recent adoption in Africa involves a creative (re)working of local cultures and religious practices, especially when religious tradition is enmeshed in intellectual as well as socioeconomic motives (the latter unaddressed by Asad). Broadening the scope of Islam as a discursive tradition allows for inclusion of converts, those not born into a particular tradition, who also engage discursively with Islamic ideas.

This flexibility of tradition lies in its translation to new contexts. Edwards (2003:13) refers to this process as *décalage,* a term borrowed from Senghor and defined as "either a difference or gap in time (advancing or delaying a schedule) *or* in space (shifting or displacing an object)." Edwards suggests "that there is a possibility here in the phrase 'in time *and* in space [italics added]' of a 'light' (*léger*) and subtly innovative model to read the structure of such unevenness in the African diaspora" (13). This process is relevant not only to the African diaspora but to all cosmopolitan communities, and Edwards attends "to the ways that discourses of internationalism *travel,* the ways they are translated, disseminated, reformulated, and debated in transnational contexts marked by difference" (7). Translating means taking a step back from the original source and adapting international ideas to local debates. Unevenness in race, class, and standard of living can be reduced through translating ideologies from one international context to another.

In addition to Qur'an and hadith, the founding texts of Asad's model, Senegalese Shi'a mastered Shi'i jurisprudence and tried, not always successfully, to translate the message of the Iranian Revolution into a new Senegalese discursive tradition. Senegalese Shi'i leaders use their status as Arabisants, those literate in Arabic who often pursued university degrees from Middle Eastern countries, to obtain a following. They find that Shi'i religious literature convincingly answers their questions about Islam that Sufi leaders had been unable to address. Yet despite their links to Iran and Lebanon they are hesitant to embrace foreign Shi'i leadership in Senegal, resistance to which has led to the emergence of various *African* Shi'i associations. Activities aiming to counter the influence of the Lebanese shaykh as Caliph Ahl al-Bayt have resulted in dividing Senegalese converts in their loyalty to different religious leaders. Shi'i Islamic authority in Senegal is grounded in a variety of factors: the socio-religious environment; knowledge formations (within which race, ethnicity, and national origins matter in the Islamic hierarchies operated by local Sufi orders); and the cosmopolitan networks of global Islamic organizations. Senegalese Shi'a therefore emphatically declare that their articulation and practice of Shi'i Islam is distinctly African, and that the religion can be separated from Middle Eastern cultural and political manifestations.

Reformist movements, either Sunni or Shi'i, are more likely to spread among Muslims who are literate in Arabic. According to the World Bank, only 39.3 percent of the Senegalese population (age fifteen and over) was literate in 2002, which increased to 49.7 percent in 2009 due to literacy programs (www.worldbank.org).

These statistics do not account for Arabic literacy, which would likely increase percentages considerably. Senegalese literate in Arabic do not always intersect with those literate in French and counted in Western statistical indicators.[1] Hastings (1997) examines the vernacular's transformation from oral to written usage, particularly for translating the Bible. Expanding on Anderson's *Imagined Communities* he argues the Bible should be seen as a lens through which the nation is imagined. He uses examples from nineteenth- and twentieth-century Africa to explore the social impact of written literature, which may be greater when most people are illiterate and the authority of the written text is mediated across certain privileged forms of orality.[2] Thus an *oral literature*, as well as a written literature, can be the medium for a people's self-imagining and the means by which Islamic authority is bestowed.

Scholars of reformist Islamic movements use various terms to describe these processes, such as *authentication*, "dependent on textual study and historical inquiry, as well as on a particular notion of rationality" (Deeb 2006:20). Authentication is linked closely to *objectification*, where "explicit, widely shared, and 'objective' questions are modern queries that increasingly shape the discourse and practice of Muslims in all social classes" (Eickelman and Piscatori 1996:38). These frameworks and developments can be applied to an African context, where literacy in Arabic and knowledge of scriptural sources is understood as one way to become a *modern* Muslim. Eickelman and Piscatori date the beginning of this process of authentication in the Middle East to events taking place in the 1980s. Other scholars argue that such movements began even earlier in Africa—in the 1930s and 1940s in Mali, and as early as 1848 in Senegal (Schulz 2008; Loimeier 2003). Senegalese converts, like Sufi marabouts and the Lebanese shaykh, have power precisely because they are literate and educated in matters of Islam.

There are many ways to utter or discursively authenticate a tradition, and Senegalese Shi'a do not share the same vision of how to educate other Senegalese about Shi'i Islam. Despite their being a small minority—a Shi'i communitas—there are numerous Shi'i institutes, a testimony to leaders' desires to carry out religious activities according to their own styles. Some, like Assan, prefer teaching: "Teaching is crucial and organizing public lectures is one way to disseminate our ideas. We organize a lot of them because people are willing and ready to attend lectures, roundtables, study days, study nights, debates, discussions.... So that is how we were able to expand interest and attract attention, most notably of young people, towards Shi'i Islam." Others work to establish Shi'i organizations that initially encouraged political involvement, but more recently concentrate activities in economic development. Yet others spread Shi'i ideas through radio or television programs. Because they arrived at Shi'i Islam from various perspectives—from Sufi, Salafi, or French education—they envision their orientation, cultural, political, and religious perspectives, and work in different ways. Iranian or Lebanese training does not matter to Senegalese Shiʿi leaders. They know one another and speak highly of the other's efforts, but work independently in their native neighborhoods or in areas they think are ripe for change.

The Embodiment of Islamic Authority

Although Islam is often envisioned as embodied in women's clothing, members of reformist Islamic movements embody Islam in books, symbolic of religious knowledge. In Shiʿi Islam religious education is also embodied in men's dress, where a certain level of knowledge is indicated in wearing the robes and turban of a Shiʿi shaykh, an honor and status bestowed upon select African Islamic scholars. Knowledge of Islamic texts featured prominently in ʿUmar's life history, as in other conversion stories recounted in chapter 6. For example, Mamadou was first exposed to Shiʿi Islam through reading al-Samawi's *Thuma Ihtadaytu*.

Books also circulate that present Shiʿa in a negative light. Youssou, who replaced ʿUmar as imam of the Ibrahim Derwiche mosque, explained that this is why some converts are reluctant to publicly proclaim adherence to Shiʿi Islam. He hypothesized that those afraid to be open about beliefs were not knowledgeable enough about the religion to defend themselves against rumors spread by Wahhabis or were not strong enough in logic to respond convincingly to people's questions. Such fear resulted from dissemination of various negative stereotypes: that Shiʿa were atheists and not Muslims; had a different Qurʾan; denied Muhammad was the prophet; and viewed Imam ʿAli as the prophet and Muhammad's companions as atheists. According to Youssou, such misconceptions were spread from inaccurate books. He gave me one of these books, which he had in his possession. *Al-Khutut al-Arida* (The Lines of Latitude: The Foundation upon Which the Religion of Twelver Shiʿism Stands) was written by al-Sayyid Muhib al-Din al-Khatib, was published in Saudi Arabia in the Islamic year of 1280 (1902 CE), and is still circulating in Senegal today. Youssou felt there were not enough books on Shiʿi Islam in Senegal. Some were available at the Lebanese Islamic Institute, and he purchased others during trips abroad, which he lent to Senegalese after Friday prayer. Other Senegalese Shiʿi organizations have more recently established libraries.

In order to read these books, to use arguments in championing Shiʿi Islam or to counter misconceptions of Shiʿa, one must be literate in the Arabic language. Thus, a primary means to authenticate Shiʿi Islam in Senegal is to develop educational institutions that teach Arabic, which is not a native Senegalese language. Many Shiʿi schools and institutes were built in the 1990s, hidden in Dakar's suburbs, in the Futa, or in the Casamance region of southern Senegal. Built in the outskirts of villages, or deep inside the suburban residential maze, the almost invisibility of institutes is a form of taqiyya (see below). Hard to find, and therefore difficult to be targeted by opponents of Shiʿi Islam, institutions cater exclu-

Senegalese Shiʿi shaykh wearing robe and turban, Dakar, 2003. Author's collection.

sively to those who are open to learning from them, Shiʿi and Sunni Muslim alike. Lebanese Shiʿa finance institutes through khums; Senegalese migrants contribute through remittances. Yet Senegalese are critical of Lebanese and Iranians for not being more generous or involved in their activities. One convert told me there are myriad institutions despite the relatively small number of Senegalese Shiʿa because the founder of each new institute hoped for Iranian funding (often to no avail).

Cherif chose a Dakar suburb "full of dance and music, not religion and scholarship" as the site for Ali Yacine Centre Islamique de Recherches et d'Informations.[3] The center was first located in a rented building in the popular residential quarter, initially consisting of a small mosque, a table and chairs for classes, and a library with two old computers. A phone booth was built in the center to help finance activities, and a large television was installed to attract passersby to the center, to use the telephone, and to discover Islam. The Islamic center in particular and Shiʿi Islam in general were publicized by the distribution of calendars promoting photos of Iranian ayatollahs Khomeini and Khamenei.[4]

These methods were successful, and in 2007 Ali Yacine moved to a larger building purchased by the Islamic center, consisting of a salon furnished with sofas and an office with two new computers, printers, scanners, a photocopier, and large stereo system, donated by ambassadors' wives. A library/prayer room is full of Shiʿi books from Iran and Lebanon and some published by Shaykh al-Zayn in Senegal. Most books are in Arabic, focusing on philosophy and Islam in general, with a few books in French, especially contributions written by Iranian Ayatollah Musavi Lari.[5] When I visited, a dozen high-school students were being tutored in math outside in the courtyard. The Franco-Islamic school offers both religious and secular lessons, including Arabic classes for adults and children, a tafsir class on Thursday nights, and philosophy and fiqh on Saturdays. The center hosts celebrations for Ramadan and Mawlud in addition to commemorating ʿAshura. Pictures of Mecca and ayatollahs Khomeini and Khamenei decorate the walls, along with photographs of Cherif with Shaykh al-Zayn and various Iranian religious and political dignitaries.

Madrasat Imam al-Baqr, the Arabic-French school ʿUmar directs, also obtains a variety of texts: the Qurʾan from Saudi Arabia, Arabic grammar books from Lebanon, Arabic math books from Nigeria, Maliki fiqh books from Tunisia, history books written by Shaykh al-Zayn, and books with French lessons from Senegal. Although it is common for Islamic schools to acquire books from many places, in Senegal many Islamic schools do not have any books at all. The fact that Shiʿi schools make books available to students attests to the importance educators place on literacy and a return to the texts. The school is financed through student fees and donations from the Lebanese community; Senegalese remittances from Gabon, America, and France; and Shiʿa in India, Lebanon, and Iran, among other sources. The student body is composed of students from all of Senegal's religious

2004

JANVIER				FEVRIER			
Lun	5	12	19 26	Lun	2	9	16 23
Mar	6	13	20 27	Mar	3	10	17 24
Mer	7	14	21 28	Mer	4	11	18 25
Jeu	1 8	15	22 29	Jeu	5	12	19 26
Ven	2 9	16	23 30	Ven	6	13	20 27
Sam	3 10	17	24 31	Sam	7	14	21 28
Dim	4 11	18	25	Dim	1 8	15	22 29

MARS				AVRIL			
Lun	1 8	15	22 29	Lun	5	12	19 26
Mar	2 9	16	23 30	Mar	6	13	20 27
Mer	3 10	17	24 31	Mer	7	14	21 28
Jeu	4 11	18	25	Jeu	1 8	15	22 29
Ven	5 12	19	26	Ven	2 9	16	23 30
Sam	6 13	20	27	Sam	3 10	17	24
Dim	7 14	21	28	Dim	4 11	18	25

MAI				JUIN			
Lun	3 10	17	24 31	Lun	7	14	21 28
Mar	4 11	18	25	Mar	1 8	15	22 29
Mer	5 12	19	26	Mer	2 9	16	23 30
Jeu	6 13	20	27	Jeu	3 10	17	24
Ven	7 14	21	28	Ven	4 11	18	25
Sam	1 8	15	22 29	Sam	5 12	19	26
Dim	2 9	16	23 30	Dim	6 13	20	27

JUILLET				AOÛT			
Lun	5	12	19 26	Lun	2 9	16	23 30
Mar	6	13	20 27	Mar	3 10	17	24 31
Mer	7	14	21 28	Mer	4 11	18	25
Jeu	1 8	15	22 29	Jeu	5 12	19	26
Ven	2 9	16	23 30	Ven	6 13	20	27
Sam	3 10	17	24 31	Sam	7 14	21	28
Dim	4 11	18	25	Dim	1 8	15	22 29

01 Janvier : JOUR DE L'AN
03 Février : TABASKI
03 Mars : TAMKHARITE
04 Avril : FÊTE NATIONALE
09 Avril : MAGAL DE TOUBA
11 Avril : PAQUES
12 Avril : LUNDI DE PÂQUES
1ᵉʳ Mai : FÊTE DE TRAVAIL

SEPTEMBRE				OCTOBRE				NOVEMBRE				DÉCEMBRE			
Lun	6	13	20 27	Lun	4	11	18 25	Lun	1 8	15	22 29	Lun	6	13	20 27
Mar	7	14	21 28	Mar	5	12	19 26	Mar	2 9	16	23 30	Mar	7	14	21 28
Mer	1 8	15	22 29	Mer	6	13	20 27	Mer	3 10	17	24	Mer	1 8	15	22 29
Jeu	2 9	16	23 30	Jeu	7	14	21 28	Jeu	4 11	18	25	Jeu	2 9	16	23 30
Ven	3 10	17	24	Ven	1 8	15	22 29	Ven	5 12	19	26	Ven	3 10	17	24 31
Sam	4 11	18	25	Sam	2 9	16	23 30	Sam	6 13	20	27	Sam	4 11	18	25
Dim	5 12	19	26	Dim	3 10	17	24 31	Dim	7 14	21	28	Dim	5 12	19	26

03 Mai : MAOULOUD - 20 Mai : ASCENSION - 6 Juin : PENTECÔTE - 7 Juin : LUNDI PENTECÔTE - 18 Août : ASSOMPTION - 1ᵉʳ Novembre : TOUSSAINT
14 Novembre : KORITÉ - 25 Décembre : NOËL - 10 Fev. Idou Ghadir - 03 Mars Achoura 2Mars Tachoura

Centre Islamique de Recherches
et d'Informations
«Aly Yacine»

GIE FALL & Co 855.60.75 / 632.60.30 - Impression -

Calendar depicting images of Iranian ayatollahs Khomeini and Khamenei, 2004. Author's collection.

Table 7.1. Madrasat Imam al-Baqr Curriculum, 2003–2004

Monday	Qurʾan	Dictation	Recreation	Fiqh	Math
Tuesday	Qurʾan	Grammar	Recreation	Arabic	French
Wednesday	Qurʾan	Hadith	Recreation	History of Islam	al-Insha (Composition)
Thursday	Fiqh	Arabic	Recreation	Education in Islam	Calligraphy
Friday	Qurʾan	Geography and Science	Recreation	ʿAqida (Islamic Belief)	Sarf (Morphology)
Saturday	French	French			

orders. The most advanced students formed a Shiʿi youth association, Jamaʿat Ahl al-Bayt, that helps the school with fundraisers and event planning. See Table 7.1 for an example of a typical week's lessons.

ʿUmar faced many problems establishing Shiʿi Islam in Senegal. When he started the school in 1992 he was just younger than forty years old, much younger than other teachers, who could not recognize a man of his age in an authoritative position, despite his impressive knowledge of Islam. Photos in his office of the mosque of Medina and the kaʿba in Mecca are meant to counter stereotypes prevalent among Senegalese Sufis that Shiʿa do not use minarets in mosques for the call to prayer or perform the hajj. ʿUmar remarked that Senegalese generally form opinions based on images; therefore showing them other images enables them to accept differences. New cosmopolitan forms of religious authority in Senegal, then, are about acquiring Islamic knowledge as well as learning how to apply this knowledge in culturally appropriate ways in order to command respect from others.

ʿUmar is not the only shaykh who keeps his feet in both Sufi and Shiʿi Islam. Youssou's mosque association meets on the first Wednesday of each month. Both Sunni and Shiʿi members joined the association and represent the mosque at religious occasions of other mosques, working to link all Muslims in Senegal. In addition to daily lessons, religious lessons are taught on Fridays and Sundays when pupils memorize Qurʾan and learn its interpretation, Islamic sciences, and hadith. Shiʿa study Jaʿfari fiqh on one side of the mosque and Sunnis study Maliki fiqh in the opposite corner. Such strategies demonstrate how Shiʿi Islam in Senegal is not intended to be a complete break with Sufi Islam; its authenticity is envisioned in the ability to integrate Sufi Muslims into institutions without requiring formal transformation of religious belief or practice, merely the exposure, at times unknowingly, to other Islamic traditions.

Schools in the Casamance region of Senegal are smaller and poorer than those in Dakar. Kolda's Shiʿi school is situated in village outskirts, and few people know of its existence. The school has two classrooms, a small cement mosque with a tin roof, a farm with sheep, goats, and chickens, a well, and a satellite dish. A Senegalese shaykh and his family reside in the school. The shaykh's office consists of two desks with benches and a small bookshelf containing fifteen books on Islam in Arabic and a few Qurʾans in French.

In Ziguinchor, the Lebanese-funded Ecole al-Rasul al-Islamiyyatu al-Sahihatu is located 5 kilometers outside town, well hidden in agricultural fields. The school's shaykh was unavailable, but a twenty-three-year-old student with plans to convert to Shiʿi Islam was willing to talk to me. He informed me that there were approximately one hundred students at the school, which opened in 1981. Students pay 1,500 CFA per month (US$3) for their studies, but after their fourth year they are no longer required to pay; he was in year four out of seven. Scholarships are available for students who cannot afford the modest tuition. The student's goal was to complete his studies, then go to Dakar in search of a scholarship to study in Iran. He claimed the school's main objective was to train students to competitively earn scholarships to study in the Middle East. I found this young man's impressions to be an informative illustration of Senegalese Shiʿi discourse; information conveyed revolved around differences that stood out most in his mind between his own religious tradition and that of his teacher. Inaccuracies, explained in endnotes, were telling of Shiʿi Islam's newness to the region. Such discourse suggests the Senegalese public has not yet developed a deep understanding of Shiʿi Islam; knowledge is based instead on contrasting superficial stereotypes.

Although this student is Tijani he studies at the Shiʿi school, open to all Muslims. Shiʿa, he told me, are known for telling the truth and not lying. They apply shariʿa law where others in Senegal do not.[6] When Shiʿa pray they place a stone on the ground, which represents the blood spilled when Husayn was "cut up into pieces and martyred." Shiʿa can pray in any mosque as long as they bring stones.[7] Shiʿa are known for extensively studying their religion, and are guardians of the gate that protects the Prophet from his enemies.[8] This makes Shiʿa unique in that they study the Qurʾan more than other Muslims. They meet every Friday morning in Ziguinchor to study the Qurʾan. They do not ask for charity (unlike Sufi talibes, who infamously beg to collect donations for marabouts). When Shiʿa die, they are buried on their backs; Tijanis are buried on their sides.[9] Shiʿa also perform ablutions differently.

According to this young student, "the only thing Shiʿa know in life is ʿAli," whom he called by his Wolofized name ʿAliou. ʿAliou was the first Shiʿi, but other companions of the Prophet were Tijanis, he tells me.[10] The martyrdom of Imam Husayn is commemorated by slaughtering a sheep, studying Qurʾan, and reciting what God said to the Prophet. They recount stories of ʿAliou and distribute candies, and people cry. Lebanese and other Shiʿi shaykhs in the region will come to this shaykh's establishment.[11]

The student explained that some Senegalese discriminate against Shiʿa; thus they keep secrets from other Muslims, who criticize Shiʿa for not praying in their mosques and preferring ʿAliou to the Prophet. A "secret" this student disclosed was that following Senegalese Sufi tradition, students worked the land, cultivating the Shiʿi shaykh's agricultural fields rich with corn, millet, mangos, potatoes, carrots, squash, papaya, and bananas without pay. Students were building a small mosque next to the school. My informant considered his Shiʿi teacher to be more honest than Tijani or Murid marabouts because instead of watching television he reads Qurʾan and books about ʿAliou. The shaykh completed his studies in Iran, where he served in the military and fought during the Iran-Iraq war, another secret, according to his student. The shaykh is strong in knowledge, said the student in awe, because he memorized the entire Qurʾan. This Tijani student informed me of the ease of becoming Shiʿi by going before the shaykh. However, Shiʿa keep their conversion secret for fear others would deem them not "good" or "real" Shiʿa because they were first Tijanis.

Islamic institutions reach a small number of people in select locations. In order to expand their population base, Shiʿi converts take advantage of the popularity of the radio in Senegal to spread knowledge about Shiʿi Islam on the air. My young informant mentioned that Zinguinchor's two Shiʿi shaykhs speak on the radio in Arabic on Fridays and Sunday nights. Their speeches are translated into Mandinka, Wolof, and Balante for the local population. A larger organized effort takes place in Dakar. Radio Dunya was the first station to sponsor a program on Shiʿi Islam, in 1994, lasting a year and a half. Shiʿi leaders spoke Wednesday nights from 12 AM to 6 AM and took audience questions. The show later moved to Friday evenings and aimed to counter Wahhabi propaganda against Shiʿa. Debates concerned differences between Sunni and Shiʿi Islam and discussed monotheism, the Qurʾan, the prophecy, and Islamic history. Radio served as publicity for Senegal's Shiʿa, and helped Senegalese discover that Shiʿi Islam is Islam, despite Wahhabi portrayal to the contrary. The program came to an end, however, when Radio Dunya's Wahhabi funders disagreed with the station's use of airtime. In particular they were opposed to Shiʿi narrations of Islamic history highlighting how Umayyids killed ahl al-bayt and Muʿawiya murdered ʿAli's sons. I spoke with the program director, who accused Shiʿa of spreading such "lies" on his airtime.

Wal Fadjri Radio began where Radio Dunya left off, creating an Islamic radio show Friday afternoons from 3:30 to 5 PM, which repeated later in the week. This show chose popular topics and invited speakers representing different Islamic schools to voice opinions. One program paired Youssou N'Dour, Senegal's most famous musician, with a Shiʿi painter to discuss what Islam says about art. The difference in these two artists' discourses about Islam and various Islamic laws that applied to their understanding of art enlightened listeners about variances in Sunni and Shiʿi Islam. Recently, to the dismay of Senegalese Shiʿa, such radio shows are becoming less frequent. Converts are using other forms of media to transmit religious views through publishing articles on Islamic history in Senegalese newspapers, speaking on Islamic television programs, and posting videos of religious lectures on websites.[12] In 2014 Institut Mozdahir International (described below) launched Senegal's first Shiʿi radio station, which broadcasts twenty-four hours of programming on religion, education, agriculture and the environment, and health seven days a week. Summaries of the daily news are broadcast in Wolof, Pular, and French languages and programming includes *anashid* (Shiʿi religious chants) in Arabic.

These sketches are examples of the formation of new religious leaders whose authority lies outside the network of Sufi marabouts, yet they are also embedded in the Sufi orders. Authenticity is established through building schools and libraries filled with books from abroad, resources not easily obtainable or affordable in a poor country like Senegal. Authority is achieved through literacy in Arabic and years of study abroad or in foreign-run religious schools in Senegal. ʿUmar describes the independent search for knowledge through books and other resources as going beyond merely inheriting one's family's tradition. For many Shiʿa this entailed migrating from the *mbotu,* the cloth that ties the baby to its mother's back, by physically leaving villages of origin and studying elsewhere (in Dakar or the Middle East).

Mass media also enables individual expressions of Islam, particularly by a younger, media-savvy generation of Muslims searching for new audiences in which to generate a following for their alternative Islamic visions. The case of Senegalese Shiʿa contributes to a growing academic focus on the role of new media in blurring the boundaries between religious renewal, secularism, politics, and popular culture through technology. An increasing public presence of religion through sound (radio, audiocassettes) and visibility (television, Internet, newspapers, magazines, books), enables populist leaders to capitalize on the aesthetic force of speech and the performative qualities of visualization (Schulz 2012). As listeners, readers, and spectators become active participants, the proliferation of actors able to create and sustain an Islamic public sphere—or an Islamic counterpublic (Hirschkind 2006)—additionally leads to a fragmentation of authority through contesting the religious status quo (Eickelman and Anderson 2003). Mass media enables a rearticulation of religion, particularly as embodied in identity politics or politics of difference—inclusive of women and based on claims to moral superiority (Schulz 2012), which challenges Western understandings of modernity as necessarily linked to the public decline of religion (Meyer and Moors 2006). There are a growing number of radio stations, television channels, newspapers, and magazines in Senegal as in other postcolonial countries (Larkin 2008) under pressure

Institut Mozdahir International bookstore, Dakar, 2013.

from organizations such as the World Bank to liberalize state-controlled media in a turn to democracy.

Challenging State Authority, Establishing Religious NGOs

In Senegal spiritual progress is thought to lead to material progress. Sufi orders exhibit a version of the Protestant ethic where work along with prayer and religious instruction are fundamental Islamic tenets. In rural areas talibes are expected to work in the name of their marabout. Spirituality attributed to work historically allowed for Murid colonization of the Senegalese countryside, enabling Bamba's followers to overcome hazards of early settlement and seize the land collectively (Cruise O'Brien 1971).[13] Senegalese migrants to urban areas—in Senegal and abroad—continue to send a portion of earnings to religious leaders. In contrast Senegalese Shiʿi spirituality is manifested in religious knowledge over manual labor, where converts follow attraction to Khomeini's ideals with reading books on Shiʿi Islam. Intellectual spirituality is expected to lead to material progress, and knowledge is shared through building schools, organizing conferences, publishing books, distributing pamphlets, and debating ideas over radio and television. Shiʿi converts hope education will result in a more sophisticated modernity than the work expected of Sufi talibes and will contribute to Senegalese economic development. Yet according to one of the "secrets" revealed by the Ziguinchor student, select Shiʿi leaders continue to follow Sufi tradition and require manual labor from students in return for instruction.

Senegalese Shiʿa are firm advocates of religious work having concrete secular benefits for society. This is evident in the work of various Shiʿi associations. In 1999 ten active members created Ansar Muhammad, the most prominent of these early groups. Objectives were to bring a cultural revolution and make Islam better known to Senegalese with the motto of "courtesy and brotherhood." Ansar Muhammad organized debates on Islam and sponsored dinners and celebrations of major Islamic holidays. Its former president Assan denied the association aimed to proclaim Senegal an Islamic state: "Our community has profound roots in Senegal and does not engage in political activism . . . because we know these issues would only, in the end, divide Senegalese and lead to useless debate. So we work to enlighten people on crucial issues that help develop their spirit and mentality, their conscience, and then will help develop their country." Other smaller associations met regularly for prayer and study meetings in various locations in and around Dakar. Individuals worked to develop Shiʿi institutions in the Futa, Kaolack, and Casamance.

When I returned to Senegal in 2007, I was surprised to find that many fledgling associations had disbanded. Some, but not all, involved in earlier organizations joined a well-financed larger institute that seemed to have suddenly emerged on the Senegalese Shiʿi scene. Press releases, however, stated this institute was initiated in 2000. Founded by a Senegalese *sharif* (who claims descent from the Prophet Muhammad and published a book on his succession, Hydarah 2008) of mixed Mauritanian and Peul origin from Kolda, Institut Mozdahir International's goals are to promote education, health, and agro-pastoral development. Mozdahir uses Shiʿi Islam and the teaching of the Prophet to "work in this world as if you will live forever and for the next world as if you will die tomorrow" (Tall 2006) to carry out development activities in the name of religion. Although leaders are intellectuals who debate Shiʿi theology, teach classes, and write books, it is no coincidence that the slogan chosen from the Prophet resembles that of the Murids. Amadou Bamba's famous phrase "work as if you would never die and pray as if you were to die tomorrow" (Creevey 1979:281) allowed agricultural labor to substitute for religious instruction. Mozdahir runs agricultural projects in the Casamance with the aim of teaching workers how to farm banana plantations and share profits in the hope of keeping young farmers rooted in Senegal and helping to prevent illegal migration, a growing problem in Africa.

When Ali Yacine Centre Islamique de Recherches et d'Informations expanded into its new building it also became an "association for sustainable human development" with plans to apply for NGO status for its work focusing on the environment, drugs, malaria, AIDS, and famine. This includes Association Fatima Zahra, a women's development organization that functions as a *tontine,* rotating credit association. It encourages women to work, for example, in selling powdered soap or vegetables in small quantities. Ali Yacine provides free medical consultations for those in the neighborhood and envisions itself as working to eradicate poverty. Cherif told me that operating merely as an Islamic organization no longer suffices without also providing services to the people. The application of religious knowledge and scriptural sources to modern discourses of development is no less authentic an aspect of Islam-as-a-discursive-tradition.

Thus the new face of Islamic reformist movements couples religious education and building mosques and institutions with extra-religious benefits. This is true in Sufi orders as well (see Samson 2009). As Karp (2002) notes, *development* and *modernity* are key terms intimately related to one another and cannot be exclusively defined. Converting to Shi'i Islam, like choosing another reformist Islamic tradition, is therefore seen as conversion to modernity but, unlike converts to Christianity who wish to become more "Westernized" (van der Veer 1996), those who choose Islam may be opposed to the modern European example often associated with colonialism and imperialism. There has been growing scholarly interest in the work of Islamic NGOs, which have been expanding activities and outreach across the African continent since the 1980s and 1990s (Benthall and Bellion-Jourdan 2003; Ghandour 2002; Kaag 2007). More than Sunni counterparts, Shi'i organizations are dependent on NGO status in order to obtain legitimacy and convince their growing network of followers of wider benefits of adhering to a minority branch of Islam.

The Spread of Islam to Africa and Other Revisionist Histories

In addition to Arabic literacy and the building of Islamic schools and NGOs, Islamic authority can be negotiated through redrafting the historical narrative of the origin and nature of Islam in Senegal. Senegalese converts uphold that Shi'i Islam has historical roots in Senegal with the tenth-century spread of Islam. This is perhaps an imagined past that contradicts, one could argue, the equally imagined Sunni version of African Islamic history accepted by historians. Larson (2000) insists upon the interdependency and complementarity, not oppositionality, of *history* (as things that happened in the past) and *memory* (as representations of past happenings in the present) as ways of apprehending and ascribing meaning to the past. Employing popular historical memories can shape the course of historical events as history and memory reproduce one another. This (re)narrated past can be used to convince others of Shi'i Islam's authenticity in West Africa.

One informant explained:

> If you talk about the Shi'i movement in Senegal you first have to go back in time, to see Shi'i Islam as it is, as an ideology, cultural practice, and form of behavior, that is a way of adopting and adapting Islam to our culture and social norms. In Senegal those who immersed themselves in Shi'i teachings fi-

nally realized that Shi⁽i Islam has long been entrenched in Senegal, since the emergence of Islam in the country.

Another Senegalese Shi⁽i leader gave a more detailed historical account:

> Islam was introduced in Senegal between the ninth and tenth centuries according to historians. . . . Islam was brought by Almoravids who were themselves influenced by Fatimid Shi⁽a. Don't you know that Morocco along with Iran were the only countries in the Muslim world not part of the Ottoman Empire? Idrisids came to Morocco as refugees fleeing ⁽Abbasids who tried to exterminate them. They settled there and founded their state, the Idrisid Empire. They are descendents of Prophet Muhammad (peace be upon him). Islam in Senegal came from Morocco. . . . In its social and religious aspects you find a lot of similarities between the two. In Morocco, ⁽Alaoui is ⁽Ali ibn Abi Talib, descendant of Imam ⁽Ali. All that goes to show that Shi⁽i Islam had an extraordinary amount of influence on the other Sufi orders here in Senegal.

Senegalese Shi⁽a argue that Islam was brought to Senegal by Almoravids in Morocco who were influenced by Fatimid Shi⁽a. Almoravids did play an important role in the development of Islam in the region. West African oral traditions connect Wolof history to Almoravids through the founding king of Jolof, said to have been a descendant of Abu Bakr b. ⁽Umar, an eleventh-century Almoravid commander (Levtzion 2000:78). Western historians, however, depict Almoravids, who did come in contact with Fatimids, as having "finally secured the victory of Sunni-Maliki Islam in the eleventh century" (Levtzion and Pouwels 2000:2). Brett documents: "In North Africa it was Berber nomads from the western Sahara who took up the anti-Fatimid call of the jurists of Qayrawān, to create the militantly Malikite empire of the Almoravids in Morocco and Muslim Spain" (2001:430). Elsewhere he writes: "Ibn Yasin [founder of the Almoravid dynasty] followed the Malikite scholars of Qayrawan in their opposition to the Fatimid Mahdi as a usurper of their authority for the law" (1999:2). Austen (2010) describes their entrance into North Africa through fighting against various dissident Kharijite and Shi⁽i sects in southern Morocco.[14] He credits Almoravids for playing a major role in unifying Islamic identity of the western Sahara and Morocco.[15] Even though Senegalese Shi⁽a depict Almoravids as sympathetic to Shi⁽i Islam from their interaction with Fatimids, Western scholars of the period clearly state that Almoravids were anti-Fatimid and strongly pro-Maliki.[16]

Senegalese Shi⁽a also refer to the spread of Shi⁽i Islam to Senegal through the Idrisid dynasty and evidence of Shi⁽i roots in Morocco through ⁽Alaouis (Hydarah 2008:132–135).[17] Cornell writes that Moulay Idris and his successors, descendants of the Prophet's grandson Hasan, brought with them to Morocco from the Arabian Peninsula "a form of archaic Shi⁽ism that was similar in many respects to Zaydism" (1998:200). The Idrisids initiated a tradition of independent dynasties

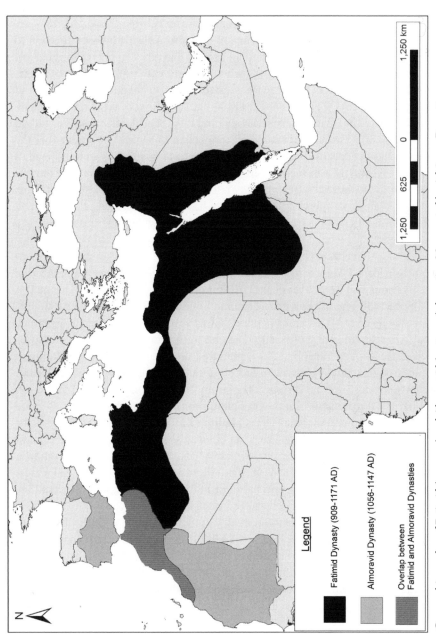

Geographic overlap of Fatimid (909–1171) and Almoravid (1056–1147) dynasties. Map created by Adrianne Daggett.

justifying their rule in Morocco by claims to descent from the Prophet, beginning in the eighth century and lasting until today. Hourani, however, depicts Idrisids as being "another challenge, both to ʿAbbasids and Fatimids" (1991:41). Yet Cornell shows that Idrisids used the Prophet Muhammad's birthday celebration to promote the cult of the Prophet and his family. Even though festival origins can be traced back to Shiʿi Fatimids, Morocco's Sunni elite supported its ritualization in order to reduce the influence of Christianity on uneducated Muslims and new converts (203). Cornell even laments that "few modern scholars have taken the Shiʿism of the Idrisids very seriously" and talks of a "doctrinal well of Idrisid Shiʿism" (224).[18] Perhaps an early Shiʿi connection to Senegal through either the Almoravids or Idrisids is a myth. However, Senegalese retelling of the spread of Islam to West Africa to include Shiʿi roots is an important attempt by converts not only to globalize the (re)emerging reformist movement but also to establish its legitimacy by demonstrating Shiʿi Islam has always been Senegalese. The aim of this foundational move is to solidly reconnect to a wider religious world and a deeper past.

Ideas of Shiʿi Islam's historicity in Senegal were also actively promoted through Iranian efforts. I came across this same notion of African history while meeting with various representatives of Shiʿi institutions in London in July 2007. One Iranian educator, who works with the Islamic College in London following a twelve-year stay in West Africa, informed me that African Sufis are Shiʿa. He explained that Africans think the only difference between Sunnis and Shiʿa is jurisprudence. Yet African Sufis, like Shiʿa, practice *tawassul*, the act of supplicating to God through a prophet, imam, or Sufi saint. Sufis and Shiʿa both practice *ziyara*, visits to shrines. They both respect the family of the Prophet and have the notion of sharifs. According to him the root of Sufism comes from Shiʿi Islam. Because of the oppression of Shiʿa in Mecca, Medina, and Karbala, the household of the Prophet disappeared and went to other countries. This is why Idris, the nephew of Imam Hasan (the son of Imam ʿAli), came to North Africa. The Iranian shaykh went so far as to claim that in West Africa there is no difference between local Islamic beliefs and Shiʿi ideas, and therefore many Africans are unaware that they are Shiʿa.

I had a similar conversation during that trip to London with the director of the World Ahlul Bayt Islamic League (WABIL), a respected Iraqi shaykh who spent much time in India as Ayatollah al-Khuʾi's wakil. Established in 1982, World Ahlul Bayt Islamic League serves Shiʿa all over the world in education, human rights, and religious teachings, and aims to strengthen the link with the Shiʿi religious leadership in Najaf. In discussing my research interests in Senegal, WABIL's director asked me when Shiʿi Islam first came to Africa. He disapproved of my answer dating this process to the 1880s to 1920s with the first wave of Lebanese migrants. He argued that scholars have proven that Islam first came to Africa through Shiʿi sayyids, descendants of Imam Hasan, the first to preach Islam in Africa. He stated that Mali was the center of religious knowledge and the pioneers of Timbuktu's religious library were also sayyids. He pointed out that Idris in Morocco and the Fatimid dynasty predated the Malikis. In fact, he claimed, a qadi (Islamic judge) was thought to have decreed that people should follow Malikis and not Fatimids, which is how Sufi Islam grew in Africa. Yet this Islamic scholar asserted that the Maliki school could not eliminate Shiʿi influences, especially among Sufi groups. Today's heads of Sufi orders are Shiʿa (if we define Shiʿa as those who believe in the spiritual leadership of ahl al-bayt, the family of the Prophet Muhammad, after the Prophet's death).

In addition to portraying Senegalese history as infused with Shiʿi influences from the time of the spread of Islam, Senegalese Shiʿa also highlight Shiʿi elements inherent in contemporary local Sufi Islam in a development of what Mandaville has called *counter-hegemonic discourses* (2001:179). They maintain that these relics exist because Sufi Islam originated from and ends in Shiʿi Islam and all Sufis follow ʿAli. "For example, consider the Tijanis. Now, if you look at their book, or books of other Sufi orders, their reference is ʿAli ibn Abi Talib for the spiritual dimension. They say that no one can transcend certain realities without going through ʿAli, because the Prophet said in a hadith: 'I am the city of knowledge, ʿAli is its door'; this is a hadith which everyone recognizes. So you have to go through the door in order to reach him."

For ʿUmar, Shiʿa and Tijanis diverged in the histories they inherited, not in theology, and his goal is to convince Senegalese of this fact. He instructed me in shared prayers and religious invocations. For example, he told me when Lebanon's Sayyid Hasan Fadlallah went to Mecca on pilgrimage he recited two invocations that Tijanis in Senegal take to be theirs exclusively, that of *salat al-fatih* and *allahumma anta al-salam wa minka al-salam* (Oh God! You are the source of peace and from you is all peace).[19] He pointed out that the invocation *ya man azhar al-jamil* (Oh, you who reveal beauty) is recited in both Iran and Senegal. Similarly, Tijanis are also thought to be from the Hasanite line and are disciples of the family of the Prophet through Ahmad al-Tijani, their spiritual guide.

ʿUmar stopped this comparison to search for a book on a bookshelf in the corner of his salon. He called over Gibril, who had escorted me to our interview, to show him something from this Tijani secret book that women are not permitted to read. The two Shiʿi men found an invocation in the name of God, his Prophet Muhammad, the Imams ʿAli, Hasan, and Husayn, and Abu Bakr, ʿUmar, and ʿUthman. ʿUmar highlighted that the names ʿAli, Hasan, and Husayn appear before Abu Bakr, ʿUmar, and ʿUthman in this Tijani book, proving his claim that the only divergence in the two branches of Islam is in their invocations. Tijanis who insist on greater differences do so out of ignorance; he cited the proverb "Ignorance is the enemy of mankind."

Are such revisionist historical accounts a matter of "silencing the past" (Trouillot 1995), the "invention of tradition" (Hobsbawm and Ranger 1992), or Ranger's (1993a) flexibly revised notion of the "imagining" of tradition? It is not my goal to determine historical facts but to examine various reasons for their different narrations. Iranian efforts were strategically aimed at combating Saudi Arabian objectives of spreading throughout Africa a Wahhabi-influenced Islam.[20] Converts deem the spread of Shiʿi Islam to be impeded by criticism from so-called Wahhabis. Wahhabis are far more numerous in Senegal and envision their role as restorers of Islam from what they perceive to be innovations, superstitions, deviances, heresies, and idolatries, especially inherent in Sufi and Shiʿi Islam. Hostility comes as well from other foreign Islamic movements, such as Jamaʿat Ibadu Rahman and other Sunni reformist movements in Africa, working their way into territories in which they were not historically embedded.[21] Power, in the form of coercion, discipline, institutions, and knowledge, gives meaning to religious symbols through social and political means (Asad 1993). Struggles for religious power are well addressed in Asad's definition of *orthodoxy*: "Wherever Muslims have the power to regulate, uphold, require, or adjust *correct* practices, and to condemn, exclude, undermine, or replace *incorrect* ones, there is the domain of orthodoxy. . . . Argument and conflict over the form and significance of practices are therefore a natural part of any Islamic tradition" (1986:15–16).

Although Iranians may be battling Saudis for influence and authority in West Africa, Senegalese converts to Shiʿi Islam envision these historical narratives along the same lines as a return to the sources of Qurʾan and hadith, popular in other reformist movements as well. Diouf (2000) argues that Senegalese Murid Sufis represent a unique cosmopolitanism and temporal trajectory rooted not in Western modernity or global Islam, but in West African history, which has always been global. Senegalese Shiʿa, in their own unique cosmopolitanism, merge North and West African history with Iranian revisions. Returning to one's roots—textual and historical—in this case pre-Sufi origins of Shiʿi Islam in Senegal, offers Shiʿa historical legitimacy over other reformist traditions, which are newer and more foreign to the region. History can offer Shiʿi Islam authenticity if it can be argued that it was initially meant to have been the dominant religious order in West Africa.

Senegalese Shiʿi Practices

Revisionist historical narratives are one strategy to translate the discursive tradition of Shiʿi Islam to the Senegalese context. Senegalese Shiʿa distinguish between religious theology as universal and religious practice as cultural, another discourse establishing Shiʿi Islam as a cosmopolitan yet autochthonous network. In adapting Khomeini's philosophy and Shiʿi Islamic law and theology without simultaneously adopting Iranian or Arab culture and traditions, Senegalese Shiʿa envision Shiʿi Islam's incorporation into Senegalese culture. In one informant's words:

> We are proud to be Senegalese. This helps us avoid losing ourselves in a process of assimilation. Because often people mistakenly understand our religious practices as imitating Iranians or Lebanese; no! We are Senegalese just like any other Senegalese and proud of being Senegalese. But being Senegalese does not prevent us from being open-minded. Our openness is key to our understanding of Shiʿi Islam as it developed in Iran; we were interested in what was happening in Iran because we are Muslims and the revolution was instigated in the name of Islam to serve interests of the Islamic umma. . . . So this is how we discovered Shiʿi Islam. Now, in order to avoid being associated with all this, we say, "We are not Iranian, we are not Lebanese." I am only giving these two examples. We are also not Saudis. We are Senegalese.

In order to authenticate Shiʿi Islam, converts market Shiʿi practices as *Senegalese*. In focusing on "intellectual" aspects of Senegalese conversion, this chapter first highlighted how books and Islamic knowledge are critical elements in new constructions of religious authority. The remainder of this chapter examines how Senegalese converts adapted certain Sufi practices; for them, this is part of what makes Shiʿi Islam *Senegalese*. Specifically, I explore the translation of four provisions of Shiʿi Islam to the Senegalese context: the marjaʿ system; taqiyya; the commemoration of Muharram; and the institution of *zawaj mutʿa*. To be Senegalese Shiʿi is to educate others and allow them to choose what religious tradition to follow, not to rigidly insist upon "correct" Islamic practice.

The Marjaʿiyya

Although not all Shiʿa in Senegal (Lebanese or Senegalese) are knowledgeable about the Shiʿi fundamental of emulating a marjaʿ, chapter 4 suggested a majority of Lebanese in Dakar follow Ayatollah al-Sistani. Senegalese converts, in contrast, are influenced by a variety of Shiʿi scholars. Some exclusively follow teachings of Ayatollah Khamenei, Khomeini's successor in Iran, but others abide by the authority of a combination of others, including al-Sistani and (before their deaths) Lebanese Muhammad Husayn Fadlallah and Ayatollah Muhammad Shirazi of Iran, popular among Gulf Shiʿa. Whereas Shiʿa typically follow rulings of only one marjaʿ, it is permissible to emulate one marjaʿ in some aspects of fiqh and another marjaʿ in other issues as long as the two marajiʿ are of equal knowledge or each is considered the expert in the particular field in which he is followed.

Cherif explained:

> Today Shiʿa reject the quest for a single guiding source that captures almost all types of knowledge. Now they are looking for various sources of specialized knowledge: for economics, we need a reference who knows Islamic economic

principles; for prayers, one who knows about rituals; for dogma, one who knows something about other dimensions of people's lives. What I am trying to say is that we need the highest authority on each issue. . . . So then you must take from this marjaʿ something, and from the other marjaʿ something, and from the other marjaʿ something. That is in our nature, as Senegalese.

Cherif personally chooses to emulate the following marajiʿ:

I follow Khamenei as well as Fadlallah, Muhammad Shirazi, and Sistani. For example Fadlallah is a thinker, . . . he talks about philosophy, sociology, and human sciences in general. He is open to a variety of issues. . . . What is special is that he also expresses himself in an extraordinary intellectual way. Like Muhammad Shirazi, who is also very good on philosophy and history. I have often listened to him. He is simple and very convincing as well. It is the same thing with Khamenei. His fiqhs are very intelligent. . . . Maybe his political responsibilities enabled him to understand more, to become more open and tolerant than other marajiʿ.

Assan's choice of spiritual references differed from Cherif's: "In Senegal we face difficulties because we do not have direct and sustained contact with great scholars of the Shiʿi community. For me, in Imam Khomeini's day (peace be upon him), I followed him closely, his speeches, the orientations he gave, and I greatly respected his fatwas. These days I follow ʿAli Khamenei, because I feel for him more than for anybody else. Even if I consider all other shaykhs my brothers, he is the one I follow."

These accounts demonstrate that there is no conformity in which marjaʿ Senegalese Shiʿa follow, and they do not limit themselves to ideas of only one marjaʿ. This fusion of marajiʿ distinguishes them from the Lebanese shaykh, who exclusively follows al-Sistani, and the Iranian embassy, which officially works under Khamenei. Abdou explained that the marjaʿ system resembles Senegal's medical system: when somebody needs surgery and the medical specialist for that particular ailment cannot be found in Senegal, they go to France or another country for the operation. The marjaʿ system works in the same way. If there is an expert in Shiʿi Islam in Senegal they approach him with questions, but given the lack of expertise they turn to Iran or Iraq. Books written by some of these marajiʿ can be found in personal libraries of converts in Arabic, French, and English translation.

Taqiyya

Concealing or disguising religious beliefs in order to protect one's self, family, or property from harm is permitted for Shiʿa at times of imminent danger. From the time of Imam Jaʿfar al-Sadiq (702–765) onward, the taqiyya doctrine became important to Shiʿa who lived as a minority among an often hostile Sunni majority. Senegal is not a country where people are oppressed; therefore Senegalese Shiʿa claim they do not need taqiyya. Nevertheless many Senegalese converts, particularly in the 1980s and 1990s when Shiʿi schools and organizations were first becoming established in Senegal, were not open about being Shiʿa and practiced dissimulation. Some proudly wore the robes and turban of a Shiʿi shaykh while others chose not to publicly mark themselves in a way that could be misunderstood by many Senegalese. For example when praying in Sunni mosques Senegal's Shiʿa hid their Shiʿi ways in order to avoid lengthy explanations to people who were unlearned, who did not have open minds, and who thought Shiʿa were mistaken in their practice of Islam. Shiʿa perform ablutions in a different manner from Sunni Muslims and use the turba (or another natural element) during prayer. Cherif pointed out that in the time of his grandfather every Muslim used to pray on natural substances, which he claimed is no longer possible with the arrival of modernity: "We have our distinctiveness as Shiʿa, but what makes us distinct is not something fundamental that could create a rift between us and others." Taqiyya allows converts to strengthen their relationship with Senegal's umma by not publicly accentuating differences in Islamic practice.

Assan explains:

> There are specific Shiʿi practices; if I am in a meeting and engage in such practices people may stop listening to me. So let's put such practices aside because what is at stake is more vital and must be protected: that is, for these people to listen to us, for them to accept us, we have to maintain dialogue with them. For that we do taqiyya. So you assess the situation according to interests at stake. Let's say I am engaging in a practice that is misunderstood that can bring people to question themselves constantly during the entire time I will stay among them, so I won't have the chance to convince them on that issue. So let's do taqiyya, in the meantime, until we are better understood, better known by those people. It is sort of a pedagogical process.

Other instances of taqiyya are intentionally building Shiʿi schools and mosques outside of city centers so they will be more difficult to locate by those who are not open to learning from them. Senegalese use of taqiyya to move adeptly between Sunni and Shiʿi spaces allows them flexibility to establish and disseminate religious beliefs and practices with minimal resistance. Their minority cosmopolitanism taught them when to publicly perform their difference and when to privately celebrate being Shiʿa.

This adaptability of taqiyya led Abdou to make a scientific analogy comparing Senegalese society to physical matter. He characterized those Senegalese as "solids" who renounced differences but lacked arguments as proof, as they were unable to change their form without breaking. This group tended to become violent when opposed and was unable to accept what is unfamiliar. In contrast "liquids" took the shape of their container, meaning this group was accepting of differences, while "gases" were free to move around in space. Abdou pointed out that all three types of "matter" exist in Senegal, but the advantage of taqiyya enables

Shiᶜa, like gases, to mix with both groups, hiding their Shiᶜi ways when with "solids" but engaging in Shiᶜi practices when with "liquids" in the hope of teaching them about Shiᶜi Islam. Lebanese Shiᶜa in Senegal, in contrast, were already identifiable as an ethnic and racial minority and had no use for taqiyya.

ᶜAshura or Tamkharit: A Day of Mourning or Celebration?

Taqiyya was a strategy most needed in the early days of establishing Shiᶜi institutions in Senegal. Senegalese Shiᶜa have more recently taken to publicly propagating historical narratives. Like revisionist accounts of the spread of Islam to West Africa, ᶜAshura divides Sunnis and Shiᶜa. The tenth day of Muharram, during which the martyrdom of Imam Husayn is commemorated, is a day of mourning and sadness for Shiᶜa but can also be a day of celebration for Sunni Muslims. In Senegal ᶜAshura overlaps with Tamkharit, a joyful occasion with carnival-like festivities, resulting in a sort of Muslim Halloween where girls dress as boys and boys as girls, and children go door to door to receive gifts to the rhythm of drums.[22] Senegalese Muslims chant nocturnal evocations on the ninth night of Muharram. The holiday evokes the obligation to give charity to help the most deprived. Members of Sufi orders fast during the day followed by a feast of couscous with beef. Tamkharit is thought to be a syncretism between Islamic rituals and pre-Islamic popular practices linked to the Lebu ethnicity's offerings to pagan divinities.[23] Others trace its origin to the time of the Umayyads, when Yazid the son of Muᶜawiya promoted a glorification of this day in celebration of his victory over Imam Husayn and his companions (Mozdahir 2007:122). Yet others consider its pagan rituals very far from Islamic prescriptions.

Over the past decade Senegalese converts to Shiᶜi Islam have begun to commemorate ᶜAshura in their own way. The practice of self-flagellation has been most controversial in Western media coverage as well as hotly disputed by Shiᶜi clerics. Senegalese Shiᶜa insist that such *Arab* or *Iranian* practices are not essential to Shiᶜi Islam, stressing in contrast their *Senegalese* or *African* Shiᶜi identity. For example ᶜUmar highlighted how religious practices reflect a people's customs and was critical of the self-flagellation (before its interdiction by Khomeini and later Khamenei) that he witnessed in Iran: "Compared to Senegal the situation is different in places such as Iran, India, Pakistan . . . you know, the Senegalese are very calm, not agitated, very sensitive even. So we give our lectures, we awaken people, because chest-beating is not something that is required by Islam. Our approach is cultural. So as Senegalese we also have our habits and customs to respect. For our part, as Shiᶜa, what we do is organize lectures—only lectures, nothing more. It is an intellectual activity."

Converts in Dakar organize public debates that cater to a Senegalese Sunni Muslim audience in a mixture of Wolof, Arabic, and French. Conferences, television and radio appearances, and books and pamphlets discuss whether ᶜAshura is a celebration or a day of mourning and play up the closeness that African Sufis also feel toward the family of the Prophet. For example, one flyer created for the 2008–2009 Muharram season advertised: "Be with Husayn or be against Husayn and the family of the Prophet." In addition to educating Senegalese about the history of the battle of Karbala, lectures and written publicity also address origins of Tamkharit, whose festivities conflict with the somber remembrance of the tragic events of Karbala.

Shiʿi converts have begun to introduce themselves into geographies of religious ceremonies in Senegal—of which they had not previously been a part—by equating the Shiʿi day of mourning with the Sufi celebration. Senegalese perform ideological and theological comparisons of ʿAshura and Tamkharit, as if these holidays were the same. Institut Mozdahir International organized a conference around the theme of "ʿAshura: A Day of Celebration or Mourning?," even publishing a French translation of the January 27, 2007, conference proceedings. Speakers from various Sunni and Shiʿi traditions came from Senegal, Mauritania, other West African countries, and France, and included religious clerics, university professors of Islamic studies, high school teachers, converts to Shiʿi Islam, privately funded researchers, and community practitioners. Many Senegalese maintain that ʿAshura/Tamkharit celebrates the Muslim New Year, albeit on the tenth and not the first of the month of Muharram.[24] Conflating Arabic and Wolof names for the date suggested that Senegalese Sufis were erroneous in their joyful commemoration of the Shiʿi day of mourning. Translating ʿAshura as Tamkharit also enabled Shiʿa to claim their belonging to Senegalese religious space.

Speakers recounted the story of the battle of Karbala and also addressed origins of Tamkharit in Senegal. Senegalese Shiʿa insisted that commemorating ʿAshura as a day of mourning should not divide the Muslim community; on the contrary it should unite them. Although there was indeed a division created on that day, this was not between Sunnis and Shiʿa; the division was instead one of humanity against inhumanity. The holiday recalls prophets' victories over trials and sharing Muslim spirituality with other religions in a demonstration of Islam's openness. Indeed, Sharif Muhammad ʿAli Aïdara, the head of Mozdahir, concluded the conference—and the published conference proceedings—with the declaration that it is the responsibility of all Muslims to pass on the message of this debate, as Islam is a religion of peace, dialogue, tolerance, and love. If Muslims accept coming together and sincerely discuss the questions that divide them, they will be able to overcome their differences (he is calling for cosmopolitanism here). Members of Senegal's Sufi orders, like Shiʿa, are also attached to the family of the Prophet Muhammad and Imam Husayn. Senegalese Shiʿa hope that through educating Senegalese about ʿAshura they will sensitize them to the sadness of this date and avoid conflict.

In the past the holiday was known only as Tamkharit, but I noticed that in January 2008 newspapers began to publish front-page announcements for a "*bonne fête d'achoura*," evidence of increased awareness in Senegal of the Shiʿi commemo-

Institut Mozdahir International 'Ashura conference, Dakar, 2008. Photo commissioned by author from event photographers.

ration, even if "happy holidays" is not the appropriate 'Ashura greeting.[25] Mozdahir's 2007 conference had become an "annual" conference by 2008 with even more attendees, and their 2009 plans included caravans that would travel the north and south of Senegal to distribute flyers to educate Senegalese Sufis about 'Ashura in an attempt to reach an even larger base than their widely attended and heavily publicized Dakar conference. As documented on their website, their director remarked that "the Prophets inspired by God's revelation were chosen by Allah because of their means to educate their community and end ignorance and bad morals" thereby linking the work of the prophets to the mandate of this Shi'i NGO to educate others through such conferences.[26] Other Shi'i organizations convened their own conferences, perhaps out of competition, or simply the need to spread 'Ashura knowledge more broadly.[27]

For example, Conseil des Oulémas d'Ahlul-Bayt, founded in 2004 by Senegalese Shi'a connected with Shaykh al-Zayn, organized their first conference on January 17, 2008 (9 Muharram). Approximately two hundred students were bused in from a school to attend the event, held outside the Lebanese-run Islamic school near Dakar's central bus station. The style of the event followed that of Senegal's Sufi orders: a tent was set up on the street, under which a table with

Conseil des Oulémas d'Ahlul-Bayt ʿAshura conference, Dakar, 2008.

microphones was placed for speakers and rows of plastic chairs for the audience, comprised of a couple hundred young school children and a few dozen adults. A cassette was playing, amplified by a loudspeaker, during the two hours between the time the event was supposed to start and the time it actually began. If one listened closely these were not the usual Sufi incantations chanted during religious events in Senegal but sad lyrics, lamenting in Arabic the tragic events that took place during the battle of Karbala in Iraq over 1,400 years ago. This drew the attention of passersby, as did the curious black banners hanging from the tent and covering the speakers' table, with images of the battle scene and verses written in colorful Arabic letters proclaiming the martyrdom of Imam Husayn and his family. The conference was led by Senegalese converts to Shiʿi Islam, dressed in Senegalese boubous or Shiʿi robes and turbans, and featured the appearance of the Iranian ambassador and a speech by Senegal's Lebanese shaykh.

A young student opened the conference by reading from the Qurʾan. The shaykhs then took turns reciting prayers in Arabic and addressing the audience with speeches about the history and significance of ʿAshura in Wolof, interspersed with phrases in French and Arabic. The first speaker announced that it is important to organize such programs in order to enlighten those in attendance. We must know more about those we honor as our role models and set as our examples: Who were they and what did they stand for? The speaker named various men chosen by God: Adam, Noah, Abraham, the Prophet and his family. He discussed how Muhammad had suffered while building the foundations of Islam and was attacked by his own people, where his relatives were the first to oppose him and his teachings. He suffered so much in Mecca that he decided to move to Medina and was pursued there as well. He then likened the suffering of Muhammad to that of ʿAli (using his Wolofized name ʿAlioune), who, like his son Husayn, had many enemies.

By beginning with the Prophet Muhammad, a noncontroversial figure in the history of Islam, this speaker eased into educating the audience about historical events key to Shiʿi Muslims. The shaykhs also familiarized students with the story of the battle of Karbala by using common Wolof sayings, such as "It is better to throw firewood in a fire that is lit by God than to try to extinguish it." They explained: "If God chose ʿAlioune then man cannot prevent his greatness before God just like man cannot put out God's fire. Therefore only by following the path of the family of the Prophet will we be salvaged from punishment on the Day of Judgment."

Speakers personalized the ʿAshura story in order to draw in the predominantly Sunni audience. They pointed out that one whose mother or father is killed would not celebrate on that day when the killing took place; it is therefore an irony when you see someone who says he loves the Prophet Muhammad celebrating the day his family was slaughtered. "The Prophet Muhammad warned that if anyone sees the right path and decides to follow another path he would be a loser. Who would see pure cassava and decide to go for the impure one?" This speaker called for the audience to teach their children to love and follow the Prophet's family.

The shaykhs were periodically interrupted by a student who sang songs in Arabic and occasionally in Wolof, reciting "no event will ever be as painful as that of Karbala; it was there where the great grandson of the Prophet was assassinated; Husayn's life ended in Karbala; what happened there was a very ugly incident." His recitations in form and tune resembled songs of Senegal's Sufi orders, but varied in content, where the singer repeatedly exclaimed, "If you love ʿAlioune snap your fingers." Clapping is considered un-Islamic, and in Senegal Muslims snap their fingers when listening to or singing religious songs. He also sang songs of praise for several of the shaykhs leading the conference, and was not alone in his praise for Lebanese Shaykh al-Zayn. The griot's praise song, originally sung to honor ruling families and nobility in Wolof, Peul, Mande, and other societies of the western Sahel, has been adapted to praise religious leaders and is a common feature at both religious and academic conferences. Typically the singing that takes place at religious ceremonies is in Arabic, and singers are not restricted to griots. Drawn from both religious and secular origins, the popular Islamic music performed at these ceremonies constitutes an important aspect of the Sufi ritual (McLaughlin 1997) and in this case has been adapted to Senegalese Shi'i rituals as well.

Conference leaders reach out to their audience of predominantly Sunni Muslims and those who are newly discovering Shi'i traditions by using formats similar to those of Sufi orders: tents and loudspeakers, music and praise singing, Wolof proverbs and phrases. Event venues are decorated with 'Ashura banners typical of those used elsewhere in the Shi'i world, yet instead of the somber black dress of other Shi'i women, Dakar's Shi'i conferences are populated with African women wearing their finest fashion—boubous of pure white or bright cheerful colors, hair nicely coiffed, makeup fully applied, and flashy gold jewelry on display. As a minority community, Senegalese Shi'a aim to teach others in order to gain more followers and to avoid conflict. Doing so necessitates forms of disseminating these new religious ideas in a manner that does not highlight fundamental differences. For that reason the commemoration of 'Ashura in Dakar does not consist of bodily rituals of self-flagellation (latam) demonstrating individual grief, solidarity with ahl al-bayt, and unison with the wider global Shi'i world. Efforts concentrate instead on uniting as *Senegalese* Muslims—who also love the family of the Prophet—through events that orchestrate a new Shi'i Islamic message through local Sufi Islamic practices.

Mut'a Marriage

Temporary marriage, zawaj mut'a, is another practice that distinguishes Sunnis from Shi'a. A pre-Islamic custom practiced by some Arabian tribes, mut'a was a temporary alliance between a woman and man, common at the time of the Prophet. The second caliph, 'Umar, outlawed this practice, viewing it as fornication. Shi'i Muslims never accepted 'Umar's ruling as legitimate, and their continued practice of mut'a marriage remained a point of contention with Sunni Muslims, who sometimes regard it as legalized prostitution. Defined as "marriage of enjoyment," mut'a involves a contract that may be performed either by the man and woman themselves or by a religious authority. A marriage payment by the man to the woman must be specified as well as the duration of the union, which may be as long or as short as the partners desire as long as they are both in agreement. The objective of mut'a marriage is sexual pleasure, and any children that result are considered legitimate. The contract is renewable, and the man may engage in an unlimited number of simultaneous temporary marriages, although he is limited to four permanent wives. The woman is allowed only one husband at a time, and she must wait a period of forty-five days before contracting another temporary marriage, long enough to ensure she is not pregnant. In most Muslim societies it is unacceptable for a young woman not to be a virgin on her (permanent) wedding night; therefore mut'a marriage is recommended only for divorced or widowed women (Haeri 1989).

Although both Lebanese and Senegalese Shi'a practice this type of marriage, it has different meanings and stigmas for each community. Mut'a marriage is a private and often socially unacceptable practice for Lebanese in Senegal, although it is becoming more frequent and visible in Lebanon (Deeb 2010). One Senegalese sociologist accused Lebanese men of using the institution to marry Senegalese women in villages and later abandon them when they married Lebanese wives. I first encountered the practice when a Lebanese man I was interviewing proposed that I become his temporary wife. He offered me a sum of 50,000 CFA (approximately US$100) for "the rights to my body" for an initial period of one month. He informed me that he had engaged in four temporary marriages since he married his (permanent) wife. I did not accept his proposal but used this encounter to broach the subject with various Lebanese men and women in the community with whom I was close.[28]

My male friends used disrespectful adjectives to describe this man, whose identity I kept anonymous, and women were horrified by my encounter. One man, who had spent some time in Lebanon, explained to me that this practice was mostly carried out in Senegal by Lebanese who had recently come from Lebanon, whom he referred to as "fundamentalists."[29] He views this type of marriage as "sex without regret" and pointed out that temporary marriage is frequently contracted by Lebanese men in Senegal with divorced women, Senegalese and Lebanese alike. He suggested that Senegalese women were attracted by the financial incentive of the contract. He views the practice as acceptable *only* when men must travel frequently without their wives or when they live in a society that enforces it. He does not see this institution as necessary today and certainly not in Senegal.

Nadia, who had spent some time during her youth in southern Lebanon, suggested that temporary marriage exists in Africa but is rare. She had a friend in Abidjan who was divorced but contracted mut'a marriage in order to legally date a Lebanese man. She defended her friend by informing me that the couple did not plan to engage in sexual intercourse immediately, but for him to even touch her arm was forbidden by Shi'i Islam unless they were married. Nadia thought temporary marriage was a good thing in theory as it regulates society and legitimizes children. Nevertheless she explained that it is only contracted in rare circumstances and is not for everyone. Another Lebanese woman told me that Shi'a refer to this type of marriage as a "secret marriage." Other women born and raised in Senegal were against this practice, considering it a way for men who are not ready to commit to a woman to pleasure themselves. The range in Lebanese responses from "rare" to "frequent" is a testimony to the private nature of this religious practice as well as certain men's use of the contract to engage in sexual relations beyond Senegal's small Lebanese female community.

Whereas those Lebanese who may engage in zawaj mut'a do so purely for pleasure, Senegalese Shi'a envision temporary marriage as a solution to social problems created by Senegal's current economic crisis. Temporary marriage allows a Senegalese man (who may not be able to afford a proper wedding until his forties) to marry in accordance with Islamic law by negotiating a private contract that suits his financial capabilities. Temporary marriage also benefits women, who can end the relationship without the stigma of divorce. A woman may insist that the man support her, pay her rent, and she can indicate whether she wishes to have sexual relations. Fatou envisioned temporary marriage as keeping order and morality in society, preventing adultery and prostitution, legitimizing children, and reducing AIDS, sexually transmitted diseases, and abortion, therefore being politically as well as economically beneficial. "It is liberating young people, those young people who are precisely sinning without even being aware of it," she declared, explaining that men and women were more free, able to agree on marriage terms outside of societal pressures, without large financial obligations or enduring social debts toward one another. Senegalese Shi‘a—both men and women, although many women are not willing to engage in this practice—perceive temporary marriage not only as a respectable institution but also as a logical one that facilitates their current economic and social reality. The discourse on temporary marriage among Senegalese converts is thus linked to African economic development and women's rights.

One male informant explained temporary marriage as follows:

> We do it in Senegal because we know that it is authorized and understood. We do it without running the risk of sinning; indeed it is quite the contrary. By contracting, for example, temporary marriage with a girlfriend, instead of carrying on in a way that could lead me to commit a sin, we marry. . . . There are many blessings in it. But this is something we can't publicize, because the Senegalese don't understand it. It is a practice the Senegalese might use to hold against us and put us in a bad position towards others.

Assan actively works to promote women's rights in Islam.

> When I mention women's emancipation I am talking about the fact that Islam, in its original form and its first goal, was to liberate women from the yokes of slavery, exploitation, seclusion, etc. Islam banished everything that impeded fulfillment of women's aspirations. . . . Temporary marriage is an intervention related to such a context. It is aimed at humanizing relationships. It is a contract that respects values. . . . A girlfriend is someone with whom you have come to a sentimental agreement, someone with whom you are in love. Now, in order to be authorized by religion, it is necessary to follow religious procedures. So the emancipation of women is not just the emancipation of women, but . . . the emancipation of society in order to avoid that society falls into anarchy.

‘Umar referred to our discussion of temporary marriage as the most beautiful question of all that I asked him. He often explains the jurisprudence of zawaj mutʿa to Senegalese and asked my forgiveness for discussing sexual matters, as he was old enough to be my father. ʿUmar pointed out that all Muslims conserved this form of marriage but Shiʿa are more loquacious than Sunnis and made this marriage provision known. He gave examples of Sunni Muslims who engaged, perhaps unknowingly, in temporary marriage. A man in the Futa owned many cows and when he took them to graze he met a young girl and fell in love. The cowherd wanted to marry her, so he gave the girl fifteen cows, spent one night with her, and then left and never saw her again. In another example, the Tijani Shaykh ʿUmar had fifty children by women he encountered during his travels so he must have engaged in temporary marriage. The men in these stories were not Shiʿa, and for ʿUmar these examples proved that temporary marriage exists in all schools of Islam. In Sunni "temporary marriages," however, the woman is not aware of the end of her marriage, which is determined by the whim of the man.[30]

Nevertheless most Sunni Muslims in Senegal do not understand temporary marriage. A scandal occurred in 2009 when a Mozdahir leader discussed temporary marriage on television, causing much outrage. He was arrested upon leaving the television studio. This incident led to a heated debate in the newspapers and on the radio, Internet, and television programs on questions of marriage and women's rights in Islam, and Shiʿi Islam in Senegal became associated with temporary marriage. Whereas Mozdahir faced some initial backlash, this incident increased publicity for the NGO, resulting in numerous phone calls inquiring how to perform this type of marriage.

*   *   *

I have outlined the historical migrations, global movements, and religious institutions that have made cosmopolitanism a constitutive feature of Senegalese Muslim self-understanding and practice. The search for modern forms of *authentic* knowledge cannot lead to social change on its own; inherent in Islamic education is the *authority* bestowed on those who are knowledgeable. With the spread of religious knowledge through books, media, and the Internet comes a broadening of the scope of religious authority and the resulting conflict with or accommodation of old political communities (Eickelman and Piscatori 1996; Roy 2004; Mandaville 2007). Religious scholars who were once revered for their guidance are losing their monopoly over religion with a growing number of educated Muslims who are literate in Arabic. Literacy enables them to turn directly to texts, often to individually acquired libraries of Islamic legal books, which they interpret themselves. The conflict is no longer about who can read Islamic texts but about who is the best interpreter of these texts. Thus, empowerment is not won through staging a coup d'état against the religious and political status quo and bringing a violent Islamic revolution to Senegal. Empowerment is achieved through inclusion and coexistence, through building Shiʿi institutions that also cater to Sunni Muslims, and through sharpening one's juridical expertise to excel in the comparison between Maliki (Sunni) and Jaʿfari (Shiʿi) law. Converts are won over through stressing complementarities of Sunni and Shiʿi Islam before revealing the perceived superiority of Shiʿi jurisprudence, by not forcing Shiʿi views on others but allowing them to be convinced on their own and at their own pace. In this way conversion to a Shiʿi alternative can bring change peacefully and maybe even promote economic development in pushing to reform Sufi orders.

Yet as cosmopolitans Senegalese Shiʿa do not envision their new religious identity as cutting all ties with their Sufi roots. Instead they endeavor to convince their Sufi brothers and sisters of the historical origins, concrete benefits, and authenticity of Shiʿi Islam in Senegal. Cosmopolitan ethics, knowledge, and connections throughout the Muslim world enable a small but growing minority of Senegalese Shiʿa to contend for religious authority in Senegal and likewise claim inclusion in the nation. Shiʿi Islam can become an alliance within the larger Sufi orders where an elite group of educated Muslims in both Sunni and Shiʿi Islam belong.

There is a struggle for religious authority in Senegal. Reformist Islamic movements, including Senegalese converts to Shiʿi Islam, are able to counter and escape Sufi dominance through promoting an alternative—and for them more comprehensive—interpretation of Islam. Building schools and libraries ensures them a following through offering other Senegalese Muslims access to this same knowledge. Religious scholars are also adjusting to and responding to the demands of this changing situation by providing religious education in Arabic. Senegal has therefore seen an increase in new (Shiʿi as well as Sufi) Islamic youth organizations. Lebanese, Iranian, and African religious scholars compete for leadership of Senegal's Shiʿi communities. Although Lebanese and Iranians have better financial resources, Senegalese converts insist that being an indigenous African leader is an important component of one's religious authenticity. Through mastering both Sunni and Shiʿi jurisprudence, Senegalese reject the authority of local Sufi marabouts *and* protest Arab and Iranian domination of Islam. In West Africa the ʿulamaʾs authority is not disappearing into a Westernized, globalized, Islamic individualism, as Roy (2004) has argued. Religious authority is shifting as scholars and newly emerging leaders develop their own Islamic networks counter to or concurrent with the status quo. Senegalese are encouraged to join this new community, advertised through conferences and media publicity catering to the general Sufi public, not only because of the more authentic version of Islam it espouses, but also for the concrete modern benefits it offers.

Those at the margins of capital-rich "global cities" are forced to seek unconventional financial networks. Senegalese Shiʿa are converting to an alternative modernity of Islam that enables converts to negotiate new economic linkages with Iran and Lebanon (as opposed to Saudi Arabia and other Sunni Arab countries).

Shi'i Islam is being negotiated in Senegal as both an activist and a peaceful religion capable of bringing about social change at the local and even national level. As Shi'a, Senegalese Muslims are able to obtain scholarships to study abroad, acquire funding for their Islamic organizations, and gain an advantage over Senegalese Sunnis in accessing employment opportunities with the Iranian embassy or Lebanese Islamic Institute. Above all, conversion to Shi'i Islam is linked to a discourse of progress and economic development where knowledge of Shi'i texts and the implementation of their ideas could bring African Shi'i modernity. Donham (1999) suggests that *development* and *democracy* replaced *revolution* in modernity's master narrative, but the case of Senegalese converts to Shi'i Islam has demonstrated that the Iranian Revolution has not been forgotten.

Conversion allows for a break with the past in order to create a new present in the hope for a better future. The reworking of history and tradition enables converts to negotiate new international linkages, whereas revisionist historical narratives of the spread of Islam attempt to locally establish Shi'i legitimacy in Senegal. Mourning the martyrdom of Imam Husayn on Senegalese soil ties peripheral West Africa to the Shi'i core in the Middle East. The institution of temporary marriage provides an Islamically permissible solution to Senegal's socioeconomic crisis. The more Shi'i leaders can demonstrate that Shi'i Islam is compatible with a Senegalese lifestyle, the more followers they convert. Shi'i Islam in Senegal is built upon cosmopolitan convergences of the new religion with the old as well as ways in which Shi'i Islam diverges from the Sufi orders. The goal is not to assimilate Senegalese Muslims into a global movement but rather to adapt Shi'i Islam to a local African context.

Proclaiming Shi'i Islam to be Senegalese is thus a demonstration of autochthony and belonging. The actions of Senegalese Shi'i institutions aim to counter not only foreign Shi'i leadership in Senegal but also the inefficiencies of the Senegalese state. Shi'i NGOs merge elite Islamic knowledge with basic services needed by the people—farming, rotating credit associations, health care—to enable Shi'i believers to be self-sustaining and lead safer, healthier lives. Such economic development activities discourage the movement's followers from illegal migration and teach them to develop the land in order to feed their families. Adapting cosmopolitan knowledge gained elsewhere to the Senegalese context is an effort to step in where the state has failed and go beyond the duties of a citizen. For Senegalese converts there is no greater proof of their loyalty to their country and love for their people than to remain in Senegal and work for a better tomorrow.

Coda
On Shi͑i Islam, Anthropology, and Cosmopolitanism

"I<small>SLAM</small>" <small>ENTERED THE</small> Western imaginary with a vengeance in 1979 with the revolution in Iran. This particular interpretation of Shi͑i Islam was broadly depicted by Western media as "militant" and closely linked to "terrorism" (Said 1997). Over the past thirty years Sunni "radical" groups, such as Hamas, al-Qa͑ida, and the Taliban, replaced Ayatollah Khomeini as "evildoers" and "bad Muslims" (Mamdani 2004). Shi͑i Islam only later returned to the forefront with the struggle for power in Iraq since the fall of Saddam Hussein in 2003, Hizbullah's reappearance in the international scene in the 2006 Lebanon War, and the presidency of Ahmadinejad in Iran (fiercely contested in the 2009 elections). Each of these Shi͑i bodies indiscriminately fell under the "war on terrorism" during the George W. Bush administration. Most recently, media coverage and policy analysis of the so-called Arab Spring put forward an abundance of unlikely comparisons of Egypt's 2011 revolution to 1979 Iran and premature suggestions of an emerging Cold War between Saudi Arabia and Iran for control of the Gulf, in particular regarding the unfortunate repression of Shi͑i protestors in Bahrain (see Leichtman 2011). Today, rereading Edward Said's classic portrayal of Western media's *covering Islam* at the time of the Iranian Revolution sadly reminds us that little has changed. Journalists and policymakers are now convinced that Shi͑a are different from Sunnis, while remaining confused about what exactly distinguishes these two branches of Islam, what relevance this has for politics, and why this distinction even matters.

Not surprisingly, there has been a surge in literature on Shi͑i Islam, with some scholars envisioning a "Shi͑a revival" (Fuller and Francke 1999; Nasr 2006), a "Shi͑i-led reformation" (Nakash 2006), or the formation of a highly contested "Shi͑i crescent" (Barzegar 2008; Khashan 2008; Mikaïl 2008) in the Middle East.[1] Scholarship highlights differences between Shi͑a in Iran and the Arab world (Fuller and Francke 1999; Nakash 2006) or expands geographic boundaries from the Mediterranean to Central Asia (Monsutti, Naef, and Sabahi 2007) or South Asia (Cole 2002). Monsutti, Naef, and Sabahi suggest that these "other Shiites," those who live outside Iran, share a common feature in their treatment as a minority by ruling Sunni elites. Mervin (2007) refers, in the plural, to "Shi͑i worlds." Yet none of these studies investigate Shi͑a in Africa.

Meanwhile "Africa" has always been seen as a "dark continent" by the West (Mbembe 2001; Mudimbe 1988). Joseph Conrad's *Heart of Darkness* remains a popular high school curricular choice, often American students' only introduction to Africa. Ferguson points out that even today "Africa" "continues to be described through a series of lacks and absences, failings and problems, plagues and catastrophes" (2006:2). He suggests that the "shadow" imagery of Africa goes beyond darkness or poor visibility to a kind of doubling (i.e., "informal economy"; "shadow state"; "alternative modernity"; African institutions as a failed copy of the Western model). Thus it is no surprise that when the media does focus on Shi'i Islam in Africa, it suggests that African chaos enables Arab terrorists to freely carry out illicit activities.

This book has endeavored to bring both Africa and Shi'i Islam out of the shadows. Unlike early case studies of colonial mimicry written by Rhodes-Livingstone anthropologists (Mitchell 1956; Mitchell and Epstein 1959), today's African cosmopolitans no longer poke fun at the Western Other in resistance. Some Africans, in despair, turn to Europe for help, desperately claiming equal rights of membership in an unequal global society (Ferguson 2002). Cosmopolitanism could be understood in terms of mimesis and alterity (Taussig 1993). Yet in focusing on Shi'i Islam—with its already anti-Western revolutionary ideologies—and in distancing myself from the Kantian Enlightenment model, I prefer to leave behind colonial baggage inherent in such analyses. Non-Western models certainly provide an alternative to the Western modern. I have thus highlighted not only French colonial cosmopolitanism but also the cosmopolitan ideologies of Michel Chiha, Leopold Sedar Senghor, and Ayatollah Ruhollah Khomeini—all of whom in different ways attempted to reconfigure universalism into various sorts of humanism, where universality was a function of disparate European/Christian, Arab, African, or Islamic particularities. It is precisely the unique ways in which cosmopolites in Senegal mold, adapt, and integrate foreign philosophies and religious practices into a distinctly African understanding that enables the assertion of their rights to membership as both "citizens of the world" and autochthons at home. In so doing they transform Shi'i Islam into a universalizing while differentiating identity that supersedes previous colonial categories of "race" (for Lebanese) and "ethnicity" (for indigenous Africans). This Shi'i Islamic humanitarianism enables a moving beyond the dominant framework for evaluating Shi'i movements in terms of political influence. The Senegalese case also demonstrates that "local, parochial, rooted, and culturally specific loyalties" can easily coexist with and do not run counter to "translocal, transnational, transcendent, elitist, enlightened, universalist and modernist ones" (Werbner 2008:14).

I have taken up Werbner's (2008) call for a new anthropology of cosmopolitanism, which I have methodologically linked to Marcus's (1995) earlier reflections on multi-sited ethnography. In moving beyond the traditional anthropological community study model I have focused more broadly on global Islamic movements and their vernacularization in one principal geographical location. I have endeavored to circumvent the limitations of many ethnographies of migration that focus on transnational ties between migrant community and country of origin to the exclusion of acknowledging the sometimes profound influence of migrants on host societies. I have also used a broad conception of religion that brings together an examination of the sacred, Shiʿi rituals, individual piety, and Islamic authorities and institutions. This led me to unravel the "webs of significance" (Geertz 1973) embedded in networks between Shiʿi Muslims in Senegal, Lebanon, Iran, and Iraq, between Sunni and Shiʿi Muslims in Senegal, and across time and space to French colonial relations with both Lebanese and Senegalese. I could have written two—more concise!—books (as I have been advised to do on multiple occasions), one on Lebanese migrants and another on Senegalese converts. Instead, I have chosen to make the larger theoretical and methodological point that in this age of globalization, multiculturalism, transnationalism, and cosmopolitanism, communities and the social movements in which they participate can be understood only through mapping out their local, national, and global intersections. This book is my version of an "ethnography of global connection" (Tsing 2004).

Others have highlighted the cosmopolitan predisposition of Shiʿi Islam. The marjaʿiyya transcends national boundaries in terms of both religious authority and the financial flow of khums (Walbridge 2001). Scholars explore how this manifests in the "Shiʿi international" of Iraq's Najaf school (Mallat 1993); contextualize Hizbullah's uniqueness as the coming "full circle" of five centuries of Lebanese-Iranian encounters (Chehabi 2006); and examine transnational Shiʿi politics through relations of Shiʿi movements in the Gulf to central religious authorities in Iraq or Iran (Louër 2008).[2] Shiʿi religious shrines and pilgrimage sites have also been globally commoditized and objectified (Pinto 2007). Shiʿi transnationalism does not impede the construction of national identities, as Shaery-Eisenlohr (2008) convincingly argues in her account of Shiʿi Lebanon. Instead, cosmopolitanism enables Shiʿa to encounter various cultural and nationalist *Lebanese, Iranian, Iraqi,* and other Shiʿi communities. In contrast to these political Middle Eastern Shiʿi identities, Senegalese converts, in a declaration of "cosmopolitan patriotism" (Appiah 1998), proclaim themselves to be founding members of a vernacular *Senegalese* Shiʿi Islamic network.

Muslim cosmopolitanism embraces religious, political, socioeconomic, and cultural difference. Shiʿi rituals—and the global and local allegiances inherent in their performances—have distinct meanings for Lebanese migrants and Senegalese converts. ʿAshura is the ultimate embodiment of collective Shiʿi identity. Whereas Lebanese turn to the Middle East in conforming their commemorative performance with traditions in Lebanon, Senegalese remake the period of mourning and remembrance into an internally focused intellectual debate with Senegal's Sufi Muslims. Lebanese in Senegal are emotionally tied to tragedies in Lebanon and Iraq, and ʿAshura instills in them a spirit of resistance. For Senegalese converts, ʿAshura is an occasion to incorporate Iranian revisionist histories into conference lectures and publications. They highlight Senegalese Sufis' own love for the family of the Prophet and in so doing, claim their place in Senegal's religious landscape through equating ʿAshura with Tamkharit.

Autochthony is the alter ego of cosmopolitanism. The Senegalese state links notions of autochthony to race, reinforced from French colonial times by politique des races. In contrast to indigenous Senegalese traditions, Shiʿi holidays for Lebanese underpin a cosmopolitan Lebanese national identity in linking the Prophet's birthday to the independence of the south of Lebanon and Ramadan to the southern Lebanese Sadr Foundation. These rituals inadvertently constitute Senegal as *not home* for Lebanese. Yet Lebanese are careful to also publicly perform their loyalty to Senegal, particularly when moved to demonstrate political solidarity with Lebanon, whose national culture integrated Muslims and Christians into a "secular" ethnic group of "Senegalese of Lebanese origin," united in order to claim their place as belonging to Senegal's history. Senegalese converts similarly counter accusations that Shiʿi Islam is not Senegalese by turning it into a fiercely vernacular and even historically African tradition. Discourses of these ritual communities were reinforced by Shaykh al-Zayn and Senegalese Shiʿi leaders embedding their religious work in NGOs with a humanitarian agenda, diluting the specific religio-political message of Shiʿi Islam while gaining legitimacy in the eyes of those who need these services. Through education, health care, economic development, working for peace in rebel separatist territories, and assisting during national tragedies, Shiʿi Islam is de-radicalized and familiarized as it caters to the African public good. This humanism was also reinforced by the universalist language of Ayatollah Khomeini, Shaykh al-Zayn, and Senegalese Shiʿi leaders, knowing when to highlight Shiʿi Islam as an all-inclusive (not foreign minority branch of) Islam. Examining Lebanese migrants and Senegalese converts together has enabled an evaluation of the development of a global Shiʿi Islamic movement translated and converted by minority communities in diverse ways that transform its conceptual framework into a humanitarian and thus (locally) universal frame of reference from which all Senegalese can benefit.

There are many differences between these two groups. Aside from varied understandings and practices of Shiʿi fundamentals such as the marjaʿiyya, temporary marriage, and even taqiyya, is the power to choose to be Shiʿa. Senegalese converts often highlight that Lebanese were born into the religion, that they are businessmen who are not educated in matters of Islam, and many are even illiterate in Arabic. The question of choice pertains to cosmopolitanism as well as religion. Lebanese left Lebanon over a century ago to escape economic hardship and political strife. Many arrived in Senegal unintentionally but found favorable conditions for their settlement. Yet French colonial and later independent Senegalese governmentality of Lebanese led to their unity as an ethnic group in order to counter various political categories and anti-Lebanese campaigns constructed around their community as a perceived threat. Excluded from Senegalese society as the economic, racial, and religious Other, Lebanese concurrently clung to cosmopolitan linkages, including Shaykh al-Zayn as a representative of Lebanon, while renegotiating the integration debate in an effort to claim (fictive) autochthony. Ironically it was their cosmopolitanism, linked to a distinct *Lebanese* national identity—not fully detached from wider sectarian politics in Lebanon—that enabled their incorporation in Senegal as a *secular* ethnic group. Although Lebanese may not have had a choice in becoming cosmopolitans or Shiʿi Muslims, I illustrated their agency in strategically using their connections to effectively minimize religion as the community's dominant identifier and in its place opting for ethnicity over race and country of origin. This was why Shaykh al-Zayn was more successful in bringing the community back to their Lebanese roots than in transforming them collectively into pious Shiʿa.

In contrast, Senegalese refer to Shiʿi Islam as an *acquired,* not *inherited,* religion. For them this was a choice involving many years of study, knowledge of Arabic, access to religious texts, and sometimes, but not necessarily, international travel. The Arabic language became another territory for Senegalese converts to resist the Western conception of Islam as portrayed by French media and to experience Shiʿi Islam even without leaving Senegal. Yet one can also question how much choice they really had, as Senegalese Shiʿa, like those who turned to other Sunni reformist movements, were searching for a solution to counter the inadequacies of the Senegalese state and dominance of Sufi orders. In demonstrating authority over "authentic" Islamic knowledge, cosmopolitanism gained them a following not only for enviable connections to Iran and/or Lebanon but also for the understated ability to incorporate new religious traditions into existing Sufi ways. Shiʿi Islam was portrayed not as a complete break with the past but as an option to improve and build upon local practice. As such, Senegalese converts were able to bypass the authority of local Sufi marabouts as well as Arab and Iranian domination of Shiʿi Islam through creating their own unique religious community. This modern form of conversion enables a mélange of foreign and indigenous religious traditions through strategic fusion of cosmopolitanism and autochthony. In this way, Shiʿa in Senegal—both Lebanese migrants and Senegalese converts—live religious lives that are not circumscribed by state borders or local customs yet are fully grounded in Senegal.

Migration, literacy, and media technologies have encouraged Muslims to connect with coreligionists beyond national boundaries and expand their knowledge about the diversity of Islam. Shiʿi Islam has simultaneously adapted to Senegalese local culture in a similar way to how Peel (2000) describes Christianity's "inculturation" by the Yoruba. Muharram commemorations resemble much more the religious debates of Senegal's Sufi orders than the passion plays of Iran. Where else would a shaykh be able to claim the title Caliph Ahl al-Bayt? As Shiʿi Islam travels to Africa it loses the (often political) spirit that exemplifies the religion in the Middle East. This ethical, moral, and flexible Shiʿi cosmopolitanism can be celebrated or hidden in response to local minority identity politics (which have also evolved over time). The universal humanitarianism of education, economic development, interethnic cooperation, and peace and conflict resolution enables Shiʿi Islam to bypass contentious political debates grounded in other national contexts, while at the same time fulfilling a political role at home in competing with other religious groups and NGOs to fill the gap left by the failure of the Senegalese state.

This brings us to the question of the Islamic umma, the "imagined community" of Muslims-at-large, for Shiʿa in Africa. There is something particular about the cosmopolitanism of Shiʿi Islam that distinguishes it from more general notions of *globalized Islam* (Roy 2004). Scholarship examining Muslim diasporas as an ever-expanding and hypothetical umma that includes formerly non-Muslim countries where Muslims now reside has neglected to examine the umma as it applies to Muslim minorities. Do Shiʿi Muslims perceive of themselves as part of the wider umma or as belonging to a more narrow and exclusively Shiʿi global Muslim community? How has the nature of Sunni dominance of the Muslim world and the often tense history of Sunni-Shiʿi relations impacted their vision? This book has explored the nature of cosmopolitan Islam for Shiʿi minority communities in a Sunni Muslim–majority African country, which is already perceived of as peripheral to the Muslim "core" in the Middle East.

Scholarship on the Qurʾanic notion of umma has recently been merged with studies of the Muslim diaspora, where faith is understood to supersede nationalism, race, and ethnicity, especially among Muslims in the West. Castells writes: "For a Muslim, the fundamental attachment is not to the *watan* (homeland), but to the *umma,* or community of believers, all made equal in their submission to Allah" (1997:15). Roy (2004) argues that Islam has become deterritorialized and globalized and is being reshaped by Western languages, cultures, and ways of life, with the loss of influence of Muslim traditional territories and cultures. Mandaville (2001) examines how Muslims are constructing new frameworks for the practice of Islamic politics in response to conditions of life in Europe and thereby *reconceptualizing* the umma through revising ideas about who, what, and where political community can be. Sayyid defines the umma as "a community of believing women and men unified by faith and transcending national state boundaries" (2000:36). He agrees that a pervasive representation of Muslim migrant communities throughout the developed world has contributed to the assertion of Muslim subjectivity and the formation of a Muslim umma. He therefore contends that even though the Muslim umma is not reducible to displaced population groups and includes the Muslim population in Muslim countries, the umma becomes the manifestation of diaspora because it is an attempt to come to terms with the limits and crisis of the nation-state.

This book calls for a moving beyond Western-centric theoretical developments, which often focus on relations between Sunni Muslims in Europe, the United States, and the Middle East. My research suggests that this ideology of the umma does not hold for a marginalized Muslim minority community in a Muslim majority country, a product of both south–south migration as well as religious conversion, which instead defines itself along reformulated ethnic, religious, and national boundaries. Whereas French colonialism sometimes did unite Lebanese and Senegalese, the trials and errors of Senegalese postindependence politics, influenced by the power of Sufi orders, did not enable Lebanese to feel at home in Senegal. One cannot ignore the contentious history between Arabs and Africans, including the Arab slave trade and African marginalization when traveling in the Middle East. This was why Amadou Bamba gained popularity as an indigenous African—not Arab—founder of the Murid Sufi order (Cruise O'Brien 1984). Lebanese could not position themselves merely as members of the wider Muslim umma in order to receive rights as African citizens; they needed to make autochthonous claims on Senegal.

Furthermore, Shiʿa in Senegal do not envision themselves as "universal Muslims," but identify with specific religious centers in the Shiʿi world. Whereas Lebanon orients Lebanese Shiʿa in Senegal, whose shaykh follows Ayatollah al-Sistani in Iraq, African converts to Shiʿi Islam in the same country are much more oriented toward Iran. Liberal-secular visions of religious pluralism have never been at odds with Shiʿi Islam or with Islam in Senegal. Far from being "counter-cosmopolitans" (Appiah 2006), Lebanese migrants and Senegalese converts to Shiʿi Islam have made cosmopolitanism their own by transforming global reformist Islam into a distinctly local Senegalese articulation and performance. They redefined the umma as a select community of global Shiʿi Muslims also inclusive of Senegalese Sufis (who, they believe, are really Shiʿa). This is certainly not the recruiting ground for al-Qaʾida and other "young, global Muslim fundamentalists" as Appiah (2006:138) defines the umma to be. To be cosmopolitan is to command religious discourses and to create a ritual community by incorporating a variety of customs and traditions. In this way a humanitarian Shiʿi universalism is refracted and reconfigured through cultural particularisms, transforming both in the process. The culture of Islam in Senegal is the coexistence—not convergence—of multiple Islamic traditions (Qadir, Tijani, Murid, Sunni reformist movements, Shiʿi, etc.). Globalization and the pursuit of authenticity have led to exposure to new religious ideas, which have created multiple discursive traditions about being Muslim in Senegal.

Glossary

Terms are in Arabic unless otherwise indicated

abaya—cloak; loosely fitting over-garment worn by some Muslim women

adhan—call to prayer

ahl al-bayt—family of the Prophet; Shiᶜa

anashid (s. nashid)—religious chants

Arabisants (French)—returned students who studied in the Middle East, often at religious centers; their Arabic training and acculturation was perceived as a difficulty in their integration into Senegal's administrative and educational system built on a French model

ᶜAshura—tenth day of the Islamic holy month of Muharram, when Imam Hussayn was killed (in 680 CE) in Karbala, Iraq

baraka—blessing or gift of grace; spiritual power

bidᶜa—innovation in Islam

boubou (French)—long flowing wide-sleeved garment worn by Muslims in West Africa

caliph—head of Senegalese Sufi order; Sunni caliphs were selected or elected successors of the Prophet in political and military leadership

fatiha—first verse of the Qurᵓan

fatwa—religious decree; ruling on Islamic law issued by a scholar

fiqh—Islamic jurisprudence

gamu (Wolof)—Tijani celebration

gris-gris (French)—talisman or amulet usually inscribed with verses from the Qurᵓan

hadith—Prophetic traditions

hajj—pilgrimage to Mecca; hajja (f.), hajji (m.), or al-hajj are honorific titles given to Muslim women or men who have completed the hajj

halal—permitted in Islam

haram—forbidden in Islam

harisa—Lebanese dish of grain and chicken eaten during ᶜAshura; each stir of the dish with a large wooden stick is thought to bring a blessing

hawza (p. hawzat)—Shiᶜi Islamic school; religious seminaries in the Middle East

hijab—headscarf; veil

husayniyya—meeting place in which to commemorate ᶜAshura

iftar—nightly break-the-fast meal during Ramadan

ijtihad—religious decisions based on reason

imam—prayer leader; Shiᶜi leader who was both political and religious guide. A Shiᶜi majority follows a series of twelve Imams from the family of the Prophet who ruled after his death in 632 CE

istikhara—guidance supplication using the Qurᵓan to request what actions are best and proper from God and to remove doubt

jebbalu (Wolof)—vow of obedience pronounced by talibes to their marabout

jihad—to struggle in the way of God

jinn—spirits or supernatural creatures in Islamic mythology mentioned in the Qurʾan; jinn can be good, evil, or neutral and are able to interfere physically with people or objects and can be acted upon

kaʿba—sacred enclosure at Mecca

khatib (f. khatiba)—orator; preacher; one who recounts the story of the death of Imam Husayn

khums—Shiʿi income tax of one-fifth

khutba—sermon delivered before Friday prayers

Korite (Wolof)—ʿId al-Fitr, feasting holiday signifying the end of Ramadan

latam—self-flagellation during ʿAshura

madrasa (p. madaris)—Islamic school; médersa (French) refers to a French-controlled Islamic school during colonial times

magal (Wolof)—"to celebrate" or "to exalt"; annual pilgrimage of Murids to Tuba

mahdi—"the rightly guided one" who is the restorer of religion and justice and will rule before the end of the world; the twelfth Shiʿi Imam believed to live in occultation

majalis (s. majlis)—"place of sitting"; religious assembly; special gathering in remembrance of Imam Husayn

marabout (French)—Islamic leader

marjaʿ [al-taqlid] (p. marajiʿ)—a source to emulate or follow

marjaʿiyya—system of highest-ranking Shiʿi leadership

marjan—protection paper containing Qurʾanic verses

Mawlud—Prophet Muhammad's birthday

mbotu (Wolof)—shawl tying a baby to its mother's back

métis (French)—children of mixed African and Lebanese (or French) parentage

métissage (French)—cross-breeding or synthesis

muezzin—the person appointed at a mosque to call Muslims to prayer

mujtahid—qualified specialist on Islamic law

mukhtasar—concise handbook of Islamic legal treatises

muqaddam—Sufi representative of an important marabout

musoor (Wolof)—head wrap

mustahab—religiously commendable

naar (Wolof)—Arab

nadba—elegy

njebbel (Wolof)—vow of obedience to a marabout

perðo mbotu (Pular)—one who migrates from one's parents' traditions; convert

qadi—judge who rules according to Islamic law

sayyid (also sharif)—honorific title given to Muslims accepted as descendants of the Prophet Muhammad through his grandsons, Hasan and Husayn; sayyids wear black turbans

shariʿa—Islamic law

Shiʿat ʿAli—partisans of ʿAli

sunna—body of Islamic law based on words and deeds of Muhammad and his successors

Tabaski (Wolof)—ʿId al-Adha, holiday commemorating the sacrifice offered during pilgrimage to Mecca by slaughtering sheep

tafsir—Qurʾanic commentary

talibe (Wolof)—Sufi disciple; student

taqiyya—Shiʿi practice of dissimulation or precaution

taqlid—emulating a marja's interpretation of Islamic law
tarjamat—Islamic biographies
tasha'a—to accept or enter the Shi'i school
tawassul—supplicating to God through a prophet, imam, or saint
ta'ziya—recitals of the sufferings and martyrdom of Husayn
teranga (Wolof)—hospitality
tontine (French)—rotating credit association
turba—block of clay from Karbala used in prayer by Shi'a
'ulama—scholar; clergy; authority on Islamic law
umma—community of Muslims-at-large
wakil—Shi'i authorized representative of a marja'
wilayat—authority invested in the Prophet and his family as representatives of God on earth
wilayat al-faqih—Ayatollah Khomeini's concept of jurist's guardianship of the state
wird—litany of Sufi prayers
zakat—2.5 percent Islamic tax on assets
zawaj mut'a—Shi'i temporary marriage
ziyara—visits to religious shrines
zu'ama—Lebanese political bosses; clientalism

Notes

Preface

1. Ginger Thompson, "U.S. Says Lebanese Bank Laundered Money for Drug Smugglers Tied to Hezbollah," *New York Times,* February 10, 2011. Benjamin Weiser, "7 are Accused of Conspiracy to Sell Drugs to Arm Taliban," *New York Times,* February 15, 2011. Helene Cooper, "Treasury Dept., Citing Six People as Operatives, Accuses Iran of Aiding Al Qaeda," *New York Times,* July 29, 2011.
2. Rick Gladstone, "U.S. Blacklists Fund-Raisers for Hezbollah," *New York Times,* June 11, 2013, http://www.nytimes.com/2013/06/12/world/middleeast/us-hits-hezbollah-with-new-sanctions .html?_r=1&.

Introduction

1. Hefner (2003:159–160) similarly coined the concept *civic pluralism,* defining a *plural* society as one that developed a high measure of social and cultural differentiation, particularly regarding ethnicity, religion, gender, ideology, and class. A *civic pluralist* society renounces any intention of repressing this pluralism and responds to its challenges in a peaceful and participatory way.
2. Often academics, using popular terms, are claiming as new what is not new at all. Cooper's (2005:117) critique of scholars' widespread use of *-itys, -izations,* and other "totalizing concepts" questions the adequacy and analytic value of similar terms. In the context of cosmopolitanism, Lawrence (n.d.) also questions how one can display an *-ism* without falling into another, which becomes its shadow opposite.
3. Political scientists, in particular Villalón (1995) and Cruise O'Brien (1996), have argued that Senegal is exceptional among African states for its long colonial experience of French sovereignty; special postcolonial relationship with France; preservation of multiparty democratic politics since independence; and above all assertion of statehood over most of its national territory through institutional networks of Sufi orders. Nevertheless, some have questioned this Senegalese exception as a result of the contested 2012 presidential elections and President Wade's unwillingness to give up power, changing the constitution and challenging notions of Senegalese democracy in the process.
4. Bayart (2000:222) defines *extraversion* as "the creation and the capture of a rent generated by dependency and which functions as a historical matrix of inequality, political centralization and social struggle."
5. Muslim and Francophone Africa were also excluded from early English-language anthropological accounts of Africa, such as those by the Manchester school (Werbner 1984) and even among anthropologists working in West Africa (Hart 1985), with the notable exception of Cohen (1969).

Introduction to Part 1

1. See Brand (2006:ch. 5) for the history, politics, and development of this ministry. The conference for businessmen was to be followed by conferences targeting engineers, lawyers, poets, artists, and other Lebanese diaspora communities.

2. I frequently heard Lebanese in Lebanon refer to Senegal as an example of the most "integrated" Lebanese community in Africa. In contrast, Senegalese did not consider Lebanese to be "integrated" enough (see chapter 2).

3. Peleikis even suggests "long-distance confessionalism" (2003:176).

4. This book included translations in French, English, Portuguese, Spanish, and Arabic.

5. Pseudonyms are used to protect informant identities with the exception of those who are public figures (such as Shaykh al-Zayn) and names published in newspaper articles.

6. Leichtman (2006) further discusses Senegalese censuses and early Lebanese demographics in West Africa.

7. Clark and Phillips (1994) write that out of 15,000 Lebanese in the 1960s, 45 percent were Christians, almost all Catholics, and 4,000 lived in the interior. In Cap Vert, Lebanese Christians represented only 29 percent of the total Lebanese population, whereas in the interior they were an 80 percent majority (Martin 1964:48).

1. French Colonial Manipulation and Lebanese Survival

1. Boumedouha clarifies that in 1932 the Lebanese association Comité Libano-Syrien was dissolved for failing to achieve its goals. In its place, two associations were created: Comité Libanais consisted of both Lebanese Christians and Muslims, and Comité Coopératif Libanais was organized mostly by Lebanese Christians. Association objectives were to defend Lebanese interests in Senegal, promote charitable works, and strengthen the relationship between France and Lebanon (1987:88–89). Associations collaborated until the mid-1930s, when they disagreed over how to defend Lebanese: whether to publish circulars and articles in local newspapers in response to French attacks or to finance another French newspaper in Dakar to send defensive articles to the metropole (101). As religious and political cleavages deepened, Lebanese Shiʿa formed an organization of their own at the end of the 1930s, Comité d'Adhésion et de Bienfaisance Libano-Syrien (116). The French administration disapproved of the formation of multiple Lebanese associations for fear this would increase intra-Lebanese strife. Boumedouha notes that religio-political leaders in Lebanon heavily influenced political loyalties of early Lebanese immigrants, who were afraid of changing their allegiance, fearing reprisals against families in Lebanon (119). He argues that intra-Lebanese strife of the 1920s and 1930s disappeared between 1939 and 1945 as the community came together as a result of World War II. Lebanese associations fell apart before independence and were replaced by Lebanese Maronite and Shiʿi religious institutions. Additionally, the Lebanese Consulate General was established in Senegal in 1946, and remained until 1961, when the uncertainty of African independence led to its dissolution. On March 3, 1969, a Lebanese diplomatic mission was reestablished, which grew into the present-day embassy.

2. The Lebanese ambassador is Maronite Catholic and the consulate officer is Sunni Muslim, despite the Lebanese Shiʿi majority in Senegal today. Syria has its own embassy.

3. The French are referring to Muslims when they mention "Syrians" in colonial correspondence. See also Kaufman (2004).

4. Bathurst is the old name of Banjul, Gambia's capital. The Gambia separates the Casamance from the rest of Senegal.

5. Most likely in the absence of a Catholic priest a Maronite couple in West Africa would also go to a pastor of a different Christian denomination for religious needs.

6. French first used the term *marabout* in West Africa to refer to members of Muslim lineages who were also clerics, ranging from obscure to well-known and including urban and rural imams or prayer leaders, teachers, scholars, preachers, saints and Sufis, amulet confectioners and diviners (Soares 2005). The term originated in North Africa from the Arabic *murabit*, used in Algeria to designate rural holy men. French corruption of the term continues to be used in North Africa today, instead of the Arabic *wali Allah* (Cornell 1998).

7. See Austen (2010); Diouf (2001); Levtzion (1987; 1994); Levtzion and Pouwels (2000); Robinson (2004); Sanneh (1997); Trimingham (1962); Willis (1979) on the history of Islam in West Africa.

8. Wolof transcribed in Arabic script was called *ajami*. Wolof continues to be written in Arabic today, but to a lesser extent than in the past and predominantly in rural areas.

9. Boumedouha documents that in 1947 the governor general of AOF invited Muhammad Sabra, the first Lebanese consulate officer, along with other diplomats, to be present during Korite (ʿId al-Fitr) prayer. Sabra joined Africans in prayer, but a few days later, at the request of colonial authorities, was recalled by the Lebanese government and replaced by a Christian (1987:260–261).

10. His daughter explained that after independence Lebanese were able to live wherever they wanted, but by then had become accustomed to life in the plateau.

11. Lebanese also secretly supported the Algerian National Liberation Front and backed President Nasser's nationalization of the Suez Canal in 1956. Many Lebanese displayed Nasser's photo in Dakar, but this did not lead to violence as it did in Ivory Coast. Lebanese in Senegal denounced the French, British, and Israeli attack against Egypt and peacefully marched in Dakar in commemoration of Nasser's death in 1970 (Boumedouha 1987:191).

12. Out of the West African colonies, Senegal had the largest French and Lebanese population and was the only colony in which these respective interests came into direct conflict. Therefore there was never as organized an effort against Lebanese in other parts of West Africa.

13. Lebanese were excluded from the Chamber of Commerce during the colonial period, but became active members after independence.

14. The paper changed its name in 1950 to *Les Echos d'Afrique Noire* when Voisin divorced his wife, who was entitled to half the value of the paper under its former name.

15. "Excess Lebanese" probably referred to newly arriving Lebanese migrants who were not yet registered or were illegal.

16. The Lebu are one of Senegal's ethnic groups who mostly live in fishing villages.

17. A neighborhood in Dakar populated by Senegalese. The French forbade Lebanese from residing outside of the plateau.

18. *"Mauvoisin"* was a shortening of Maurice Voisin, but also a pun on *"mauvais libanais,"* a phrase Voisin used repeatedly.

19. Les Phalanges, known as Kataʾib in Arabic, is the political and military force of Lebanon's Maronite Church, founded by Pierre Gemayel in 1936.

2. Senegalese Independence and the Question of Belonging

1. This differed from the definition of Césaire, who coined the term *Negritude,* of "simply recognition of the fact of being black, and the acceptance of that fact, of our destiny of black, of our history and our culture." Vaillant differentiates the two: "for Césaire Negritude was primarily an attitude; for Senghor it was an objective reality" (1990:224).

2. "Then" in the first sentence refers to a 1937 speech in Dakar when Senghor acknowledged both he and Senegal were "Afro-French."

3. See also "Les Fondements de l'Africanité ou Négritude et Arabité" (Senghor 1977:105–150).

4. Boumedouha notes the Senegalese government ironically ended the Africanization process, as middle and senior management staff preferred to work for Lebanese and French firms, which offered higher salaries than government service (1987:239).

5. I cannot confirm these figures.

6. See Diop and Diouf (1990:138–148). Diouf replaced Senghor in 1981.

7. The ferryboat between Dakar and Ziguinchor sank on September 26, 2002, resulting in a national tragedy with almost two thousand victims.

8. Leichtman (2006) includes examples of Lebanese outside Dakar, perceived as more "integrated."

9. See also Lefebvre (2003).

10. See Diarra and Fougeyrollas (1969) for an early study of Senegalese stereotypes.

11. He was forced to resign in 2005 after a 2–2 draw with Togo hurt the Lions' qualification chances for the 2006 World Cup.

12. *Alliance Info,* n.d., 18.

13. If a Lebanese man is polygamous, he tends to have one Senegalese and one Lebanese wife. Lebanese have Senegalese mistresses, and métis children are proof of these relations, although formal marriages are rare.

14. A Lebanese intellectual used the term "hybrid" to refer to his community. On hybridity see Bhabha (1994); Anthias (2001); Werbner (2001); Kraidy (1999).

15. The oldest Lebanese religious institution in Senegal is Notre Dame du Liban, founded in 1952. The church runs two schools: Ecole Maternelle was built behind the church in 1957 and Collège Notre Dame du Liban was inaugurated in 1960. The church even displays a crèche during Christmas with multiracial miniature figures representing the family of Jesus. See Leichtman (2013).

16. I was told that approximately 10,000–11,000 Lebanese hold Senegalese citizenship and 3,000–4,000 hold French nationality.

17. Farid currently has Senegalese, Lebanese, and Sierra Leonean citizenship. His stepmother (his father's second wife) holds Moroccan and Lebanese citizenship. His brothers and half-brothers have Lebanese and Senegalese nationality, and additionally one holds French nationality, two others have Moroccan nationality, and one became American.

18. There are approximately 2 million French living outside France. The three other representatives in West Africa are of French origin.

19. Signs were bilingual in French and English.

3. Shiʿi Islam Comes to Town

1. A religious leader's following is contingent upon personal charisma. Anthropologists have long analyzed charisma of shaykhs, kings, and other leaders (Crapanzano 1973; Geertz 1983; Gilsenan 2000; Lindholm 1990). Cruise O'Brien (1988) likewise applies Weber's concept of charismatic authority to African Sufi Islam. The relationship between charisma and authority is also a central issue in Shiʿi Islam, discussed in relation to the twelve Imams (Halawi 1992) and contemporary Shiʿi leaders, such as Musa al-Sadr (Ajami 1986; Halawi 1992; Mervin 2000).

2. From my consultation with Sabrina Mervin, ʿAbdul Munʿam al-Zayn does not appear to be directly related to the influential al-Zayn family of Nabatiye, Lebanon.

3. Musa al-Sadr knew ʿAli al-Zayn and presided over ʿAbdul Munʿam's marriage in Lebanon.

4. Some Lebanese pay this tax; others do not.

5. Hasan is a pseudonym; I have not altered names of extended family members.

6. I am using his name as he is a public figure.

7. Mansur was Sy's son by birth, Barud's spiritual brother.

8. It is not uncommon for Lebanese to be awarded such honors or to proudly display medals and photos with influential authorities in offices as symbols of integration. Barud, however, had more awards than any other Lebanese I encountered.

9. The name comes from Um Kalthum's song *wulid al-huda* (birth of guidance). The Islamic Institute was initially called al-Huda before the women's organization took that name.

10. I am using his name.

11. A Moroccan bookstore specializing in Sunni and Shiʿi literature sells two *marjan* (protection papers containing Qurʾanic verses) from Lebanon. One dates from 1946, but the owner claimed he does not sell these to anyone as few remained (he sold one to me for 2500 CFA, US$5. He received in 2002 a shipment of six hundred pages of a newer version that sells for 500 CFA (US$1).

12. Translated by the author from French. I have chosen to use standard spelling for Arabic transliteration into English. In publications the shaykh spells his name using French orthography.

13. It is common in Lebanon and other Arab countries to display photos of political figures. While Musa al-Sadr is commonly portrayed in Lebanon, it is for his political, rather than religious, leadership (Deeb 2006).

14. He has a home in the south of Lebanon, which I visited; it is rumored to be valued at $1 million. This is a multifloor construction in a village outside Tyre with acres of land growing oranges, figs, and grapes. The shaykh has a personal library in his Lebanese residence.

15. Lebanese Sunnis now have their own mosque, built by a woman in memory of her son who died in a car accident, and led by a Sunni shaykh who arrived in Dakar from Lebanon in 2012.

16. The Islamic Institute has its own printing press.

17. Zahra is Prophet Muhammad's daughter.

18. At its height there were 150 Lebanese families living in Kaolack, around 2,000 people. In 2002 there were 30 families, approximately 250 individuals. Lebanese typically have large extended families. In 2014 I was told that there were perhaps only five Lebanese families remaining in Kaolack.

19. A hall used for the commemoration of the battle of Karbala. The Islamic Institute uses this lecture hall for all large community gatherings.

20. In Sunni Islam, representations of human figures are forbidden in places of prayer. Shiʿi Islamic tradition allows display of imagery, and a banner of the battle of Karbala is a common ʿAshura decoration.

21. Kufa was the final capital of Imam ʿAli and one of five Iraqi cities of great importance to Shiʿa.

22. Zaynab is the sister of Imam Husayn, whose family was killed during the battle of Karbala.

23. When I met with Shaykh al-Zayn in 2014 he informed me that he hired a second shaykh from Lebanon to assist him in leading the community in their religious needs. This has allowed him to work part time at the Islamic Institute, freeing up more time to write books and to travel.

24. Organization of the Islamic Conference, which changed its name to Organization of Islamic Cooperation in 2011, held a second meeting in Dakar in 2008. These were the only meetings held by the organization in sub-Saharan Africa, a point of great pride for Senegalese and an attestation of the importance of Islam in Senegal. For a published collection of Shaykh al-Zayn's speeches see El-Zein (1993).

4. Bringing Lebanese "Back" to Shiʿi Islam

1. I spent two weeks in Dakar in June 2006—one month before the start of the war—and returned for six weeks the following summer. Although I was not present at the protest, events were well documented on the Lebanese embassy's website.

2. The full text of this speech can be found at http://www.solidariteliban.com (accessed July 15, 2008). This website contains a timeline of the war's events, including disturbing images from Lebanon and documentation of the Dakar protest.

3. Syria, which has long dominated Lebanon's foreign policy and has supported Hizbullah, maintained troops in Lebanon from 1976 to 2005. Iran has a long history of relations with Lebanon and backs Hizbullah.

4. The shaykh was thought to have Amal leanings, although he famously helped negotiate the release of French hostages taken by Hizbullah in the 1980s.

5. Louër (2008) contends that despite their transnational pledge, Shiʿi Islamic movements have always targeted a particular nation-state.

6. Middle Eastern and African airlines banned smoking much later than Western carriers.

7. Occasionally the school enrolls students of other nationalities, including Europeans and Americans. Lebanese Christians study Arabic there, although the Maronite church also provides Arabic lessons, albeit in a less formal manner.

8. This is a point of debate, and some Shiʿi scholars have argued in favor of following a deceased marjaʿ (such as Ayatollah al-Khuʾi) under certain circumstances.

9. Fadlallah died in 2010. These interviews were conducted in 2003. Fadlallah's status as marjaʿ was disputed.

10. I am equating the Arabic term *hijab*, commonly translated as "veil," with the French word *foulard*, "headscarf." These terms are used interchangeably in Senegal. Lebanese most often cover their hair, ears, and throat, and a rare Lebanese woman will wear a face veil with a slit for the eyes. College al-Zahra enforces the young age of eight or nine for students to don the veil.

11. Lebanese metonymically refer to the first ten days of Muharram as "ʿAshura." Technically, the term refers only to the tenth of the month, when the battle at Karbala took place. Some Lebanese in Senegal (and in Lebanon) continue to hold mourning gatherings for three days after the tenth; others continue mourning forty days after the tenth.

12. In Iraq and Pakistan ʿAshura is marked by passion plays reenacting the story, with men beating themselves with heavy chains, self-flagellating in mourning for the martyrdom of Husayn. This *latam*, ritualized striking of one's body in grief, is also practiced in Lebanon, although Islamic authorities are trying to reform such "anti-Islamic" practices and are encouraging Lebanese to donate blood to a blood bank instead of shedding blood in the streets (Deeb 2005). Lebanese in Senegal do not perform these activities.

13. See Fischer (1980) and Aghaie (2004) on the use of "the Karbala paradigm" during the Iranian Revolution.

14. The following Sunday was Mother's Day.

15. Israel withdrew from southern Lebanon on May 25, 2000.

16. Everything else was conducted entirely in Arabic.

17. During all official occasions involving Lebanese, Senegalese politicians are enthusiastic about Lebanese integration and contributions to Senegal. The Senegalese public does not always share this viewpoint, as described in chapter 2.

18. It is also significant that Berri was born in Sierra Leone. Not only do Lebanese in Senegal have ties with other Lebanese communities throughout West Africa, in particular Ivory Coast, but Lebanese from Africa also hold important political positions in Lebanon.

19. Mermier and Picard (2007). See also Deeb (2008); Mervin (2008); Shaery-Eisenlohr (2008).

20. "Les Libanais ont manifesté jeudi à Dakar contres les raids israéliens," *Panapress*, http://www.grioo.com/pinf07373.html (accessed July 15, 2008). For other descriptions of protests in Senegalese newspapers see "La chaîne de solidarité libano-sénégalaise," *Le Quotidien*, July 21, 2006, 4; Yakhya Massaly, "Les libanais du Sénégal manifestent contre les attaques," *Walfadjri*, July 21, 2006, 2; Daouda Mané, "Marche de solidarité avec le peuple libanais," *Le Soleil*, July 21, 2006, 3.

21. "La chaîne de solidarité libano-sénégalaise," *Le Quotidien*, July 21, 2006, 4.

22. "Les Libanais du Sénégal veulent la fermeture de l'ambassade d'Israël," *Le Quotidien*, July 22–23, 2006, 4.

23. "La communauté libanaise ne doit pas dicter la politique étrangère du Sénégal," *Le Quotidien*, July 25, 2006, 8.

24. Qana was first shelled by Israeli artillery on April 18, 1996, resulting in a large number of civilian deaths and injuries. The second airstrike by Israel on July 30, 2006, hit an apartment building, killing many civilians, especially children (Volk 2010).

25. For a summary of Shaykh al-Zayn's politics during the war and his linking the 2006 Lebanon War to the battle of Karbala, see Amadou Gaye, "Cheikh Abdel Monem El Zayn 'Cette guerre fera tomber les régimes arabes non solidaires au Hezbollah,'" *Le Soleil*, August 18, 2006, 19.

26. I was told that approximately 3,000 Lebanese were in attendance in addition to one Senegalese government representative.

27. Victims included relatives of those in Senegal.

28. His Free Patriotic Movement is comprised of thousands of Lebanese members from different religious sects, including a significant number of Muslims.

29. Lebanese political parties flew some with Lebanese citizenship from Senegal to Lebanon in order to vote.

5. The Vernacularizaton of Shiʿi Islam

1. A feature news report called Senegalese "néo-chiites" (*Wal Fadjri*, September 2, 2003).

2. Diop died on June 24, 2014, in Morocco. His body was flown back to Senegal to be buried in Kaolack.

3. At the time of the revolution these could be found at Université Cheikh Anta Diop's Arabic Department.

4. According to an article by *Le Messager* (Aïdara 2003). I have not verified these figures.

5. *Ahl al-bayt*, family of the Prophet, is another term for Shiʿa. *Allah salimuhum*, may God give them peace, follows names of deceased.

6. I maintain French orthography. This is a poor translation. The shaykh is not named caliph of the Prophet Muhammad's family, but of their followers, the Shiʿa. SAWS is the Arabic acronym for "may God bless Him and give Him peace," recited after referring to the Prophet.

7. Media in Senegal is referred to as *presse alimentaire*, where for a small fee journalists will publish anything.

8. Zonis and Brumberg (1987) refer to the 1984 conference as the first annual meeting; Halliday writes of a 1980 meeting.

9. Zakzaki leads the Islamic Movement in Nigeria and has a large following who are thought to be Shiʿa.

10. Houchang Chehabi (personal communication) informed me of this and that Iranian officials denied attempts to export the revolution to Africa; therefore official statements are dif-

ficult to find. The Iranian government was more interested in East and Southern Africa at that time. Wilfried Buchta (personal communication) assumes any serious attempts to export the revolution to Africa came to a halt with the elimination of Mehdi Hashemi in 1987; nevertheless the Ahmadinejad government took renewed interest in Senegal in particular. Both scholars noted that the Iranian Foreign Ministry's think tank, Institute for Political and International Studies (IPIS), published a journal in Persian about Africa and books on Iran's relations with African states.

11. Niass currently heads a party called Frap, associated with Parti Démocratique Sénégalais (PDS).

12. Fatemeh Sadeghi informed me that there were many demonstrations in Tehran in the early 1980s, both in support of and in protest against the revolution. This depiction of a united defense of the Republic is Toure's interpretation, likely based on official discourse presented during his visit.

13. He claims to have innocently served time for the threat his brother posed to Senegal's political stability.

14. Later funding was obtained from Algeria and various Senegalese Tijani sources.

15. Niass's book cover portrays a photo of him in full "Iranian" dress with the president.

16. Journalists wrote anonymously at first.

17. Association Culturelle Imam al-Khuʾi teaches Qurʾan classes in Paris, attended by African Shiʿa from Burkina Faso, Cameroon, Ivory Coast, Mali, Martinique, Senegal, and Sierra Leone. Its director provided me with a list of twenty names of Muslims who had written to him from Senegal requesting books in French on Shiʿi Islam, money, or other assistance.

18. *Le Témoin* reported the closure was due to financing certain Senegalese religious movements (August 3, 1993, 8).

19. See *Le Soleil*, February 12, 1990, 5; February 11, 1991, 10–11; February 11, 1992, 5; February 11, 1993, 4; February 12, 1993, 3; February 13–14, 1999, 10; and February 8, 2003.

20. *Le Soleil*, April 2, 1990, and May 13, 1991.

21. *Le Soleil*, December 22, 2001.

22. For more information on the 2003 visit see "Wade Wanting Better Ties with Iran," *Iran International*, no. 27 (January 2004), http://www.iraninternationalmagazine.com/ issue_27 /text/wade.htm; on the 2006 visit see Mamadou Sèye, "Énergie, Prospection Pétrolière, Industrie: Le Sénégal bénéficie des solutions iraniennes," *Le Soleil*, June 28, 2006; "Communiqué conjoint de la visite officielle de Son Excellence Me Abdoulaye Wade, président de la République du Sénégal en République Islamique d'Iran: du 26 au 28 juin 2006 (du 5 au 7 Tir 1385 de l'Hégire solaire)," *Le Soleil*, June 29, 2006.

23. "Stronger OIC Agenda would Better Serve Muslims," http://www.islam-pure.de/imam /news/news2008/02_2008.htm, February 28, 2008.

24. "Senegal Stresses Expansion of Ties with Iran," Fars News Agency, July 29, 2007. There was also an intensification of economic ties between Senegal and Iran, including discussions of building in Senegal a petrochemical refinery and factory for assembling automobile parts from Iran's car manufacturer Iran Khodro, the construction of professional schools, financial assistance from Iran for preparations for the OIC summit in Dakar, and approval of Senegal's use of OIC funds to aid in the fight against poverty. Iran promised scholarships for Senegalese students to specialize in nuclear physics and a team of Iranian experts to study Senegal's production system in order to transfer knowledge in agricultural engineering. See D. Sarr Niang, "Conseil des Ministres: L'Iran prête à executer tous les accords signés avec le Sénégal," *Le Soleil*, August 3, 2007.

25. "Suite a notre article 'L'Iran se positionne.' Réaction de l'ambassade d'Iran à Dakar," *Le Témoin*, September 7, 1993, 9.

26. As chapter 4 has shown, this changed as a result of the 2006 Lebanon War.

27. "Senegal–Iran: From Friendship to Diplomatic War," *Afrik-News*, February 25, 2011, http://www.afrik-news.com/article19020.html.

28. Robinson (2004:42) and Levtzion and Pouwels (2000:ix) write of the "Africanization" of Islam. I prefer not to use this term, which is too general and tainted a concept, but refer to this process as vernacularization of Islamic traditions.

29. I am grateful to Irfan Ahmad for suggesting the applicability of this concept.

6. Migrating from One's Parents' Traditions

1. "Joseph's" son's name, Khomeini, is not a pseudonym.

2. Usually Senegalese women take their husbands' religion; in this case Muslim women are not permitted to marry non-Muslims, so Joseph's father converted to Islam.

3. Today the national station no longer holds a monopoly on news in Senegal, with the arrival of French television stations and a proliferation of recently established Senegalese competition. One can also purchase Arabic satellite TV.

4. Such policies were famously referred to by Iranian writer Jalal al-e Ahmad as "Westoxication." See Diouf (2000) for a discussion of Senegalese alternative modernities in the context of the Murid trade diaspora.

5. I acknowledge that many Muslims do not consider the change in affiliation from Sunni to Shi'i Islam a conversion. Niezen writes: "For most reformers 'conversion' is too strong a word to describe their change in religious orientation. . . . The reformers themselves perceive change as being from laxity and ignorance to rigour and enlightenment. They usually see themselves as having always been Muslims, albeit earlier in life misguided ones" (1990:420). Yet Nakash (1994) notes that Iraqi tribesmen who converted from Sunni to Shi'i Islam perceived change in religious status as such, and used the term *rawafid,* meaning "rejection" of and "defection" from Sunni dogma. Senegalese Shi'a are not opposed to the term *conversion,* although they do not use this word. In Wolof *tuub* refers to complete reversal from an attitude of denying to one of accepting, too radical a concept for Senegalese Shi'a, and one not used for "people of the book." *Tajdid* in Arabic (*renouveller* in French) is sometimes heard, translated as "religious renewal" or "revival." Most often used is the Arabic term *tasha'a,* literally translated as "to be affiliated with or partisan of" and meaning "to accept or enter the Shi'i school."

6. Not all African reformist movements insist on literacy in Arabic. See Samson (2009) and Janson (2009).

7. See also Keane (2007).

8. Cherif insisted I use his name and acknowledge his religious center in my work. I am using the honorific title by which he is known, indicating his alleged descent from the Prophet's family, and the actual name of his institute and others in Senegal as they are often written about in newspapers.

9. Like many sayyids, Imam Khomeini claims to be able to trace his genealogy back to the Prophet Muhammad. Senegalese Sufis as well as Shi'a feel closeness to the family of the Prophet. Although interlocutors mention this point, Khomeini's spiritual leadership was due to charisma and other personal qualities and not to his ascendancy.

10. This is the Senegalese Islamic Institute attached to the Grand Mosque of Dakar, not the Lebanese-run institute.

11. A sociologist at Université Cheikh Anta Diop called the movement "literary Shi'ism," not political Shi'ism.

12. I have not used pseudonyms for Cherif's children.

13. Khomeini resided in Paris from October 12, 1978, to January 31, 1979.

14. Ho (2006:31) developed a similar concept of *local cosmopolitans* in relation to the long history of the Hadrami diaspora, those who, while embedded in local relations, also maintain connections with distant places and articulate a relation between different geographical scales.

15. Youssou died in 2008. A Senegalese Shiʿi who lived in the United States replaced Youssou as imam, but prefers not to wear Shiʿi robes and turban.

16. A dozen women are also in attendance.

17. Ayatollah al-Khuʾi was alive at the time the book was written; he died in 1992.

18. *Prière sur le Prophète* is translated as "blessed be his name."

19. Inheritance rights are more generous under Shiʿi Islam than Sunni Islam. The wife receives from her husband as part of the marriage contract the *mahr,* a mandatory amount of money and/or possessions. The wife also has the right to maintenance; the husband is obligated to provide her with food, shelter, and clothing. Muslim women are expected to acquire the appropriate education to raise and educate their children with proper morals. If a woman has the skills to work outside the home for the good of the community, she may do so as long as her family obligations are met. Shiʿi women have the right to earn money, own property, enter into legal contracts, and manage their own assets. Shiʿi religious scholars have heavily debated women's religious and political leadership.

20. Fatou, for example, dresses in an imported veil and during our interview was wearing a short-sleeved shirt. She wears conservative Western-style clothing, as do many Senegalese young adults. Members of the Sunni Ibadu Rahman movement are characterized by wearing the Iranian chador. Wives of male Shiʿi converts often dress in African boubous with the *musoor,* matching cloth wrapped around the head. Khady and more observant Senegalese women wear an additional headscarf to cover their ears. Khady's dress thus changed to become more conservative, yet remained African.

21. Similar terms were used to refer to Peul (or Fulbe), who joined the nineteenth-century jihad movement (Hanson 1994).

Interlude

1. The shaykh taught Arabic from the Islamic Institute before a separate Arabic Language Institute was built in 1998.

2. This is a common Sunni stereotype.

3. Only grand mosques can conduct Friday prayer.

7. The Creation of a *Senegalese* Shiʿi Islam

1. See Ka (2002) and Ware (2009) for histories of Islamic schooling in Senegal.

2. Jack Goody (1987; 2000) wrote several books comparing oral and written cultures and exploring the transformative effects of literacy, including in West Africa.

3. Ali Yacine refers to Ale (the family of) Yasin, a term invoking the Prophet's family through the sacred hadith, Surat al-Yasin.

4. Distributing calendars to clients at the start of each new year publicizing one's business is common in Senegal. Calendars often portray glossy photos of Sufi marabouts.

5. Sayyid Mujtaba Musavi Lari established the Office for the Diffusion of Islamic Culture Abroad in Qom in 1980. This organization prints Qurʾans and copies of his translated works for

free distribution among individuals, institutions, and religious schools in Africa and elsewhere. See www.irib.ir/worldservice/Etrat/English/Nabi/Besat/sea11.htm (accessed July 31, 2008).

6. Senegalese Shiʿa do not call for the application of a narrow and politicized interpretation of Islamic law, as do Muslim reformists in Nigeria, Sudan, and northern Mali.

7. The turba, a clay tablet that rests between the forehead and ground during prostrations, sometimes comes from Karbala and represents the battle that led to Imam Husayn's death. However, Shiʿa may pray on any natural substance, such as a leaf or stone.

8. A Shiʿi hadith.

9. The head of the corpse must face Mecca.

10. At the time of the Prophet there were no divisions in Islam. The Tijani order developed much later.

11. He described how Lebanese came in cars to the institute, located outside town. Cars are a sign of wealth and starkly contrast the poverty and simplicity of this institute.

12. One such article "Oui, les Chiites sont des musulmans!" (*Le Soleil,* May 12 and 13, 2001) responded to a previous article, "Les chiites sont-ils des musulmans?" (*Le Soleil,* May 5, 2001).

13. This "work ethic" has most often been attributed to Murids but is also prominent in other Sufi orders.

14. Austen (2010) states that prior to the Almoravids' rise in the mid-eleventh century, small communities of Ibadi Kharijite merchants had represented Islam in the desert. Fatimids put an end to the Ibadi Tahert state in 909 and adopted a doctrine of *kitman* (concealment of beliefs) in response. He suggests "there is no direct evidence about whether this practice was followed in the southern Sahara and Sudan, but it would have made good sense in a region where Muslim merchants constituted a very small minority among populations with whom they wished to maintain peaceful trading relations" (85–86).

15. Cornell (1998:126) describes in more detail than other scholars how Sunni Islam met serious competition in North Africa from Shiʿa.

16. Michael Bonner helped clarify period history and pointed me to some of these sources.

17. ʿAlaouis were an offshoot of Shiʿi Fatimids who ruled North Africa from Egypt. The term ʿAlaoui (or ʿAlevi in Syria) suggests an adherent of ʿAli, the Prophet's son-in-law, and accentuates the religion's similarities to Shiʿi Islam. The ʿAlaoui dynasty took over rule in Morocco in the mid-seventeenth century. I am presenting these historical accounts in reverse chronological order as they were presented to me, in order of importance.

18. Austen writes that Idrisids "never established very firm or wide-ranging political or Shia religious authority, but did bring Islam to the 'Far West' of the Muslim world" (2010:84). He considers Almohads the last rulers to champion any form of Shiʿi Islam in North Africa. He credits them for bringing the Maghreb and southern Spain under a single rule, but states that Shiʿi theology proved to be an obstacle in maintaining loyalty of their subjects who preferred to follow established beliefs and practices of Sunni Islam (85). I have not heard Senegalese discuss Almohad rule in relation to their interpretation of the spread of Shiʿi Islam to West Africa.

19. Tijanis accord special blessing to recitations of *salat al-fatih:* Oh God bless our Master Muhammad (peace be upon him) who opened what had been closed, and who is the Seal of what had gone before, he who makes the Truth Victorious by the Truth, the guide to thy straight path, and bless his household as is due of his immense position and grandeur.

20. The term *Wahhabi* refers to an Islamic movement that purports to be orthodox, named after Saudi Arabian founder Muhammad ibn ʿAbd al-Wahhab (1703–1792). This name is rarely used by members of the group today and was first designated by their opponents. Also known as *Salafism,* the movement accepts the Qurʾan and hadith as fundamental texts and advocates a puritanical and legalistic theology in matters of faith and religious practice.

21. See Augis (2002) for discussion of the spread of Orthodox Sunni Islam to Dakar's female students who joined the Ibadu Rahman movement; Janson (2005) on the Gambian following of Tabligh Jamaᶜat; and Schulz (2008) on Islamic moral renewal among Sunni women in Mali.

22. The name comes from two words: *tam*, to demonize, and *kharit*, which means friend. Everything is permitted on this day, even to demonize one's friend without fear of retribution.

23. Rawan Mbaye, university professor and Tijani leader, informed me of a custom to pay offerings to Lebu divinities by filling a calabash with food (typically couscous with beef) on the ninth day of Muharram. If the calabash is empty the next morning the divinity is believed to have taken his share.

24. For additional Qurʾanic events and a description of other Tamkharit customs see http://www.au-senegal.com/La-Tamxarit.html?var_recherche=tamkharit (accessed September 17, 2007).

25. The Wolof greeting for Tamkharit is *deweneti,* meaning "may I be in a position to wish you a happy new year next year."

26. http://www.mozdahir.com/interventions-de-cherif/discours-de-cherif-achoura-2008.html (accessed March 1, 2009).

27. See Leichtman (2012) for a complete account of these ᶜAshura conferences.

28. A Senegalese Shiᶜi also proposed over Skype that I engage in temporary marriage with him during a subsequent visit to Dakar, an offer I also declined.

29. The man who suggested mutᶜa marriage to me was born in Senegal and raised in a popular Senegalese neighborhood away from the "Lebanese ghetto." He had, however, traveled to Lebanon more than twenty times.

30. Senegalese Sufis do not practice *nikah ᶜurfi,* Sunni marriage without an official contract. Secret marriage does exist, called *takku suuf* in Wolof. For example, a man may marry a widow who faces economic difficulty after her husband's death.

Coda

1. See also Fouad Ajami, Vali R. Nasr, and Richard N. Haass, "The Emerging Shia Crescent Symposium: Implications for U.S. Policy in the Middle East," panel meeting, Council on Foreign Relations, New York, June 5, 2006, http://www.cfr.org/publication/10866.

2. Shaykh al-Zayn was also trained in Najaf under Ayatollah al-Khuʾi and Sayyid Muhammad Baqir al-Sadr, and thus extends this "Shiᶜi international" to Africa. Shaery-Eisenlohr (2008) contests Chehabi's portrayal of Hizbullah as part of a recurrent pattern of historical relations between Iran and Lebanon, making a clear distinction between pre- and postrevolutionary Iranian–Lebanese ties.

References

Secondary Sources

Abdullah, Zain. 2010. *Black Mecca: The African Muslims of Harlem.* New York: Oxford University Press.

Abou, Sélim. 1998. *Liban déraciné: Immigrés dans l'autre Amérique.* Paris: L'Harmattan.

Abrahamian, Ervand. 1993. *Khomeinism: Essays on the Islamic Republic.* Berkeley: University of California Press.

Abu-Lughod, Lila. 1991. "Writing against Culture." In *Recapturing Anthropology: Working in the Present,* ed. R. G. Fox, 137–162. Santa Fe: School of American Research Press.

Afary, Janet, and Kevin B. Anderson. 2005. *Foucault and the Iranian Revolution: Gender and the Seductions of Islamism.* Chicago: University of Chicago Press.

Aghaie, Kamran. 2004. *The Martyrs of Karbala: Shiʿi Symbols and Rituals in Modern Iran.* Seattle: University of Washington Press.

Aguilar, Mario I. 1995. "African Conversion from a World Religion: Religious Diversification by the Waso Boorana in Kenya." *Africa* 65 (4): 525–544.

Ahmad, Irfan. 2011. "Immanent Critique and Islam: Anthropological Reflections." *Anthropological Theory* 11 (1): 107–132.

Ajami, Fouad. 1986. *The Vanished Imam: Musa al Sadr and the Shia of Lebanon.* Ithaca, N.Y.: Cornell University Press.

Akyeampong, Emmanuel K. 2006. "Race, Identity and Citizenship in Black Africa: The Case of the Lebanese in Ghana." *Africa* 76 (3): 297–323.

Alfaro-Velcamp, Theresa. 2007. *So Far from Allah, So Close to Mexico: Middle Eastern Immigrants in Modern Mexico.* Austin: University of Texas Press.

Anderson, Benedict. 2006 [1983]. *Imagined Communities: Reflections on the Origins and Spread of Nationalism.* London: Verso.

Anthias, Floya. 2001. "New Hybridities, Old Concepts: The Limits of 'Culture.'" *Ethnic and Racial Studies* 24 (4): 619–641.

Appiah, Kwame Anthony. 1998. "Cosmopolitan Patriots." In *Cosmopolitics: Thinking and Feeling Beyond the Nation,* ed. Pheng Cheah and Bruce Robbins, 91–114. Minneapolis: University of Minnesota Press.

———. 2006. *Cosmopolitanism: Ethics in a World of Strangers.* New York: W. W. Norton.

Arsan, Andrew. 2010. "The Ties That Bind: The Political Sentiments of Shiʿa Migrants in Senegal, 1919–1960." In *Politics, Culture and the Lebanon Diaspora,* ed. Paul Tabar and Jennifer Skulte-Ouaiss, 278–293. Newcastle upon Tyne: Cambridge Scholars Publishing.

Asad, Talal. 1986. *The Idea of an Anthropology of Islam.* Occasional Paper Series, Center for Contemporary Arab Studies. Washington, D.C.: Georgetown University Press.

———. 1993. *Genealogies of Religion: Discipline and Reasons of Power in Christianity and Islam.* Baltimore: Johns Hopkins University Press.

———. 1996. "Comments on Conversion." In *Conversion to Modernities: The Globalization of Christianity*, ed. Peter van der Veer, 263–273. New York: Routledge.

———. 2009. "Free Speech, Blasphemy, and Secular Criticism." In *Is Critique Secular? Blasphemy, Injury, and Free Speech*, ed. Talal Asad, Wendy Brown, Judith Butler, and Saba Mahmood, 20–63. Berkeley: Townsend Center for the Humanities, University of California.

Augis, Erin. 2002. "Dakar's Sunnite Women: The Politics of Person." Ph.D. thesis. Department of Sociology, University of Chicago.

Austen, Ralph A. 2010. *Trans-saharan Africa in World History*. New York: Oxford University Press.

Austin-Broos, Diane. 2003. "The Anthropology of Conversion: An Introduction." In *The Anthropology of Religious Conversion*, ed. Andrew Buckser and Stephen D. Glazier, 1–12. Lanham, Md.: Rowman and Littlefield.

Babou, Cheikh Anta. 2007. *Fighting the Greater Jihad: Amadu Bamba and the Founding of the Muridiyya of Senegal, 1853–1913*. Athens: Ohio University Press.

Balda, Justo Lacunza. 1993. "The Role of Kiswahili in East African Islam." In *Muslim Identity and Social Change in Sub-Saharan Africa*, ed. Louis Brenner, 226–238. London: Hurst.

Barth, Fredrik. 1969. *Ethnic Groups and Boundaries: The Social Organization of Culture Difference*. Boston: Little, Brown.

Barzegar, Kayhan. 2008. "Iran and the Shiite Crescent: Myths and Realities." *Brown Journal of World Affairs* 15 (1): 87–99.

Batran, A. A. 1979. "The Kunta, Sīdī al-Mukhtār al-Kuntī, and the Office of *Shaykh al-Tarīqa'l-Qādiriyya*." *Studies in West African Islamic History* 1: 113–146.

Baubock, Rainer. 2003. "Towards a Political Theory of Migrant Transnationalism." *International Migration Review* 37: 700–723.

Baum, Robert M. 1990. "The Emergence of a Diola Christianity." *Africa* 60 (3): 370–398.

Bayart, Jean-François. 2000. "Africa in the World: A History of Extraversion." *African Affairs* 99: 217–267.

Bayat, Asef, and Bahman Baktiari. 2002. "Revolutionary Iran and Egypt: Exporting Inspirations and Anxieties." In *Iran and the Surrounding World: Interactions in Culture and Cultural Politics*, ed. Nikki R. Keddie and Rudi Matthee, 305–326. Seattle: University of Washington Press.

Beck, Ulrich. 2006. *The Cosmopolitan Vision*. Cambridge: Polity.

Beeman, William O. 1995. "Iranian Revolution of 1979." In *The Oxford Encyclopedia of the Modern Islamic World*, ed. John L. Esposito, 232–236. New York: Oxford University Press.

Behrman, Lucy C. 1970. *Muslim Brotherhoods and Politics in Senegal*. Cambridge, Mass.: Harvard University Press.

Benthall, Jonathan, and Jérôme Bellion-Jourdan. 2003. *The Charitable Crescent: Politics of Aid in the Muslim World*. London: I. B. Tauris.

Bhabha, Homi K. 1994. *The Location of Culture*. London: Routledge.

———. 1996. "Unsatisfied: Notes on Vernacular Cosmopolitanism." In *Text and Nation: Cross-Disciplinary Essays on Cultural and National Identities*, ed. Laura Garcia-Moreno and Peter C. Pfeiffer. London: Camden House.

Bierwirth, Chris. 1999. "The Lebanese Communities of Cote D'Ivoire." *African Affairs* 98: 79–99.

Boone, Catherine. 1992. *Merchant Capital and the Roots of State Power in Senegal, 1930–1985.* Cambridge: Cambridge University Press.

———. 2003. *Political Topographies of the African State: Territorial Authority and Institutional Choice.* Cambridge: Cambridge University Press.

Boumedouha, Said. 1987. "The Lebanese in Senegal: A History of the Relationship between an Immigrant Community and its French and African Rulers." Ph.D. thesis. Centre of West African Studies, University of Birmingham.

———. 1992. "Change and Continuity in the Relationship between the Lebanese in Senegal and Their Hosts." In *The Lebanese in the World: A Century of Emigration,* ed. Albert Hourani and Nadim Shehadi, 549–563. London: I. B. Tauris.

Bowen, John R. 1993. *Muslims through Discourse: Religion and Ritual in Gayo Society.* Princeton, N.J.: Princeton University Press.

Brand, Laurie A. 2006. *Citizens Abroad: Emigration and the State in the Middle East and North Africa.* Cambridge: Cambridge University Press.

———. 2010. "National Narratives and Migration: Discursive Strategies of Inclusion and Exclusion in Jordan and Lebanon." *International Migration Review* 44 (1): 78–110.

Brenner, Louis. 1984. *West African Sufi: The Religious Heritage and Spiritual Search of Cerno Bokar Saalif Taal.* Berkeley: University of California Press.

———. 2001. *Controlling Knowledge: Religion, Power and Schooling in a West African Muslim Society.* Bloomington: Indiana University Press.

Brett, Michael. 1999. *Ibn Khaldun and the Medieval Maghrib.* Aldershort: Ashgate Variorum.

———. 2001. *The Rise of the Fatimids: The World of the Mediterranean and the Middle East in the Fourth Century of the Hijra, Tenth Century CE.* Leiden: Brill.

Brink-Danan, Marcy. 2011. "Dangerous Cosmopolitanism: Erasing Difference in Istanbul." *Anthropological Quarterly* 84 (2): 439–474.

Buchta, Wilfried. 2001. "Tehran's Ecumenical Society (*Majmaᶜ al-Taqrīb):* A Veritable Ecumenical Revival or a Trojan Horse of Iran?" In *The Twelver Shia in Modern Times: Religious Culture and Political History,* ed. Rainer Brunner and Werner Ende, 333–353. Leiden: Brill.

Buggenhagen, Beth. 2012. *Muslim Families in Global Senegal: Money Takes Care of Shame.* Bloomington: Indiana University Press.

Calhoun, Craig. 2003. "'Belonging' in the Cosmopolitan Imaginary." *Ethnicities* 3 (4): 531–553.

Casanova, José. 1994. *Public Religion in the Modern World.* Chicago: Chicago University Press.

Castells, Manuel. 1997. *The Rise of the Network Society.* Oxford: Basil Blackwell.

Caswell, Nim. 1984. "Autopsie de l'ONCAD: La Politique Arachidière au Sénégal, 1966–1980." *Politique Africaine* 14: 39–73.

Chalabi, Tamara. 2002. *The Shiᶜis of Jabal ᶜAmil and the New Lebanon: Community and Nation-State, 1918–1943.* Basingstoke: Palgrave.

Chavez, Leo R. 2001. *Covering Immigration: Popular Images and the Politics of the Nation.* Berkeley: University of California Press.

Chehabi, H. E., ed. 2006. *Distant Relations: Iran and Lebanon in the Last 500 Years.* London: I. B. Tauris in association with the Centre for Lebanese Studies.

Chiha, Michel. 1994 [1966]. *Lebanon at Home and Abroad.* Beirut: Fondation Chiha.

Clark, Andrew F., and Lucie Calvin Phillips. 1994. *Historical Dictionary of Senegal*. 2nd ed. Netuchen, N.J.: Scarecrow Press.

Clifford, James. 1992. "Travelling Cultures." In *Cultural Studies*, ed. Lawrence Grossberg, Cary Nelson, and Paula A. Treichler, 96–116. London: Routledge.

Cohen, Abner. 1969. *Custom and Politics in Urban Africa: A Study of Hausa Migrants in Yoruba Towns*. Berkeley: University of California Press.

Cohen, William B. 2003 [1980]. *The French Encounter with Africans: White Response to Blacks, 1530–1880*. Bloomington: Indiana University Press.

Cole, Juan R. I. 2002. *Sacred Space and Holy War: The Politics, Culture and History of Shiʿite Islam*. London: I. B. Tauris.

Comaroff, Jean, and John L. Comaroff. 1991. *Of Revelation and Revolution: Christianity, Colonialism, and Consciousness in South Africa*. Vol. 1. Chicago: University of Chicago Press.

———. 2000. "Millennial Capitalism: First Thoughts on a Second Coming." *Public Culture* 12 (2): 291–343.

———. 2001. "Naturing the Nation: Aliens, Apocalypse and the Postcolonial State." *Journal of Southern African Studies* 27 (3): 627–651.

Comaroff, John L., and Jean Comaroff. 2009. *Ethnicity, Inc*. Chicago: University of Chicago Press.

Conklin, Alice L. 1997. *A Mission to Civilize: The Republican Idea of Empire in France and West Africa, 1895–1930*. Palo Alto, Calif.: Stanford University Press.

Cooper, Frederick. 1996. *Decolonization and African Society: The Labor Question in French and British Africa*. Cambridge: Cambridge University Press.

———. 2005. *Colonialism in Question: Theory, Knowledge, History*. Berkeley: University of California Press.

Copans, Jean. 1980. *Les marabouts de l'arachide: La confrérie mouride et les paysans du Sénégal*. Paris: Le Sycomore.

Cornell, Vincent. 1998. *Realm of the Saint: Power and Authority in Moroccan Sufism*. Austin: University of Texas Press.

Coulon, Christian. 1981. *Le marabout et le prince: Islam et pouvoir au Sénégal*. Série Afrique Noire 11. Paris: Éditions A. Pedone.

Crapanzano, Victor. 1973. *The Hamadsha: A Study in Moroccan Ethno-Psychiatry*. Berkeley: University of California Press.

Creevey, Lucy E. 1979. "Ahmad Bamba 1850–1927." *Studies in West African Islamic History* 1: 278–307.

Crowder, Michael. 1968. *West Africa under Colonial Rule*. London: Hutchinson.

Cruise O'Brien, Donal B. 1971. *The Mourides of Senegal: The Political and Economic Organization of an Islamic Brotherhood*. Oxford: Clarendon Press.

———. 1984. "La filière musulman: Confréries soufies et politique en Afrique noire." *Politique Africaine* 1 (4): 7–30.

———. 1988. "Introduction." In *Charisma and Brotherhood in African Islam*, ed. Donal B. Cruise O'Brien and Christian Coulon, 1–31. Oxford: Clarendon Press.

———. 1996. "The Senegalese Exception." *Africa* 66 (3): 458–464.

———. 1998. "The Shadow-Politics of Wolofisation." *Journal of Modern African Studies* 36 (1): 25–46.

Cruise O'Brien, Rita. 1972. *White Society in Black Africa: The French of Senegal*. Evanston, Ill.: Northwestern University Press.

Cummings, William. 2001. "Scripting Islamization: Arabic Texts in Early Modern Makassar." *Ethnohistory* 48 (4): 559–586.

Dabashi, Hamid. 2011. *Shiʿism: A Religion of Protest.* Cambridge, Mass.: Belknap Press of Harvard University Press.

Deeb, Lara. 2005. "Living Ashura in Lebanon: Mourning Transformed to Sacrifice." *Comparative Studies of South Asia, Africa and the Middle East* 25 (1): 122–137.

———. 2006. *An Enchanted Modern: Gender and Public Piety in Shiʿi Lebanon.* Princeton, N.J.: Princeton University Press.

———. 2008. "Exhibiting the 'Just-Lived Past': Hizbullah's Nationalist Narratives in Transnational Political Context." *Comparative Studies in Society and History* 50: 369–399.

———. 2010. "Sayyid Muhammad Husayn Fadlallah and Shiʿa Youth in Lebanon." *Journal of Shiʿa Islamic Studies* 3 (4): 405–426.

Della Porta, Donnatella, and Sidney Tarrow. 2005. "Transnational Processes and Social Activism: An Introduction." In *Transnational Protest and Global Activism,* ed. Donnatella Della Porta and Sidney Tarrow, 1–17. Lanham, Md.: Rowman & Littlefield.

Devji, Faisal. 2008. *The Terrorist in Search of Humanity: Militant Islam and Global Politics.* New York: Columbia University Press.

Dia, Mamadou. 1985. *Memoires d'un militant du tiers-monde.* Paris: Publisud.

Diagne, Souleymane Bachir. 2011. *African Art as Philosophy: Senghor, Bergson and the Idea of Negritude.* Calcutta: Seagull Books.

Diarra, Fatoumata Agnès, and Pierre Fougeyrollas. 1969. "Relations inter-raciales et inter-ethniques au Sénégal." Unpublished manuscript. Dakar: Institut Fondamental d'Afrique Noire (IFAN).

Dilley, R. M. 2004. *Islamic and Caste Knowledge Practices among Haalpulaar'en in Senegal: Between Mosque and Termite Mound.* Edinburgh: Edinburgh University Press.

Diop, Abdoulaye-Bara. 1981. *La société Wolof. Tradition et changement. Les systèmes d'inégalité et de domination.* Paris: Karthala.

Diop, Momar Coumba, and Mamadou Diouf. 1990. *Le Sénégal sous Abdou Diouf: État et société.* Paris: Karthala.

Diouf, Mamadou. 2000. "The Senegalese Murid Trade Diaspora and the Making of a Vernacular Cosmopolitanism." *Public Culture* 12 (3): 679–702.

———. 2001. *Histoire du Sénégal: Le modèle islamo-wolof et ses peripheries.* Paris: Maisonneuve et Larose.

Diouf, Mamadou, and Mara A. Leichtman. 2009. *New Perspectives on Islam in Senegal: Conversion, Migration, Wealth, Power, and Femininity.* New York: Palgrave Macmillan.

Donham, Donald L. 1999. *Marxist Modern: An Ethnographic History of the Ethiopian Revolution.* Berkeley: University of California Press.

———. 2002. "On Being Modern in a Capitalist World: Some Conceptual and Comparative Issues." In *Critically Modern: Alternatives, Alterities, Anthropologies,* ed. Bruce M. Knauft, 241–257. Bloomington: Indiana University Press.

Edwards, Brent Hayes. 2003. *The Practice of Diaspora: Literature, Translation, and the Rise of Black Internationalism.* Cambridge, Mass.: Harvard University Press.

Eickelman, Dale F., and Jon W. Anderson. 2003 [1999]. *New Media in the Muslim World: The Emerging Public Sphere.* Bloomington: Indiana University Press.

Eickelman, Dale F., and James Piscatori, eds. 1990. *Muslim Travellers: Pilgrimage, Migration, and the Religious Imagination.* Berkeley: University of California Press.

———. 1996. *Muslim Politics.* Princeton, N.J.: Princeton University Press.

El-Solh, Raghid. 2004. *Lebanon and Arabism: National Identity and State Formation.* London: I. B. Tauris in association with the Centre for Lebanese Studies.

El-Zein, Abdul Hamid. 1977. "Beyond Ideology and Theology: The Search for the Anthropology of Islam." *Annual Review of Anthropology* 6: 227–254.

El-Zein, Al-Sheikh Abdul Monem. 1993. *Kalimat wa-Mawaqif.* Beirut: Markaz Jawad.

———. 2001. *L'Islam: Ma Doctrine et Ma Loi.* 5eme édition. Dakar: l'Institution Islamique Sociale.

Engelke, Matthew. 2004. "Discontinuity and the Discourse of Conversion." *Journal of Religion in Africa* 34 (1–2): 82–109.

Esposito, John L., and François Burgat, eds. 2003. *Modernizing Islam: Religion in the Public Sphere in Europe and the Middle East.* New Brunswick, N.J.: Rutgers University Press.

Faist, Thomas. 2000. "Transnationalization in International Migration: Implications for the Study of Citizenship and Culture." *Ethnic and Racial Studies* 23 (2): 189–222.

Farah, Douglas. 2004. *Blood from Stones: The Secret Financial Network of Terror.* New York: Broadway Books.

Farsoun, Samih K. 1970. "Family Structure and Society in Modern Lebanon." In *Peoples and Cultures of the Middle East: An Anthropological Reader,* ed. Louise E. Sweet, 2: 257–307. New York: Natural History Press.

Fatton, Robert, Jr. 1987. *The Making of a Liberal Democracy: Senegal's Passive Revolution, 1975–1985.* Boulder, Colo.: Lynne Rienner Publishers.

Ferguson, James. 1999. *Expectations of Modernity: Myths and Meanings of Urban Life on the Zambian Copperbelt.* Berkeley: University of California Press.

———. 2002. "Of Mimicry and Membership: Africans and the 'New World Society.'" *Cultural Anthropology* 17 (4): 551–569.

———. 2006. *Global Shadows: Africa in the Neoliberal World Order.* Durham, N.C.: Duke University Press.

Filfili, Nadra. 1973. *Ma vie: 50 ans au Sénégal.* Beirut: L'imprimerie Ghorayeb.

Fischer, Michael M. J. 1980. *Iran: From Religious Dispute to Revolution.* Cambridge, Mass.: Harvard University Press.

Fischer, Michael M. J., and Mehdi Abedi. 1990. *Debating Muslims: Cultural Dialogues in Postmodernity and Tradition.* Madison: University of Wisconsin Press.

Fisher, Humphrey J. 1973. "Conversion Reconsidered: Some Historical Aspects of Religious Conversion in Black Africa." *Africa* 43 (1): 27–40.

———. 1985. "The Juggernaut's Apologia: Conversion to Islam in Black Africa." *Africa* 55 (2): 86–108.

Fuller, Graham E., and Rend Rahim Francke. 1999. *The Arab Shiʿa: The Forgotten Muslims.* New York: St. Martin's Press.

Gabbert, Wolfgang. 2001. "Social and Cultural Conditions of Religious Conversion in Colonial Southwest Tanzania, 1891–1939." *Ethnology* 40 (4): 291–308.

Gberie, Lansana. 2002. "War and Peace in Sierra Leone: Diamonds, Corruption and the Lebanese Connection." Occasional Paper #6. Diamonds and Human Security Project, Partnership Africa Canada.

Geertz, Clifford. 1968. *Islam Observed: Religious Development in Morocco and Indonesia*. Chicago: University of Chicago Press.

———. 1973. "'Internal Conversion' in Contemporary Bali." In *The Interpretation of Cultures,* 170–189. New York: Basic Books.

———. 1983. "Centers, Kings, and Charisma: Reflections on the Symbolics of Power." In *Local Knowledge: Further Essays in Interpretive Anthropology,* 121–146. New York: Basic Books.

Gellar, Sheldon. 1982. *Senegal: An African Nation between Islam and the West*. Boulder, Colo.: Westview Press.

———. 1987. "Circulaire 32 Revisited: Prospects for Revitalizing the Senegalese Cooperative Movement in the 1980s." In *The Political Economy of Risk and Choice in Senegal,* ed. Mark Gersovitz and John Waterbury, 123–159. London: Frank Cass.

Gellar, Sheldon, Robert B. Charlick, and Yvonne Jones. 1980. *Animation Rurale and Rural Development: The Experience of Senegal*. Ithaca, N.Y.: Rural Development Committee, Center for International Studies, Cornell University.

Gellner, David N. 2005. "The Emergence of Conversion in a Hindu-Buddhist Polytropy: The Kathmandu Valley, Nepal, c. 1600–1995." *Comparative Studies in Society and History* 47 (4): 755–780.

Gellner, Ernest. 1981. *Muslim Society*. Cambridge: Cambridge University Press.

Gersovitz, Mark, and John Waterbury. 1987. *The Political Economy of Risk and Choice in Senegal*. London: Frank Cass.

Geschiere, Peter. 2009. *The Perils of Belonging: Autochthony, Citizenship, and Exclusion in Africa and Europe*. Chicago: University of Chicago Press.

Geschiere, Peter, and Francis Nyamnjoh. 2000. "Capitalism and Autochthony: The Seesaw of Mobility and Belonging." *Public Culture* 12 (2): 423–452.

Ghandour, Abdel-Rahman. 2002. *Jihad humanitaire: Enquête sur les ONG Islamiques*. Paris: Flammarion.

Gilsenan, Michael. 2000 [1982]. *Recognizing Islam: Religion and Society in the Modern Middle East*. London: I. B. Tauris.

Glick Schiller, Nina. 2005. "Long-Distance Nationalism." In *Encyclopedia of Diasporas: Immigrant and Refugee Cultures Around the World,* ed. Melvin Ember, Carol R. Ember and Ian Skoggard, 570–580. New York: Springer.

Glover, John. 2007. *Sufism and Jihad in Modern Senegal: The Murid Order*. Rochester, N.Y.: University of Rochester Press.

Goody, Jack. 1987. *The Interface between the Written and the Oral*. Cambridge: Cambridge University Press.

———. 2000. *The Power of the Written Tradition*. Washington, D.C.: Smithsonian Institution Press.

Gualtieri, Sarah M. A. 2009. *Between Arab and White: Race and Ethnicity in the Early Syrian American Diaspora*. Berkeley: University of California Press.

Guarnizo, Luis Eduardo. 1998. "The Rise of Transnational Social Formations: Mexican and Dominican State Responses to Transnational Migration." *Political Power and Social Theory* 12: 45–94.

Guarnizo, Luis Eduardo, Alejandro Portes, and William Haller. 2003. "Assimilation and

Transnationalism: Determinants of Transnational Political Action among Contemporary Migrants." *American Journal of Sociology* 108: 1211–1248.

Guèye, Cheikh. 2002. *Touba: La capitale des mourides.* Paris: Karthala.

Haeri, Shahla. 1989. *Law of Desire: Temporary Marriage in Shiʿi Islam.* Syracuse, N.Y.: Syracuse University Press.

Halawi, Majid. 1992. *A Lebanon Defied: Musa al-Sadr and the Shiʿa Community.* Boulder, Colo.: Westview Press.

Hall, Stuart, in conversation with Pnina Werbner. 2008. "Cosmopolitanism, Globalisation and Diaspora." In *Anthropology and the New Cosmopolitanism,* ed. Pnina Werbner, 345–360. Oxford: Berg.

Halliday, Fred. 1986. "Iranian Foreign Policy since 1979: Internationalism and Nationalism in the Islamic Revolution." In *Shiʿism and Social Protest,* ed. Juan R. I. Cole and Nikki R. Keddie, 88–107. New Haven, Conn.: Yale University Press.

Halm, Heinz. 1997. *Shiʿa Islam: From Religion to Revolution.* Princeton, N.J.: Markus Wiener Publishers.

Hamer, John H. 2002. "The Religious Conversion Process among the Sidama of North-East Africa." *Africa* 72 (4): 598–627.

Hanf, Theodor. 1993. *Coexistence in Wartime Lebanon: Decline of a State and Rise of a Nation.* London: I. B. Tauris.

Hannerz, Ulf. 1990. "Cosmopolitans and Locals in World Culture." *Theory, Culture and Society* 7: 237–251.

——. 2004. "Cosmopolitanism." In *A Companion to the Anthropology of Politics,* ed. David Nugent and Joan Vincent, 69–85. New York: Blackwell.

Hansen, Thomas Blom, and Finn Stepputat. 2005. "Introduction." In *Sovereign Bodies: Citizens, Migrants, and States in the Postcolonial World,* ed. Thomas Blom Hansen and Finn Stepputat, 1–36. Princeton, N.J.: Princeton University Press.

Hanson, John. 1994. "Islam, Migration and the Political Economy of Meaning: Fergo Nioro from the Senegal River Valley, 1862–1890." *Journal of African History* 35 (1): 37–60.

Harrison, Christopher. 1988. *France and Islam in West Africa, 1860–1960.* Cambridge: Cambridge University Press.

Hart, Keith. 1985. "The Social Anthropology of West Africa." *Annual Review of Anthropology* 14: 243–272.

Hartman, Michelle, and Alessandro Olsaretti. 2003. "'The First Boat and the First Oar': Inventions of Lebanon in the Writings of Michel Chiha." *Radical History Review* 86: 37–65.

Harvey, David. 1990. *The Condition of Postmodernity: An Enquiry into the Origins of Cultural Change.* Cambridge: Blackwell.

Hastings, Adrian. 1997. *The Construction of Nationhood: Ethnicity, Religion and Nationalism.* Cambridge: Cambridge University Press.

Hefner, Robert W. 1993. "Introduction: World Building and the Rationality of Conversion." In *Conversion to Christianity: Historical and Anthropological Perspectives on a Great Transformation,* ed. Robert W. Hefner, 3–44. Berkeley: University of California Press.

——. 2003 [1999]. "Civic Pluralism Denied? The New Media and *Jihadi* Violence in Indonesia." In *New Media in the Muslim World: The Emerging Public Sphere,* 2nd ed., ed. Dale F. Eickelman and Jon W. Anderson, 158–179. Bloomington: Indiana University Press.

———, ed. 2005. *Remaking Muslim Politics: Pluralism, Contestation, Democratization.* Princeton, N.J.: Princeton University Press.

Held, David. 2010. *Cosmopolitanism: Ideals and Realities.* Cambridge: Polity.

Hill, Joseph. 2007. "Divine Knowledge and Islamic Authority: Religious Specialization among Disciples of Baay Ñas." Ph.D. thesis. Department of Anthropology, Yale University, May.

———. 2012. "The Cosmopolitan Sahara: Building a Global Islamic Village in Mauritania." *City and Society* 24 (1): 62–83.

Hirschkind, Charles. 2006. *The Ethical Soundscape: Cassette Sermons and Islamic Counterpublics.* New York: Columbia University Press.

Hitti, Philip K. 1957. *Lebanon in History from the Earliest Times to the Present.* London: Macmillan.

Ho, Engseng. 2002. "Names beyond Nations: The Making of Local Cosmopolitans." *Études Rurales* 163/164: 215–231.

———. 2006. *The Graves of Tarim: Genealogy and Mobility across the Indian Ocean.* Berkeley: University of California Press.

Hobsbawm, Eric, and Terence Ranger, eds. 1992 [1983]. *The Invention of Tradition.* Cambridge: Cambridge University Press.

Hodgkin, Elizabeth. 1998. "Islamism and Islamic Research in Africa." In *Islam et islamismes au sud du Sahara,* ed. Ousmane Kane and Jean-Louis Triaud, 197–262. Paris: Karthala.

Hodgson, Dorothy L. 2011. *Being Maasai, Becoming Indigenous: Postcolonial Politics in a Neoliberal World.* Bloomington: Indiana University Press.

Hoesterey, James B. 2012. "Prophetic Cosmopolitanism." *City and Society* 24 (1): 38–61.

Horton, Robin. 1971. "African Conversion." *Africa* 41 (2): 85–108.

———. 1975a. "On the Rationality of Conversion, Part I." *Africa* 45 (3): 219–235.

———. 1975b. "On the Rationality of Conversion, Part II." *Africa* 45 (4): 373–399.

Hourani, Albert. 1991. *A History of the Arab Peoples.* New York: Warner Books.

Hourani, Albert, and Nadim Shehadi, eds. 1992. *The Lebanese in the World: A Century of Emigration.* London: I. B. Tauris.

Humphrey, Michael. 1998. *Islam, Multiculturalism and Transnationalism: From the Lebanese Diaspora.* London: I. B. Tauris.

———. 2004. "Lebanese Identities: Between Cities, Nations and Trans-Nations." *Arab Studies Quarterly* 26: 31–50.

Hunter, Shireen T. 1990. *Iran and the World: Continuity in a Revolutionary Decade.* Bloomington: Indiana University Press.

Hydarah, Sharif Muhammad Ali. 2008. *The Facts of the Prophet's Succession.* Beirut: Dar al-Mahajja al-Baydaa.

Ifeka-Moller, Caroline. 1974. "White Power: Social-Structural Factors in Conversion to Christianity, Eastern Nigeria, 1921–1966." *Canadian Journal of African Studies* 8 (1): 55–72.

Ikenga-Metuh, Emefie. 1987. "The Shattered Microcosm: A Critical Survey of Explanations of Conversion in Africa." In *Religion, Development and African Identity,* ed. Kirsten Holst Petersen, 11–27. Uppsala: Scandinavian Institute of African Studies.

Irvine, Judith T. 1974. "Caste and Communication in a Wolof Village." Ph.D. thesis. University of Pennsylvania.

Jahanbegloo, Ramin, ed. 2004. *Iran: Between Tradition and Modernity.* Lanham, Md.: Lexington Books.

Janson, Marloes. 2005. "Roaming about for God's Sake: The Upsurge of the Tabligh Jamaᶜat in The Gambia." *Journal of Religion in Africa* 35 (4): 450–481.

———. 2009. "Searching for God: Young Gambians' Conversion to the Tabligh Jamaᶜat." In *New Perspectives on Islam in Senegal: Conversion, Migration, Wealth, Power, and Femininity,* ed. Mamadou Diouf and Mara A. Leichtman, 139–166. New York: Palgrave Macmillan.

Jenkins, Richard. 1986. "Social Anthropological Models of Inter-Ethnic Relations." In *Theories of Race and Ethnic Relations,* ed. John Rex and David Mason. Cambridge: Cambridge University Press.

Ka, Thierno. 2002. *Ecole de Pir Saniokhor: Histoire, enseignement et culture arabo-islamiques au Sénégal du XVIIIe au XXe siècle.* Dakar: n.p.

Kaag, Mayke. 2007. "Aid, *Umma,* and Politics: Transnational Islamic NGOs in Chad." In *Islam and Muslim Politics in Africa,* ed. Benjamin F. Soares and René Otayek, 85–102. New York: Palgrave Macmillan.

Kahn, Joel S. 2008. "Other Cosmopolitans in the Making of the Modern Malay World." In *Anthropology and the New Cosmopolitanism,* ed. Pnina Werbner, 261–280. Oxford: Berg.

Kane, Ousmane. 1998. "Introduction." In *Islam et islamismes au sud du Sahara,* ed. Ousmane Kane and Jean-Louis Triaud, 5–30. Paris: Karthala.

———. 2011. *The Homeland is the Arena: Religion, Transnationalism, and the Integration of Senegalese Immigrants in America.* New York: Oxford University Press.

Kane, Ousmane, and Leonardo Villalón. 1995. "Entre confrérisme, réformisme et islamisme, les Mustarshidīn du Sénégal." *Islam et Sociétés au Sud du Sahara* 9: 119–201.

Karam, John Tofik. 2007. *Another Arabesque: Syrian-Lebanese Ethnicity in Neoliberal Brazil.* Philadelphia: Temple University Press.

Karp, Ivan. 2002. "Development and Personhood: Tracing the Contours of a Moral Discourse." In *Critically Modern: Alternatives, Alterities, Anthropologies,* ed. Bruce M. Knauft, 82–104. Bloomington: Indiana University Press.

Kaufman, Asher. 2004. *Reviving Phoenicia: In Search of Identity in Lebanon.* London: I. B. Tauris.

Keane, Webb. 2002. "Sincerity, 'Modernity,' and the Protestants." *Cultural Anthropology* 17 (1): 65–92.

———. 2007. *Christian Moderns: Freedom and Fetish in the Mission Encounter.* Berkeley: University of California Press.

Keddie, Nikki R. 1995. *Iran and the Muslim World: Resistance and Revolution.* London: Macmillan.

———. 2002. "Introduction." In *Iran and the Surrounding World: Interactions in Culture and Cultural Politics,* ed. Nikki Keddie and Rudi Matthee, 3–11. Seattle: University of Washington Press.

Kepel, Gilles. 2002. *Jihad: The Trail of Political Islam.* London: I. B. Tauris.

Khalaf, Samir. 1971. "Family Associations in Lebanon." *Journal of Comparative Family Studies* 11 (2): 235–250.

———. 1977. "Changing Forms of Political Patronage in Lebanon." In *Patrons and Clients in Mediterranean Societies,* ed. Ernest Gellner and John Waterbury, 185–202. London: Duckworth.

Khashan, Hilal. 2008. "The Myth of the Shiʿi Crescent." *Shiʿa Affairs Journal* 1: 41–51.

Khater, Akram Fouad. 2001. *Inventing Home: Emigration, Gender, and the Middle Class in Lebanon, 1870–1920.* Berkeley: University of California Press.

Khuri, Fuad I. 1968. "The African-Lebanese Mulattoes of West Africa: A Racial Frontier." *Anthropological Quarterly* 41 (2): 90–101.

Klein, Martin A. 1968. *Islam and Imperialism in Senegal: Sine-Saloum 1847–1914.* Stanford, Calif.: Stanford University Press.

Knauft, Bruce M. ed. 2002. *Critically Modern: Alternatives, Alterities, Anthropologies.* Bloomington: Indiana University Press.

Kraidy, Marwan M. 1999. "The Global, the Local, and the Hybrid: A Native Ethnography of Glocalization." *Critical Studies in Mass Communication* 16: 456–476.

Kuehn, Thomas. 2012. "Translators of Empire: Colonial Cosmopolitanism, Ottoman Bureaucrats and the Struggle over the Governance of Yemen, 1898–1914." In *Cosmopolitanisms in Muslim Contexts: Perspectives from the Past,* ed. Derryl N. MacLean and Sikeena Karmali Ahmed, 51–67. Edinburgh: Edinburgh University Press in association with the Aga Khan University.

Labaki, Boutros. 1993. "L'émigration libanaise en Afrique Occidentale sud-saharienne." *Revue Européene des Migrations Internationales* 9 (2): 91–112.

Laremont, Ricardo, and Hrach Gregorian. 2006. "Political Islam in West Africa and the Sahel." *Military Review* (January–February): 27–36.

Larkin, Brian. 1997. "Indian Films and Nigerian Lovers: Media and the Creation of Parallel Modernities." *Africa* 67 (3): 406–440.

———. 2008. *Signal and Noise: Media, Infrastructure, and Urban Culture in Nigeria.* Durham, N.C.: Duke University Press.

Larson, Pier M. 1997. "'Capacities and Modes of Thinking': Intellectual Engagements and Subaltern Hegemony in the Early History of Malagasy Christianity." *American Historical Review* 102 (4): 969–1002.

———. 2000. *History and Memory in the Age of Enslavement: Becoming Merina in Highland Madagascar, 1770–1822.* Portsmouth, N.H.: Heinemann.

Launay, Robert. 2004 [1992]. *Beyond the Stream: Islam and Society in a West African Town.* Long Grove, Ill.: Waveland Press.

Lawrence, Bruce B. 2010. "Afterword: Competing Genealogies of Muslim Cosmopolitanism." In *Rethinking Islamic Studies—From Orientalism to Cosmopolitanism,* ed. Carl W. Ernst and Richard C. Martin, 302–327. Columbia: University of South Carolina Press.

———. 2012. "Muslim Cosmopolitanism." *Critical Muslim* 2.

———. n.d. "Muslim Cosmopolitanism in the Age of Globalization." Paper presented at the conference Beyond Islamic Studies: De-Essentializing the Study of Muslim Societies, Michigan State University, April 7, 2011.

Lefebvre, Guillaume. 2003. "La communauté guinéenne de Dakar, une intégration réussie?" In *Etre étranger et migrant en Afrique au XXe siècle. Enjeux identitaires et modes d'insertion. Volume II: Dynamiques migratoires, modalités d'insertion urbaine et jeux d'acteurs,* ed. Catherine Coquery-Vidrovitch, Odile Goerg, Issiaka Mandé, and Faranirina Rajaonah, 133–150. Paris: L'Harmattan.

Leichtman, Mara A. 2005. "The Legacy of Transnational Lives: Beyond the First Generation of Lebanese in Senegal." *Ethnic and Racial Studies* 28 (4): 663–686.

———. 2006. "A Tale of Two Shiʿisms: Lebanese Migrants and Senegalese Converts in Dakar." Ph.D. thesis. Department of Anthropology, Brown University.

———. 2009. "Revolution, Modernity and (Trans)National Shiʿi Islam: Rethinking Religious Conversion in Senegal." *Journal of Religion in Africa* 39 (3): 319–351.

———. 2010. "Migration, War, and the Making of a Transnational Lebanese Shiʿi Community in Senegal." *International Journal of Middle East Studies* 42 (2): 269–290.

———. 2011. "Iran, Shiʿi Muslims, and the Arab Spring in Retrospect." Special issue on The (R)evolution of the East. *Islamic Monthly* (Summer/Fall): 47–49.

———. 2012. "The Africanization of ʿAshura in Senegal." In *Shiʿism and Identity: Religion, Politics and Change in the Global Muslim Community,* ed. Lloyd Ridgeon, 144–169. London: I. B. Tauris.

———. 2013. "From the Cross (and Crescent) to the Cedar and Back Again: Transnational Religion and Politics among Lebanese Christians in Senegal." *Anthropological Quarterly* 86 (1): 35–74.

Leichtman, Mara A., and Dorothea Schulz, eds. 2012. "Muslim Cosmopolitanism: Movement, Identity, and Contemporary Reconfigurations." Special Issue. *City and Society* 24 (1).

Lesser, Jeffrey. 1999. *Negotiating National Identity: Immigrants, Minorities, and the Struggle for Ethnicity in Brazil.* Durham, N.C.: Duke University Press.

Levitt, Matthew. 2004. "Hizbullah's African Activities Remain Undisrupted." *RUSI/Jane's Homeland Security and Resilience Monitor.* March 1. http://www .washingtoninstitute.org/print.php?template=C06&CID=463.

Levitt, Peggy. 2008. "Religion as a Path to Civic Engagement." *Ethnic and Racial Studies* 31: 766–791.

Levitt, Peggy, and Nina Glick Schiller. 2004. "Conceptualizing Simultaneity: A Transnational Social Field Perspective on Society." *International Migration Review* 38 (3): 1002–1039.

Levtzion, Nehemia. 1987. "Merchants vs. Scholars and Clerics in West Africa: Differential and Complementary Roles." In *Rural and Urban Islam in West Africa,* ed. Nehemia Levtzion and Humphrey J. Fisher, 21–37. Boulder, Colo.: Lynne Rienner Publishers.

———. 1994. *Islam in West Africa: Religion, Society and Politics to 1800.* Hampshire: Variorum.

———. 2000. "Islam in the Bilad al-Sudan to 1800." In *The History of Islam in Africa,* ed. Nehemia Levtzion and Randall L. Pouwels, 63–91. Athens: Ohio University Press.

Levtzion, Nehemia, and Randall L. Pouwels, ed. 2000. *The History of Islam in Africa.* Athens: Ohio University Press.

Lincoln, Bruce. 2003. *Holy Terrors: Thinking about Religion after September 11.* Chicago: University of Chicago Press.

Lindholm, Charles. 1990. *Charisma.* Cambridge: Basil Blackwell.

Lofland, J., and N. Skonovd. 1981. "Conversion Motifs." *Journal for the Scientific Study of Religion* 4: 373–385.

Loimeier, Roman. 1998. "Cheikh Touré. Un musulman Sénégalais dans le siècle. Du réformisme à l'islamisme." In *Islam et islamismes au sud du Sahara,* ed. Ousmane Kane and Jean-Louis Triaud, 155–168. Paris: Karthala.

———. 2003. "Patterns and Peculiarities of Islamic Reform in Africa." *Journal of Religion in Africa* 33 (3): 237–262.

Louër, Laurence. 2008. *Transnational Shia Politics: Religious and Political Networks in the Gulf.* New York: Columbia University Press.

MacLean, Derryl N. 2012. "Introduction: Cosmopolitnisms in Muslim Contexts." In *Cosmopolitanisms in Muslim Contexts: Perspectives from the Past,* ed. Derryl N. MacLean and Sikeena Karmali Ahmed, 1–9. Edinburgh: Edinburgh University Press in association with Aga Khan University.

Magassouba, Moriba. 1985. *L'islam au Sénégal: Demain les mollahs?* Paris: Karthala.

Mahmood, Saba. 2005. *Politics of Piety: The Islamic Revival and the Feminist Subject.* Princeton, N.J.: Princeton University Press.

———. 2009. "Religious Reason and Secular Affect: An Incommensurable Divide?" In *Is Critique Secular? Blasphemy, Injury, and Free Speech,* ed. Talal Asad, Wendy Brown, Judith Butler, and Saba Mahmood, 64–100. Berkeley: Townsend Center for the Humanities, University of California.

Makdisi, Ussama. 2000. *The Culture of Sectarianism: Community, History and Violence in Nineteenth-Century Ottoman Lebanon.* Berkeley: University of California Press.

Mallat, Chibli. 1993. *The Renewal of Islamic Law: Muhammad Baqer as-Sadr, Najaf and the Shi'i International.* Cambridge: Cambridge University Press.

Mamdani, Mahmood. 1996. *Citizen and Subject: Contemporary Africa and the Legacy of Late Colonialism.* Princeton, N.J.: Princeton University Press.

———. 2004. *Good Muslim, Bad Muslim: America, the Cold War and the Roots of Terror.* New York: Pantheon.

Mancabou, Mewlon Nzalé Ange Constantin. 1998–1999. "Les Libanais de Dakar: La greffe inachevée du cèdre au baobab." Thesis. Centre d'Etudes des Sciences et Techniques de l'Information (CESTI), Université Cheikh Anta Diop de Dakar.

Mandaville, Peter. 2001. *Transnational Muslim Politics: Reimagining the Umma.* London: Routledge.

———. 2007. *Global Political Islam.* London: Routledge.

Mandel, Ruth. 2008. *Cosmopolitan Anxieties: Turkish Challenges to Citizenship and Belonging in Germany.* Durham, N.C.: Duke University Press.

Marcus, George E. 1995. "Ethnography in/of the World System: The Emergence of Multi-Sited Ethnography." *Annual Review of Anthropology* 24: 95–117.

Mark, Peter. 1978. "Urban Migration, Cash Cropping, and Calamity: The Spread of Islam Among the Diola of Boulouf (Senegal), 1900–1940." *African Studies Review* 21 (2): 1–14.

Marsden, Magnus. 2008. "Muslim Cosmopolitans? Transnational Life in Northern Pakistan." *Journal of Asian Studies* 67 (1): 213–247.

Mbembe, Achille. 2001. *On the Postcolony.* Berkeley: University of California Press.

———. 2002. "Les nouveaux Africains: Entre nativisme et cosmopolitanisme." *Esprit* 10: 65–74.

McGovern, Mike. 2011. *Making War in Côte d'Ivoire.* Chicago: University of Chicago Press.

———. 2013. *Unmasking the State: Making Guinea Modern.* Chicago: University of Chicago Press.

McLaughlin, Fiona. 1997. "Islam and Popular Music in Senegal: The Emergence of a 'New Tradition.'" *Africa* 67 (4): 560–581.

Melly, Caroline. 2010. "Inside-Out Houses: Urban Belonging and Imagined Futures in Dakar, Senegal." *Comparative Studies in Society and History* 52 (1): 37–65.

Mermier, Franck, and Elizabeth Picard. 2007. *Liban, une guerre de 33 jours.* Paris: Editions La Découverte.

Mervin, Sabrina. 2000. *Un réformisme chiite. ʿUlama et lettrés du Ǧabal ʿAmil, de la fin de l'empire Ottoman à l'indépendance du Liban.* Paris: Karthala.

———. 2002. "Les yeux de Mûsâ Sadr (1928–1978)." In *Saints et héros du Moyen-Orient contemporain,* ed. Catherine Mayeur-Jaouen, 285–300. Paris: Maisonneuve & Larose.

———, ed. 2007. *Les mondes chiites et l'Iran.* Paris: Éditions Karthala et Institut français du Proche Orient.

———, ed. 2008. *Le Hezbollah. État des lieux.* Paris: Sindbad.

Meyer, Birgit. 1998. "'Make a Complete Break with the Past.' Memory and Post-Colonial Modernity in Ghanaian Pentecostalist Discourse." *Journal of Religion in Africa* 28 (3): 316–349.

———. 1999. *Translating the Devil: Religion and Modernity among the Ewe in Ghana.* Edinburgh: Edinburgh University Press.

Meyer, Birgit, and Annelies Moors. 2006. *Religion, Media, and the Public Sphere.* Bloomington: Indiana University Press.

Middle East Intelligence Bulletin Staff. 2004. "Hezbollah and the West African Diamond Trade." *Middle East Intelligence Bulletin.* June/July, http://www.meib.org /articles/0407_12.htm.

Mikhaïl, Barah. 2008. "Iran and the 'Shiʿite Crescent' Theory: How to Transform a Scarecrow into a Giant." *Shiʿa Affairs Journal* 1: 13–20.

Mitchell, J. Clyde. 1956. "The Kalela Dance: Aspects of Social Relationships among Urban Africans in Northern Rhodesia." Rhodes-Livingstone Papers 27. Manchester University Press.

Mitchell, J. Clyde, and A. L. Epstein. 1959. "Occupational Prestige and Social Status among Urban Africans in Northern Rhodesia." Africa 29: 22–39.

Momen, Moojan. 1985. *An Introduction to Shiʿi Islam: The History and Doctrines of Twelver Shiʿism.* New Haven, Conn.: Yale University Press.

Monsutti, Alessandro, Silvia Naef, and Farian Sabahi, eds. 2007. *The Other Shiites: From the Mediterranean to Central Asia.* Bern: Peter Lang.

Moreau, René Luc. 1982. *Africains musulmans: Des communautés en mouvement.* Paris: Présence Africaine.

Moussavi, Ahmad Kazemi. 1996. *Religious Authority in Shiʿite Islam: From the Office of Mufti to the Institution of Marjaʿ.* Kuala Lumpur: International Institute of Islamic Thought and Civilization.

Mozdahir. 2007. *Achoura: Jour de fête ou jour de deuil?* Dakar: Institut Mozdahir International.

Mudimbe, V. Y. 1988. *The Invention of Africa: Gnosis, Philosophy and the Order of Knowledge.* London and Bloomington: James Currey and Indiana University Press.

Nakash, Yitzhak. 1994. *The Shiʿis of Iraq.* Princeton, N.J.: Princeton University Press.

———. 2006. *Reaching for Power: The Shiʿa in the Modern Arab World.* Princeton, N.J.: Princeton University Press.

Nasr, Vali. 2002. "The Iranian Revolution and Changes in Islamism in Pakistan, India, and Afghanistan." In *Iran and the Surrounding World: Interactions in Culture and Cultural Politics,* ed. Nikki R. Keddie and Rudi Matthee, 327–352. Seattle: University of Washington Press.

———. 2006. *The Shia Revival: How Conflicts within Islam Will Shape the Future.* New York: W. W. Norton.

Niasse, Sidy Lamine. 2003. *Un arabisant entre presse et pouvoir.* Dakar: Editions Groupe Wal Fadjri.

Niezen, R. W. 1990. "The 'Community of Helpers of the Sunna': Islamic Reform among the Songhay of Gao (Mali)." *Africa* 60: 399–424.

Nock, A. D. 1933. *Conversion: The Old and the New in Religion from Alexander the Great to Augustine of Hippo.* London: Oxford University Press.

Norton, Augustus Richard. 1987. *Amal and the Shiʿa: Struggle for the Soul of Lebanon.* Austin: University of Texas Press.

———. 1994. "Musa al-Sadr." In *Pioneers of Islamic Revival,* ed. Ali Rahnema, 184–207. London: Zed Books.

———. 2007. *Hezbollah: A Short History.* Princeton, N.J.: Princeton University Press.

Nussbaum, Martha. 1994. "Patriotism and Cosmopolitanism." *Boston Review* 19 (5). http://bostonreview.net/BR19.5/nussbaum.php.

Omi, Michael, and Howard Winant. 1986. *Racial Formation in the United States: From the 1960s to the 1980s.* New York: Routledge.

Ong, Aihwa. 1999. *Flexible Citizenship: The Cultural Logics of Transnationality.* Durham, N.C.: Duke University Press.

———. 2006. *Neoliberalism as Exception: Mutations in Citizenship and Sovereignty.* Durham, N.C.: Duke University Press.

Osanloo, Arzoo. 2009. *The Politics of Women's Rights in Iran.* Princeton, N.J.: Princeton University Press.

Østergaard-Nielsen, Eva. 2003. "The Politics of Migrants' Transnational Political Practices." *International Migration Review* 37: 760–786.

Paillard, Jean. 1935. *La Fin des Français en Afrique Noire.* Paris: Les Œuvres Françaises.

Péan, Pierre. 2001. *Manipulations Africaines.* Paris: Plon.

Peel, J. D. Y. 2000. *Religious Encounter and the Making of the Yoruba.* Bloomington: Indiana University Press.

Peleikis, Anja. 2003. *Lebanese in Motion: Gender and the Making of a Translocal Village.* Bielefeld: Transcript.

Picard, Elizabeth. 2002. *Lebanon, a Shattered Country: Myths and Realities of the Wars in Lebanon.* Rev. ed. Teaneck, N.J.: Holmes & Meier.

Pinto, Paulo G. 2007. "Pilgrimage, Commodities, and Religious Objectification: The Making of Transnational Shiism between Iran and Syria." *Comparative Studies of South Asia, Africa and the Middle East* 27: 109–125.

Piot, Charles. 2010. *Nostalgia for the Future: West Africa after the Cold War.* Chicago: University of Chicago Press.

Pollock, Sheldon, Homi K. Bhabha, Carol A. Breckenridge, and Dipesh Chakrabarty. 2000. "Cosmopolitanisms." *Public Culture* 12 (3): 577–589.

Ranger, Terence. 1993a. "The Invention of Tradition Revisited: The Case of Colonial Africa." In *Legitimacy and the State in Twentieth-Century Africa,* ed. Terence Ranger and Olufemi Vaughan, 62–111. London: Macmillan Press.

———. 1993b. "The Local and the Global in Southern African Religious History." In *Conversion to Christianity: Historical and Anthropological Perspectives on a Great Transformation,* ed. Robert W. Hefner, 65–98. Berkeley: University of California Press.

Redfield, Robert. 1956. *The Little Community.* Chicago: University of Chicago Press.

Reinkowski, Maurus. 1997. "National Identity in Lebanon since 1990." *Orient* 38: 493–515.

Robinson, David. 2000. *Paths of Accommodation: Muslim Societies and French Colonial Authorities in Senegal and Mauritania, 1880–1920.* Athens: Ohio University Press.

———. 2004. *Muslim Societies in African History.* Cambridge: Cambridge University Press.

Rosander, Eva Evers. 1997. "Introduction: The Islamization of 'Tradition' and 'Modernity.'" In *African Islam and Islam in Africa: Encounters between Sufis and Islamists,* ed. David Westerlund and Eva Evers Rosander, 1–27. Athens: Ohio University Press.

Roy, Olivier. 2004. *Globalized Islam: The Search for a New Ummah.* New York: Columbia.

Rubin, Michael. 2008. "Iran's Global Ambition." *AEI Middle Eastern Outlook.* March 17. http://www.meforum.org/article/1873.

Saadeh, Edmond Khalil. 1952. *The Lebanon in the World: Guide of the Lebano-Syrians Emigrants in Western and Equatorial Africa.* Beirut: L'Universelle Impression & Edition.

Sachedina, Abdulaziz Abdulhussein. 1988. *The Just Ruler (al-sultan al-ᶜadil) in Shiᶜite Islam: The Comprehensive Authority of the Jurist in Imamite Jurisprudence.* New York: Oxford University Press.

Said, Edward W. 1997 [1981]. *Covering Islam: How the Media and the Experts Determine How We See the Rest of the World.* New York: Vintage Books.

Salibi, Kamal. 1988. *A House of Many Mansions: The History of Lebanon Reconsidered.* Berkeley: University of California Press.

Samson, Fabienne. 2009. "Islamic Identities of Protest and Citizen Mobilization in Senegal: Two New Movements within Sufi Orders." In *New Perspectives on Islam in Senegal: Conversion, Migration, Wealth, Power, and Femininity,* ed. Mamadou Diouf and Mara A. Leichtman, 257–272. New York: Palgrave Macmillan.

Sanneh, Lamin. 1997. *The Crown and the Turban: Muslims and West African Pluralism.* Boulder, Colo.: Westview Press.

Şaul, Mahir. 2006. "Islam and West African Anthropology." *Africa Today* 53 (1): 2–33.

Sayyid, Bobby S. 2000. "Beyond Westphalia: Nations and Diasporas—The Case of the Muslim *Umma*." In *Un/settled Multiculturalisms: Diasporas, Entanglements, Transruptions,* ed. Barnor Hesse, 33–50. London: Zed Books.

Schulz, Dorothea E. 2006. "Promises of (Im)mediate Salvation: Islam, Broadcast Media, and the Remaking of Religious Experience in Mali." *American Ethnologist* 33 (2): 210–229.

———. 2008. "(Re)turning to Proper Muslim Practice: Islamic Moral Renewal and Women's Conflicting Assertions of Sunni Identity in Urban Mali." *Africa Today* 54 (4): 21–43.

———. 2012. *Muslims and New Media in West Africa: Pathways to God.* Bloomington: Indiana University Press.

Searing, James F. 2002. *"God Alone Is King": Islam and Emancipation in Senegal: The Wolof Kingdoms of Kajoor and Bawol, 1859–1914*. Portsmouth, N.H.: Heinemann.

———. 2003. "Conversion to Islam: Military Recruitment and Generational Conflict in a Sereer-Safen Village (Bandia), 1920–38." *Journal of African History* 44 (1): 73–95.

Seesemann, Rüdiger. 2011. *The Divine Flood: Ibrahim Niasse and the Roots of a Twentieth-Century Sufi Revival*. New York: Oxford University Press.

Sene, Diégane. 1997. "Un journal à l'assaut des 'Levantins.' 'Les Echos Africains' et le 'Problème Libanais' en AOF (1947–1948)." *Revue Africaine de Communication*, Centre d'Etudes des Sciences et Techniques de l'Information, Université Cheikh Anta Diop de Dakar (Novembre–Décembre).

Senghor, Léopold Sédar. 1977. *Liberté III. Négritude et civilisation de l'universel*. Paris: Éditions du Seuil.

———. 1980. *La poésie de l'action: Conversations avec Mohamed Aziza*. Paris: Éditions Stock.

———. 1993. *Liberté 5: Le dialogue des cultures*. Paris: Éditions du Seuil.

Shaery-Eisenlohr, Roschanack. 2008. *Shiʿite Lebanon: Transnational Religion and the Making of National Identities*. New York: Columbia University Press.

Simmons, William S. 1979. "Islamic Conversion and Social Change in a Senegalese Village." *Ethnology* 18 (4): 303–323.

Simpson, Edward, and Kai Kresse, eds. 2008. *Struggling with History: Islam and Cosmopolitanism in the Western Indian Ocean*. London: Hurst.

Skrbiš, Zlatko. 1999. *Long-Distance Nationalism: Diasporas, Homelands and Identities*. Aldershot: Ashgate.

Smith, Robert C. 1997. "Transnational Migration, Assimilation, and Political Community." In *The City and the World: New York's Global Future*, ed. M. E. Crahan and A. Vourvoulias-Bush, 110–132. New York: Council on Foreign Relations.

Soares, Benjamin F. 2005. *Islam and the Prayer Economy: History and Authority in a Malian Town*. Ann Arbor: University of Michigan Press.

———. 2006. "Islam in Mali in the Neoliberal Era." *African Affairs* 105: 77–95.

———. 2007. "Rethinking Islam and Muslim Societies in Africa." *African Affairs* 106: 319–326.

Soysal, Yasemin Nuhoglu. 1994. *Limits of Citizenship: Migrants and Postnational Membership in Europe*. Chicago: Chicago University Press.

Steene, Gwenda Vander. 2008. "'Hindu' Dance Groups and Indophilie in Senegal: The Imagination of the Exotic Other." In *India in Africa, Africa in India: Indian Ocean Cosmopolitanisms*, ed. John C. Hawley, 117–147. Bloomington: Indiana University Press.

Stoler, Ann Laura. 1997. "Carnal Knowledge and Imperial Power: Gender, Race, and Morality in Colonial Asia." In *The Gender/Sexuality Reader: Culture, History, Political Economy*, ed. Roger N. Lancaster and Micaela di Leonardo, 13–36. New York: Routledge.

Stoller, Paul. 2002. *Money Has No Smell: The Africanization of New York City*. Chicago: University of Chicago Press.

Takim, Liyakat N. 2006. *The Heirs of the Prophet: Charisma and Religious Authority in Shiʿite Islam*. Albany: State University of New York Press.

Taraf (épouse Najib), Souha. 1994. "L'espace en mouvement. Dynamiques migratoires et territorialisation des familles Libanaises au Sénégal." Ph.D. thesis. Université de Tours.

Taussig, Michael. 1993. *Mimesis and Alterity: A Particular History of the Senses*. New York: Routledge.

Tignor, Robert L. 1987. "Senegal's Cooperative Experience, 1907–1960." In *The Political Economy of Risk and Choice in Senegal,* ed. Mark Gersovitz and John Waterbury, 90–122. London: Frank Cass.

Traboulsi, Fawaz. 2007. *A History of Modern Lebanon.* London: Pluto Press.

Triaud, Jean-Louis, and David Robinson, eds. 2000. *La Tijâniyya: Une confrérie musulmane à la conquête de l'Afrique.* Paris: Karthala.

Trimingham, J. Spencer. 1962. *A History of Islam in West Africa.* London: Oxford University Press.

Trouillot, Michel-Rolph. 1995. *Silencing the Past: Power and the Production of History.* Boston: Beacon Press.

———. 2002. "The Otherwise Modern: Caribbean Lessons from the Savage Slot." In *Critically Modern: Alternatives, Alterities, Anthropologies,* ed. Bruce M. Knauft, 220–237. Bloomington: Indiana University Press.

Tsing, Anna L. 1993. *In the Realm of the Diamond Queen: Marginality in an Out-of-the-Way Place.* Princeton, N.J.: Princeton University Press.

———. 2004. *Friction: An Ethnography of Global Connection.* Princeton, N.J.: Princeton University Press.

Turner, Victor. 1969. *The Ritual Process: Structure and Anti-Structure.* Chicago: Adeline.

Vaillant, Janet G. 1990. *Black, French and African: A Life of Léopold Sédar Senghor.* Cambridge, Mass.: Harvard University Press.

van der Laan, H. L. 1975. *The Lebanese Traders in Sierra Leone.* Mouton: The Hague.

———. 1992. "Migration, Mobility and Settlement of the Lebanese in West Africa." In *The Lebanese in the World: A Century of Emigration,* ed. Albert Hourani and Nadim Shehadi, 531–547. London: I.B. Tauris.

van der Veer, Peter, ed. 1996. *Conversion to Modernities: The Globalization of Christianity.* New York: Routledge.

———. 2002. "Colonial Cosmopolitanism." In *Conceiving Cosmopolitanism: Theory, Context, and Practice,* ed. Steven Vertovec and Robin Cohen, 165–179. Oxford: Oxford University Press.

Vertovec, Steven, and Robin Cohen, ed. 2003. *Conceiving Cosmopolitanism: Theory, Context, and Practice.* Oxford: Oxford University Press.

Villalón, Leonardo A. 1995. *Islamic Society and State Power in Senegal: Disciples and Citizens in Fatick.* Cambridge: Cambridge University Press.

———. 1999. "Generational Changes, Political Stagnation, and the Evolving Dynamics of Religion and Politics in Senegal." *Africa Today* 46 (3–4): 129–147.

———. 2000. "Moustarchidine of Senegal: The Family Politics of a Contemporary Tijan Movement." In *La Tijâniyya. Une confrérie musulmane à la conquête de l'Afrique,* ed. Jean-Louis Triaud and David Robinson, 469–497. Paris: Karthala.

———. 2004. "Senegal." *African Studies Review* 47 (2): 61–71.

Viswanathan, Gauri. 1998. *Outside the Fold: Conversion, Modernity, and Belief.* Princeton, N.J.: Princeton University Press.

Volk, Lucia. 2010. *Memorials and Martyrs in Modern Lebanon.* Bloomington: Indiana University Press.

Walbridge, Linda S. 1997. *Without Forgetting the Imam: Lebanese Shi'ism in an American Community.* Detroit: Wayne State University Press.

———, ed. 2001. *The Most Learned of the Shi'a: The Institution of the Marja' Taqlid.* Oxford: Oxford University Press.

Ware, Rudolph T., III. 2009. "The Longue Durée of Quran Schooling, Society, and State in Senegambia." In *New Perspectives on Islam in Senegal: Conversion, Migration, Wealth, Power, and Femininity*, ed. Mamadou Diouf and Mara A. Leichtman, 21–50. New York: Palgrave Macmillan.

Weiss, Max. 2007. "'Don't Throw Yourself Away to the Dark Continent': Shiʿi Migration to West Africa and the Hierarchies of Exclusion in Lebanese Culture." *Studies in Ethnicity and Nationalism* 7 (1): 46–62.

Werbner, Pnina. 2001. "The Limits of Cultural Hybridity: On Ritual Monsters, Poetic License and Contested Postcolonial Purifications." *Journal of the Royal Anthropological Institute* 7 (1): 133–152.

———. 2006. "Vernacular Cosmopolitanism." *Theory, Culture and Society* 23: 496–498.

———. 2008. "Introduction: Towards a New Cosmopolitan Anthropology." In *Anthropology and the New Cosmopolitanism*, ed. Pnina Werbner, 1–29. Oxford: Berg.

Werbner, Richard P. 1984. "The Manchester School in South-Central Africa." *Annual Review of Anthropology* 13: 157–185.

———. 2002. "Cosmopolitan Ethnicity, Entrepreneurship and the Nation: Minority Elites in Botswana." *Journal of Southern African Studies* 28 (4): 731–753.

Westerlund, David, and Eva Evers Rosander, eds. 1997. *African Islam and Islam in Africa: Encounters between Sufis and Islamists*. Athens: Ohio University Press.

Wilder, Gary. 2005. *The French Imperial Nation-State: Negritude and Colonial Humanism between the Two World Wars*. Chicago: University of Chicago Press.

Willis, John Ralph. 1979. "Reflections on the Diffusion of Islam in West Africa." *Studies in West African Islamic History* 1: 1–39.

Wimmer, Andreas, and Nina Glick Schiller. 2002. "Methodological Nationalism and Beyond: Nation-State Building, Migration and the Social Sciences." *Global Networks* 2: 301–334.

Wright, Bonnie L. 1989. "The Power of Articulation." In *Creativity of Power: Cosmology and Action in African Societies*, ed. W. Arens and Ivan Karp, 39–57. Washington, D.C.: Smithsonian Institution Press.

Zaman, Muhammad Qasim. 2005. "The Scope and Limits of Islamic Cosmopolitanism and the Discursive Language of the ʿUlamaʾ." In *Muslim Networks from Hajj to Hip Hop*, ed. miriam cooke and Bruce B. Lawrence, 84–104. Chapel Hill: University of North Carolina Press.

Zamir, Meir. 1985. *The Formation of Modern Lebanon*. London: Croom Helm.

Zonis, Marvin, and Daniel Brumberg. 1987. *Khomeini, The Islamic Republic of Iran, and the Arab World*. Harvard Middle East Papers 5. Cambridge, Mass.: Center for Middle Eastern Studies, Harvard University.

Zubaida, Sami. 2002. "Middle Eastern Experiences of Cosmopolitanism." In *Conceiving Cosmopolitanism: Theory, Context and Practice*, ed. Steven Vertovec and Robin Cohen, 32–41. Oxford: Oxford University Press.

Newspaper and Magazine Articles, Colonial Reports, Films, and Gray Literature

Aïdara, Abdel Karim. 2003. "Trente-quatre années au service de l'islam au Sénégal: Cheikh Abdul Monem El Zein, un atypique cheikh chiite au Sénégal . . ." *Le Messager* 84, December 2, 4.

Castéran, Christian, Killian Kra, and Pierre Weiss. 1999. "Des Africains pas comme les autres." *Jeune Afrique Economie* 289: 14–27.

Charbonneau, René. 1959. "Le problème Libano-Syrien en Afrique noire." In *Comptes rendus mensuels des séances de l'Académie des Sciences d'Outre-Mer par M. le Secrétaire Perpétuel*. Vol. 19. Séances des 6 et 20 Mars et 17 Avril. Paris: Académie des Sciences d'Outre-Mer.

Cissé, Mamadou. 2004. "Renforcement de l'axe Dakar-Bayrouth: Le président du parlement Libanais au Sénégal." *Le Soleil*, March 6.

Diop, Mohamed Bachir. 1997. "Ni mythe, ni tout à fait réalité, mais les jalons sont posés." *Le Témoin* 338, February 25–March 3, 8.

Drame, Alioune. 1984. "Fermeture de l'ambassade d'Iran: Coup d'arrêt." *Le Soleil*, February 6.

Gavron, Laurence, and Cheikh Tidiane Ndiaye. 1999. *Nar Bi – Loin du Liban*. Documentary film.

Guèye, Doudou. n.d. "Afro-Libanais: Ils sont Sénégalais!" *Nation* 6.

Gyldèn, Axel. 2002. "Le succès et sa rançon." *L'Express*, October 24.

"Les Sénégalo-Libanais: Une communauté de champions." *Nation* 6–7.

Mangoné, Fal. 1958. "Le problème Libano-Syrien en A.O.F." *Centre de Hautes Etudes Administratives sur l'Afrique et l'Asie Modernes* November 29.

Martin, V. 1964. *Notes d'Introduction à une étude socio-religieuse des populations de Dakar et du Senegal*. Dakar: Fraternité Saint Dominique.

Ndiaye, Mamadou Oumar. 1997. "Quelle intégration pour les communauté etrangères?" *Le Témoin* 338, February 24–March 3, 5.

Seck, Ndiougou W., Idrissa Diop, and Abdel K. Aïdara. 2003. "Cheikh Abdul Monem El Zein: Des réalisations pour soigner l'âme et corps." *Le Messager* 84, December 2, 4.

Sow, Penda Télémaque. 1998. "Sortir de son ghetto." *L'info* 34, November 19, 2.

Tall, Al Hadj Khaly. 2002. "Cheikh Abdoul Moneim Zein khalife de la famille du Prophète au Sénégal." *Le Soleil*, May 28, 5.

———. 2004. "Dakar: La rue Tolbiac devient rue du Liban." *Le Soleil*, March 9.

———. 2006. "Organisations islamiques au service du développement: Les exemples de 'Mozdahir.'" *Le Soleil*. July 14. http://www.lesoleil.sn/imprimertout.php3?id_rubrique=355 (accessed July 31, 2008).

Thibault, Jean. 1976. "Les Libanais en Afrique: Parasites ou agents de développement?" *Voix d'Afrique* 24, October 4–17.

Touré, Al Hadj Cheikh. 1982a. "J'ai été en Iran." *Etudes Islamique* 13: 8–10.

———. 1982b. "Retour à l'Iran." *Etudes Islamique* 15.

Youssef, Jihad. 1994. "Senegal: Efforts to Strengthen Its Deeprooted Islam." *Noor Al Islam: Islamic Cultural Magazine* 51–52: 3–14.

Archives Nationales de Sénégal (ANS)

Circulaire de la Direction des Affaires Politiques et Administratives à le Gouverneur Général de l'A.O.F. 5 Novembre 1922. 19G24(108).

Ministère des Colonies à Monsieur le Gouverneur Général de l'Afrique Occidentale Française. 20 Avril 1923. 19G24(108).

Le Ministre des Colonies à Monsieur le Gouverneur Général de l'Afrique Occidentale Française. 18 Décembre, 1933. 19G1(1).

La France grande protectrice de l'Islam. *Paris-Dakar* 625:1. 19 Fevrier 1938. 19G6(17).

Renseignements. 25 Janvier 1945. 21G8(1).

Renseignements. 31 Mai 1945. 21G8(1).

Renseignements. 6 Juin 1945. 21G8(1).

Renseignements (50 – Source Indigène–Bonne). 14 Juin 1945. 21G8(1).

Le Gouverneur du Sénégal à Monsieur le Gouverneur Général, Direction des A.P.A.S. et Direction de la Sûreté Générale. 18 Juin 1945. 21G8(1).

Renseignements. 25 Juin 1945. 21G8(1).

Series 21G23(17).

Diégane Sene's Archive Collection/ANS:

Rapport sur la situation des Libano-Syriens en Afrique Occidentale Française et au Togo, par la Direction Générale des Affaires Politiques, Administratives et Sociales de l'Afrique Occidentale Française, 1945.

Note sur le Comité "HACHEM." 3 Octobre 1946.

Le Consul Général du Liban à S.E. Monsieur le Haut-Commissaire Gouverneur General de l'A.O.F. 21 Mai 1947.

La liberté de la presse ne devrait pas permettre les attaques contre la dignité des gens, ni les articles pouvant porter atteinte aux relations internationales. Si nos émigrés d'Afrique sont devenus 'jaunes' c'est parce qu'ils ont verse leur sang rouge dans ce continent noir. *Al Hayat*, 15 Juillet 1947, Légation de France, Service d'Information.

Un cri du Sénégal. *Al-Amal*, 18 Juillet 1947, Légation de France, Service d'Information.

Copie à l'intention du Bureau Politique d'une réponse faite par les Echos Africains à Monsieur Pierre Gémayel. 7 Août 1947.

Monsieur le Haut Commissaire de l'Afrique Occidentale Française par Maurice Voisin. 7 Août 1947.

Extraits d'un lettre de M. Voisin à Monsieur le Gouverneur du Sénégal du 8 Août 1947.

Copie d'un tract diffusé ce jour, 14 Décembre, par Maurice Voisin concernant une plainte déposée contre la Directrice des Echos d'Afrique Noire par le Consul du Liban à Dakar. 14 Décembre 1953.

Copie d'une pétition comportant 8 signatures et mise en circulation le 16 Décembre par Abou Jaoudi Edmond, 2 Rue des Essarts, pour protester et mettre en garde les autorités contres les attaques de Maurice Voisin. 17 Décembre 1953.

Compte-rendu succint du meeting, organisé le Samedi 19 Décembre 1953, au Cinéma Alhambra par Maurice Voisin. 21 Décembre 1953.

Albert-Henry. Les minorité étrangères en Union Française. Le problème Libano-Syrien en A.O.F. *La Croix du Sud*, 3–9 Juillet 1954, 1, 8.

Index

Page numbers in *italics* indicate photographs and illustrations.

Mara A. Leichtman is Associate Professor of Anthropology and Muslim studies at Michigan State University. She is editor (with Mamadou Diouf) of *New Perspectives on Islam in Senegal: Conversion, Migration, Wealth, Power, and Femininity.*